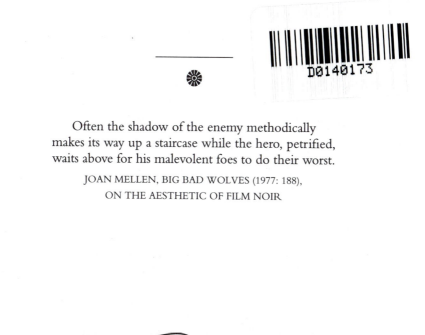

Often the shadow of the enemy methodically
makes its way up a staircase while the hero, petrified,
waits above for his malevolent foes to do their worst.

JOAN MELLEN, BIG BAD WOLVES (1977: 188),
ON THE AESTHETIC OF FILM NOIR

thomson.com

changing the way the world learns

To get extra value from this book for no additional cost, go to:

http://www.thomson.com/wadsworth.html

thomson.com is the World Wide Web site for Wadsworth/ITP
and is your direct source to dozens of on-line resources.
thomson.com helps you find out about supplements,
experiment with demonstration software, search for a job,
and send e-mail to many of our authors. You can even
preview new publications and exciting new technologies.

thomson.com: *It's where you'll find us in the future.*

CONTEMPORARY ISSUES IN CRIME AND JUSTICE SERIES

Todd Clear, *Series Editor*

Popular Culture, Crime, and Justice

FRANKIE Y. BAILEY

State University of New York at Albany

DONNA C. HALE

Shippensburg University

West/Wadsworth Publishing Company

I(T)P® An International Thomson Publishing Company

Belmont • Albany • Bonn • Boston • Cincinnati • Detroit • London • Madrid
Melbourne • Mexico City • New York • Paris • San Francisco • Singapore
Tokyo • Toronto • Washington

Criminal Justice Editor: Sabra Horne
Assistant Editor: Claire Masson
Senior Editorial Assistant: Kate Barrett
Marketing Manager: Mike Dew
Senior Project Editor: Debby Kramer
Production: Forbes Mill Press
Copy Editor: Robin Gold
Print Buyer: Karen Hunt
Permissions Editor: Peggy Meehan
Cover Designer: Dean Charlton
Compositor: Thompson Type
Printer: Malloy Lithographing
Cover Printer: Phoenix Color Corporation

 This book is printed on acid-free recycled paper.

Printed in the United States of America
1 2 3 4 5 6 7 8 9 10

For more information, contact Wadsworth Publishing Company, 10 Davis Drive, Belmont, CA 94002, or electronically at http://www.thomson.com/wadsworth.html

International Thomson Publishing Europe
Berkshire House 168-173
High Holborn
London, WC1V 7AA, England

International Thomson Editores
Campos Eliseos 385, Piso 7
Col. Polanco
11560 México D.F. México

Thomas Nelson Australia
102 Dodds Street
South Melbourne 3205
Victoria, Australia

International Thomson Publishing Asia
221 Henderson Road
#05-10 Henderson Building
Singapore 0315

Nelson Canada
1120 Birchmount Road
Scarborough, Ontario
Canada M1K 5G4

International Thomson Publishing Japan
Hirakawacho Kyowa Building, 3F
2-2-1 Hirakawacho
Chiyoda-ku, Tokyo 102, Japan

International Thomson Publishing GmbH
Königswinterer Strasse 418
53227 Bonn, Germany

International Thomson Publishing Southern Africa
Building 18, Constantia Park
240 Old Pretoria Road
Halfway House, 1685 South Africa

Library of Congress Cataloging-in-Publication Data

Bailey, Frankie Y.
    Popular culture, crime, and justice / Frankie Y. Bailey, Donna C. Hale.
      p. cm.
    Includes bibliographical references and index.
    ISBN 0-534-51975-X
    1. Crime in popular culture—United States. 2. Crime in mass media—United States.
  3. Criminal justice, Administration of—United States—Public opinion. 4. Public opinion—United States
    I. Hale, Donna C. II. Title
    HV6789.B25 1997
    364.973—dc21

97-24853

Contents

Foreword

I love Columbo. The way he seems to know instinctively exactly who the murderer actually is, despite the apparent evidence to the contrary, leaves me in awe. And then his careful, plodding way of breaking down the alibi, and eventually piecing together the inescapable truth, is simply astounding. I also admit I just love his needling, irritating way of seeming to be on his way out the door, only to turn on the surely-by-now perspiring criminal and say, in that annoyingly offhand way, "Oh, yes . . . one more thing . . ."

Yes, I love Columbo, but there is very little truth in him. Murders are rarely the results of careful plots carried out by the rich and famous. Detection is almost never the process of destroying a seemingly irrefutable alibi. Arrests do not follow carefully explained proofs to astounded culprits. Columbo is, after all, a television character, based not at all on reality, but on favorite American fantasies about reality. So I love Columbo even though I know there is about as much relationship between him and the real world as there is between Batman and the real world.

On the other hand, it would not be the case that Columbo is irrelevant to American images of crime. To the contrary, he is one of the innumerable, nightly episodes of crime data Americans expose themselves to every day, day after day, week after week. In a peculiar way, these presentations about crime and justice are as much or more important as contexts for the formulation of crime policy as is actual crime, actual punishments. Americans learn what they know about crime and justice from the popular media-commercial news and entertainment, especially. And what they know—what they think they know—can often be but a distorted version of reality, for the popular media are not as interested in informing us as in commanding our attention, not as interested in "the truth" as in good stories. Indeed, even the "true crime stories" now so popular offer the viewer a subtly slanted, truncated idea of crime and justice.

Because media are so important in the public conception of crime, I am especially pleased to announce the addition of this book, *Popular Culture, Crime and Justice,* to the Wadsworth Issues in Crime and Justice Series. The Wadsworth Series specializes in the coverage of important topics that receive too scant attention in the major textbooks, yet remain critically important to a fuller understanding of crime and justice. The Series seeks to provide its readers with timely, current analyses of important issues that more general textbooks are able only to introduce, if they are addressed at all.

Professors Bailey and Hale have provided us with an outstanding new addition to the Series, a book that fits with excellence our editorial objectives. This is a book that considers how popular culture presents—and thus helps form—images of reality about crime and justice. The contributors include some of the most active recent scholars in the field of crime and justice, and their work shows how creative thinking and analysis can help us better understand this elusive topic. The study of popular culture is relatively recent and uses innovative methods of content analysis and linguistic interpretation. Scholars who work in this area use these unconventional techniques to uncover the meaning of the messages to which we are exposed in our daily media fare.

The contributors to this volume have done an extraordinarily valuable job of documenting the popular media contribution to images of crime and justice. The chapters herein cover an array of topics, from the created images of censorship social movements to the everyday newsmaking of crime coverage by journalists. They show how popular presentation of crime and criminals, justice and justice officials, can reinforce stereotypes, promote inaccurate views of social reality, and mislead social consensus about the problem of crime.

If we are to confront the problem of crime with any effectiveness, our actions must be based on a real understanding of crime and its consequences. Unfortunately, the main source of information on this topic—the public media—is not always an accurate foundation on which to form useful judgments. This book goes a long way to explaining, and showing, why the media provide a distorted reality on crime and justice. I commend the volume to you, the reader.

Todd Clear
Series Editor

Preface

T he idea for this volume grew out of a telephone conversation we had one day. We both agreed that such a volume was needed, and we thought it would be "fun" to put one together. Almost three years later, we are ready to admit it was also a lot of hard work. But we did have fun. We were able to immerse ourselves in an area of research—popular culture, crime, and justice—that we both find intriguing.

In this text, we examine how the criminal justice system (police, courts, and corrections), criminal justice participants (professionals, victims, and offenders), and the criminal justice process are presented in popular culture. The term "popular culture," as we are using it here, incorporates and subsumes "mass media" (that is, newspapers, magazines, television, radio, movies). The chapters in this volume address the interrelationship between criminal justice and popular culture from a variety of perspectives. The methodologies employed by the contributors include historical research, observational research, and content analysis. The prologue and Chapter One provide a general overview and introduction to the topic. In Part One, the two contributors offer provocative theoretical perspectives on understanding popular culture. In Part Two, the focus is on censorship. The two contributors look, respectively, at the furor in the 1940s and 1950s over juveniles and crime comic books and at recent crusades against controversial forms of popular culture. In Part Three, the contributors focus on the depiction of crime and justice by journalists. The final section, Part Four, is about the images of criminal justice professionals (female police and attorneys) and of prisons in popular films.

When we discussed the audience for this book, we wanted it not only to be adoptable for courses in criminal justice and criminology and sociology, but also to be used by researchers and students in communications/mass media and women's studies courses. Just as importantly, we wanted it to be accessible to a general audience whose contact with the criminal justice system is limited to reading about it in their daily newspaper or watching a "cop show" on television. We hope this book will make both audiences more aware of how their perceptions of the criminal justice system are shaped by popular culture.

So now the volume is done. And there are some people we want to thank. First of all, the contributors. We couldn't have done it without you. Thanks also to Ray Surette, who encouraged us in this undertaking. And we thank the reviewers who helped us to shape this volume with their lively input and helpful comments: Richard R. E. Kania, Guilford College; Lawrence F. Travis, University of Cincinnati; Randy Blazak, Portland State University; Elizabeth Z. McGrath, Loyola University of Chicago; Michael Hallett, Middle Tennessee State University; Stephanie Kane, Indiana University; Gregg Barak, Eastern Michigan University. We also would like to thank Sabra Horne, the criminal justice editor at Wadsworth, and her incredibly efficient staff. And Carla Firey, a master's student at Shippensburg University, who assisted in the preparation of the final manuscript, including the index. And, finally, we wish to offer our sincere appreciation to Cindy Prieto, Rockefeller College computer consultant, who nursed us through our computer crises. Thanks, Cindy!

On a more personal note, Donna C. Hale thanks her mother, Jewel Fitzpatrick Puckett, who advised her from childhood not to take at face value what she read and saw, and to always keep an open mind. This sound advice has been invaluable in both Donna's life and research endeavors. Also, she dedicates this book to the memory of Dixie, the Scottish Terrier, who was by her side during most of the time the research for this project was taking place. Dixie enjoyed the research process and always got her fair share of the popcorn!

Frankie Y. Bailey dedicates this book to her parents, Bessie Fitzgerald Bailey and the late Frank Bailey who let her watch television while she was doing her homework and gave her money for those Saturday matinees.

Popular Culture

Popular culture comprises the amusements that occupy the nation's leisure times; it reflects the interests, manners, and tastes of its diverse audience. It includes the popular arts—the movies, stage, television and radio, journalism, fictional writings, and the poetry and other forms of expression that appeal to the majority; and it includes fads and fashions in dress and speech, sports, and styles of interaction that draw the interest of audiences.

INCIARDI AND DEE (1987: 85)

Forms of popular culture are largely created and maintained through mass media.

SNOW (1983: 9)

Making sense of crime and criminalization means paying close attention to culture.

FERRELL AND SANDERS (1995: 7)

※

Prologue

Some Unpopular Thoughts about Popular Culture

RAY SURETTE

THE ALLURE OF POPULAR CULTURE

Reading the following essays brings a basic question about popular culture to mind. Why is popular culture so popular? Both its entertainment and its news components currently enjoy immense popularity. Like most Americans, I relish the entertainment products provided by the popular culture. I look forward to reading my low-grade, stereotype-laden, predictable adventure and science-fiction novels. I like a good adventure or action film with lots of special effects and implausible plots. This entertainment is popular with me simply because it takes me to places that don't exist. When I pick up or see a popular culture entertainment piece, I am seeking a pleasurable escape from reality. In sum, I enjoy popular culture's ability to entertain me and transport me. I am not seeking knowledge or enlightenment. I want to see something that I will not see otherwise, to have described to me experiences that I will not personally experience. I want a brief visit to a constructed world that does not exist to experience events that do not happen. The entertainment products of popular culture are play. With it my mind goes barefoot and enjoyably stump-stupid for awhile.

Where popular culture's entertainment is escapism, popular culture's news is voyeurism for me. News as entertainment gives me knowledge about a world, but not much knowledge about my world. I realize that the popular news usually informs me about real events and real people, but these events and people do not seem connected to me. Popular news tells me about distant, rare events; about the lives of people caught in extreme circumstances; and about bizarre crimes, spectacular trials, and extraordinary situations. Analogous to popular culture's entertainment, I pay attention to popular culture's news because I find it interesting, not because I find it particularly useful or relevant to my personal life. The reality described to me in popular news sometimes fascinates me, but seldom does it strike me as realistic or relevant.

I am therefore not surprised that the content of popular culture both in entertainment and news is significantly different from my experience and, I believe, from most people's experiences. Popular culture has to be different from my reality to gain and maintain my interest. I do not seek out novels about professors or academia. Nor do I expect popular culture's news to give me a picture of the actual world I am likely to encounter. Popular entertainment allows me to escape my reality; popular news gives me filtered, molded snippets of the abnormal events of the world. Thus, the primary element of popular culture's popularity is that it presents a different experience from reality—an escape from the normal using a construction of the unusual. So what's the problem? How can anything that's so much fun and so obviously unrealistic be bad?

THE PROBLEM WITH POPULAR CULTURE

Concern with popular culture arises when people forget or do not realize that popular culture is an extract of reality. Even when it is presented as a snapshot of reality as in the popular news, aspects of reality are extracted, recast, and marketed. Popular culture takes a specific, narrow slice of the world and reshapes it as a constructed image of reality. And even when we recognize popular culture as unrealistic, the continued exposure to the content of popular culture influences our view of reality—its influence increasing as alternate sources of information are less available (Adoni and Mane, 1984). Like candy to cavities, a diet heavy on popular culture will rot one's perceptions of reality.

The reason for this influence is the manner in which people develop a picture of reality in their minds. The process is the same for everyone, although the end result, your personal idea of reality, can be highly individualistic. The process called the social construction of reality works as follows: Under this view, people create reality—the world they believe exists—from their personal knowledge and from knowledge gained from social interactions with other people. People then act in accordance with their constructed view of reality. Individuals gain the knowledge from which they construct their social realities from various sources (Altheide, 1984; Quinney, 1970; Tuchman, 1978). The first source, termed "experienced reality," is the directly experienced world (Adoni and Mane, 1984). Experienced reality is limited to a relatively few personal experiences, but because experienced reality provides direct world knowledge, it has a powerful influence on our constructed reality. Other world knowledge acquired socially and collectively constitutes our "symbolic reality." In sum, your symbolic reality comprises all the events you didn't witness but believe occurred, all the facts about the world you didn't personally collect but believe to be true, and all the things you believe to exist but haven't personally seen. Knowledge from your experienced and your symbolic reality is mixed together, and from this mix, each individual constructs his or her "world." Not surprisingly, individuals with access to similar knowledge and who frequently interact with one another tend to construct similar social realities. The constructed reality is perceived as the "real" world by each individual—what we individually believe the world to be like. This reality is subjective because it differs among individuals because their experienced realities differ. However, people of the same background will usually see the world more alike than different because they share the same symbolic reality and much of the same experienced reality. This socially constructed subjective reality leads to social behavior. The objective world and its symbolic representations are fused into individual consciousness and provide the basis for individual social actions (Adoni and Mane, 1984: 326). People act according to how they believe the world is.

Underlying this framework is an overriding interest in American popular culture and the mass media. This is because, in advanced societies like the United States, most of our knowledge of the world, and hence the bulk of our reality, is obtained socially from our "symbolic reality," and popular culture; the media are centrally involved in the distribution of knowledge from these other sources (Altheide, 1984). Media information is not accepted uncritically but, rather, is part of the social construction of reality competition (Ericson, 1991: 242). The competition involves claims and claimsmakers who compete with one another to have their particular construction of reality widely accepted. Claims are the descriptions and explanations regarding the extent and nature of a phenomenon. These statements are promoted as facts about something in the world. For example, "crime is out of control" is a claim about the condition of crime in society. Claimsmakers are the promoters, activists, professional experts, and spokespersons involved in forwarding specific claims about a phenomenon (Best, 1991: 327). Claimsmakers do more than draw attention to particular social conditions, they shape our sense of what the problem is. Each social condition can be constructed in many different ways. For example, crime can be constructed as a social, individual, racial, sexual, economic, justice, or technological problem, and each construction implies different policy courses and solutions. The most important result of the social reality construction competition is that the winning dominant construction directs public policy. The social policies and the solutions sought are tied to claims of the successful winning construction.

The media's role is that of playing field for the social construction competition between claimsmakers. Claimsmakers compete for media attention, and the media tend to favor those who are dramatic, sponsored by powerful groups, and related to established cultural themes. The media also act as a

claims filter, making it difficult for those outside the popular cultural mainstream to access the media and establish their claims. The sources of knowledge people use to socially construct reality vary in importance with the mass
media increasing in importance as other sources decline (Cohen and Young,
1981b; Lichter, 1988). Because we get no more than a glimpse of world events
firsthand, we must depend on the social construction of reality created by the
media (Hans and Dee, 1991; Nimmo and Combs, 1983; Tuchman, 1978).
The degree of media contribution to an individual's construction of reality is a
function of that individual's direct experience with various phenomena and
consequent independence from the media for information (Adoni and Mane,
1984: 327).

In the end, popular culture emerges as one of three dominant social construction of reality engines. The most significant remains our personal experiences and information we receive from people close to us. This is our
conversational knowledge base and, with our own experiences, provides the
foundation of our reality. Popular culture, distributed through the mass media
and composed of popular news and entertainment, is the second information
engine. Because the popular culture contains a common, shared set of world
knowledge that is pervasively distributed via the mass media, popular culture
has emerged as a main engine in the social construction of reality process. In
final effect, the media establish powerful frames for perceiving the world while
they control the distribution of shared social knowledge. The content of this
shared knowledge is mostly determined in the gyrations of popular culture.
The third engine is knowledge supplied by various organizations, institutions,
and agencies that collect and disseminate data, information, and claims about
the world. Popular culture and the elements of the third engine have an inter-
dependent symbiotic relationship through the mass media because the agencies and institutions depend on the media for wide distribution of their
knowledge and claims, and the media depend on these organizations for credible knowledge to market and distribute.

POPULAR CULTURE—WHAT DOES
IT MEAN FOR CRIME AND JUSTICE?

For most of the history of criminology and criminal justice studies, this question has not been a mainstream concern. When it has been explored, this issue
has been approached in a simplistic fashion under the assumption that effects
follow automatically from content. Recently, however, the academic study of
popular culture has begun to catch up with the long-standing public interest
in its effects. Currently, most Americans feel that the news media emphasis on
violent crime combined with violent movies and television are a major reason
why the United States has more violent deaths than other countries (Harris
Poll, 1994). Popular culture's news and entertainment has also had important

effects on crime and justice in America, historically exemplified by the impact of popular culture products such as *Uncle Tom's Cabin* in the mid nineteenth century on slave laws, the film *I Am a Fugitive from a Chain Gang* on correctional practices in the 1920s, and the recent effects of the movie *Silence of the Lambs* and the reporting of serial murders in the news on "Three Strikes and You're Out" legislation (Jenkins, 1994; Shichor and Sechrest, 1996).

The perception of popular culture as a legitimate area of crime and justice study was invigorated in 1990 by Graeme Newman's article "Popular Culture and Criminal Justice" (Newman, 1990). Since this article was published, the study of the relationship between popular culture and crime and justice has enjoyed an ever-expanding field of research. The following essays reflect the latest ventures in this exploration and belie the notion that the relationship between popular culture and crime and justice can be safely ignored. As described in the opening chapter by Frankie Bailey and Donna Hale, the essays focus on the content and effects of popular culture concerning crime and justice along two main divisions—entertainment (historically tied to detective stories) and news (historically traceable to gallows sermons). The first is the popular culture found in movies, videos, novels, and comic books, to name a few contemporary outlets. The second is popular journalism produced as entertainment to be consumed as entertainment. As the subsequent essays reveal, this infotainment-styled news is found within special programs, news magazines, and daily local newscasts. The essays in this book advance our understanding of popular culture's role in the realm of crime and justice in many ways.

Focusing first on perspectives for understanding popular culture, Peter Manning in a discussion of television describes the concept of media looping and its relationship to the popular culture's impact on the construction of social reality. In media looping, media content is extracted from one context or component of the media and reused and reframed in another. It is not unusual for looping to result in new ambiguous media realities. These looping effects are observed by Manning both in real events that are mediated, such as the Rodney King beating and the Oklahoma City bombing, and in created-for-media pseudo-events in shows like *Cops*. A hyperreality results in which the media-generated reality loops and interweaves with our unmediated personal reality. Bringing to mind Plato's "shadows on the cave wall," Manning harbingers a future where crime and justice will be understood and experienced through the popular culture's reality mixing bowl.

In Chapter 3, while focusing on popular movies, Newman takes an initial step in moving the tradition of content analysis of popular culture's violence from the mere counting of violent acts to an understanding and incorporation of the context of violence within stories. He provides a methodological model that can be applied to other areas of popular culture, crime, and justice research. What he terms the language of violence must be considered to adequately examine the effects of violent media on viewers' subsequent violent behavior. Toward this effort, he offers a typology of movie violence that can serve as a foundation for subsequent research. Based on classifications of violence as either instrumental violence (goal-oriented, rational, logically planned) or expressive violence (explosive emotional act), Newman examines the encoding and enplotting of violence. Encoding involves the context and rationale of the violence portrayal, enplotting describes the techniques that use violence to enhance or resolve story-line problems. This approach leads to a detailed typology of movie violence that goes a long way toward increasing the comprehension of entertainment violence.

The theme of censorship and deviance is covered by two essays by Amy Nyberg and Jeff Ferrell that provide a sense of history to the area and a glimpse of future developing trends. First, using comics, Nyberg provides an excellent review and discussion of the social construction of a social problem, in this case delinquency, and the role of the media as both villain and moderator. In the late 1940s, increased concern about delinquency coupled with and fed by increased popular press coverage resulted in the public implicating popular culture and specifically radio, the movies, and comic books as causes of delinquency. Comics were the most vulnerable target, and Nyberg describes the claims and claimsmakers that abounded in the 1950s battle to assign cause and enact legislation aimed at the comic book industry. The 1950s story of comics is a description of one installment in a recurring moral crusade in America that regularly aims at some component of the popular culture.

Ferrell updates this moral crusade history and signifies its recurring nature in an examination of the social construction process through which popular culture is criminalized. Reviewing recent attacks on rap and heavy metal music, Ferrell discusses the periodic attempts to reconstruct popular culture as criminal and to establish its effects as criminogenic. The social reconstruction relies on obscenity arguments to portray popular culture as criminal and on copycat effects to portray popular culture as criminogenic. What is ironic is that the popular culture, which is largely developed and delivered through the mass media, finds itself criminalized through the same mass media. Popular culture is seen to be both dependent on the mass media for its life and to be demonized by it.

Focusing next on the popular culture news, or popular everyday journalism, the questions of how events come to be news and the news' social influence are addressed by a set of essays by Steven Chermak; Jeffrey Ross; Kenneth Tunnell; Neil Websdale and Alexander Alvarez; and Katherine Bennett, W. Wesley Johnson, and Ruth Triplett. A highly selective gatekeeping process regarding crime and justice news is revealed. The end result of this selective gatekeeping, the content of the popular crime and justice news is refined throughout the essays. Opening this discussion, Chermak expands our understanding of the crime news gatekeeping process and the role of news sources in the creation of crime news. He observes that crime news sources have varying, sometimes conflicting, goals in providing crime information and that the relationship and past interactions between the news' sources and the journalists strongly influence access and the selection process.

Along similar lines, Ross describes the process by which police violence events come to be known, selected, and constructed as popular news of police violence. Looking at the gatekeeping process in detail, Ross reports that a parallel gatekeeping process exists to filter police violence events into news of police violence. As with general crime news, it is equally unlikely that news of police violence will be representative of all police violence, and, like terrorist acts of violence, most police acts of violence go unreported. In sum, what is newsworthy police violence is what the news media agencies decide is newsworthy after a long arbitrary organizational, highly idiosyncratic gatekeeping process that is largely separate from the significance of these events to either the police or the public. The end result, as with much crime and justice news, is information about police violence that is not typical of police violence.

Tunnell's chapter discusses the content analysis of newsmagazine television programs, a currently popular form of infotainment programming. Television newsmagazine programming is found to be very similar to popular news. What makes these programs worrisome is that they are expanded, in-depth stories that create the image that an issue is being discussed from multiple sides. These programs have the feel of context, without the reality of context. Like most popular news, high profile, sensationalist crimes and criminals are emphasized with a focus on individual, random, stranger-on-stranger acts of violence. Television newsmagazines also continue the process of commodification (the packaging and marketing of crime information for popular consumption), which has a long history. Newsmagazines continue the general popular culture's portrayal of crimes and criminals within constructions that are nearly always simplistic and individualistic.

Websdale and Alvarez in their chapter and Bennett, Wesley, and Triplett in their chapter discuss the effects and social role of crime and justice popular news. Bennett, Wesley, and Triplett employ the concept of reintegrative and disintegrative shaming to describe two possible opposite effects of the popular culture on the social reaction to offenders. The popular culture is shown to usually portray offenders in stigmatizing constructions. Reintegrative shaming occurs but significantly less often. Websdale and Alvarez use a related concept of tainting to discuss how the popular news discredits the perpetrators of homicide-suicides. Coverage of these dual acts of violence are also seen to be similar to most crime and justice news that focuses on the individual aspects of each event and downplays the social pattern of their occurrence. The focus is on dramatic entertainment criteria with a recitation of details about individual offenders and crime scenes. Social structure contexts such as references to a history of domestic violence are downplayed.

The other major stream of popular culture, the admittedly entertainment flow, is discussed in the remaining chapters. The crime and justice entertainment images of popular culture are examined in four chapters by Donna Hale; Frankie Bailey, Jocelyn Pollock, and Sherry Schroeder; Robert Freeman; and Derral Cheatwood. Collectively, the chapters reveal that although some changes are evident, the bulk of popular culture's crime and justice content remains depressingly stereotyped.

Along these lines, the stereotypical portrait of women found in the popular culture is discussed by Donna Hale regarding policewomen and by Frankie Bailey, Jocelyn Pollock, and Sherry Schroeder regarding female attorneys. Hale explores the portrayal of policewomen in films from 1972 to 1995. Although she finds that there has been an upsurge of policewomen films in the last 13 years, social stereotypes of women still dominate the content. Hale reports that the sexual nature of the policewomen determines her portrayal most often. Two policewomen stereotypes are found to be common: hypermasculine policewomen (male demeanor and characteristics) and hyperfeminine policewomen (sexual, pleasure creatures). For policewomen in films, myths of femininity remain evident.

Similarly Bailey, Pollock, and Schroeder examine the images of female attorneys in popular films. Female attorneys appear to fare somewhat better than policewomen in films in that some aspects of their real world are accurately portrayed. The films do reflect the formerly scarce numbers of female lawyers, the gender-based attitudes prevalent toward women lawyers, and the existence of the femininity-achievement conflict that pits the traditional female social role against their functioning as effective attorneys. However, women lawyers, like policewomen, are likely to have their sexuality and sexual relationships dominate their portrayals and to be more often shown as young, white, single, and childless. They also share with male portrayals the unrealistic overemphasis on dangerous and sensational criminal law cases.

An area long ignored and still understudied is the portrait of corrections found in the popular culture. In response, Robert Freeman and Derral Cheatwood in two separate chapters look at those images. Freeman looks at the images of corrections, which he summarizes as a "smug hacks" image. Regarding the entertainment content of popular culture concerning corrections, Freeman reports that correction's films are stuck in the pre-1960s days of corrections and highlight the harshness of prison life. He also observes that the news media focus on the negative aspects of corrections, emphasizing negative acts of both inmates and staff. And as with film, when positive images of corrections are shown in popular news, the inmates are more likely to be the ones shown positively. The historical animosity between corrections personnel and the media and corrections' tendency to avoid and bar the news media has left the public with few alternative sources of information to construct their image of corrections. Freeman points out that this vacuum encourages public acceptance of the stereotypes of corrections found in the entertainment portions of popular culture.

Cheatwood likewise looks at prison life as depicted in films while offering a typology of prison films. He observes that although prison films are the primary source of public information about prisons and corrections in general, prison films compose just 1 percent of all films. Having few personal dealings with corrections and few media portraits from which to choose, most of the public is doubly limited in their access to alternative correctional information sources. Members of the public must therefore construct their reality of the world of corrections from severely biased and restricted knowledge.

THE FUTURE OF POPULAR
CULTURE, CRIME, AND JUSTICE

The essays in this book raise many issues concerning popular culture, crime, and justice. Returning to my initial query about the popularity of popular culture, escapism and voyeurism do not explain the dominance of crime and justice in popular culture's content, nor the emphasis within the crime and justice content on violent predatory crime (Surette, 1994). This myopic focus on violent predatory crime is tied to a long historical interest in crime and justice as theater (Ball, 1981; Surette, 1992), and the palatable explanation of crime that predatory crime presents to the public. Crime and justice has been a source for story lines since antiquity, and predator criminality, though constructing crime as a frightening (and hence entertaining) phenomena, also presents crime as caused by individual-based deficiencies, thus freeing the public from any causal role. The popular culture's construction of crime and justice is deeply rooted in our cultural heritage, particularly our tradition of individualism and our preexisting social stereotypes. The belief in individual responsibility and individual-based explanations for crime is the primary image reflected in our popular culture (Bullah, Madsen, Sullivan, Swidler, and Tipton, 1985; Gans, 1988) and has significant impact on crime and justice policies. Pointed out repeatedly in these chapters, the popular culture's focus on individual responsibility for crime is distressing not because it is incorrect but because it is fragmentary. As Tunnell astutely reports, such a perspective on criminal behavior leaves societal influences unquestioned and puts forth half the problem as if it were the whole problem. To look only at individual responsibility is to look away from any social responsibility.

The popularity of the violent predatory crime is also likely caused by a downward comparison effect. Downward comparison is a psychological process in which one feels better about his or her own situation if shown someone in a worse one. Therefore, a popular culture image of violent urban crime would have a soothing effect on middle-class suburban America by holding a crime and justice construction of reality that is more violent and dangerous than what they are experiencing. And as this violent urban crime is shown as caused by individual deficiencies like greed and innate evilness, the apparently better-off-by-comparison rest of America can enjoy a guilt-free boast regarding the crime situation. In another ironic evolutionary trend, recent films have tended toward more one-dimensional characters and stories within violent action portraits that are closer to fantasy while some of the more sophisticated multidimensional characters and stories appear in the comics.[1] In general, however, these essays show that the evolution of the content of popular culture is mostly more of the same—recycled story lines and stereotypes with more graphic violence, sex, and special effects.

One particularly distressing finding of these essays is the continued low visibility of minorities and the invisibility of minority women. When portrayed, women of all races have a tacked-on sexual message that contains numerous images of dominance and submissive sexual relationships linked to sexual coercion and violence. Paradoxically, in the same popular culture, women are given the additional burden of having professionalism somehow cancel their femininity. A successful woman in the popular culture is frequently unwomanly. Smart, effective, and professional females employed in crime and justice—as found in the popular culture—are rare. When these traits are attributed, it often means the female's sexuality is repressed.

The future of popular culture's crime and justice news is that popular culture will continue to merge news and entertainment and that the marketing of crime and justice will continue to increase. What effect these loops will have on the crime and justice gatekeeping process is less clear. The availability of video and new media technologies has already created a new genre of programs termed "reality programming" that rely heavily on images of real crimes, criminal investigations, and criminal justice agency activities as fodder for entertainment programs (Cavender and Fishman, Forthcoming). It will be interesting to see what affect video in public hands has on the reporting of police violence and other types of crime news—as pictures invariably increase the newsworthiness of an event as the videotaping of the Rodney King beating exemplifies. Whether the application of entertainment criteria to the selection of crime news has plateaued is not known, but there is no indication of its decline. This book teaches us that to understand the future of news, we must understand the history of entertainment and employ an associated analysis.

It is safe to say that popular culture will remain a dominant social construction engine, so that influence in the popular culture realm will remain highly important. In that the content of popular culture continues to be distorted and biased, the debunking of its content remains a crucial task (Barak, 1994a). As these chapters point out, this task is especially needed in the crime and justice area because of limited alternative information sources and becomes increasingly necessary the farther into the criminal justice system you look. To the extent that the dynamics of the popular culture define criminalization and the working of the criminal law and criminal justice system, then the urgency of comprehending this process and the links between popular culture's content, the public's construction of crime and justice, and society's crime and justice policies is apparent. This work provides a step in that direction.

The most important observation running through these essays is the social construction competition that is ongoing. The ultimate competition is not for the construction of crime and justice but is for influence over the popular culture's social construction engine. The mass media and the popular culture they construct and legitimize are the grand prizes. If you influence the symbol-creating and symbol-defining engine of a society, you create the social reality of that society. And if a particular perspective of social reality gains control of a social construction engine, other constructions will never be competitive. The ultimate significance of the social construction of moral crusades and panics in crime and justice is that they set the stage for future access to and enhanced influence on the general social construction machinery. Winning one social construction contest puts us in a better position for future contests. For in crime and justice, perceptions have a nasty habit of becoming reality.[2]

NOTES

1. For a discussion, see Newman (1993) and Williams (1994).

2. For a discussion of changes in the reality of criminal justice to accommodate perceptions of criminal justice, see Kappeler, Blumberg, and Potter (1996).

1

❀

Popular Culture, Crime, and Justice

FRANKIE Y. BAILEY
AND DONNA C. HALE

It's a case of intergalactic law and order.

NETWORK PROMO FOR AN EPISODE OF *STAR TREK: DEEP SPACE NINE*[1]

We like stories about outlaws who live outside the social order. We imbue them with all kinds of romantic legends. That's our particular mythology, whether it's Wyatt Earp or Eliot Ness or Al Capone.

DIRECTOR BRIAN DEPALMA ABOUT HIS CRIME FILMS[2]

INTRODUCTION

On May 19, 1996, the last first-run weekly episode of *Murder, She Wrote* was broadcast on CBS. *TV Guide* noted in a "Close-Up": "After a dozen years and 286 'slayings,' *Murder* gets the ax, closing a chapter in TV history as the longest-running mystery drama" (*TV Guide*, 1996: 91).

Murder, She Wrote had enjoyed a much longer run than either the show's creators or the network anticipated (Meyers, 1989: 277–278). It was atypical of television mystery series because the sleuth Jessica Fletcher (played by Angela Lansbury) was a woman in her sixties, a former English teacher turned crime writer, a widow who lived in a small town in Maine. There was little sex or on-screen violence, no high-speed chases or shoot-outs to jolt the audience to attention. And yet for more than a decade, *Murder, She Wrote* had dominated its time spot, beating out the competition.

One reason offered for the success of the show was that until its final season, it had followed CBS's powerhouse Sunday newsmagazine *60 Minutes*. Perhaps after receiving a dose of "doom and gloom" from the newsmagazine, the Sunday audience sought "a breath of relief" in the form of a whodunit

(Meyers, 1989). In Jessica Fletcher's world, bad things happened (sometimes to good people), but at the end of the hour, Jessica solved the mystery. The murderer was taken into custody by the police. Order was restored.

Actually, *Murder, She Wrote* was in the tradition of the "classic detective" story. Since the "golden age" of detective fiction, commentators have pondered the pleasures and rewards such fiction offers readers (Allen and Chacko, 1974; Symons, 1985; Wells, 1929). Whatever its attractions, in the twentieth century, the detective story is a staple of popular culture.

Stories of fictional crime and punishment capture our imagination, and as Quinney writes, "Social reality begins in the imagination" (1970: 291). For crime and justice, social reality might well begin with what Quinney describes as a "generalized criminal mythology, conceptions of crime [that] are diffused throughout the populations" (281). However, our construction of beliefs about crime are "mediated by the social context of diffusion and by the interpersonal relations associated with the adoption of criminal conceptions" (281). Or, put another way, we gain the knowledge from which we construct social reality from four sources: (1) personal experiences, (2) significant others, (3) groups and institutions, and (4) the mass media (Surette, 1992: 4).

The mass media and other forms of popular culture are what concern us here. In *The Mythology of Crime and Criminal Justice*, Kappeler, Blumberg, and Potter assert that the "media are mythmakers" (1996: 7). This, they argue, is a reason for concern because the media (along with other institutions, such as the government) offer us distorted images of crime, criminals, and law enforcers. We are presented with distorted pictures of the seriousness of crime and its social location. On *Murder, She Wrote*, the fictional town of Cabot Cove, Maine, Jessica Fletcher's hometown, had five murders each television season (Meyers, 1989: 280), giving it perhaps the highest small-town murder rate in America.[3] The victims were drawn from Jessica's middle- and upper-class friends, acquaintances, and business associates. The victims, like their murderers, were usually white. The murderers were motivated more often by greed and convenience than by passion. Both victims and murderers were atypical of real life.

One might argue that it is unlikely that the audience who tuned in each Sunday night to watch Jessica Fletcher solve another mystery perceived the show as a serious source of information about real life crime. However, Grant asserts that reality-based (video verité) crime shows such as *Cops* and *America's Most Wanted* are not necessarily a more reliable source for such information. She states, "The verité form presents the story as objective even though, as in other fiction, verité has been edited to tell a story from a particular perspective [that of the police]" (1992: 61). These stories are "decontextualized," stripped of their relation to the social space occupied by the alleged offenders.[4]

At the same time, crime has long provided material for other types of programming, including talk shows, daytime dramas, and situation comedies. Among these, talk shows have come under fire from critics. The 1990s version of the daytime talk show has been described as "trash TV" or "tabloid talk" and condemned by critics as "unprofessional, exploitative, sleazy" (Grant, 1992: 17). Caldwell cites as an example of this tabloid format a February 1993

Geraldo show broadcast during the ratings sweep period. The show had as its subject "men who murder their wives" (1995: 223). The program began with the airing of a videotaped (caught on camera) murder of a woman by her husband. Caldwell reports that among Geraldo's guests that day was a woman who had "survived 'five gun blasts' to the face and abdomen" (223). The overall tone of the show "suggested that this particular matrimonial ritual was not uncommon" (223).

Of course, as Rose points out, "the personalities of TV talk show hosts shape the nature of their programs" (1985: 341). In the wake of media and public scrutiny following recent incidents involving traumatized guests, several hosts have publicly declared their intention to tone down the sensational nature of their shows.

Even so, the standard format of the daytime talk show (that is, audience participation, lively or highly emotional talk, limited speaking time for each guest) seems to be problematic for the discussion of some topics. For example, on a recent episode of *Oprah* (1/12/96), actress Sally Field appeared to discuss her new movie, *Eye for an Eye*, in which she played a mother whose teenage daughter was raped and murdered. Joining Field and host Oprah Winfrey were the members of a real-life support group for parents of murdered children. The parents shared their reactions to the film (which the studio audience had viewed) and expressed their own feelings of rage toward the murderers of their children and their desire for vengeance if they could not obtain justice. Later in the show, a psychologist (and author) whose own child had been murdered joined the group to offer advice to the parents (and to the listening audience) about dealing with such destructive emotions. But we wonder if, because of the nature of the talk show format, such an emotion-laden topic can be examined without some degree of sensationalization. Was the presence of the psychologist "as expert" sufficient to place the topic of "parents of murdered children" (and vigilante violence) in perspective for the viewing audience?

The audiences of daytime dramas ("soap operas") are also exposed to crime. Since the days when they were broadcast on radio, these dramas have had crime as an element. Matelski finds that toward the end of the 1940s "crime emerged as an important plotline theme, especially in the area of juvenile delinquency. This direction was reflective of the times, for Americans were becoming increasingly concerned about youth crime in their country" (1991: 34). Crime remains an important theme. Most daytime dramas (including *General Hospital*, *All My Children*, *The Guiding Light*, *As the World Turns*, and *The Young and the Restless*) number police officers, private investigators, or attorneys among their continuing characters. In Matelski's review of the plotline themes of soap operas between 1983 and 1990, four of the nine story lines most likely to air during rating sweeps periods were crime or mystery-related: (1) the discovery of key clues in some type of crime or mystery, (2) court cases, (3) criminal arrests, and (4) investigations (usually involving international travel) (34). On soap operas, attempted murder, rape, and kidnapping are among the trials and tribulations suffered by the characters. However, some types of crimes generate troubling plotlines. Several years ago, critics voiced concern about a disturbing trend in which soap opera rapists were being transformed into romantic leading men. In fact, the love affair between one of daytime television's most popular couples, *General Hospital's* Luke and Laura, "started with a rape and ended at the altar" (Logan, 1993: 13).

Crime has also found its way into television situation comedies (sitcoms). Over the years, several situation comedies have featured law enforcement officers as their protagonists. These shows include *Car 54, Where Are You?* (1961–1963), *The Andy Griffith Show* (1960–1968), and *Barney Miller* (1975–1982). The first two shows were played strictly for laughs. But as Kania and Tanham note of *Barney Miller,*

> Even comedy in the 1970s had a strong current of realism and a human touch. *Barney Miller* . . . had a realism lacking in both the earlier comedy and serious police drama programs. The mixed bag of cops, criminals, clients, and complainants accurately portrayed the typical casework of real police officers (1987: 36).

Another comedy of the 1970s—not about police officers but about a blue-collar family—*All in the Family* (1971–1979) also had more realism than TV audiences had come to expect from sitcoms. During the course of the show, Archie Bunker, his wife Edith, his daughter Gloria, and his son-in-law Michael (a.k.a. "Meathead") were all victims of urban crime. One particularly memorable episode of this ground-breaking sitcom (see Mintz, 1985) dealt with the beating death of "Beverly," a female impersonator and friend of the Bunker family. Another episode was about Edith Bunker's frightening encounter with a serial rapist who tricked his way into her home.

In the 1990s, crime in the news sometimes provides the punchline of the sitcom plots. For example, a recent episode of *Murphy Brown* offered a parody of the real-life O.J. Simpson trial.[5] Sitcom journalist Murphy, in court to challenge a traffic citation, found herself provided by her network with a "dream team" of high-powered defense attorneys. This *Murphy Brown* episode reflects what Rushkoff describes as the "house of mirrors within mirrors [that] is the American mediascape" (1994: 20). He asserts that we function in a "datasphere" in which "media viruses spread rapidly if they provoke our interest" (10). Thus a real-life crime saturates the news media and then becomes a part of general popular culture in the form of made-for-television movies, monologues by late-night talk-show hosts, plotlines for dramas or situation comedies, and even as bumper stickers, Halloween masks, tee shirts and other collectibles.

But what was the relationship between popular culture and crime before our age of high technology and mass audiences?

FROM VILLAGE TO METROPOLIS

In the beginning were Cain and Abel, Biblical murderer and victim. Renowned mystery writer, scholar, and editor Ellery Queen writes, "The first recorded murder was complete with victim, criminal, motive, and—inferentially—weapon; we know that 'Cain rose up against Abel his brother, and slew him'" (1969: 3). British writer and scholar Dorothy Sayers, in the introduction to her anthology *The Omnibus of Crime* (1929), supports this view that some of the earliest tales of murder and intrigue can be found in the Bible. Other sources of such stories are the myths and folktales of ancient peoples. Evident in early folk cultures is the fascination humans have demonstrated for murder and other dastardly deeds.

Zipes describes the folktale as an oral narrative through which the common people expressed the "manner in which they perceived nature and their social order and their wish to satisfy their needs and wants" (1979: 5). The history of the folktale is an ancient one. In the nineteenth century, the fairy-tale arose in the western world as "the mass mediated cultural form of the folktale" (12). And in these fairytales, as in the folktales, were villains, victims, and dastardly deeds.

In his seminal analysis of the meaning of fairytales, *The Uses of Enchantment*, Bruno Bettelheim writes, "In fairytales, as in life, punishment or fear of it is only a limited deterrent to crime" (1976: 9). Attitudes that "crime does not pay" and that "the bad person always loses out" are what make fairytales useful teaching tools. The child, according to Bettelheim, identifies with the hero of the tale who struggles and overcomes (9).[6]

In the close-knit rural villages, information about crime was conveyed by word of mouth. Stories of local crimes became the basis for folk songs and ballads. With the movement from village to town and city and the development of technology came a transition from folk culture to mass culture. But crime remained a topic of popular interest, and some folk culture narrative forms made the transition into mass mediums. An example of such a transition is the "murdered girl" ballad. This ballad form tells the story of a naive young woman who is seduced by a young man. When she becomes pregnant and begins to talk of marriage, the young man kills her. As Coffin observes, "the formula is often so strong that fact simply melts under its power and vanishes among the clichés" (1975: 100). In the nineteenth century, this formula was adopted in sensational stories depicting the demises of real-life victims such as Naomi Wise (1808) and Pearl Byran (1896) (Coffin, 1975: 101–107).[7] This also was the formula used by novelist Theodore Dreiser in *An American Tragedy* (1925), his fictionalized retelling of the 1906 Adirondack murder of Grace Brown by Chester Gillette. One of the two movies based on the case was *A Place in the Sun* (1951).[8]

Other real-life crimes also received ballad treatment. These ballads tell stories ranging from the exploits of Western outlaws such as Billy the Kid and Jesse James to the saga of a scorned woman who kills the man who "done her wrong" ("Frankie and Johnny").[9] These ballads and the perspectives they represent prompt questions about how Americans perceive crime and justice. Or as Chambliss and Mankoff (1976) put it, "Whose law? What order?" In popular culture narratives, individuals who break the law have sometimes been presented as heroes.

Kooistra observes that throughout American history, a small group of individuals who rob and kill have nonetheless been "commonly perceived as heroes. . . . These are outlaws who have been transformed from ordinary criminals into legendary figures" (1990: 217). At the same time, those racial and ethnic groups that historically have been outside the American mainstream have created their own popular culture in which the status of folk hero is bestowed on real-life and fictional characters who are strong enough to challenge the status quo and defy the rules of the dominant society (Dance, 1987; Frye, 1980; Mirande, 1987). For example, there is "Stagolee" (or "Stackolee"), the African American folklore hero. There is the Native American warrior Geronimo and also the Mexican American social bandit Joaquin Murieta.

Clearly, there exists in American society an ambivalence about crime that is reflected in our popular culture. In this respect, literary crime can serve as "an ambiguous mirror of social values" (Cawelti, 1976: 77). For example, in nineteenth-century England and America, the domestic circle was "the focal point of conceptions of morality and social authority." And yet, "the literature of crime and the actual crimes that most fascinated the public were primarily the murders of relatives . . . These were the staples of the classical detective story and the great Victorian murder trials" (77).

One of the more famous examples of this "malice domestic" was the late nineteenth-century case of Lizzie Borden, the New England spinster accused of the ax murders of her father and stepmother. For more than a century, this unsolved double murder case has continued to fascinate scholars, mystery buffs, and the general public. It not only has been the basis for a nursery rhyme, biographies, novels, short stories, and true crimes books, but has also been the subject of ballets and operas. A classic episode ("The Older Sister") of the television show *Alfred Hitchcock Presents* opens a year after the trial. Acquitted of the murders, Lizzie Borden is living with the suspicions of those around her. And, in this fictional solution to the crime, she also lives with her own devastating knowledge of who actually committed the murders. In "The Older Sister," Lizzie Borden is presented as a stalwart heroine who has unselfishly allowed herself to be blamed for the crimes committed by Emma, her sister.[10]

If Lizzie Borden had lived in colonial New England and had been convicted of double murder, she might well have been sentenced to death. In that event, she would probably have been the subject of a "gallows sermon." Prepared by ministers for the execution of condemned criminals, these sermons were "effectively marketed and distributed" to the general public (Cohen, 1993: 4). The first book printed in Boston was an execution sermon prepared by Increase Mather (Cohen, 1993: 8).[11] Between 1674 and 1825, more than 75 volumes (often with the prisoner's confession included) were issued in the region (10). Prominent among the contributors to the genre were ministers Increase and Cotton Mather, father and son. But during the course of two centuries, the control of the literature of crime and punishment passed from the ministers to the attorneys and the publishers. Gallows sermons were superseded by newspaper accounts, trial reports, and novels. The "framing" of the criminal that had once been religious was now secular. The starring role in the drama had passed from charismatic minister to charismatic attorney (several of whom became early media celebrities) (Cohen, 1993).

In the country as a whole, the nineteenth century brought industrialization, urbanization, immigration, and the expanding marketplace. Papke finds that during the period 1830 to 1900, "an immense variety of crime-related products traveled every avenue into the cultural marketplace" (1987: xvi). These products included broadsheets, pamphlets, and newspaper articles about crime. They also included novels and stories. In addition, "police chiefs, detectives, and criminals composed memoirs, confessions, and crime-stopping kits" (xiv).[12]

Among the detectives who engaged in this type of composition were Allan Pinkerton (see Klein, 1994) and William J. Burns. Pinkerton published several volumes about the activities of his operatives and their infiltration of groups such as "The Molly Maguires." Burns, the head of the Burns International Detective Agency who would later be J. Edgar Hoover's predecessor at the Bureau of Investigation, became famous enough to be a "front-page detective" (Hunt, 1990). His activities attracted not only newspaper coverage but a derogatory comic strip (later "Mutt and Jeff") commissioned by newspaper publisher William Randolph Hearst (Hunt, 1990: 47). In his own efforts at self-promotion, Burns lectured and wrote about his cases.

During this period, as new crime-related products entered the marketplace, the crime genres that are still a part of our popular culture came into being.

CRIME, JUSTICE, AND GENRE FORMULAS

In her critique of Hollywood films, Mellen writes, "As every culture has norms and dominant values defining what is 'masculine' and 'feminine,' our films have been made in the service of quite specific images and ideals of manliness" (1977: 7). She asserts, "The ideal man of our films is a violent one" (3). She finds this to be true not only of males who portray criminals and outlaws but also of those who represent law and order:

> By the late sixties and seventies the job of the screen male who would be "masculine" and "strong" becomes the overt protection of a social order in danger of collapse. In an era of deteriorating cities, unemployment, and escalating violence, the hero is not the underdog but the cop, the more brutal the better. (24)

Mellen is quoted at length here because her analysis touches on a number of issues relevant to crime genres in popular culture. Specifically,

Who is the hero and what makes him heroic?

How are evolving crime genres related to changing social conditions?

What are the roles assumed by women and others who are not white males in these genres?

We will address these questions later. But, first, we should define *genre*. Writing about the genre film, Schatz states, "[It] involves familiar, essentially one-dimensional characters acting out a predictable story pattern within a familiar setting" (1981: 6). Their familiarity with characters, setting, and story line means that film literate audiences have no difficulty distinguishing a western from a gangster movie or a horror film from a romance.

Each genre (or type) of film has its own conventions, but as Schatz observes, "All film genres treat some form of threat—violent or otherwise to the social order" (1981: 26). The threat and the resulting conflict are "indigenous" to the environment (that is, western frontier town or urban inner-city neighborhood) of a genre film and "reflect the physical and ideological struggle" for control (26).

These comments about genre films apply to other mediums. Stories that are pleasing to audiences are told and retold, moving across mediums. They are reduced to formulas that are "a combination or synthesis of a number of specific cultural conventions with a more universal form or archetype" (Cawelti, 1976: 6). Berger observes that genres are important in the study of popular culture because

> They enable us to talk about the relationship of texts to other texts in terms of form as well as content. The concept of intertextuality . . . suggests that texts are often related to one another on content level. That is, they borrow (sometimes inadvertently) from one another . . . (1992: xiii).[13]

American crime genres reflect European (particularly British) influence. They also reflect a reaction to that influence. The roots of crime fiction are located in the distant past, but modern crime fiction is generally said to have begun with Edgar Allan Poe, "the father of the mystery short story."[14] Sayers asserts that in Poe's five tales of "ratiocination" written between 1840 and 1845, the "general principles of the detective story were laid down forever" (1929: 10). In these stories, Poe introduced now familiar conventions of detection fiction such as the red herring and the puzzle or cipher story. But Poe's greatest contribution to the genre was the creation of his brilliant, eccentric amateur detective, Monsieur C. Auguste Dupin. In three stories narrated by his nameless friend, Monsieur Dupin solves cases that have baffled the police. One of these stories, "The Murder of Marie Roget," is based on the real-life unsolved murder of a New York City "shop girl" named Mary Rogers. In the story, Poe has Dupin provide a solution to the crime.

But for all Dupin's brilliance, he was later upstaged by another nineteenth century fictional detective. Building on the conventions Poe—an American writing about a brilliant French detective—had laid down, Arthur Conan Doyle, a British physician turned writer, created Sherlock Holmes, consulting detective. Holmes resides at 221-B Baker Street with his friend, Dr. John Watson. When unoccupied with crime solving, Holmes succumbs to ennui, to which he responds by playing his violin or taking a seven-percent solution of cocaine. Holmes and Watson debuted in a *Study in Scarlet* (1887) and were soon read and beloved on both sides of the Atlantic. It was Holmes (of the logical and scientific, if somewhat eccentric mind) that other would-be detective writers rushed to imitate.[15] As a character, Holmes made a successful transition from print to film to radio and eventually to television. In his deerstalker cap, magnifying glass in hand, Holmes has even turned up in Madison Avenue ads.

This concept of the detective as a talented nonprofessional became the basis for the "classic detective" fiction created during the "golden age" of detective fiction. The characters created by British writers such as Agatha Christie, Dorothy Sayers, and G.K. Chesterton solve their crimes in country manors, English villages, and on isolated islands. Golden age fiction emphasizes plot and puzzle. It invites the reader to indulge in "armchair detection" with little wear and tear on the reader's emotions. The characters are aristocratic or military or at least well-bred and respectable. Violence happens offstage.

Writers such as Ellery Queen, S.S. Van Dine, and Rex Stout offered readers American versions of the classic detective. But in the 1920s, a new kind of detective fiction that reflected both its pulp magazine origins and the changes occurring in American society appeared. In his essay, "The Simple Art of Murder," Raymond Chandler writes of his contemporary Dashiell Hammett: "Hammett gave murder back to the kind of people who commit it for reasons, not just to provide a corpse, and with the means at hand, not handwrought dueling pistols, curare, and tropical fish" (1934: 16). Hammett was one of the writers of "tough guy" or "hard-boiled" detective fiction who emerged in the United States. Appearing first in the pages of "pulp magazines,"[16] these writers created protagonists who were tough, at times violent, even brutal. But according to Chandler, creator of "Philip Marlowe," the tough guy detective was "the best man in his world" (1934: 20). He was a professional ("private eye") with an office (usually shabby) and a desk (usually with a bottle of liquor in the drawer). He was a loner who struggled to maintain his personal integrity and to do his job in a world of gangsters, dangerous women, brutal cops, corrupt politicians, and depraved rich.[17]

In both classic detective fiction and hard-boiled fiction, the agents of official law enforcement are peripheral characters. They are often ineffective, sometimes stupid or (in tough-guy fiction) brutal. Nineteenth-century novelists such as British writer Charles Dickens had introduced police officers as positive characters in their novels.[18] But in the nineteenth-century atmosphere of distrust of the official police and the early twentieth-century environment of corruption, police officers did not prosper as fictional heroes.[19] Not until the 1940s did the police procedural novel firmly establish the police officer in this role (Dove, 1982).

In counterpoint to these crime genres that presented a heroic detective were those formulaic stories that offered the outlaw or gangster as hero. Manchel maintains that although there had been earlier depictions of gangsters in films, director D.W. Griffith's 1916 film *Intolerance* "cemented many characteristics of gangster films" (Manchel, 1978: 17). With the coming of Prohibition, the gangster films that moviegoers saw in movie theaters bore increasing resemblance to reality. Film stars Edward G. Robinson and James

Cagney, who played tough, urban gangsters, had their real-life, sometimes equally flamboyant counterparts.[20] With the arrival of the new sound technology, the gangster film came into its own, bringing "the punchy slang of city streets, the screech of burning tires, and the chatter of tommy guns" into the theater (Toll, 1982: 159).

During the Great Depression, which began with the 1929 stock market crash, the movie industry slid into a slump (Toll, 1982: 162). Box office receipts were down. At the same time, the industry was receiving increasing pressure from interest groups who wanted less sex and violence in the movies. For years, the movie industry had been dodging censorship efforts by these reform groups. In 1934, the Roman Catholic bishops and the nation's chiefs of police "decided to support the censorship campaign" (Powers, 1983: 67–68). The bishops organized the Episcopal Committee on Motion Pictures in November 1933 and established a membership division, the Legion of Decency. American Catholics joining the Legion pledged to protest against "vile and unwholesome motion pictures" that were a "grave menace to youth, to home life, to country, and to religion" (68).

When other groups joined the Catholics in this movement, the movie industry resurrected the Production Code that had been proposed by movie industry troubleshooter Will Hays (see Vaughn, 1990). However, when the International Association of Chiefs of Police formed a committee to persuade Hollywood to do something about the way police characters were portrayed, Hollywood "was eager to cooperate" (Powers, 1983: 68). MGM created a short subject series *Crime Does Not Pay* (70). The studios asked for "an exemption to the antigangster rules" so that they could work in "the public interest" (71). This time the police officer would be the hero. The gangster would be replaced by the G-man. And audiences would still get plenty of action (Powers, 1983).

Thus the (first) cycle of gangster films gave way to a cycle of films about government agents (G-men). J. Edgar Hoover, though he knew the value of good publicity, was not completely happy with the movie industry's tendency to turn federal law enforcement officers into "action heroes." He attempted to persuade the media to follow his "formula," in which the agent was presented as a part of an organization, a team player. Hoover was not altogether successful in his efforts.

For its part, the movie industry shifted gears by recasting its leading men. Stars such as James Cagney and Edward G. Robinson, who had made their film careers playing gangsters, now switched to the other side. An ad campaign for *G-Men* (1935), the "first important piece of popular entertainment based on the history of the FBI" (Powers, 1983: 52) proclaimed: "Hollywood's Most Famous Bad Man Joins the G-Men and Halts the March of Crime" (Toll, 1982: 163). The movie starred James Cagney.

G-Men and the other films in this cycle contributed greatly to the creation of the "mythology" of the "G-Men," who like Hoover and the real agents of the FBI were engaged in a war against the "public enemies." This mythology was strengthened as it evolved in comic strips, in superhero comic books, on the radio, and later on television.

By the 1940s, all the crime genre formulas had been established. Television and societal changes would bring variations on these formulas. But these would be variations on familiar themes.

HOLLYWOOD FILMS, 1940s–1990s: FROM SMALL TOWN DANGERS TO DANGEROUS GHETTOS

In 1940, Thornton Wilder's Pulitzer Prize-winning play (1938) about small town life was made into a film. Director Alfred Hitchcock admired *Our Town* so much that he invited Wilder to write a movie script for him. The result was *A Shadow of a Doubt* (1943) in which Wilder and Hitchcock explored the darker side of small-town life (Levy, 1991: 74–75). In this film, young Charlie, recently graduated from high school and stifled by life in a small town, is delighted when her Uncle Charlie, her mother's brother and her own namesake, arrives for a surprise visit. To her distress, she soon learns he is one of the two men suspected of being the "Merry Widow Killer," a psychopath who preys on wealthy widows. Levy (1991) asserts that this film, like others made during the 1940s, reflects an "ambivalence and cynicism" about small-town life.

Another such film is Orson Welles's *The Stranger* (1946) in which Welles as a Nazi war criminal hides out in an American college town, posing as a professor. He marries the town sweetheart and judge's daughter Mary, played by Loretta Young (Levy, 1991: 83). In both films, the villains are pursued by detectives who force the young women (niece Charlie and wife Mary) to face the truth about the men they love and admire. These shattering revelations are in keeping with another film trend of the period in which women found themselves involved with men who threatened their physical or mental well-being. These films include the Hitchcock classic *Suspicion* (1941), in which shy bride Joan Fontaine suspects charming husband Cary Grant intends to kill her, and director George Cukor's *Gaslight* (1944), in which suave Charles Boyer plots to drive wife Ingrid Bergman insane. (This subgenre of "woman in jeopardy" has become a staple of modern films, with such examples as *Sleeping with the Enemy* [1991]).

The postwar period was also the height of what the French looking at American films dubbed *film noir*. In these films, darkness and lurking shadows are both real and symbolic. The protagonists are caught in a web of lies and deceits, propelled by ambitions, lust, or greed. Often the restless or rootless hero is drawn to a beautiful and alluring woman (*femme fatale*). The attraction proves disastrous for one or both of them. The ending is often an ironic twist of fate. Examples of film noir include *Detour* (1945), *The Strange Love of Martha Ivers* (1946), *The Postman Always Rings Twice* (1946), and *The File on Thelma Jordan* (1949).

Some gangster films of the period also had a *noirish* sense of darkness and threat. In *Kiss of Death* (1947), for example, Richard Widmark provides a prototype for the grinning psychotic killer as he pushes a wheelchair-bound, elderly woman down a staircase. In this film, ex-convict Victor Mature, trying to go straight, is menaced by both his former criminal associates and the agents of law enforcement who want his cooperation.

By the 1950s, the crime films being produced by Hollywood reflected the political and social climate in which juvenile rebellion, Communism, and the Cold War were focal points for popular fears. Among the films dealing with the battle of federal law enforcement against the Communist threat was *I Was a Communist for the FBI* (1951). The demand for cooperation with Congressional investigating committees and obliquely the ethics of becoming an informer were addressed in *On the Waterfront* (1954), the Marlon Brando–Rod Steiger classic about organized crime and union labor. Teen rebellion and its causes were examined in *Rebel without a Cause* (1958) with James Dean, Natalie Wood, and Sal Mineo, the victims not only of their own adolescent confusion but also of insensitive, neglectful, or incompetent adults. And in *The Defiant Ones* (1958), the racial concerns that were beginning to enter the public consciousness were addressed as convicts Tony Curtis and Sidney Poitier, chained together and at each other's throats, attempted to escape a sheriff's posse.

The 1960s brought Ian Fleming's novels about British agent James Bond to movie audiences. Agent 007 did (still does) battle with the forces of world domination and destruction. Dressed with sartorial elegance, driving sports cars, and equipped with state of the art weapons and gadgets, Bond romanced beautiful women and demolished villains in settings that ranged from London to Jamaica to the Swiss Alps. In outer space or on the Orient Express, Bond was superbly masculine and invincible. He made the Cold War look like fun. In contrast were the more sober *The Spy Who Came Out of the Cold* (1965), which looked at the grimmer realities of espionage, and *Dr. Strangelove: Or How I Learned to Stop Worrying and Love the Bomb* (1964), which offered a satiric take on the Cold War, offering not a dashing and lethal spy but a crazed Air Force general.

The 1960s and 1970s also witnessed the return of stylish gangster films. *Bonnie and Clyde* (1967) stars Warren Beatty and Faye Dunaway as two "pretty looking people" (according to the movie's theme song). For the two, robbing banks is both occupation and romantic adventure.[21] In *The Godfather* (1972), based on Mario Puzo's best-selling novel, the members of a Mafia family headed by a strong-willed patriarch love each other and conduct their business as honorably as possible. However, they accept the necessity of using violence to deal with dishonorable men and the members of rival crime families. In these two movies, the criminal emerges once again as both protagonist and tragic hero.

This question of who should be perceived as hero and who as villain was also shown in the films of the late 1960s, 1970s, and early 1980s, which dealt with hippies, war veterans, and minorities. For example, in *Easy Rider* (1969), director Dennis Hopper's counterculture commentary on American values, two drug-using/selling motorcyclists take off on an odyssey across the South-west from California to New Orleans. In *Joe* (1970), the attempts of a bigoted blue-collar father to "protect" his daughter from her drug-using, hippie boyfriend end in tragedy. In *First Blood* (1982), Vietnam vet Rambo, both heroic and disturbed, wages his own one man war when he is mistreated by a small town sheriff.

This was also the period when Sidney Poitier, in the film *In the Heat of the Night* (1965), ushered in a new era of films featuring African American protagonists. Poitier played Virgil Tibbs, a Philadelphia homicide detective caught up in the investigation of a murder in a southern town. He was followed in theaters by black private detectives such as John Shaft (*Shaft*, 1971) and by criminals such as "Priest," the drug-dealer who wants to make one more big score in *Super Fly* (1972). These films ushered in the era of so-called "black exploitation" films that presented violent black heroes (who were sometimes criminals), villainous white bigots, and brutal, corrupt, or stupid white police officers. Aimed at a predominantly black urban audience, the films often distressed both critics and community leaders. They also presented new images of African American heroes.

But even as this period marked gains for those who had formerly been excluded from mainstream society, it was also a period of conflict, apathy, and backlash. In the 1970s, the United States finally withdrew from a foreign "conflict" that had become a no-win situation. This conflict in Vietnam resulted in a massive loss of lives and had torn the country apart as people took sides about American involvement in Southeast Asia. At the same time, in the wake of the marches, demonstrations, and urban riots (or rebellions) of the 1960s and early 1970s, there was a call for "law and order" on the homefront.

In Hollywood films of the 1970s, Clint Eastwood as police detective "Dirty Harry" Callahan became symbolic of the kind of policing that was necessary in urban cities gone out of control.[22] He was (in the tradition of Western heroes) a lean, tall man with a gun. He was a loner, protecting the innocent, the helpless, and the unappreciative. He was expected to do the "dirty" jobs, such as dealing with sickos and psychopaths. But his hands were cuffed by bureaucratic red tape and Supreme Court decisions that made life easier for the "bad guys" than for the cops.

Dirty Harry has been described as a "vigilante cop" who takes the law into his own hands. But in *Magnum Force* (1973), while dealing with a group of young cops who have formed their own hit squad to deal with criminals who evade the system, Harry says, "I hate the goddamn system. But until someone comes along with some changes that make sense, I'll stick with it" (Bailey, 1993: 41). Harry bends the rules, but in his own opinion, he still works within the system. The visual image of "Dirty Harry" with his huge gun and narrowed gaze and the visual image of Charles Bronson in *Death Wish* (1974) with his huge gun and chilling smile symbolize the philosophy of both the cop and the citizen vigilante films of the 1970s: In an urban frontier outpost, a death-dealing gunfighter is needed.

Gibson has identified what he describes as the "paramilitary culture in post-Vietnam America" (1994). In real life, this paramilitary culture is reflected in the popularity of men's adventure magazines, gun collecting, war games, and, at the extreme, militia movements. In films, the "warrior hero" is often a vigilante hero. Gibson quotes the police detective/former Vietnam vet played by Mickey Rourke in *Year of the Dragon* (1985): "This is a fucking war and I'm not going to lose it, not this one. Not over politics . . . This is Vietnam all over again . . . " (Gibson, 1994: 34).

Faced with an ineffectual or corrupt bureaucracy at the municipal, state, federal, or sometimes international level, the warrior hero does what is necessary to "win" the war—or at least the battle in which he is currently engaged. In the 1980s and 1990s, this warrior hero is often portrayed by actors such as Steven Seagal, Sylvester Stallone, Arnold Schwarzenegger, and Jean Claude Van Damme—an "action hero" who is truly invincible, and the only hope for cities and citizens under siege.

In a parallel development, since the 1980s, young African American filmmakers have been among those who have offered images of crime and violence centered in the urban inner city. In films such as *Boyz N the Hood, New Jack City, Menace II Society, Juice, Fresh,* and *Clockers,* the protagonists and the criminals are the young black men caught in the poverty and violence of a ghetto subculture. In the alternate economy of this subculture, they are drawn into gangs and drug-dealing. They become both the violent offenders and the victims of violence.[23]

But during these decades when Hollywood films offered both sex and violence and social commentary, what was happening on television—that other medium in which the crime genres evolved?

TELEVISION CRIME GENRES:
FROM *DRAGNET* TO *NYPD BLUE*

In 1949, *Dragnet* premiered on the radio. In 1953, it moved to television (1953–1959). Star and producer Jack Webb's vision of the police officer as by-the-book law enforcer provided the model for other successful police shows, including *Adam-12* (1968–1975). But in 1967 when *Dragnet* returned to television, its law and order message seemed confrontational when aimed at marijuana smoking hippies and other representatives of the 1960s counterculture. By the 1980s, the cops on *Hill Street Blues* were battling both their own demons and a criminal justice system depicted as ineffectual. *Hill Street Blues* heralded the movement toward the police dramas that are part soap opera, part biting sitcom, in which the officers acknowledge and struggle with the complexities of policing a diverse society.

In between *Dragnet* and *Hill Street Blues* was a long line of television crime shows falling into the genres (or subgenres) of police procedure, private eye, amateur detective, or espionage. During the first 20 years of television crime drama, it was generally the private eyes and amateur sleuths who brought color and personality to the small screen. Radio sleuths such as *The Thin Man* and *Ellery Queen* made the transition to television. And 1958 became the year when "the detective genre entered the 'hip age.'" Private eyes were more "debonair and their exploits were accompanied by a jazz (or at least a finger-snapping) score." (Norden, 1985: 40). These hip PI shows included *Peter Gunn* and *77 Sunset Strip*. By the early to mid 1960s, the popularity of James Bond spawned TV spy shows such as *The Man from U.N.C.L.E.* By the late 1960s, the emphasis was again on the ordinary gumshoe, but sometimes with a gimmick. Private eyes such as *Barnaby Jones* (a senior citizen detective) or *Cannon* (a portly detective) were popular. So was *Mannix*, who was in the tradition of the ordinary gumshoe—but who had an African American secretary.

In the 1970s the *Rockford Files*, *Charlie's Angels*, and *Hart to Hart* all premiered, presenting detectives who were, respectively, low-key and likeable, beautiful, or wealthy. Actually, Jennifer and Jonathan Hart were all three, and they had a cute dog and a gravel-voiced housekeeper named Max.

In the 1980s, former model turned actor Tom Selleck brought his own twist to the TV private eye genre as a former Navy officer who lived on the estate of a mysterious millionaire. *Magnum, P.I.* combined humor and action and had wide audience appeal.

Also in the early 1980s, Pierce Brosnan, who later became the new James Bond, played *Remington Steele*, the con man who pushed his way into the life and the detective agency run by a strait-laced female PI (Norden, 1985: 40–50).

In the meantime, police shows such as *Ironside* (1967–1975), *Columbo* (1971–1977), *Kojak* (1973–1978), and *Baretta* (1975–1978) offered police officers with personality and with a wheelchair, raincoat, lollipop, and bird, respectively. During this period, police procedurals also began to reflect the changes occurring in society as a result of the women's movement and civil rights activism. More women and minorities were entering the police ranks. Even as *Hawaii Five-O* (1968–1980), strong on law and order ("Book 'em, Dano"), offered an occasional Asian archvillain, other shows presented a more liberal facade. For example, *The Rookies* and *Mob Squad* presented teams of officers who were both young and interracial. *Mob Squad* also included a female undercover officer. *Amy Prentiss* and *Get Christie Love* featured women in starring roles; they were short-lived shows. Angie Dickinson as Sergeant Pepper Anderson enjoyed more success with *Police Woman* (1974–1978). And on *Hill Street Blues* (premiering 1981), Officer Lucy Bates was a female officer, out on the street with a male partner. Officer Bates was later promoted to sergeant. But not until *Cagney and Lacey* (1982–1988) were two female detectives paired as partners. Even then the controversy surrounding the show forced a cast change to make Christine Cagney more "feminine." After a series of up and downs, including cancellations, the show was finally repackaged to attract a female audience. It remained a police procedural, but it was a cop show that dealt with the personal lives of the two female characters and included treatment of "women's issues" such as abortion, sexual harassment, and date rape (see D'Acci, 1994).

By the 1990s, male cops too were dealing with personal issues that affected their lives on the job: Police officers on shows such as *NYPD Blue* and *Homicide* were angst-ridden, flawed, but still committed to their profession. And on cable-networks, the police procedural ventured into genre-bending on such shows as *Forever Knight,* featuring a homicide detective who is also a vampire, and *The Sentinel,* with a detective who possesses heightened sensory perception. And occasionally a police show has picked up where another left off. *Miami Vice* was the most stylish cop show of the 1980s. *New York Undercover* has followed in *Vice's* footsteps with music, drug lords, fashion, and cool young cops.

CONCLUSION

In this chapter, we have examined the evolution of popular culture depictions of crime and justice from folklore to urban crime films. What we have seen is that matters of crime and justice (or injustice) have always evoked popular interest. Humans have always shared with each other stories of good and evil, murder, and revenge. But since the nineteenth century with the improvements in technology that have made a "mass culture" possible, stories of crime and justice have been commodities packaged and offered to consumers in newspapers, magazines, novels and, later, on radio, in film, and on television. Today crime and justice is even a commodity for cyberspace.

And yet some contemporary formulas for telling these stories have their roots in ancient times and folk culture. In our mass culture, these formulas have evolved into crime genres that are a part of popular culture as entertainment. The boundaries separating entertainment and more serious forms of mass media are becoming increasingly more blurred. Crime stories broadcast on the evening news provide material for monologues by late-night talk-show hosts. Crimes committed by entertainers and athletes become the focus of reports by network news programs. The packaging of entertainment and news shows are sometimes difficult to distinguish. But crime and justice permeate all these forms of popular culture.

Rushkoff has described "Courtroom TV" (all courtroom programming, from the now defunct *L.A. Law* to the *Court TV* channel) as "popular cultural forums" where we "evaluate our rules and customs" (1994: 52). On programs such as *Law & Order,* we see stories straight out of the headlines—from the death penalty in New York State to assisted suicide. We watch as these issues are debated by the cops, the lawyers, and everyone else involved in the case of the week. In these popular culture forums, the uninhibited exploration of issues of crime and justice take place. In these forums, many people are exposed to ideas and concepts that help shape their perceptions of reality. Therefore, we agree with those scholars (Chase, 1986; Ferrell and Sanders, 1995; Nevins, 1995; Newman, 1990; Porsdam, 1994) who have urged us to incorporate the study of popular culture into our academic disciplines.

In the chapters that follow, the contributors examine a range of issues having to do with popular culture, crime, and justice. As we will discuss in our epilogue, much is still to be explored about this intersection of culture, deviance, and criminal justice.

DISCUSSION QUESTIONS

1. Bailey and Hale assert that there is an innate human interest in crime and justice and that this is one reason for the interrelationship between crime and justice and popular culture. Explain why you agree or disagree.

2. The authors look at the social changes that have affected crime and justice as popular culture. What were (are) those changes?

3. The authors discuss crime as depicted in popular culture genres. What is a genre? How can one genre be distinguished from another? Does a movie such as *Natural Born Killers* (about two young serial killers), which includes animation and a sitcom-like sequence, create "genre confusion" in its audience?

4. Why do the authors think the study of popular culture should be incorporated into the curriculums of disciplines such as criminology, criminal justice, and the law? Explain why you agree or disagree that popular culture has relevance to these disciplines?

NOTES

1. This promo ran on Channel 11, New York City, on April 13, 1996, at 12:30 A.M. The episode advertised was about the arraignment of Federation officer Commander Worf for the destruction of a civilian Klingon vessel during battle— a depiction of a futuristic judicial proceeding.

2. DePalma made this comment during an interview with Lee (1993). As does the promo for *Deep Space Nine*, this comment by DePalma illustrates the manner in which crime and justice and law and order themes permeate popular culture, from science fiction and westerns to gangster films.

3. The rest of the season Jessica Fletcher, successful mystery writer, traveled around the country and abroad to visit friends and relatives, to do research, or to promote her books. Where Jessica went, murder followed.

4. See also Rushkoff (1994) and Caldwell (1995) who consider reality-based programming within the context of television in general. Cavender and Bond-Maupin describe reality television such as *America's Most Wanted* and *Unsolved Mysteries* as "a hybrid programming format in that a news

or public service format is imposed on entertainment to produce a new television genre" (1995: 215).

5. Ironically, before making his media debut as a defendant in a real-life double murder case, Simpson, the football player turned actor, had appeared as a security guard in the disaster film *The Towering Inferno* (1974) and as a detective in the wacky *Naked Gun* movies (1988, 1991, 1994). Even before that Simpson played a homicide detective in the made-for-television movie *A Killing Affair* (1977). Elizabeth Montgomery, best-known as TV witch "Samantha" on *Bewitched*, was the female partner with whom he had an interracial affair. Montgomery herself also starred as a crafty Lizzie Borden (*The Legend of Lizzie Borden*, 1975) who dealt with the matter of blood-stained clothing by committing the murders of her father and stepmother in the nude. Montgomery's last role was in the made-for-television movie based on the memoirs of Miami crime reporter Edna Buchanan.

6. In *Seductions of Crime*, in his chapter on "righteous slaughter," Katz refers to the example of Dorothy, the heroine of the children's book *The Wizard of Oz*. Dorothy

"in rage after the witch has snatched one of her silver shoes," launches a "lethal" and "moral attack" on the wicked witch (1988: 29).

Children might also be exposed to another type of tale—the "urban legend; anthropologists and other scholars have been interested in how these stories come into being. For example, Best and Horiuchi (1995) have analyzed news stories (1958–1983) about Halloween sadism ("the razor blade in the apple") to understand the social construction of such modern tales of crime and villainy.

7. See Tunnell (1995a) for his discussion of these ballads and crime and punishment in bluegrass music. Also see Franklin (1978) for his discussion of the influence of the prison experience on folk songs and the blues.

8. For discussion of this case, see Brandon (1986). The first movie about the case resulted in a lawsuit by Minerva Brown, Grace's mother, who complained that the movie contained "false, untrue, slanderous, libelous, and defamatory matter" (Brandon, 1986: 335). Mrs. Brown and the studio, Paramount, settled out of court.

9. See Coffin (1975) for discussion of "Frankie and Johnny" (or "Frankie and Albert"), one of the more durable of the American crime ballads. The ballad was apparently based on a nineteenth-century murder case and was probably composed by an African American. As with most ballads, it has multiple variations. Gaining widespread popularity, the song was used by the Leighton Brothers in their vaudeville act and was soon-to-be Hollywood sex symbol Mae West's trademark song in her Broadway musical *Diamond Lil*. It was the title of an Elvis Presley movie (*Frankie and Johnny*, 1966). In an Agatha Christie movie, *Death on the Nile* (1978), Mia Farrow, who played the woman scorned, belts out a few of the lyrics before she shoots her lover.

10. The TV episode begins when an aggressive female reporter barges into the Borden house to get an interview with Lizzie on the first anniversary of the murders. She tells Emma, "the older sister,"

that living with Lizzie "must be trying on the nerves." The reporter then offers a reconstruction of what happened in the house that morning as she tries to get Emma to admit that Lizzie did it. Outside the house, a neighborhood child is singing the nursery rhyme: "Lizzie Borden took an ax . . . " The eager reporter writes down the words of the song to include in her news story.

Today the legend of Lizzie Borden lives on in Fall River, Massachusetts, where the house Ms. Borden moved into after her acquittal was recently converted into a bed-and-breakfast inn. Guests can enjoy an authentic "morning of the murders" breakfast.

11. As Cohen notes, "Few civic occasions aroused as much popular interest in early New England as public hangings" (1993: 3). These hangings were "prominent among the extraordinary communal events addressed by early New England ministers" (3). Crime and punishment in New England has gained its place in popular culture in novels such as Nathaniel Hawthorne's *The Scarlet Letter* (1850) and Arthur Miller's play about the 1692 Salem witch trails, *The Crucible* (1953). Salem, Massachusetts, has also become a popular tourist attraction.

12. See Papke's discussion of the loss in nineteenth century "cultural work" of critical perspective on crime. Papke asserts that during the antebellum period, "with cities burgeoning and industrializing and emergent social groups struggling to define their relationship with one another, cultural work regarding crime briefly became more fluid" (1987: 181). But by the 1890s when "specialization, genre, professional, and bureaucratic institutionalism assumed hegemonic roles . . . the reporting, imaging, and remembering of crime lost its critical thrust" (181). In the twentieth century, Papke sees occasional examples of this critical thrust in "the hard-boiled school of detective fiction, black prison writings of the 1960s and 1970s, and the television series *Hill Street Blues*" (182).

13. Berger observes that there is an interesting philosophical question about

whether or not genres can actually exist (1992: 4–5). In his own use of the concept, he states,

As I use the term, a genre is more comprehensive than a formula. Consider the mystery, for example. Within this genre, one might have a number of different kinds of mysteries. . . . Each of these would be a subgenre with a somewhat different formula, though each would involve solving some mystery . . . (43)

Berger compares his own perspective to that of Cawelti who does take a formulaic approach to texts (31).

14. Poe is honored by the Mystery Writers of America (MWA) as their patron saint. At an annual banquet, the organization awards "Edgars" for achievement in various categories of mystery writing. In an example of "medical sleuthing" worthy of an episode of the television series *Quincy, M.E.* (1976–1983), a cardiologist at the University of Maryland Medical Center recently reported the results of his study of Poe's final days. The cardiologist theorizes that instead of dying of alcohol poisoning as has been commonly believed, Poe actually died of encephalitic rabies (Crenson, 1996: 8A).

15. See Panek (1987) for his discussion of the development of the detective story. Also see Landrum, Browne, and Browne (1976), including the introduction to the volume in which the editors offer a brief but informative overview of the evolution of detective fiction (and the detective) from adventure stories, penny dreadfuls, and chapbooks to modern genre fiction.

16. The most famous of these crime/mystery/adventure magazines was *Black Mask*, founded in 1920 by H.L. Mencken and George Jean Nathan, who soon sold their financial venture. Under the guidance of legendary editor Captain Joseph T. ("Cap") Shaw, *Black Mask* became the most famous and the best of the crime magazines (Binyon, 1989: 38).

17. Talleck points out, "Tough-guy fiction is a product of a particular social context and a literary style, and it reached its apogee in the thirties, flourishing alongside, and indeed related to the proletarian fiction engendered by the Depression"

(1976: 247). Both Ernest Hemingway, who wrote the short story "The Killers" (1927), and William Faulkner, author of *Sanctuary* (1931), are "affiliated" with this style of fiction (Talleck, 1976: 248). Although best known as a Southern novelist, Faulkner was one of the scriptwriters for the movie version of Raymond Chandler's detective novel *The Big Sleep* (1939) (Gidley, 1976). Two works by Faulkner, *Knight's Gambit* (1949) and *Intruder in the Dust* (1948), feature detection by attorney Gavin Stevens and his nephew.

18. Charles Dickens had written magazine articles about British policing before his creation of "Inspector Bucket" in *Bleak House* (1853). Dickens based this character on a real police detective, Inspector Charles Field. Dickens's friend and contemporary Wilkie Collins created "Sergeant Cuff" to investigate the mystery of the missing jewel in *The Moonstone* (1868) (Binyon, 1989: 3–4). In America, Anna Katherine Greene, often credited as "the mother of the mystery novel" and the daughter of a prominent criminal attorney, introduced police detective Ebenezer Gryce in her 1878 novel, *The Leavenworth Case* (Binyon, 79–80).

19. In the United States, there was continued concern about political control of urban police departments. As late as 1931, the Wickersham Commission reported on the "corrupting influence of politics" (Friedman, 1993: 359). The Commission also found police involvement in both corruption (bribes and grafts) and police brutality. However, a movement was already underway by police administrators such as O.W. Wilson and August Vollmer to make police departments more professional with improved standards and training. But as popular culture depictions of modern urban police departments such as *Serpico* (1973) (based on the story of real-life cop Frank Serpico) and *Prince of the City* (1981) suggest, in policing as in other professions, the ideal is not always realized.

20. For example, "Legs" Diamond gained fame not only for his dancing style but also for his ability to survive repeated murder attempts. He finally died in Albany, New York, and was immortalized in

film and in a novel (*Legs*) by Pulitzer Prize winning novelist William Kennedy. In Chicago, Al Capone evaded charges based on his activities as a gangster, but finally "took a fall" for income-tax evasion. *Scarface* (1932), the movie produced by millionaire Howard Hughes, was based on Capone's life as an underworld kingpin. The movie's release was slowed by the Hays Office's concern about the graphic violence. When it finally premiered, Capone was already serving time in federal prison (see Clarens, 1980). Capone has had repeated reincarnations not only in the television show *The Untouchables* but also in the movie of the same title starring Kevin Costner as Capone's nemesis, federal agent Eliot Ness. Earlier, in 1983, Brian DePalma, the director of *The Untouchables* (1987), had remade *Scarface*. In that update, the setting was Miami, and the gangster kingpin was a Cuban refugee.

21. See O'Kane (1992) for his discussion of outlaw ballads and the rural outlaw (such as Bonnie and Clyde) as folk hero. Movie critic Hal Hinson writes that the film *Bonnie and Clyde* (1967) offered a "startlingly modern perspective on violence and crime and the American gangster myth" (1995: 291). Some critics were shocked or outraged by the violence.

22. The "Dirty Harry" persona was invoked in the world of politics when a president (quoting the film cop's challenge to a perpetrator at whom he had his gun pointed) invited reporters to "Go ahead. Make my day." In the 1996 election year, candidates engaged in political discourse about being "tough" on crime continued to use popular culture references to make their point. Republican candidate Robert Dole said, in berating the crime policies of his Democratic opponent, "[President Clinton] talks like Dirty Harry but acts like Barney Fife [the incompetent deputy on *The Andy Griffith Show*]." (Powell, 1996, A-3).

23. See Giroux's discussion of these films in *Fugitive Cultures* (1996). Giroux writes, "Although the violence in these films is traumatizing in an effort to promote an antiviolence message, it is also a violence that is hermetically sealed within the walls of the black urban ghetto" (42).

PART I

✳

Understanding Popular Culture

Most professional scientists understand that facts are phenomena that become meaningful only through identification procedures and interpretations framed by theories. Facts do not speak for themselves; they emerge through theoretical frameworks that may be as general and mundane as commonsense knowledge, as far reaching as quantum mechanics, or as specific as genetics. (Snow, 1983: 13)

The scholars who study popular culture come from a variety of disciplines, including psychology, sociology, criminology, criminal justice, women's studies, anthropology, history, and literature. Their approaches to research and analysis are influenced not only by their specialized training but also by the theoretical perspectives they choose to adopt. Strinati (1995: 3) finds that differences among theoretical perspectives are reflected in arguments about three related themes:

- What or who determines popular culture
- The influence of commercialization and industrialization on popular culture
- The ideological role of popular culture

The leading theories of popular culture include (1) Marxism, (2) Feminism, (3) Structuralism and Semiology, and (4) Postmodernism (Strinati, 1995).

Rooted in the critique of capitalist societies developed in the nineteenth century by Karl Marx and Friedrich Engels, Marxist analysis postulates,

Everything is shaped, ultimately, by the economic systems of a society, which, in subtle ways, affects the ideas that are instrumental in determining the kinds of arrangements they will make with one another, the institutions they will establish, and so on. (Berger, 1991: 34)

Although Marxist analysis takes various forms, the basic premise is that in capitalist societies there is an ongoing conflict between the bourgeoisie and the proletariat. As Berger notes, the "notion—that the masses of people are being manipulated and exploited by the ruling class—is one of the central arguments of modern Marxist cultural analysis" (1991: 37).

Obviously, a Marxist analysis of crime and justice in popular culture would look at what Spring describes as the "ideological management" of ideas as "a source of power" (1992: 2). This same interest in culture and power is at the heart of feminist analyses of popular culture that focus on gender relationships in a historically "patriarchal" (male-dominated) society. Whereas Marxism emphasizes class, feminism emphasizes gender. Harding writes,

> Feminist researchers have argued that traditional theories have been applied in ways that make it difficult to understand women's participation in social life....They have produced feminist versions of traditional theories... (1987: 3)

Having perhaps less of an overtly political stance than either Marxism or feminism, structuralism and semiology focus on the "deep structure" of systems ranging from human languages to literary texts. Structuralism is based on work done by Ferdinand de Saussure before World War I. But much of what was formerly called structuralism is now called semiotics (or semiology). Semiotics is

> The science of signs. It stresses that "meaning," even when it seems natural or inherent, is always the result of social conventions; also, it analyzes culture as a series of sign systems. (Culler, 1996, no page)

Semiotics is concerned with codes. As Fiske explains, "A code is a rule-governed system of signs, whose rules and conventions are shared amongst members of a culture and which is used to generate and circulate meanings in and for the culture" (1987: 4). Fiske adds, "What passes for reality in any culture is the product of that culture's codes, so "reality" is always already encoded..." (5)

And, finally, postmodernism, which

> Hold[s] that the consumption of information has replaced the production of things. The media, which used to report (or distort) reality, have *become* reality. (Brown, 1995: 2)

These theoretical perspectives need not be mutually exclusive. For example, Barak, in outlining an approach to media, crime, and justice, proposes "constitutive criminology":

> An emerging theoretical model...that combines insights from two older traditions [symbolic interaction and labeling] and from a more recently developed synthesis of postmodernism and cultural Marxism. (1995: 142)

Fiske, discussing his approach to "cultural studies," describes a perspective derived from "particular inflections of Marxism, semiotics, poststructuralism, and ethnography" (1987: 1).

Aside from the theoretical perspective of the scholar, there is the matter of research methods. Harding (1987: 2) states, A research *method* is a technique for (or a way of) proceeding in gathering evidence." She notes that these techniques tend to fall into three categories: (1) interrogation of informants, (2) observing behavior, and (3) examining historical traces and records. In the chapters that follow, several of the contributors interrogated (surveyed or interviewed) informants. At least one contributor engaged in observation of behavior. Others examined records or—here—popular culture texts.

Several contributors use a technique called content analysis. Wimmer and Dominick state, "Many definitions of content analysis exist" (1994: 3). The technique dates back to World War II when intelligence units analyzed popular songs played on European radio stations as a part of their effort to keep track of troop movements. By 1952, the technique "had gained recognition as a tool for media scholars" (163). As a tool, content analysis allows the systematic examination of a selected sample (for example, of popular films or newspaper articles). Content analysis is quantitative, but it also allows for qualitative interpretation. In the chapters that follow, the contributors who use this technique discuss it in the context of their research.

But first, in the two chapters in this section, Manning (on television) and Newman (on popular films) introduce approaches to "decoding" the messages found in media texts.

2

❋

Media Loops*

PETER K. MANNING

INTRODUCTION

Television is a fundamental source of modern experience, affecting the economy, politics, and interpersonal relations, yet how it accomplishes such massive influence is controversial. Clearly, television is an industry (Gitlin, 1986), an entertainment medium (Mitroff and Bennis, 1993), and a producer of images and perceptions (Epstein, 1974). Though viewers see television as providing a window on the world, its quintessential claim is that it communicates immediacy and poignancy to viewers and so shapes the experience of the modern life (Epstein, 1974: 39; Miller, 1988; Mitroff and Bennis, 1993). Television plays with time and space by collapsing real lived experience into media events and enabling viewers to travel the world visually from their livingroom couches. This capacity has political implications: Television's power to shape politics and meanings is realized through selectively projecting and framing reality, thus creating a *sense of the immediate and real* and endlessly reproducing it visually (Benjamin, 1964; Poster, 1990).

Television is, on the one hand, an industry characterized by commercial ends and marketing strategies and, on the other hand, is a medium that creates cultural experiences for viewers. Viewers see themselves perhaps, but they also construct social meanings and resist conventional definitions (Fiske, 1987).

---

* This paper has been revised for this volume. It is a part of a series of papers on media and policing: "Interactional Shadows" (1995a); "Reflexions" (1995b); and "Dramaturgy, Politics, and the Axial Media Event" (1996).

Television shapes the drama of modern life as well as influences theories of modern life that emphasize reflexive experience. Much as nineteenth century philosophers such as Baldwin, Cooley, and Mead explored interpersonal relations, modern analysts should examine the modes of influence through which television works to incorporate this into social theories (Manning, 1996). To do this requires us to see how television is seen by those who view it and how it achieves its influence and its cultural and social impact.

Television captures a kind of reality. In everyday life, we encounter others who are embodied, who smell, move, and speak. We are rooted in this primary reality. Think of encounters as naturally organized activities that can be shaped and changed in many ways. How do strips of naturally organized social *activity* (Goffman, 1974: 10), basically face-to-face interactions, differ from transformations of that primary reality? How is a movie, a play, or a television program different from everyday life? In some way, images shown on television are selective, rationally constructed, edited, and stylized representations. Television creates *media events*. Some media events, to be discussed later, are political and produce major changes in social realities. Understanding this transition from activity to event is essential if we are to understand how television credibly represents the real. "Real," as defined here, is the outline of the possible, the pattern of constraints and limits on human choice. The *transformation* of activities into events, and media looping to affect, shape, and recreate social activities and other media events, illuminates the processes of shaping of social reality in a media-driven society.

Television entertains, distracts, reports, and engages attention, but not all television is intended to be a stylized mirror (a true, accurate, and valid reflection) of society. Naturally organized activities shown as televised events make an implicit claim of representing the real, whereas dramatizations, comedies, and entertainments claim artistic and aesthetic purposes.

Television represents society through stylized images, but it also represents images. Once shown, a media event (for example, several minutes of news film) can be reshown in either an identical or dissimilar social context. When an image is shown in another context, reframed by the media, I term it a *media loop*. Looping, reshowing an image, is a common and perhaps essential media practice found on news, sports and feature programs, and game and talk shows. Media images are constantly recycled, reproduced in a new context, and reexperienced. This is the basis for the argument that television is highly self-referential (Miller, 1988).

Once an event is filmed (or digitalized), it can be altered in another significant fashion. It can be reshown in a new form or *genre*. A genre is a category of artistic work with a characteristic style, form, or content. Examples of genres are poetry, essays, short stories, novellas, and novels. Consider the range of media genres: organized social activities (for example, sporting events or live telecasts); edited versions of an event reshown (for example, Great NBA playoffs); comedies, dramas, soap operas, and made-for-entertainment vignettes (MTV, CTV, or VH1); and previously formatted performances now filmed (concerts, operas, plays).

Each of these genres can be transformed into another genre (a type of program or artistic presentation). Think of football "highlights" programs devoted to showing terrible collisions, elusive fumbles, or funny post-touchdown dances that convert a live game into a comedy. When genres are so transformed, realities are made problematic. Genre conversion occurs when the form of the event is changed, but the content remains.

Genres can be mindfully conflated when simulation, or infotainment reenactments, are the basis for a program (for example, *Rescue 911*; *America's Most Wanted*). In these programs, a constructed reality is presented as the dramatic and true picture of the crisis, and the "real events" represent a mere incomplete shadow. This is true because, by dramatic conceit, the viewer knows that the rescue occurred or the victim did not die, and cues to how that happened are given by voice-over narration, the introduction of the host, and preview clips ("teasers"). But at the same time, film is shown of the actual scene, rescue workers, and actual family members.

It seems likely that just as readers are oriented to the meaning of texts by cues that establish perceptually the existence of a literary form and museum patrons to visual artistic conventions to interpret categories of pictures (Baxandall, 1972), viewers know and recognize television's genres. They can differentiate, arguably, a genre transformation from the reshowing of an image. Compare a parody of a presidential speech on *Saturday Night Live* with film clips of past presidential speeches shown on a news program. The latter is a loop and a change in genre.

If an image is reshown in a new context without genre change, then *intertextuality* results—one image is embedded in another (Eco, 1986: 200; Fiske, 1987: 108–127). In other words, looping sometimes produces intertextuality. If an image is metaphorically a "text," showing previous presidential nominating speeches at political conventions during convention coverage is intertextuality. Specifically, the differences between the two images (previous speeches just after a current speech) when contrasted create meaning. Thus, the aesthetics of television shape the visual experience of watching, and the connection and flow of images is as important as the images themselves.

Several kinds of loops appear to exist. They range from the simple to the more complex. An instant replay (reshowing in close-up a play from a game) is an example of a *simple loop*. Lawrence Welk reruns with new introductions (framing) by Welk are a more complicated *rerun loop*. An archival news film of a past event shown on a contemporary news program is a *past-recreating loop*. When one media features a story developed by another media, when *Hard Copy* reports a story and shows the cover of *Newsweek* as a source, it is an *intramedia loop*. When stories and images are linked by a common theme, as when one live event (a disaster) is tied to another (a previous disaster) through pictures, a *linking loop* is created. When a reconstruction such as *Rescue 911* shows film, actual settings, and voices, an *ambiguous loop* appears. It is not clear what is being looped into what. When such loops appear, they create meaning on the margins—that is, as a result of the juxtaposition of two images a different or third meaning emerges.

Media representation and looping laminate realities or layer them and interweave types of experience in a single visual experience. We see and experience several things at once. Although each media genre is a form of representation, the rules by which genres are framed, converted from social activity to media event, and looped differ. Transforming activity into events, and events into media looping, each create differences. Two important differences are discussed here. Differences between (1) social activity and a representation and (2) the representation and the represented representation.

These two differences are explored here in connection with an analysis of how television symbolizes and represents. I analyze three media events that spawned loops: (1) the video of the Rodney King beating in Los Angeles in March 1993, (2) a simulated event activity—an episode of *Cops*, and (3) media coverage of the bombing of a federal building in Oklahoma City, Oklahoma, in April 1994.[1] Because media represent these events to those who are distant from and unfamiliar with them, this created imagery shapes political processes and contributes to political knowledge (Edelman, 1988).

A MEDIA-DRIVEN SOCIETY

The media and politics are interrelated because modern societies are media-suffused (Gergen, 1991) and much of political relevance is seen on television. The modern political stance is one of observation, or passive amusement, much like watching Michael Jackson perform at the halftime of a Super Bowl Game. The "postmodern society" (Denzin, 1986), "postmodernism" (Jameson, 1992), "the society of the spectacle" (Debord, 1983), "the cinematic society" (Denzin, 1995), and the "surveillance society " (Lyon, 1994) are idealized and abstracted ideal types that suggest the increasing role of media in society. The types feature media effects prominently and they selectively highlight the visual and reflective facets of contemporary society. To understand the role of media and media loops we should first consider how television frames reality.

THE FRAMING OF REALITY

The way television is viewed means that it is *framed*, or understood, as a benign fabrication meant to entertain (Goffman, 1974: 83). Television conveys images within well-recognized genres governed by tacit conventions. These conventions facilitate organizational production of the images and audience interpretation of them.

Not all television genres frame or reproduce social reality, in the sense of attempting to accurately represent or "mirror" society. Consider the range of nonrealistic television genres and their functions: MTV, quiz shows, sitcoms, and soap operas are heavily formulaic and framed as "make believes" or "contests." These shows are shaped for and by television, although the genre is borrowed from radio, the theater, or vaudeville. Comedies, dramas, and action shows are shown. Some genres combine other genres: "Infomation" shows combine "news," "current events," and gossip; "talk shows" weave together scandal, shaming, and degradation ceremonies; and reconstructions and edited versions of reality such as *Rescue 911*, *True Stories of the Highway Patrol*, and *Cops* use up-close pictures of police work taken by a handheld camera, and "live" footage to convey verisimilitude. Live shows, such as the coverage of disasters, sporting events, and "eyewitness reports" of local news, are closer to ongoing social activities.

Each genre is recognized by viewers, as are the techniques television producers use to establish reality (Epstein, 1974: 152–180; Fiske, 1987; Kappeler, Blumberg, and Potter, 1995: 24–26). Television's production process, decision-making, management, and technology all systematically frame strips of activity as media events. Television's chief product is framed or bracketed social reality that is perceived, interpreted, and interpolated within the viewers' mundane social worlds (Fiske, 1987, 1994; Taylor and Mullan, 1986).

Yet, once in the television frame, motivated aspects of image-presentation are suppressed by viewers. The processes implied by the active verb "transform," fashioning everyday activities into televised images, are bracketed or set aside by viewers. Viewers manage to maintain a sense that television is entertainment, not reality, and be riveted by television's rendition of social life. They maintain personal interpretations of the meaning of events and generalized typifications of such events. Viewers willingly suspend disbelief in recognizable yet unseen cognitive mechanisms, the motives behind programming, the elaborate staging of shows, the violation of time (flashbacks and flashforwards) and space (driving 100 miles an hour in a New York street) conventions and so sustain the verisimilitude of realist television genres (Fiske, 1987).

REALITY RULES

To argue that television frames reality is to contend that viewers translate events on the small screen into a rendition of a near-life, even when they recognize that it is entertainment. Granted that social life provides us with codes to make sense of events, indicated by labels we use such as "disaster," "play," "fight," and "debate," how do we see television, with a small screen, bright color, amplified sound, and programming as real? Raymond Williams (1974) aptly notes that television represents a continuous succession or flow of images that follow no laws of cause and effect, but convey the cultural experience of watching television. However, partitioning, clustering, and drawing connections between images, especially in conveying reality, requires cognitive work.

The cognitive processes that describe how the typical viewer sees television as real can be expressed in a simplified fashion as *reality rules* (Manning, 1996). These rules describe the cognitive work necessary to convert the rapidly flickering images of television into a believable mini-portrait of society. The rules guide exploration and elaboration of relationships between activities, the media (both as structure and process), media logic, and the viewer. Although a variety of interpretive rules might be imagined, these suffice to structure thought (as grammar forms a sentence without a speaker's awareness) and produce a consistent sense of reality. Television's adherence to these rules suggests that realism is a background against which we can contrast other televised social realities (Fiske, 1987: 22).

The first rule for watching television as if it were representing the real, or "mirroring society," is the *veridicality rule*. The image (bundle of images as a message) represents reality most convincingly when images captured in "real time" typify the key elements of activities and, conversely, do not typify other activities. The assumption that television is a kind of reality mirror is indicated partially by the veridicality rule. The second, a *sampling rule*, defines any display of images as a nonrandom, purposively selected, collection displayed for an intended (dramaturgical) purpose or purposes that contain key elements defining the typical character of such an image. This rule sees messages as a sample of images drawn from a range of possible images that effectively conveys that activity. A third rule for pinning down the sense of televised reality is the *ordering and sequencing rule*: An image, or image set, once established as "real," will be seen continuously as such. A corollary of the ordering and sequencing rule is that further instances of this image set will be connected to the first metaphorically. A metaphoric theme, once set, is held. An image will be seen as an example of a continuing pattern of association until otherwise defined. A fourth rule for stabilizing imagery and granting it verisimilitude is the *framing rule*: a sequence of images is what it is framed to be, and no other. The rule is based on the metaframe of television reality, how television generally works to produce its effects (Manning, 1996; Meyrowitz, 1979). A fifth rule is the *coherence rule*, which links images, narrative explanation (if offered), and patterned imagery. This rule, if it holds, ensures that a series, once seen, will be seen again as a series and that words and images maintain an apparent iterative quality. A sixth rule guiding the shaping of television's reality is the *salience rule*, which states that the key elements (salient points) in a series of images will remain so over time. These rules can be used to compare media events. Let us now apply these rules.

ACTIVITIES, MEDIA
EVENTS, AND MEDIA LOOPS

The Rodney King Beating, Video and Media Event

The story is perhaps familiar. Around 12:20 A.M. on March 3, 1991, after a chase in which he was pursued by officers from several police departments, Rodney King and two passengers, all African American males, were stopped near a park in suburban Los Angeles. George Halliday heard a commotion and used a handheld video camera to film the beating from his balcony for about 20 minutes. Several officers attacked and kicked King, delivering some

56 blows, while he writhed helplessly on the ground with a taser gun cord attached to his neck.[2]

The quality of the video connotes actual activities filmed in real time (Rule #1, veridicality). The film displayed an icon showing date and lapsed time in minutes and seconds. This situated the activity temporally and the unfocused, crude video film bespoke realism. (The film was somewhat grainy, the camera tilted and moved, and the clarity of the image varied). The silent film, showing shadowy distant figures, captured the action eerily. The lights of the circled police cars partially illuminated the deeply shadowed scene.

The sampling rule (Rule #2, sampling) works here. The brief flickering images efficiently conveyed the core defining elements of a violent event: repeated blows, absence of intervention of bystanding officers, a victim on the ground, and the easily recognizable nightsticks, uniforms, cars, weapons, and paraphernalia of the modern police. The video tape was edited for effect. During the trial of four officers for the beating, it was admitted that the video, in spite of its raw, unedited appearance, had been edited by KTLA and other stations (Goodwin, 1995). These images of violence, flickering in the half-light, punctuated by silent brutal blows, suppress other information. What is shown is dramatic, unusual, and newsworthy. As framed and shown, the film was intended to represent a sample of real LAPD activities, not a rehearsal, fabrication, theater, or a joke.

In time, the film was seen as a part of a larger narrative and connected to American police violence (Kappeler, Sluder, and Alpert, 1994: 145). It became a point in an unfolding series (Rule #3, ordering and sequencing) foretelling further future violence (riots ensued following the acquittal of two of the tried officers). This sequence of images was given metaphoric meaning by commentators when clustered as "police violence," "racism," and "resisting arrest." Further, the story was framed as "news," an instance of police violence eliciting national and international reaction (Rule #4, framing).

The discourse describing the activity and the imagery cohered (Rule #5, coherence). Although the tape was edited, scenes were omitted and, clearly, other versions of the tape might reveal other facets and perhaps disconfirming evidence, this was not discussed in the media until the trial. The activity was described as police violence and subsequent stories were linked by the media metaphorically and connected to the original event.

The term, "the King beating," evolved as the label for the filmed event. The theme of police violence toward minorities set the nature of subsequent media questions. The salient feature, "police violence against minorities" remained highlighted (Rule #6, salience). The questions asked, especially during coverage of the officers' trials, focused on individual motivations of the police, but the motivations of Halliday, the reporters, owners, or management of the television stations were not questioned. This video was "news" and represented real events. The question of whether this activity was "representative" of the behavior of Los Angeles officers was never raised because it was assumed.

In sum, the beating was shown first as "news" and then looped in as background or a context for stories of King's leaving the hospital, being stopped, and being rearrested; the two trials of the officers accused of beating King; the riots following their first acquittal; and so on. The beating became a linchpin in a series of stories and took on political reality partly because of its repeated showings (Jacobs, 1996).[3] The beating has not, to my knowledge, been transformed and embedded in another television genre.

Realistic Simulation and Looping: *Cops*

Cops is one of several police "infotainment shows" that combine artistic production values with action footage and stage police work as real (Surette [1992: 67] lists 10 programs in 1989–1991). These shows are stylized, designed, and marketed versions of policing—commercial products, not *cinema verité*. *Cops*, for example, presents vignettes of police-public interaction filmed originally in selected cities (Las Vegas, Nevada; Portland, Oregon; Memphis, Tennessee; and elsewhere). A camera team with handheld cameras and microphones accompanies officers as they encounter the public, on raids, while pursuing suspects, and during routine patrol. The wobbling cameras, fuzzy and blurred images, alternating close-ups and distant shots, interpolated and "amateurish" in quality, suggest real events, real people, and real time. The audio, varying in fidelity and volume, conveys raw sound. Officers sometimes turn to the camera and speak directly to the viewer, "We think he panicked when he saw us following him . . . " Mock warnings (a voice-over by an announcer) are provided: "The people shown were only arrested; their guilt or innocence will be determined at a later date." "The suspect was arrested, and subsequent decisions will be made." Like *Dragnet*, legal decisions are reported—"X did not appear for his trial date, and his bond was revoked."

Cops is a simulation of policing. The activity is framed as quasi-real, a true copy. Officers and administrators of the police departments filmed have contractual rights to edit the tapes, censor, and remove scenes. The tapes are edited further by the show's producers to heighten dramatic incidents; remove dubious violent, illegal, or racist incidents; and polish and create apparent continuity in the narrative ("Cops," *Parade Magazine*, Summer, 1993). Participating officers see themselves enacting roles as cops and recognize it as a performance selectively emphasizing certain role requirements and functions (Hallett and Powell, 1995). How does this near-version of police activities fit the reality rules?

The first part of the veridicality rule (#1) holds. Changes in the lighting, camera angle, volume of the voices, and film quality, as well as the blanked-out faces of the apprehended, and rapid jump cuts from one scene to the next, could have been fabricated. They connote realism. The second part of the veridicality rule does not hold. The images might represent something else—a drama, an entertainment, a reenactment, a false presentation, a rehearsal, or training. The show could be either staged or authentic; both or neither.

The sampling rule (#2) holds; however, the sampling of images is accomplished with an intense commercial dramaturgical purpose. The selection and length of the episodes, officers featured, the length of each scene, and officers' comments are intentional. The hours of film are edited, synthesized, and shaped, and the content is subject to manipulation and selectivity, interweaving life and theater.

The ordering and sequencing rule (#3) is marginally applicable. The show is punctuated by commercials and scenes are shown with voice-over narration. These mark *Cops* as a production, as do its edited and slightly artificial quality, stylized format, and punctuation, usually after or before a particularly dramatic and tense moment, when officers face the camera and explain slowly and ponderously the course of events. Gaps in the sequence of events are not explained so that what is missing is suppressed and is irrelevant to the story (but not to the activity).

The framing rule (#4) is ambiguously relevant because events are framed as televised versions of policing, not as a naturally occurring sequence of unaffected policing events. The sampling rule constrains what is shown, how it is framed, and why.

The coherence rule (#5) holds in this case because *Cops* is a named television program listed in the television guide with time and channel. Each episode begins and ends in much the same way: the title is shown, introduction given, and the theme music, "Bad Boys," is played. This format appears whenever *Cops* is shown. These frame the show, provide a sustaining anchor for assumptions of continuity, and omit other potentially intrusive matters.

The salience rule (#6) holds in that certain identifiable features shape the content of every episode. These recycled features are partially a result of media format (Altheide and Snow, 1994) that requires repeated prominent features weekly. The focus on service-oriented police work perhaps adds another dimension: continuity in content (Hallett and Powell, 1995).

In sum, television transforms policing into an event, *Cops*, in accordance with modified media reality rules. Social activities, naturally occurring, are filmed, edited, and made commercially engaging. *Cops* is then looped, like the King video, into the world, viewed by police as an exemplar of their work (Hallett and Powell, 1995), videotaped so that its contents can be studied by sociology classes, and used as lecture material and "data" for research papers and books. In this sense, it becomes part of the reflexive dialogue of the society.

A Double Echoing Loop: The Oklahoma City Bombing

In the two previous examples, policing was transformed and looped after an event had occurred, with television's production values as salient guides. Events created during television coverage of natural disasters or untoward events (riots, assassinations, sudden deaths, or terrorist acts), are driven by an odd assemblage of realist conceits (Dayan and Katz, 1993) that present edited, selectively screened snapshots of an event rarely seen (the actual explosion, earthquake, or hurricane) to be labeled "live coverage."

After the bombing of a federal building in Oklahoma City on the morning of April 11, 1995, live television coverage appeared within an hour on CNN and continued through the day. Other national networks rushed correspondents there within hours. It was framed first as an Arab terrorist act and reframed the following day as a domestic terrorist act (when McVeigh was arrested). The bombing was then connected to the FBI/ATF attack on the Waco compound and, by extension, the FBI sharpshooter's killing of a woman and child at Ruby Ridge, Idaho. The story had been given a story-structure, metaphoric reality and was looped back to *double echo* other activities and media events. How does this kind of television reflect reality according to the rules?

The veridicality rule (#1) holds because some events, usually reported via "talking heads" with the destroyed building in the background, are shown as they unfold. The coverage is carried via interviews (with the police chief, fire chief, head of rescue operations, emergency medical workers, and, later, relatives of victims). These representative anecdotes are seen as part of a coherent sequence illustrating a type of event that is both fateful and consequential. The images shown are not unique, or uniquely representative; they are of routine disasters, events that punctuate modern, risky life.

The sampling rule (#2) that asserts that the images shown are a sample of real activities holds, but the natural order of activities apparently drives the coverage, rather than media coverage or production decisions exclusively driving the events shown (Epstein, 1974). Nevertheless, willful direction, production, and sampling occurs. The sampling of images, both of time and content is based on preestablished organizational, economic (advertising obligations, programming commitments and schedules, and competing news stories), and occupational values (Epstein, 1974). Events can be only partially typified and stereotyped, only partially controlled and executed with dramaturgical purpose, because of the unknown exigencies of disasters.

The ordering and sequencing rule (#3) is weakly descriptive because the images are punctuated by commercial breaks, other programs, talking heads, and voice-over narration. The salience of order and sequence is heightened by the reported, naturally unfolding activities. In the bombing, the ordering-sequencing rule was violated by the intrusion of new knowledge. The bombing was not "another Arab terrorist bombing." A new order sequence focal point was found to organize and make meaningful unfolding activities during the course of the coverage. The bombing was redefined as a case of domestic, anti-government and ideologically based terrorism.

The framing rule (#4) is powerful because events are framed as televised versions of naturally occurring events, unfolding dramatically and vividly before the viewer's eyes. "You are there" is the conceit, even though there is little action intrinsic to a destroyed and crumbling building. This framing is asserted, even though the journalistic device of the story line emerged quickly to shape activities into events and "stories" (Epstein, 1974).

The coherence rule (#5) arose through continuous coverage and the emergent story line. The story was linked first to "Arab terrorists," then to the unfolding underlife of the militia and chauvinistic patriotic movements. Then several subtexts emerged: the search for villains, coconspirators, and condemnatory evidence. Tertiary stories then emerged: When will normalcy return? Who are the victims? How is the city recovering? Each of these is a preformatted mode of resurrecting reality (Epstein, 1974: 152–180).

The salience rule (#6) works for each definition or framing. In the first story line, certain selected facts are used to document the story, but other facts are found once the point of the story (the perpetrators) changed. Framing and reframing changed the salience of bits of facts and images.

REALITY AND REALITY RULES

Let us compare the rules in connection with the three events analyzed. In both the King video and *Cops*, the "real-time" assumption holds, as does the veridicality rule. Scenes are shown as if they were real-time activities; they unfold for the viewer in a provocative fashion. The viewer is a "fly on the wall" watching with no role in shaping the event's dynamics. The second part of the veridicality rule is dubious in *Cops* because elements are staged for the camera (officers speaking to the viewer and voice-over narration) that define the meaning of the images. The Oklahoma City bombing coverage on the scene is edited for time and extensiveness, interlarded with the daily television schedule and shown in news specials. Live, on-the-scene reports are included. The conceit is "you are there," and it is the immediate sort of real-life drama viewed up close at which television excels.

The sampling rule in the King video holds because television edits for reality, picking and selecting the angles, shots, and duration of given segments. *Cops* is doubly edited (by the police and by the television producers) for the same reasons: intentionally to reproduce what might be seen as real, exciting, and engaging by the viewer! Theater and life are interwoven. In both, the images shown are selected from a known set of images previously produced. The sampling rule in the bombing story is more complex given that on-line editorial decisions are made, but live coverage is created and orchestrated by directors and producers who switch between scenes, reporters, cameras, story lines, and locations attempting to create narrative order(s). The fiction of "on-the-scene live" is perhaps true initially, but virtually never true once the cameras, crews, and reporters are in place and mobilized by decisions of the producers. In created-for-television images, the criteria for sampling are aesthetic rather than a measure of the representativeness of the images from a pool of possible. The criteria for low art such as television comedies and music videos resemble high art—coherence, beauty, resonance and catharsis, characterization, and so on. The audience differs, but the model remains art, not life.

The King video and the *Cops* show are set in the context of other naturally occurring activities, whereas in the Oklahoma City event, the unfolding story was redefined in the course of the coverage. The ordering and sequencing rule holds—neither the King video nor *Cops* broke frame or departed from the original designation.

The framing rule holds in all five instances, but the framed genre is different in each case, and some ambiguity was seen in the liminal character of *Cops*. Each was framed initially as it was to be seen, even though some intermixing of genres occurs. The bombing remains labeled a "disaster."

Table 2-1 Events

Rules	King Video	Cops	Oklahoma City Bombing
Veridicality Rule	Real time	Real time, partially	"Live"
Sampling Rule	Edited for key elements	Edited for key elements	Edited and responsive to activities
Ordering & Sequencing Rule	Theme holds	Theme holds	Theme—focal point changes
Framing Rule	News	Infotainment	"Disaster"
Coherence Rule	Framed to be as it is	Framed to be as it is	Continuous coverage and emergent story line
Salience Rule	Elements remain	Elements remain	Elements change

Both the coherence of images and the salience rule work in *Cops* and the King video. The media in the Oklahoma City presentations altered the salience of some key event elements as story lines and the defining elements emerged. Looked at comparatively, the activities are assembled using slightly different "weightings" to each rule. This suggests how television partitions its realities.

MEDIATED POLITICS AND CULTURE

Three types of mediated reality were discussed: two police videos, one an activity that became a media event and a simulation, and one a recreation of modern, urban American policing shown as entertainment. The third was a bombing that became the basis for continuous coverage and linkage to other story lines (Epstein, 1974: 169–174). Each of the three maintains a framed reality, but different realities are framed. Looping permits the media to alter the nature of a framed reality by embedding, or rekeying, one image inside another. The outer rim, so to speak, defines the meaning of matters inside (Goffman, 1974: 82).

Differences exist between the meaning of televised events as revealed in the application of the reality rules. Media events and *axial media events* are transformations of live activity. Although Dayan and Katz (1993) use "media events" to refer to televised, already ritualized activities that are massively ceremonial and socially significant, the term is used here to explore media's power to amplify in political significance activities that might otherwise be invisible and insignificant. Some media events of an erstwhile banal character are axial, or historic moments that uncover the fault lines of societies, dramatic turning points in consciousness and collective life. Media reflect and create these *axial visual events*, events that portend change, whether ceremonially enhancing solidarity or reducing it, while engaging massive audiences.

The most important effect of media loops and the creation of media events is that the events become political reality. Simulation or hyperreality lurks inevitably when media loops are involved. Activities become events cast within a media genre. The media genre rekey other genres and mix events and persons (as when Chief Gates plays himself in a police show), or reenact or reconstruct dramatic and risk-filled episodes using professional actors and some of the actual participants or their voices. Rescue personnel appear as disembodied voices via audio or play themselves (*Rescue 911*). Media events can also be looped as news, as the King example illustrates.

These suggest the now familiar trail of media effects on social relations, especially the direct controlling effects of the media in the last 10 years. Programs such as *America's Most Wanted* have led repeatedly to suspects being turned in to the police, and local "crime stoppers" shows are very popular.[4] Altheide (1992) argues that the media perform directly as an integral part of the shaming and punishment process.[5]

When media events attain political significance, they are soon interwoven tightly with actual events. Media revelations of misconduct have become an almost essential feature of contemporary definitions of "scandal." Consider some loops with wide political ramifications.

In the O.J. Simpson murder case, LAPD Detective Mark Fuhrman testifies and subsequently is found to have perjured himself. The apparent perjury raises questions about the credibility of other evidence he has presented. The media publicize his lies and interview the Chief of the LAPD, Willie Williams, who deploys damage control tactics on the *Good Morning, America* show, announcing that the LAPD is investigating carefully Fuhrman's previous cases. Fuhrman retires and returns to the trial, only to take the Fifth Amendment. A lawyer for a defendant now in prison as a result in part of Fuhrman's testimony files an appeal requesting that his client's case be reheard.

Now consider a second media loop. Television reporters interviewed and filmed officers in the LAPD and elsewhere, inquiring about their reactions to media reactions to Fuhrman's televised remarks. When the interview with an officer was shown on the news, Fuhrman's voice is played from a tape made by the female witness who accused him of racism, while a still picture of him testifying is shown in a small box at the corner of the screen! *USA Today* (August 30, 1995: 3) quotes Cliff Ruff, President of the LAPD's Police Protective League, "We just got over Rodney King, and now they're implying there's a bunch of racist cops out there again." The media promote further complex intertextuality and reflexivity. The *Washington Post* (August 31, 1995: A16) prints, "The Fuhrman tapes are, in effect, the missing sound track from the Rodney King videotape, some blacks said, a verbal articulation of the anger and hatred that motivated white police officers to flail at King with their nightsticks as he lay prone."

The workings of television, decisions of television executives, and public response create political realities, some of which have direct behavioral effects. Television's event-spawning machinery has the capacity to create private realities that are the underside of the public realities and image-making. This is seen in emergent forms of visual social control by FBI investigators and state police (police use of computer identities on the Internet to lure pedophiles into illegal proposals), the prosecution of Jake Baker for simulating a killing in a chat room on the Internet, and the resonance of chat room and other on-line communications, some sponsored by newspapers (such as the *Detroit Free Press*), with axial media events such as the King beating, the Simpson trial, and the Oklahoma City bombing. Private and public forms of social control become intermingled as well.

Television creates realities, and through television's transformative processes, looping and simulation, symbolic reality, or *hyperreality* (Poster, 1990), is interwoven and competes for veridicality with direct unmediated personal experience. Hyperreality is created when images refer to other images, rather than to social activities of embodied people. Because of the seductive power of the television-viewing experience, and the foreshortening of all forms of communication, increased varieties of simulation, media looping, and reality construction loom ahead. Complicated media loops, virtual and cyber realities, and forms of hypertext (arbitrarily linked texts) by which we assemble our lives, selves, and imagery will become more common.

DISCUSSION QUESTIONS

1. What does Manning mean when he states, "Television creates *media events*"? If this is true, what are the implications for television coverage of crime and justice?

2. What is a *media loop*?

3. What are the "reality rules" identified by Manning? What examples does he offer of how television frames reality? What other examples can you think of?

NOTES

1. Consider here the work of Altheide, (1986); Elliot, (1972); Elliot and Golding, (1979); and Gitlin, (1986).

2. For details of the King affair, see books by the Christopher Commission, 1991, and Jacobs (1996), the *L.A. Times* (1992), Gooding-Williams (1993), and Owens, 1994.

3. Televised stories shown in 1992 following the filming connected the King video iteratively to the investigation of police brutality in Los Angeles (the 1991 Christopher Commission), the pressure on Chief Gates to resign, his resignation, the appointment of Willie Williams from Philadelphia as Chief of the LAPD, Gates'

attempt to promote officers loyal to him in June near the time of his promised resignation, comments of Mayor Bradley on Gates' action, the trial and retrial of Officers Koon, Powell, Brisneo, and Wind, and so on. Willie Williams resigned in March 1997.

4. These apparently real mock-ups of policing are not easily distinguished by content from fictional media versions of police work, for example, *Dragnet, Adam-12*, (both Jack Webb Productions), *Hawaii Five-O*, and, more recently, *Hill Street Blues, NYPD Blue*, and *Homicide*. Officers in the LAPD can see themselves portrayed in reruns of Jack Webb Productions.

LAPD chiefs, "Jack" Horrall and William Parker, advised Webb about the image of the LAPD they wished portrayed, and the LAPD supplied technical assistance for the production of the shows (Gates, 1993: 325–326). The police see and participate in media activities, some of which are planned and staged explicitly for the media (Gates, 1993). As chief of the LAPD, William Parker hired the first police department press relations officer in 1951 (Gates, 1993: 44). Chief Daryl Gates (1993: 326) appeared as himself in at least two episodes of *Hunter* (a show about the LAPD starring ex-Rams football star, Fred Dwyer).

5. In some cases, media coverage produces apparent changes in police practice. *Newsweek* (September 4, 1995: 25) claims that as a result of publicity surrounding the Rodney King incident, the Los Angeles police have changed their behavior. They now have ethics discussions at roll-call, at which officers are warned to be careful or "they'll be roomin' with Stacey" (Herbert, 1997).

3

❄

Popular Culture and Violence:

Decoding the Violence of Popular Movies[*]

GRAEME NEWMAN

INTRODUCTION

Violence figures very strongly in the popular movies of the American mass entertainment media.[1] Violence in war, crime, and horror movies has been popular since the first motion pictures were made.[2] Many policy makers have expressed concern about the possible effects that violence in the mass media might have on its viewers (Cater, 1975). An enormous amount of research has been conducted to investigate whether violence in the mass media does increase aggressiveness of its viewers—whether children or adults. Although policy makers and politicians are generally disposed to claim that the evidence supports the contention of the negative effects of viewing violence on mass media, the scientific evidence is not at all clear.[3] Recently, in an influential report on violence, the National Research Council did not focus on media violence as a major cause of violence in American Society (National Research Council, 1992).

A major difficulty in measuring the effects of the violence on mass entertainment media is that its portrayal on movies and TV shows is so varied, the settings and contexts of violence so diverse, that it is difficult to generalize from the findings of one study to another. Previous empirical studies have not examined the *language of violence*. They have assumed that the context within

[*]This is a revised version of a paper prepared for the International Workshop on Realities and Countermeasures for Violent Crime, Korean Institute of Criminology, November, 1993.

40

which violence occurs is not as important in affecting the viewer's subsequent violent behavior, as is the violence itself. For example, the classic studies of modeling aggression by Bandura (1973), in which young children watched various scenes of adults verbally chastising children, focused more on viewing the aggression itself, rather than its coded context: the power relationship between the adult and child, the defenselessness of the child, and so forth.

I contend that the coding of violence might be of crucial significance in estimating its effect on viewers. Before we can measure the effects of media violence on its viewers, we must first analyze the contexts and varieties of contexts in which violence is portrayed. Thus, in this chapter, I make a first, preliminary attempt to develop a systematic way to decode the language of violence as it is presented on one mass entertainment medium, popular movies. I have confined this chapter to popular movies simply as a way to cut the enormous amount of raw mass entertainment material that awaits analysis. Clearly, we could apply the same approach to TV series, advertising, popular music, and many other genres (using the term as defined by Berger, 1992).[4] However, even confining myself to popular motion pictures still leaves an enormous amount of material to cover. Actually, it is impossible to do so. I have chosen the "texts" of popular movies (by which I mean to make a rough distinction between these movies and "minority interest," "artistic," or "cult" movies). Thus, I would include in my subject matter movies such as *Taxi Driver* or *The Godfather*, but I would not include a movie such as *Videodrome*. I accept that this distinction is somewhat arbitrary and probably should be empirically based (such as using the gross revenues of motion pictures as an indicator of "popularity" or mass appeal). The problem with such a definition of "popular," however, is that movies that turned out to have a significant impact on subsequent movies might not have initially been "popular." I have therefore taken quite a bit of license in deciding which movies are "significant" examples of violence coding and which are not. Furthermore, because there are so many movies whose dominant theme is violent, it would be impossible for me to review every one. I have therefore confined myself to developing a model for analyzing the language of violence, drawing on such popular movies that seemed to me to most clearly demonstrate or elucidate the model I have developed. This is an admittedly self-serving methodology. I expect that many will disagree with my classification of some movies and general typing of some of them. The sea of mass media violence is so vast, however, that I think it is justified to make a start, if somewhat arbitrary, to impose an order or framework from which to begin a systematic discussion and to identify some of the more basic issues.

DEFINING VIOLENCE

To decipher how violence is encoded into popular movies, we must first attempt to define violence, or at least outline the boundaries of what is violence and what is not. This in itself is a difficult task because the word "violence" is a favorite word of moralists, who often identify behaviors they disapprove of by calling them violent. On the other hand, because the encoding of violence into plots and images on popular movies is so sophisticated, it is sometimes difficult to see that violence is a dominant theme. Indeed, a recent example is the movie *Unforgiven* in which there are scenes of quite shocking violence, yet this movie has been portrayed by the popular media as "anti-violence." The same could even be said of *Natural Born Killers*, in which Oliver Stone weaves together shocking scenes of violence with a theme that critiques the media exultation of serial killers.

The definition of violence put forward by the recent National Research Council study of violence (1992) defines all violence as an *intentional act*. Yet, this influential study also points out that violence is a highly diverse phenomenon. If we confined ourselves to this narrow definition, a great deal of violence that is depicted on popular movies would be passed over. And, it is not at all clear what is an intentional act of violence and what is not. If we consider the research of most of this century, the assumption that all violence (or even any violence) is an intentional act is plainly wrong, or at least a gross oversimplification (Newman, 1978). I propose, therefore, a broader definition: *Violence is a series of events, the course of which or the outcomes of which, cause injury or damage to persons or property.* This definition is very broad. It encompasses both human violent actions as well as events that might not have an immediate human element or cause, such as natural disasters (though human behavior, as we shall see, might be encoded into such violent contexts). Human violent actions, according to our definition might or might not be intentional. We have also left open *how much* injury or damage would be necessary to define a series of actions as "violent." The actions themselves might not be "violent"; for example, pulling the trigger of a gun is not a violent act in itself compared with beating someone to death with a baseball bat. However, the outcomes of pulling the trigger of a gun might be very violent.

TYPES OF VIOLENCE

If we examine the research of this century on the causes of violence, we find that research psychologists have generally classified violence into two types: (1) instrumental and (2) expressive (Newman, 1978). Instrumental violence is that violent behavior used by individuals (and sometimes by groups) to achieve a particular goal or end. The assumption generally is that violence is therefore a rational or cognitive process: The individual knows what he or she wants and decides that the way to get it is through violence. The most obvious form of this violence is violent revolutionary or terroristic behavior, which is clearly underwritten by a political ideology that provides the rationale or "justification" for the use of violence as the *means* to the end—in this case, the overthrow of a government. At a micro level, a teenager might decide that he is persecuted unjustly by a tyrannical father and choose to kill him. Or, violence to defend oneself from an immediate attack is seen as "instrumental." Clearly, the instrumental type of violence fits neatly into the definition of violence as "intentional."

The other view of violence as expressive argues that violence is largely an explosive phenomenon, which generally erupts as an expression of deep emotional forces and feelings, such as rage, anger, hatred, frustration. Thus, the boy who kills his father is driven by rage or frustration. The assumption is that it is not his conscious intention to kill the tyrannical father, he is driven to it.

Both these types of violence are used extensively in popular movies. By definition, the expressive view of violence tends to see the individual as less responsible (in a legal and moral sense) because he is seen as less in control of his actions because of the explosive nature of the emotions that force his actions to violence (although the more conservative view would be that, even so, individuals have to learn to control their emotions). However, the contexts within which these types of violence are set vary widely. For example, the model of violence portrayed in the *Godfather* movies is highly instrumental. The Godfather carefully plans and chooses the appropriate level and timing of violence so it has the maximum effect on his enemies. Those who use violence expressively ("Sonny" for example, the "hothead" in *Godfather* I) are viewed as less than adequate. In general, this series of movies advocates violence as an effective means of establishing and maintaining order. The hotheaded violence (expressive) is seen as order breaking. In this sense, the use of violence by the Godfather, even though graphically portrayed at times, conveys an ideology of its "beneficial use"—that is, maintaining a tradition and an order. And because this general lifestyle incorporates violence as a natural part of everyday life, and is mixed in to many scenes of "the family" (an extended one) at the dinner table—a classic family scene evocative of positive and warm feelings—this instrumental violence can be made to seem a positive force: as "good violence," even though it is administered by a crime syndicate.

We should see, however, that when violence is enmeshed into a lifestyle, its "rationality" might not be quite so apparent. In *Reservoir Dogs* for example, because the order of life is disturbed by an informer among the thieves, the violence of "doing business" that the film implies (see Newman and Bouloukos, 1993) is usually at a low level (but with the threat of serious violence always present), what would have been instrumental violence is transformed into expressive and explosive violence that ultimately destroys all the thieves. Thus, the rational use of violence (its controlled use to carry out the business of doing robbery) is overtaken by emotional or expressive violence that is unleashed because of the breakdown of trust among the members of the criminal gang.

Many dramas and sagas pit instrumental violence against expressive violence. For example, in the *Star Wars* epic, Luke Skywalker is the young "hothead," eager to go off and destroy his enemies without a moment's thought. He has to be trained by an arduous and laborious process to gain control of "the force." The force, we must eventually conclude, is the emotive or expressive force of violence itself. When Luke finally learns to control himself, he learns that with some planning, forethought, and organization, much greater violence can be brought to bear on one's enemies, and far more serious violence effected than the mere outbursts of a teenager.

Similarly, the portrayal of the lone gunman in the Wild West as the "cool" and deliberate gunfighter, supports the instrumentalist ideology that surrounds the portrayal of violence in the classic Western. The lone gun is portrayed as cool and emotionless. Indeed, in the most recent western—Eastwood's Academy Award winner, *Unforgiven*—the aging gunfighter is constantly presented as the cool, emotionless fighter. This portrayal is embedded into dialog that pretends that the gunfighter was not responsible for his past violent deeds (including the killing of women and children)—he was, says the hero, drunk most of the time. Killing while under the influence of alcohol or any other drug is, of course, similar to the model of expressive violence: It is implied that the violent individual is "not responsible" or "not in control" of his aggression. At the same time, this sophisticated movie develops the hero's character as one in which he cares about his children (though he leaves them home alone for two weeks while he goes off to work as a hired killer), who seems to be "against" violence, yet is doing it for the money, so he can feed his kids. As well, his nemesis, the local sheriff, is a man who knows only violence as a way to carry out his job. The sheriff (the villain) is portrayed as the extremely violent man, the hero (the criminal) as the one who wants "nonviolence." But the plot is structured in such a way as to make it all but inevitable that the hero will "go back to" violence. The sheriff provokes him, and in the end, as the hero must defend himself, he pulls off an incredibly violent massacre of all the several law enforcement officers around him—and this movie was portrayed by the media as "antiviolence!" The provocation, of course, provides the rationale or "excuse" for the hero to return to his old ways, and the ways for which the audience is waiting: an explosion of violence that will wipe away his enemies in one fell swoop.

If we keep in mind this general contrast between the two basic kinds of violence, we can now extend the analysis of the use of violence in movies to examine the kinds of rationales that are used to make the violence seem "acceptable" or even "good" in service of the story and the main characters of the popular movie. This transformation of violence is achieved by two main processes: (1) the encoding of violence and (2) the enplotting of violence. By encoding violence, I mean both the contexts and rationales within which violence is portrayed. A variety of rationales enhance both the use of expressive and instrumental violence. It should be noted, of course, that probably no movie is purely one or the other. Sometimes there is a conflict of opposites (Berger, 1992) when expressive violence is pitted against instrumental violence. By enplotting violence, I mean the techniques that use violence to enhance or resolve problems in the actual plot. *Enplotting* involves essentially *techniques*. *Encoding* involves essentially contexts and images that amount to hidden or explicit rationales.

ENCODING INSTRUMENTAL VIOLENCE

1. *Rebellion Against Injustice.* The *Star Wars* epics brilliantly provide this rationale for the use of violence. The "enemy" (Darth Vader and his crew) are portrayed as dark, evil, and violent, bent on totally destroying Luke Skywalker's "good" people. The complete and utter destruction of the enemy seems a perfectly reasonable reaction to the crass injustices perpetrated by the enemy.

2. *Vengeance.* Evening up the score is a well-established justification for the use of violence, motivated, some would say, by an expressive or emotional urge to correct a deeply perceived wrong (such as the killing of a loved one as in *Death Wish*), to a studied and instrumental process of carefully getting even. The *Death Wish* movies are the best example of this justification for violence, although the motive appears in many movies (Marongiu and Newman, 1987, Newman, 1993). This is also a good example of the expressive aspect of violence lying behind the instrumental aspect. In *Death Wish*, the motive for violence is highly emotional. The method is highly instrumental. The way in which the initial victimization is used in the plot, though it appeals to the expressive aspect of violence, also provides the unassailable rationale or "excuse" for violence. Movies that manage to blend the expressive into the instrumental aspects of violence tend to be the most effective in conveying their message.

3. *Rebellion Against Bureaucracy.* This is the essential theme of the *Dirty Harry* policing movies. Here is the "lone gunman" (the "cool" character taken from the Western) who seems only concerned with catching the crooks and giving them their due. Alas, the policing bureaucracy (and the politicians who control it) keep interfering with his work and making it all but impossible for him to carry out his real duty of catching sleazy, violent crooks. So, Dirty Harry uses violence (violence which is, of course, against the law if used officially by the policing bureaucracy) that most effectively (and very satisfyingly to the audience) dispatches criminals forthwith. The violence is therefore portrayed as clearly not legal but certainly justifiable and a "good thing" as far as the audience is concerned. The famous line "go ahead, make my day" was even paraphrased by President Ronald Reagan—a curious presidential approval of a fantasy that reflects almost exactly the model of government death squads that operated in Argentine's Dirty War (Graziano, 1992).

4. *Problem Solving.* James Bond must find out who is transporting gold, or why an operative has disappeared. He has many seemingly impossible problems to solve. He solves his problems with two skills: He is extremely talented at almost any contest (such as card playing, cheating, skiing, and of course, his prowess as a lover), and he uses violence to find his way through the puzzle, to collect the information he needs to solve the problem of who is the villain, and what he is up to. The traditional private-eye movies (for example, Mike Hammer) also use this rationale for violence.

5. *Extracting Confessions*. James Bond, Dirty Harry, Superman, and Batman all use violence (that is, threats and actual physical force) against individuals to get them to "talk." In this way, violence serves an important function to help these heroes gain the information they need to catch the villain. Needless to say, mobsters in crime movies are depicted as using violence for the same reasons—they can extract the information they need from their enemies (usually reserved for those among them who are "informers"). Perhaps the most brutal scene in which violence is used to extract information from the victim is that in *Reservoir Dogs*, where the so-called psychopath (one without apparent emotion—not unlike the heroes of the west, who are, interestingly not portrayed as psychopaths)—cuts off the ear of the policeman he has caught, ostensibly to obtain information concerning who was the informer among them.

6. *Demonstrate Authority*. The emperor Ming in the Flash Gordon movie constantly applies violence, seemingly whimsically, against those under him. The sheriff in *The Heat of the Night* and *Mississippi Burning* uses violence to demonstrate his authority. It is a way of appealing to the sense of powerlessness of the masses. Authority is portrayed as brutal and arbitrary, and violence enhances this brutality. Rarely do we see violence used in this context presented in a positive light. It is as if violence is only acceptable when used from those of lower position in the social or political hierarchy. However, the ways in which authority (that is, order) are reinforced through the use of violence is to depict societies (usually imaginary ones) in which order has disappeared. Violent chaos is almost always depicted as the result of a breakdown of order (for example, *Escape from New York, Mad Max, Road Warrior*). When violence is to be used by authority and portrayed as "good" it must be split from the authority structure—thus the Dirty Harry movies.

7. *Expose Corruption*. The *Dirty Harry* movies provide the scenario for the use of violence as the only way to demonstrate to the authorities the corruption in their midst. And, when the corruption is at the highest level (the top supervisor of the cop in *Witness*, for example), extreme use of violence is thoroughly recommended. In the movie *Witness*, we are given the opportunity to observe a small community of Amish that lives according to an ethic of nonviolence. But this nonviolence is no match for the violence that erupts from the corrupt dominant society. The scene in which Book (the hero), despite the disapproval of the Amish, beats up a hoodlum who bullied one of his Amish friends, beautifully demonstrates this contrast of cultures. And, further, when real corruption catches up to the hero on the Amish farm, the pacifism of the Amish is clearly no match for the focused and deadly violence of corrupt policemen. Only the hero, using superior intelligence, and an unwavering commitment to violence, can get rid of the aggressors.

8. *Establish Order*. It seems a contradiction in terms to suggest that violence can be used to establish order because we tend most commonly to think

of violence as breaking down order, going against it. But, if chaos reigns (or is perceived to reign), then violence is often used as a ploy to introduce order. The movie series that effectively portrays this rationale for violence is the *Batman* saga in which order seems to have been lost because of the evil machinations of the Joker, the Penguin, and other bizarre criminals and politicians, who seem devoted to destroying the society that created them. Batman employs massive violence to bring back the order and calm of Gotham City. On a micro level, the movie *Dirty Dozen* condones the use of violence as a means to train the 12 criminals who are to be prepared for a dangerous military mission in World War II. In the two movies *Road Warrior* and *Mad Max*, we are presented with a scene where there is no order, as we think of it. Rather, society is dominated by marauding bands and individual thugs. Massive violence imposes a semblance of order among the groups and brings about a balanced "order" that is based on a kind of feuding structure (see Lynch and Newman, 1987).

9. *A Higher Morality.* The violence of the movie *The Untouchables* was considerable—both from the mob and from the government agents. Even the mouse-like character, the accountant from the Treasury Department, (who actually came up with the way to nail Capone) was sucked into the use of violence to fight a battle with the mob. The good cause was, of course, enforcing prohibition and putting the mob out of business. Considerable violence was used by government authority to win the battle for the higher cause. Eliot Ness was clearly embarked on a moral crusade. The particularly brutal scene of Capone beating one of his henchmen to death with a baseball bat because he was displeased with him, conveyed to the audience that the Mob's violence was unjustified, sadistic, and primitive and that in comparison, the government's violence was more than reasonable.

10. *Conflict Resolution.* On first impression, this rationale for violence seems oxymoronic because violence *is* conflict. Yet, if we study movies in which there are seemingly irresolvable conflict-disagreements between individuals or groups, we see that violence is often used as the way to resolve the conflict. For example, in the *Godfather* movies, there is a constant competition and conflict between rival gangs. Using violence is seen as a way to redress and return to an equilibrium, that is, resolve the conflict. Similarly, in the movies *Colors* and *Boyz N the Hood*, rival gangs or groups of teenagers perceive conflict and use violence to settle scores and resolve conflict. Of course, other factors are often involved as well—such as "honor," which is seen to have been insulted or lost by certain actions of an opposing gang (such as disrespectful treatment of a gang member's girlfriend or trespassing on another gang's "turf.") Violence is regarded as a means to resolve the conflict. Family feuds are similarly portrayed in this way (Lynch and Newman, 1987).

ENCODING EXPRESSIVE VIOLENCE

1. *Stereotyping of Ethnic Groups.* The epic *Lawrence of Arabia* demonstrates this way of portraying, through graphic scenes of violence—the animalistic, "uncivilized" nature of certain races and ethnic groups. Thus, the Arabs in *Lawrence of Arabia* are depicted as animal-like in their desire to spill their enemies' blood. The Englishman Lawrence also indulges in this behavior—but the movie carefully shows how this was the action of a "fallen man," of a civilized man who had sunk to the level of the bloodthirsty Arabs.

2. *Teenage Rebellion.* Rarely do teenage movies portray teenagers as using violence in anything but an expressive, uncontrolled way. The movie *Outsiders* perhaps portrays this teenage violence best. Violence is portrayed as impulsive, senseless, and explosive. The classic *The Wild Ones*, depicting a motor bike gang's "senseless" violence is perhaps the best example.

3. *Nature.* Violence is depicted as part of the natural world. The violence of natural disasters such as earthquakes, floods, droughts, fires, and so forth is a favorite movie theme. We are invited to view natural violence in awe, yet as a challenge to human character—as a plotting tool, as we shall see later.

4. *The Beast.* The forces of nature also reside in animals. From *Godzilla* to *Jaws*, creatures from nature have served as the vehicles through which violence is "justified" in the sense that it is the natural way in which these particular "beasts" behave. Yet, many of the movies (*Jaws* for example) also manage to show that those who get eaten by these beasts sort of deserved it—that is, they do obviously silly things, take obviously silly risks that place them right in the path of the beast. So what's the shark to do? Eat them, of course. *Jurassic Park* also follows this basic premise. Through their foolishness and arrogance, humans create the situations in which they become the victims of the violence of nature that remains, though terribly vicious, "innocent" of its destructiveness.

5. *Going It One Better.* What set the James Bond movies apart when they first appeared was the explicit statement that 007 was "licensed to kill." The villains are unbelievably violent and callous. It takes an extra ruthless and extra violent hero to beat these villains at their own game. *Die Hard* does just that. The hero is the only chance that the innocent people who are the victims of the villains, have of survival. Although the villains in the *Die Hard* movies are portrayed as callous and "misguided" (and highly instrumental—not even for a higher cause, but for a "low" one: money) the level of violence and destruction that is eventually visited on them by the hero is enormous, yet seems "deserved."

6. *War.* This is perhaps the most widely established justification for violence. Ordinary people are sent to the battlefield where they must use violence that they otherwise would rather not. They learn how to kill, and be killed. Even the so-called "antiwar' movies in the post-Vietnam genre do

not so much oppose violence itself but, rather, place the violence in the context of that particular war. These people end up killing lots of people, often in the heat of the moment, with highly expressive violence, after which they feel remorse. But, "that's war." They had to do it.

7. *Fun.* The Roadrunner cartoons and many others like them allow audiences to laugh at the most outrageous acts of violence. No matter how well the wolf lays his plans, he fails to catch the roadrunner and his failure ends in insufferable violent destruction (but not death, of course), at which the audience laughs hysterically. Why is this funny? In these movies, the intended victim becomes the hero—for so often the roadrunner behaves in such a way as to cause the destruction of the scheming wolf. Cartoon violence is used to even greater effect in *Who Framed Roger Rabbit?*, where cartoon characters are subjected to untold tortures and violence, while being mixed into a regular private eye movie with "real" humans and a classic private-eye character.

8. *Mysticism.* Violence has mystical qualities. It issues out of the imaginary beast or monster that resides in the dark recesses of humanity, of the deep unconscious fears of each individual. The "bogey man" is used to typify this type of violence, which is enacted through a human looking person, who is in some way possessed by this mystical obsession of violence. The "bogey man" in the *Friday the 13th* series uses this concept to the fullest. The model of the "beast within" was graphically portrayed in the various versions of *Jekyll and Hyde*, *Dracula*, and of course, *The Exorcist* and other Satan movies. It is worth noting, however, that the violence of these demonic characters is used to justify equally harsh violence on behalf of the "victims" who must defend themselves. This cleansing of "violence by the innocents" is a well-established contextual trick in the use of violence in movies. How many parents would forbid their children from watching *The Wizard of Oz* because of the violent death that is finally dealt to the "bad" witch? Recently, however, it has been argued that the "modern" horror movie has broken away from the classic horror film, and more closely reflects the escalating real violence in society today (Crane, 1995).

9. *The Madman.* *Silence of the Lambs* was a powerful portrayal of the madman as violent. This was the prototype diabolical killer who just likes to kill and is expert enough to plan his killings and carry them out successfully without being caught—or at least most of the time. Yet even with this movie, we are treated to two different orders of psychopathic killers. The "lower order" is the sexually deviant serial killer who is depicted as the sleazy, pathetic pervert. This is the most common serial killer type portrayed in popular movies (for example, the killer in *Play it Again Sam*, and in *Dirty Harry*). But the smart, super-intelligent killer Hannibal, in *Silence of the Lambs* is portrayed as functioning at a higher level than the ordinary serial killer. His violence is simply brilliant, and we are invited to admire his ingenuity and talent. Indeed, it wins him his freedom. His use of violence as highly instrumental places the contrasting expressive violence of the pervert on a lower level.

10. *Vengeance.* Vengeance fits neatly into both instrumental and expressive violence encoding.

11. *Sex.* When women are involved in violent movies, it is virtually certain that the Freudian based link between sex and violence will be exploited. Domination and violence are a popular theme whether by men over women (for example, *Sleeping with the Enemy*), women over men (for example, *Basic Instinct*), or men over men (for example, *Deliverance*).

ENPLOTTING VIOLENCE

I use this term to describe the use of violence to enhance and resolve problems with plots in popular movies. Although I have outlined the various ways in which violence has been encoded into the overall structure of the movies, I have not addressed the actual techniques that are used when violence is employed as a major plot enhancer. The following is a list of techniques:

1. *Simultaneity.* A number of movies from different genres employ the plot technique of building up more and more problems that have to be resolved by the hero. They mount up so much that it seems that the hero will not be able to deal with them. The solution is saved to the end, or near the end, of the movie: In one fell swoop, the hero solves all the problems, sometimes in one scene (*Unforgiven*), or at least in a quick succession of scenes (*Godfather*). Violence eradicates all enemies, unpaid debts, plot leftovers. This works by building audience expectations throughout the movie that "something will happen in the end that will resolve all this." The final scene in *Reservoir Dogs* takes this plotting technique to its ultimate extreme.

2. *The Shock Scene.* The movie *Bonnie and Clyde* built toward what the audience knew was going to be an inevitable showdown between Bonnie and Clyde and the police. In the "shocking" scene (which by today's standards was not terribly graphic, but in the 1960s was a milestone in movie portrayal of violence) Bonnie and Clyde are ambushed, and their bodies are shown flung in all directions in super-slow motion, as they are riveted by bullets.

3. *The Torture Scene.* Torture scenes convince the audience of the evil nature of the torturer (unless he happens to be working in the service of a good cause, see earlier). The torture scene in *Reservoir Dogs*, for example, focused the drama on the psychopathic killer, so that the audience could enjoy the torture, while knowing that this was something that *they* would not do but a psychopath would.

4. *Revelation of the Body.* Horror movies especially depend on the shock or fascination value of showing detailed close ups of maimed or severed parts of the body, as realistically as possible. The fascination with blood and other bodily parts obviously is what makes horror movies appealing. Much more could be said about this fascinating encoding process. A

number of serial killers as described by Leyton (1990) appear to be motivated by a frenzied search of the human insides—some dissect their victims, seemingly looking for something in their entrails. Looking inside the body, the revelation of the insides, an inaccessible place to all but a select few people in our society (that is, surgeons) reveals the "secret" of the human insides.

5. *The Hook.* A violent scene early in the movie, particularly if it is graphic and startling, can "hook" or grab the attention of the viewer. The early scene in the bathroom at Penn Central station in *Witness*, for example, grabs attention and makes up for the lack of violence in the movie until toward its end. Sometimes the reverse works. For example, the viewer is "hooked" by the good natured chatting amongst the gangsters in the first scene of *Reservoir Dogs*, which is then shattered by the graphic scene of one of the gangsters lying in the back of a getaway car covered in blood from a gunshot to the stomach. But the important point is that the technique depends on shock value by using violence in contrast with scenes of calm and friendship.

6. *Innovative Destruction Techniques.* There seem to be no end of the creative ways in which the aggressor brings about the death of the victim. A new implement (for example, the fluid metal arm of the *Terminator II* that directly pierces the head of the victim) satisfies (and creates) the demand for "special effects" of violence. A paper could be written on this enplotting aspect of violence alone. I suspect that the technological achievements that depict violence in such realistic and inventive ways are the very reason that it is done at all.

7. *Violent Chase Scene.* Always a popular attraction. It is widely believed that the chase scene in *Road Warrior* is what made the movie so popular. Automobiles and violence are constantly tied together. Fiery accidents are almost always the result of a chase scene—a "must" scene in all James Bond movies, and rarely left out of a cops and robbers movie. The *Lethal Weapon* series uses this technique to the full extent, providing innovative ways to destroy and burn up vehicles.

8. *Fire.* Psychoanalysts argue that fire appeals to the most primitive part of the human psyche. Freud noted in his classic *Civilization and its Discontents* that man's relationship with fire has, since the beginning of civilization, been one of power and control. Special effects have contributed greatly to fire use in recent years. Individuals running around as they are burned alive have become common. The explosion and destruction of whole buildings has become essential in all action movies. The explosive destruction of the great American icon, the automobile, is an essential in all action and cops and robbers movies.

9. *Blood.* This is a special form of revelation of the body—the blood of life, always a bright color, and with spectacular spurting special effects. Since the violent scene in *Bonnie and Clyde*, special effects have escalated in their attempt to outdo previous killing scenes. The most blood in any recent movie was that of the stomach wound of Mr. Pink in *Reservoir Dogs*.

10. *Contest of Opposites.* Berger (1992) has demonstrated how popular and well this technique works. Opposites are pitted against each other, although they can also have a hidden thread that links them mysteriously together.[5] For example, Darth Vader turns out to be Luke Skywalker's father, and the audience waits patiently for the inevitable showdown between the "bad" and the "good" warriors. Literature has a long tradition of opposites and "twins" (Girard, 1972).

11. *Music.* Who would have thought that Beethoven could accompany scenes of personal violence so easily? Yet the apparently civilized classical music manages to rivet the viewer's attention all the more to the rapes and beatings in *A Clockwork Orange.* In this way mundane violence is transformed into the profound. Violence becomes fascinating, not only viscerally, but intellectually. Or, in a different sense, the 1970s music that accompanies the entire movie of violence in *Reservoir Dogs*, uses nostalgic humor to contrast with the terrible violence: for example when Mr. White dances around his torture victim, listening to the song, "Stuck in the Middle with You."

12. *Comedy.* Although humor is used as a way of encoding violence, comedy is also used as an enplotting technique to make the otherwise violent characters more appealing. The humorous friendship between the two cops in the *Lethal Weapon* series is an excellent example of the enplotting technique. Their friendship is based on constant patter of violent verbal abuse. The technique is also applied in *Who Framed Roger Rabbit?*

13. *Loser Wins.* The hero almost always starts out with many handicaps. He usually doesn't know what's going on, is physically smaller than his opponent, doesn't seem as ruthless, and doesn't have anyone else to help him. But he is driven by one thing: a principle of higher morality than that of his opponent. So, even though he is inevitably beaten up throughout the movie, in a final massive struggle (hand to hand combat or shoot-out is preferred), the hero wins. The *Rocky* series exemplifies this plot technique.

14. *Primal Scene of Absolute Injustice.* A scene of absolute injustice establishes the plot structure for the entire movie: the hero's family or loved one is violated unmercifully, such as Batman's parents robbed and shot before his eyes as a young child; the family of a successful businessman raped in *Death Wish*; Jesse James's mother beaten by Yankee soldiers, and many more.

15. *Board Game Plot.* The detective in private eye movies struggles through the plot as if it were a board game. Violence traps him at every move, he is beaten up and loses his "clue," and he is forced back to "go." Sex distracts him, he is again beaten by the villains, and he seemingly loses all the progress he had made. Finally, usually a massive show of violence by the villains, often killing off the hero's lover or friend, forces him to focus on the puzzle and, by using unmitigated violence, to pursue the villains.

16. *Ritual Predictability*. Violent acts and sequences are repeated and eagerly awaited by the audience. We know that James Bond will use a close to magical technological wonder to escape from an impossible situation in which his demise seems assured. We expect these "close calls" to occur several times throughout the movie. We expect the action hero to be the victim of horrendous violence many times throughout the movie. It happens predictably, ritualistically. Particular types of violent scenes are anticipated: the violent chase scene, the violent fisticuffs, the violent sword or knife fight, the violent gun battle. Various action movies specialize in these predictable violent events that are repeated several times through the movie.

CONCLUSIONS: VIOLENCE, GENRE AND POPULAR CULTURE

Do particular genres in popular movies employ particular enplotting and encoding patterns of violence? It is likely that they do, although I hasten to add that it is particularly difficult to classify movies into genres, not to mention the controversy that surrounds the definition of what genre means in the first place (see Berger, 1992 for a discussion of this concept.) I will use the term genre in this chapter to refer to a general classification of types of movies along traditional lines, for example, westerns, crime, war, drama, and so forth as outlined by Kaminsky (1974). I propose the following allocation of encoding and enplotting according to the variety of popular movie genres. It should be emphasized that these are only rough approximations, and the movies I have selected are highly idiosyncratic. I hope, however, that this offers a beginning to the mapping of the language of violence as it is portrayed in popular motion pictures. No doubt, many of the encoding and enplotting factors of violence cut across several genre lines. As well, the genre classification I have adopted is not altogether satisfactory because many of the categories overlap. Other classification schemes could easily be developed according to different criteria. Table 3-1 should be seen as exploratory or preliminary only. Basically, it summarizes the main points made in this chapter.

Wright (1975), among others, has implied that popular movies describe personalities and promote ways of behaving that are models for what we are supposed to be and the ways we should act. Wright's particular thesis was that westerns mirror the contemporary economic institutions and belief structures of American society. That movies reflect the times in which they are produced seems to me to be a truism. The exact process by which they express the economic relations of a particular economy and society, however, is not at all clear. Obviously, many popular movies make lots and lots of money. But many movies that are made to be popular movies *lose* lots and lots of money. It is particularly difficult to predict ahead of time, even with modern publicity and

**Table 3-1 Patterns of Encoding and
Enplotting Violence According to Film Genre**

Genre	Encoding	Enplotting
Gangster	Instrumental violence maintains order and tradition—*Godfather* series.	Simultaneity of violence; innovative killing scenes—strangling in car, horse's head in bed.
Action	Instrumental violence for a greater cause, against a great aggressor. Fire and blood—*Rocky* series, *Die Hard*.	The great contest. Against all odds, hero wins after being heavily beaten up. Loser wins. Ritual violent scenes.
Private eye	Instrumental violence for information, solving the puzzle. Do what regular police can't do—*Mike Hammer*. Expressive violence hampers his progress.	Hero preoccupied with women and booze and violence. Solves the case in spite of himself. Board game plot.
Super Hero	Instrumental violence to maintain order broken by criminals—*Superman, Batman*.	Special effects of violent super powers.
Spy	Instrumental violence against an evil megalomaniac by the world's savior—James Bond saves the world in the name of Great Britain and wins woman through violence.	Great chase, great contest, innovative technology of violence. Ritual repetition of violent scenes.
Cop	Violence against bureaucracy and corruption—*Dirty Harry* series. The unofficial use of violence by the authorities. Women saved from sexual violence.	The cool hero, straight shooter always wins and abuses his bosses at every turn. Ritual chase, destruction scenes.
Horror	Revelation of the body, violence as mystical—*Friday 13th* series. The demon within. Justifies violence by "innocent victims." Sexual violence: Women raped by madman.	Innovative ways of killing, suspense build-up (fool places himself/herself in path of the killer who never really dies), close ups of bodily parts and decaying flesh. Remarkable special effects.

marketing methods, which movies will be box office hits. The causal link claimed by Wright between economy of society and popular culture is an assumption that bears little meaning, unless we can first describe and analyze the actual structure and coding of violence that occurs in the texts themselves. Even then, although we can make links to the society and culture that are reflected in the language of violence in movies at a particular point in time, we do not know in which direction the causal links work. That is to say, we do not know whether violence in popular movies reflects the consciousness of culture, or whether violence in movies produces the violent consciousness of culture. More recent work of deconstructionists would argue that the content of popular culture material itself develops an impetus of its own, thus affecting

Table 3-1 *Continued*

Genre	Encoding	Enplotting
War	The supreme justification for violence—*A Bridge Too Far*. "Good" people forced to violence by war.	Mass battle scenes. Vilification of "the enemy" whose violence is sadistic and unjustified.
Western	The cool gunfighter defends the weak against bullies—*Unforgiven*.	Hero is an amazing sharp-shooter. Audience waits for the "showdown." Ritual gun fights.
Science Fiction	Instrumental violence of good against evil. Instrumental violence to save humanity from mass destruction—*Star Wars* epic, *Terminator* series.	Special weapons, great contest of opposites. Scenes of mass destruction. Innovative killing—Terminator II's arms that turn into swords. Apocalyptic opening scenes.
Comedy/Humor	Highly instrumental violence made funny—destruction without death— *Road Runner, Who Framed Roger Rabbit?*	The aggressor always fails. Long fall to earth a favorite scene.
Crime Drama	Expressive violence when order breaks down. Instrumental violence breaks down order—*Reservoir Dogs*. Sexual violence a favorite—*Silence of the Lambs*.	Innovative torture scenes. Despicable character construction.
Crime Humor	Expressive violence supports buddy loyalty. Verbal abuse between the buddies made humorous—*Lethal Weapon* series, *Who Framed Roger Rabbit?*	Impossible chase scenes (hero catches fleeing automobile on foot), explosions of buildings and automobiles. Hero seems indestructible.
Historical Epic	Instrumental violence made to seem expressive: particular groups labeled as "blood-thirsty"—*Lawrence of Arabia*, many biblical movies. Expressive violence: heroine raped by despot.	Graphic, bloody battles scenes with thousands of "extras." Despot enslaves woman or women.

mass consciousness and the structure of culture itself (McKenna, 1991). But culture and popular culture did not magically appear in the twentieth century. Rather, they have a long history.[6] It would seem prudent to hold both views and see popular culture patterning and coding of violence as an historical process. That is, there can be no unidirectional causal link between popular culture and mass consciousness: The process is one of successive feedback between one and the other. Thus, "the starting point of study should be to analyze the content and media of popular culture as a way to understanding the kind of consciousness it represents, no matter whether one takes it on face value, or as an important key to another level of consciousness that lies behind it" (Newman, 1990). This chapter has made a tentative step in that direction.

DISCUSSION QUESTIONS

1. What does Newman identify as a major difficulty in measuring the effects of mass media violence? Why does he think it is important to decode "the language of violence"? Do you think it is important to decode the language of violence? Why or why not?

2. How does Newman define violence? What two types of violence does he identify? Can you think of movies other than those mentioned by Newman in which either or both of these types of violence are displayed?

3. According to the author, what rationales are used to make violence "acceptable" within the context of a movie? Can you think of movies in which the use of violence is presented as unacceptable?

NOTES

1. Various researchers estimate that from 30 percent to 80 percent of prime time TV viewing is dominated by violent themes. The figure depends on the definition of "prime time" and the breadth of the definition of "violence." For reviews, see Newman (1990) and Surette (1992: 32–34).

2. For example, *The Story of a Crime* (1905? Zecca-director), treats us to the guillotine in the final scenes of the movie. *The Great Train Robbery* (1903) gave the first dramatic close-up of a gun shot into the camera. These were followed by the many gangster and war movies of the 1950s, not to mention the perennial westerns that featured violence and mayhem.

3. For a balanced review of both experimental and field studies, see Gerda (1985: 160–163). Though advocating a form of limitation of violence on media, Gerda nevertheless concludes that "the case that watching violence on media causes aggressive behavior...is not proven...nor is it likely to be." (1985: 259). After a careful review of the same body of research,

Surette (1992: 108) concludes that "overall...without proving conclusively,...we are a more aggressive society because of our mass media."

4. A new genre, video games, has also emerged in recent years, promising to challenge scholars of the modeling aggression even more. Violent games such as *Night Trap* or *Mortal Kombat* in which Kano hacks off heads of opponents and rips out still pulsing hearts actively engage the players in the violence. Kids no longer sit passively on the couch watching the action. They become part of the action, that is, part of the violence.

5. Levi-Strauss (1967) has demonstrated effectively the deep cultural origins of this phenomenon as it is played out by mythic heroes.

6. See for example, the excellent work on the history of the comic (Kunzle, 1973), as well as historical accounts of popular culture and high and low culture (Chase, 1986; Newman, 1990).

❋

Censorship and "Deviance"

On November 4, 1907, Chicago became the first major city to establish a system of prior censorship by authorizing the police department to deny a permit to any film it judged "immoral" or "obscene." (Walsh, 1996: 7)

Efforts to control the production or dissemination of popular culture products deemed immoral or obscene by governments or by citizen interest groups are as old as human societies. These efforts continue in varied forms. For example, in December 1983, legal scholar Catherine McKinnon and feminist writer/activist Andrea Dworkin organized hearings before the Minneapolis, Minnesota, city council. Their goal was the enactment of an ordinance that would have pornography identified as discrimination against women (Russell, 1993). Their effort was ultimately unsuccessful. However, the model ordinance symbolizes protests against degrading women by the commercialization of sex.[1]

Voiced concerns about the degradation of women are not limited to protests against pornography. Faludi (1991) asserts that men in popular culture and elsewhere are waging an "undeclared war against women." Wilson, after surveying rape in popular R-rated films, asks "How far will Hollywood go in exploiting the act of rape?" (1988: 608). However, Dowell, in a somewhat calmer voice, wonders if the "new erotic films [that] place sex in violent context" (1988: 65) might be a throwback to the films of the 1940s and 1950s in which sex was also linked to violence. Those films, she suggests, reflected the confusion in society as men and women worked out "a tense new adjustment to a more independent role for women in bed and out of it" (65).

In violent R-rated "slasher" movies, adult women are not the only objects of violent attacks in a sexual context. Often the "disposable" victims in these films are teenagers. Recently, Joe Bob Briggs, the host of TNT's *Monster*

Vision offered this laconic commentary about the plot of the horror movie, *Friday the 13th*: "Kids have sex. Kids get butchered because they're having too much sex" (Briggs, 1996).

The level of sex and violence in films, on television, in music, and elsewhere in mass culture products that are available to both adult and youthful consumers has generated both concern and activism by various citizen groups. Responding to this public concern, Congress and the president have enacted legislation requiring a "V-chip" on new television sets that will allow parents to control their children's consumption of violent programming. Recently, the television industry introduced a "rating" system for television shows similar to that used by the movie industry. According to media critic Michael Medved (1992), such legislation and such rating systems for television and films are necessary because Hollywood has "an addiction to violence."

Of particular concern to those who share Medved's view is the impact mass media violence (and sex) might be having on young people. This concern about the impact of popular culture on youth is not new. It is linked to concern about young people as consumers. Writing about the 1950s, a period when this anxiety became particularly acute, Biskind observes,

> A number of factors had conspired to create the new youth culture, ranging from World War II, which sent parents off to war or factory jobs, leaving kids to their own devices; to postwar affluence; the baby boom; the erosion of authority of the father; and last, but by no means least, the recognition by business that teen-agers would buy everything from records to Clearasil, that they constituted in short, a market (1983: 197–198).

Young people as consumers of popular culture has always troubled those who perceive popular culture as "throwaway culture" or "low culture" (Panati, 1991). But as Acland (1995) observes, there have been periods when perceptions of popular culture as a "social threat" were exacerbated. The 1950s was one such period. Another was the 1930s when the Payne Fund completed its research on the effects of movies on young people and concluded that cinematic images did indeed affect the attitudes and behavior of adolescent moviegoers. One volume culled from the study was titled *Our Movie-Made Children* (1933).

Today possible sources of injury to America's youth are said to include role-playing games such as "Dungeons & Dragons" (Lancaster, 1994); videogames (Anderson and Ford, 1987; Cooper and Mackie, 1986); rap music (Rose, 1994); and heavy metal music (Singer, Levine, and Jou, 1993). There is also concern about the R- and X-rated materials that are available in cyberspace.

This continuing discourse about youth and popular culture (or perhaps "youth culture") elicits questions about parental, media, and governmental responsibilities for protecting youth and overseeing their activities. And, like the pornography debate, the debate about the effects of media violence also raises questions about censorship.

In the two chapters that follow, the contributors examine the process by which popular culture forms become identified as "deviant" and become the focus of efforts to control their creation and distribution.

NOTE

1. Many feminist scholars draw a distinction between "erotica" and "pornography." They see erotica as presenting images of mutually pleasurable sexual activity between consenting adults without those elements of degradation, domination, or violence that they assert are found in pornography.

4

❊

Comic Books and Juvenile Delinquency:

A Historical Perspective

AMY KISTE NYBERG

C *rime Does Not Pay*, the first crime comic book, debuted in 1942.[1] Borrowing its format from the true crime magazines popular in the 1930s, the comic book based its stories on actual criminals and their crimes. In five years, sales jumped from 200,000 to nearly a million copies a month, making *Crime Does Not Pay* one of the best-selling newsstand publications of all time (Benton, 1993: 33).

The success of *Crime Does Not Pay* encouraged other comic book publishers to develop crime comics, and in the years following World War II, comics with titles such as *True Crime Comics, Justice Traps the Guilty, Crimes by Women,* and *Crime Suspenstories* appeared on the newsstand. Crime comics became the most popular comic book genre between 1947 and 1954.

At the same time, the American public was becoming increasingly concerned about juvenile delinquency. The reasons why delinquency became an issue in postwar America are complex, but one impact of the growing worry over youthful offenders was the implication of the mass media as a possible cause.[2] This chapter explores the relationship between ideas about delinquency and beliefs about media effects to help explain how and why comic books became the center of a national controversy in the years following World War II.

Although media coverage helped reinvent the crisis for America in the 1940s and 1950s, juvenile delinquency was not a new problem. Theories about juvenile delinquency passed through three distinct phases: theories that attributed delinquency to hereditary factors, theories that suggested delinquency was the result of environmental factors, and theories that studied delinquency as a psychological disorder.[3]

Early ideas about the causes of juvenile delinquency centered on behavior as a product of heredity and maintained that misbehavior was the result of "bad blood" and weak moral character. Responsibility for controlling children traditionally rested with the family. But the shift from a rural to an urban society, with its growing legion of children who lived in poverty in American cities, forced the public to take note of juvenile misbehavior and to devise an institutional system to handle the problem. The earliest institutions were "houses of refuge," chartered by cities and states and run by private charities. The first opened its doors in New York City in 1825. These gradually evolved into state-run reform schools. These institutions were populated by destitute children; many had committed no crime at all.

In the mid-nineteenth century, this rigid, class-based view gave way to an increasing recognition of the complex causes of delinquency. Philanthropic organizations, such as the New York Children's Aid Society formed in 1853, began to advocate placing children with frontier families as an alternative to reform schools. In doing so, these organizations demonstrated a growing awareness of social and environmental factors in children's behavior.

This shift led to a decreasing emphasis on the control of delinquent children. Acknowledging that a child's surroundings could be a contributing factor to delinquency, reformers turned their attention to improving conditions in the cities as a way to prevent delinquency. Delinquency was no longer perceived as a moral weakness but, rather, as a response to an unwholesome environment. These progressive reformers saw the state as a caretaker, rather than as an instrument of punishment, and pressed for changes in the juvenile justice system. This call for changes in the treatment of children became part of the larger reform movement at the turn of the century that targeted a number of urban problems.

At the end of the Progressive Era, the responsibility for social welfare passed from philanthropic organizations to the growing ranks of professional social workers and an increasingly complex governmental bureaucratic system designed to address social ills. With the introduction of Freudian psychology and rise of the mental hygiene movement in the 1920s, researchers began to explore psychological causes of behavior problems, including juvenile delinquency. As delinquency was embraced as a mental health issue, child guidance clinics were set up; nearly a third of all psychiatric clinics established by 1930 specialized in treating children. The publication of *Mental Conflicts and Misconduct* by William Healy in 1917 was the first application of Freudian psychology theories to delinquency. As a result, environmental explanations for delinquency fell out of favor, and the search for causes of juvenile misbehavior focused on family conflicts.

The definition of delinquency as a psychological problem, rather than social in origin, was the dominant opinion of experts on juvenile delinquency following World War II. There might be a relationship between culture and behavior, these experts conceded, but the family environment was still the primary site of investigation into the causes of delinquency (Gilbert, 1986:

132). These experts predicted that World War II would result in a rise in delinquency because of the disruption of the family as men entered military service and women entered the labor force.

Even after the war, fears about delinquency did not disappear. Historian James Gilbert traces this continued concern to three factors. First, the increased interest in juvenile delinquency meant that more attention was given to the topic in the popular press, making the problem more noticeable. Second, law enforcement agencies, prodded by public opinion, increased their monitoring of teenage behavior, resulting in more arrests and generating statistics that supported reports of an increase in delinquency. Third, changes in youthful behavior meant that delinquency was redefined to encompass a broad range of activities not previously considered delinquent (Gilbert, 1986: 71).

The American public, faced with the emergence of a highly visible teenage culture following World War II, was both puzzled and alarmed by the changing behavior of children. In an effort to understand what was happening, the public embraced a theory that helped explain these changes in simple terms: Modern mass culture, including radio, the movies, and comic books, was turning children into delinquents (Gilbert, 1986: 71).

This was not the first time such accusations had been made about mass media. Anthony Comstock, the founder of the New York Society for the Suppression of Vice, was instrumental in getting Congress to establish stronger laws against obscenity in the 1870s. The success of Comstock's antipornography crusade in the years following the Civil War encouraged him to broaden his censorship activities to include dime novels and story papers.

Comstock was convinced that any unwholesome reading had a detrimental effect on all readers, but he believed children were especially vulnerable to the influence of inappropriate literature. In 1884, he published a book titled *Traps for the Young*, in which he provided a number of examples of young people led astray by reading the wrong sort of books. He argued that the popular literature of the day encouraged disobedience to parents. He encouraged parents to boycott the shops that sold such material (Comstock, 1884: 42). Comstock's crusade against the dime novel introduced the idea that mass media could have harmful effects on children.

Concerns over media effects on children surfaced again with the birth of the movies. The first comprehensive study of the effects of movies, the Payne Fund studies published in 1933, provided the impetus for the film industry to impose a self-regulatory code. The industry's willingness to censor itself satisfied the public, and efforts to pass legislation restricting film were dropped. Broadcasters, following the lead of the film industry, also adopted regulatory codes that addressed public concerns about the impact of radio, and later television, on children in the audience.[4]

After World War II, mass media were once again targeted as causes of delinquency, and there was broad public support for the regulation of the mass media industries. As Gilbert explains,

> For many Americans, mass culture in this equation solved the mystery of delinquency. It was an outside force guided from media centers in New

York and Hollywood. It affected all classes of children. It penetrated the home. And it appeared to promote values contrary to those of many parents. It seemed, in other words, to be the catalyst that provoked generational conflict. Thus, as the movement to control delinquency grew in the early 1950s, one of the most important corollary developments was the impulse to investigate, control, and censor mass culture. (Gilbert, 1986: 77–78)

The medium singled out in this battle over children and culture was the comic book. Comic books were especially vulnerable because of public perceptions that they were aimed specifically at children and because they were the least regulated of any mass medium. When publishers abandoned superhero fantasy for real-world crime and horror, the American public took note. And there emerged a leader for this new crusade against the comic book—Dr. Fredric Wertham.

Wertham's credentials were impressive, and he was quickly embraced as a leading expert in the field. He was born in Germany on March 20, 1895, emigrating to the United States in 1922 after he received an invitation from Dr. Adolf Meyer, director of the Phipps Psychiatric Clinic at Johns Hopkins Hospital, to join his staff.[5] Wertham left Johns Hopkins in 1932 to take a position as senior psychiatrist in the Department of Hospitals of New York City. Between 1933 and 1936, he was successively the psychiatrist in charge of the alcoholic, children's, and prison wards of Bellevue Hospital. From 1936 to 1939, he served as the director of the Mental Hygiene Clinic at Bellevue. In 1940, he became director of psychiatric services at Queens Hospital.

In 1946, Wertham, who was concerned about the lack of access minorities had to adequate psychiatric care, opened a low-cost clinic in a Harlem church basement staffed with volunteer psychiatrists and social workers (*Time*, 1947: 50). Treatment of children was emphasized at the Lafargue Clinic because more than half of the delinquent children to enter New York City's juvenile justice system were from Harlem. Wertham's interest in comic books was stimulated by his work with the children at the clinic when he noticed his young charges were spending a great deal of time reading comic books. He and his colleagues began a systematic study of the effects of comics on children. After a two-year investigation, Wertham concluded that comic books had a harmful effect on their young readers. The results of his research were made public in an article written by Judith Crist titled "Horror in the Nursery," which appeared in *Collier's* March 27, 1948, pages 22–23.

Crist illustrated Wertham's points with anecdotal information gleaned from case histories of children the psychiatrist treated, a technique Wertham used successfully himself in later articles and books. Sandwiched between the horror stories of children who acted out the comic book stories they read, however, were several key ideas that would be repeated throughout his decade-long fight against comic books.

First, Wertham wanted his audience to realize how popular comic books were. He pointed out that some of his young patients reported reading as many as 20 a week. Second, he saw himself as "a voice for the thousands of troubled parents, who, like myself, are concerned primarily with their children's welfare." Wertham told Crist he had heard parents express anxiety about comic books literally hundreds of times in letters and during conferences. Third, he attacked those in his profession who served as consultants to the publishers, noting that many of them were "psycho-prima donnas" who did no clinical work with children. He refuted their claims that comic books were simply healthy outlets for aggression.

Finally, and perhaps most important, Wertham pressed for legislation against comic books. If publishers were unwilling to clean up comic books, he argued, "the time has come to legislate these books off the newsstands and out of the candy stores."

Wertham also organized a symposium, titled "The Psychopathology of Comic Books," held the same month the *Collier's* article appeared. A summary of the proceedings were published in the *American Journal of Psychotherapy*. Wertham used the material he prepared for the symposium to write an article for *Saturday Review of Literature*. It appeared May 29, 1948, and was titled "The Comics...Very Funny!" (pages 6–7) It was condensed for the August issue of *Reader's Digest*, and letters to Wertham poured into the offices at both publications, many of them offering help or advice for a national movement to get comic books off the shelves. It also triggered police action against comic books in more than 50 cities (Gilbert, 1986: 98–99).

In August, Wertham repeated his charges against comic books at the Seventy-Eighth Annual Congress of Correction of the American Prison Association in a paper titled "The Betrayal of Childhood: Comic Books." He once again called for legislation against comic books, noting that if the Pure Food and Drug law can protect children's bodies, then "surely the minds of children deserve as much protection."

Wertham's attacks on comic books have been dismissed by many as the work of a naive social scientist who was suggesting a simplistic cause-and-effect relationship between comic book reading and behavior.[6] However, a close study of Wertham's work reveals that although Wertham singled out comic books as a factor in juvenile delinquency, he was very careful to point out that there was no direct, linear relationship between reading comic books and delinquent behavior. His argument was more complex. He explored the relationship between culture and individuals, and he believed that the social and cultural matrix in which individuals existed had been largely ignored by psychiatry in its efforts to understand individual behavior. Wertham's goal was to establish a social psychiatry in which an understanding of culture's role must necessarily play a prominent part.[7]

Wertham believed that juvenile delinquency was a social, rather than an individual, problem. He insisted that juvenile delinquency was a mass phenomenon that could not be understood or remedied "by redefining it simply as an individual mental disorder" (Wertham, 1954: 157). The solution to juvenile delinquency was to be found in social controls because the problem was too widespread for the individual family to handle. Wertham's belief that psychiatry should serve as an instrument of social reform alienated him from his medical colleagues, but his ideas about mass media's effects on children struck a responsive chord and played a significant role in the campaign against comic books in postwar America.

The publication of Wertham's research stimulated an interest in legislation against comic books at the local, state, and national levels, and Wertham was called to give expert testimony. He spoke several times before the New York Joint Legislative Committee to Study the Publication of Comics, formed in March 1949 to make recommendations about legislation. Although the legislature passed a bill outlawing crime comic books that year, it was vetoed by Governor Thomas Dewey on the grounds it was unconstitutional. Wertham also convinced Senator Estes Kefauver, head of the Special Senate Committee to Investigate Organized Crime, to investigate the comic book industry. Wertham helped formulate a questionnaire sent out in August 1950 to law enforcement officials, educators, child guidance experts, comics publishers, and their advocates. The results failed to provide strong evidence of a relationship between comic books and delinquency, and the Kefauver committee dropped its inquiry into comic books.

Although Wertham was pushing for legislation against comic books as a means of controlling children's access, pressure groups took matters into their own hands after Wertham's attack made the problem of comic books one of national proportions. One group that sought to control comic books was the Catholic Church. Through its National Office of Decent Literature (NODL), established in 1938 and patterned after the highly successful Legion of Decency, which targeted unacceptable films, the church began reviewing comic books in 1947. The stated goals of the NODL program were to remove objectionable comic books and other publications from places of distribution accessible to youth, to encourage publishing and distribution of good literature, and to promote plans to develop worthwhile reading habits during formative years (Gardiner, 1958: 110).

NODL distributed lists of acceptable comics, and Catholic Church members were urged to use the lists in local "decency campaigns." Teams of two or three visited retailers who carried comic books and asked them to remove any the team found objectionable. Lists of stores that cooperated were announced in church and printed in parish publications. The decency crusades targeted retailers rather than publishers because "most of the filthy books and magazines are put out deliberately by publishers who know that they will sell. They are not interested in their effect on youth, and cannot be reasoned with" (Gardiner, 1958: 115).

Another group that obtained national status as reviewers of comic books was the Committee on Evaluation of Comic Books in Cincinnati, formed in June 1948. Unlike NODL, the committee confined its activities to reviewing comic books. It was headed by Jesse L. Murrell, a Methodist minister from Covington, Kentucky. Murrell supervised a reviewing staff of approximately 130 individuals including women with children, educators from both public and parochial schools, PTA members, juvenile court workers, librarians, clergymen, and members of the business community. The results were made available to anyone for a nominal fee to cover mailing. In addition, *Parents'*

Magazine published the committee's list each year (Murrell, 1954: 114). In 1954, even a comic book such as *Superman* was rated as being objectionable because it depicted criminal acts or moral violations (even if legally punished) and because it featured "sinister creatures" portrayed in a grotesque, fantastic, or unnatural way. Funny animal books like *Tweety and Sylvester* were about the only titles to receive the no-objection rating (Murrell, 1954: 49).

Even though such pressure groups received national attention, their impact was limited to cities where groups organized "decency crusades." There was still no legislation regulating the sale of comic books. In an effort to rekindle interest in such legislation, Wertham collected his articles and lectures describing his research on the effects of mass media violence into a book-length study. *Seduction of the Innocent* was published in spring 1954, but excerpts were printed in the November 1953 issue of *Ladies' Home Journal* in an article titled "What Parents Don't Know about Comic Books." The publication of Wertham's article followed the announcement of the formation of a Senate Subcommittee on Juvenile Delinquency. That committee was charged with making a full and complete study of juvenile delinquency in the United States, with exploring the extent and character of the problem, and with determining its causes and contributing factors. In its report, the committee noted that it had received a vast amount of mail from parents concerned about the possible effect of mass media on their children. The report noted, "This led to an inquiry into the possible relationship to juvenile delinquency of these media" (U.S. Senate, 1955).

The Senate committee conducted three types of investigations—community investigations, investigations of special problems, and investigations of relevant federal programs. The goal of community investigations was to determine the scope of the problem of juvenile delinquency in various cities selected. During its first year, the committee conducted hearings in Washington, Boston, Philadelphia, Chicago, Denver, El Paso, San Diego, Los Angeles, San Francisco, and Miami (U.S. Senate Judiciary Subcommittee, 1954).

In addition to holding hearings in various cities, the committee also dealt with the subjects of runaways, the desertion of children by their fathers, the sale of babies for adoption, auto theft among juveniles, the problems of American Indian children, drug use among juveniles, and pornography. Federal programs were examined as well, with the committee considering legislation that would assist various federal agencies in coordinating their efforts to control juvenile delinquency. But the task of the committee that drew the most public attention was its investigation of the relationship between mass media and juvenile delinquency.

The hearings on comic books were held in the United States Court House in New York City on two days in April and one day in early June, 1954. The committee selected New York because most of the comic book publishers were based there. The senators called 22 witnesses and accepted 33 exhibits as evidence. Among the witnesses were four comic book publishers, four experts on the effects of comic books on children (including Wertham), and seven people involved with some aspect of distribution.

Though declaring itself neutral in the debate over media effects, the committee looked for evidence to challenge the contention by experts that comics had little or no effect on most children. This was accomplished by a selective examination of the material and by discrediting those who testified in defense of comics. This was in keeping with the pattern of other Congressional investigations, where the committee perspective was determined before the actual work began and the investigations served as little more than dramatization of the committee's point of view (Moore, 1974: 242).

Before the start of the hearings, the Senate committee's staff had requested that the Library of Congress compile a survey summarizing all the studies they could locate on the effects of crime comics on the behavior of children (U.S. Senate Judiciary Subcommittee, 1954). In this report, the library staff noted that there had been few scientific investigations of the influence of mass media on juvenile delinquency. In its report, issued nearly a year after the Juvenile Delinquency Subcommittee concluded its hearings on comic books, the committee noted that there were "marked differences of opinions among experts" concerning the effects of comic books on juvenile delinquency. There was a need for large-scale research studies to understand the impact of crime and horror comic books on the behavior of children. In the meantime, the report noted, the country "cannot afford the calculated risk involved in feeding its children, through comic books, a concentrated diet of crime, horror, and violence" (U.S. Senate, 1955).

The solution, concluded the report, was not federal censorship. Rather, the publishers should take primary responsibility for censoring comic books. The committee, of course, had no way to enforce its recommendations, but it did not have to—the industry had formed the Comics Magazine Association of America in the fall of 1954 and implemented a program of self-censorship that, combined with pressure from the distributors, wholesalers, and retailers, brought sweeping changes. Such regulations, modeled on what had been successful in film and broadcasting, helped diffuse anti-comic book sentiment among the public.

The idea of a self-regulatory code was nothing new for the comic book industry. The publishers had already made one attempt, through the trade association known as the Association of Comics Magazine Publishers, to police themselves following Wertham's first assault on the industry in the late 1940s. In addition, several companies had their own editorial codes, often formulated with the help of child guidance experts. But such measures were not enforced strictly enough to satisfy critics. In August 1954, the publishers held an organizational meeting and agreed to adopt a code that would eliminate horror comics completely and place strict regulations on the content of crime comics. The new organization became known as the Comics Magazine Association of America and is still in existence today.

Taking its cue from what had proved successful for the film industry, the comic book industry sought a "czar" with the proper credentials to administer its new code. On September 16, the industry appointed Judge Charles F. Murphy to the post. Murphy would direct the Comics Code Authority office, which established a system of pre-publication review. The entire contents of a comic book had to be approved by the office before it could be printed. All comic books approved by Murphy's office were entitled to publish the "Seal of Approval" on their cover.

The code consisted of 41 specific regulations that CMAA President John Goldwater, one of the publishers of Archie Comics, labeled as "problem areas" in comic books. He added,

> Taken together these provisions constitute the most severe set of principles for any communications media in use today, restricting the use of many types of material permitted by the motion picture code and the codes for the television and radio industries. (Goldwater, 1964: 24)

Under the code, crime comics could continue to be published, but all such titles had to adhere to strict rules concerning the presentation of such stories. Without ever admitting that depiction of crime led young readers to become juvenile delinquents, the code nonetheless placed an emphasis on portraying crime in a negative light, on creating respect for established authority, on depicting commission of crime in such a way that young readers would not be tempted to imitate what they read, and on making sure that the excess violence was purged. Other sections of the comics code forbid the publication of horror comics, provided guidelines for dialogue and language, regulated the depiction and costumes of female characters, and handed down rules about how publishers were to deal with the topics of sex and marriage.

The comics code remained in effect for the next 17 years. Then Marvel Comics broke new ground in 1970 by producing a mainstream comic book dealing with drugs (a topic forbidden under code guidelines) and publishing and distributing the comic without code approval. By doing so, Marvel forced the CMAA to reevaluate the code. At their meeting in June 1970, the publishers agreed to consider revisions to the code at a subsequent meeting (Comics Magazine Association of America, 1970). Those revisions, which reflected the ways in which social conditions and concerns had changed since the 1950s, were adopted in December, and publishers agreed the new code would go into effect February 1, 1971. Many of the restrictions on the presentation of crime and horror were liberalized. For example, publishers were no longer prohibited from presenting crimes "in such a way as to create sympathy for the criminal." The prohibition against presenting details and methods of a crime was amended to read, "with the exception of those crimes that are so far-fetched or pseudo-scientific that no would-be lawbreaker could reasonably duplicate." Figures of authority, such as policemen and government officials, could now be shown committing an illegal act; however, "it must be declared as an exceptional case and the culprit pay the legal price" (Comics Magazine Association of America, 1971).

The code was revised a second time in 1989, and the emphasis on what material would be prohibited reflected the changing nature of comic book content. Crime and horror were de-emphasized, demonstrating that this area was no longer the major concern of comic book publishers, and the guidelines dealing with sex were expanded.

Although ideas about juvenile delinquency and media effects have changed since the 1950s, the vulnerability of the comic book industry to outside criticism remains a concern to publishers and retailers alike. Recent Congressional investigations of violence in television and video games has once again raised fears that the comic book industry could face the same sort of problems that it did in the 1950s. One comic book fan, in a letter published January 14, 1994, in the weekly *Comics Buyer's Guide*, concluded: "With television and movies coming under increasing attack from certain factions including the religious right, are comic books next to be in the spotlight? This could be the beginning of the 1950s all over again."

DISCUSSION QUESTIONS

1. According to Nyberg, what three distinct phases can be identified with regard to theories of juvenile delinquency from the nineteenth century to the 1940s? How did the theories about juvenile delinquency affect social policy?

2. Why did comic books become a focal point of public concern about juvenile delinquency? Do you think public concern about a mass medium such as comic books is justified if the primary audience is young people? Why or why not?

3. What kinds of censorship efforts were directed at comic books? What response(s) were made by the comic book industry? Do you think mass media industries such as the comic book, movie, or television industries can effectively regulate themselves? Should they be required to engage in such self-regulation?

NOTES

1. From the beginning, comic books featured crimefighting in stories about policemen and private detectives and in titles featuring costumed superheroes fighting crime. But comic book historians make a distinction between these comics and crime comics, defining crime comics as those that focused on the criminal and the crime rather than on the heroics of the crimefighter.

2. For a thorough discussion of juvenile delinquency and postwar culture, see Gilbert, 1986.

3. The following discussion of the history of juvenile delinquency is drawn from these two sources: Mennel (1973) and Hawes (1971).

4. For a more in-depth discussion of media regulatory codes, see Cowan (1979); deGrazia and Newman (1982); Leff and Simmons (1990); Rowland, Jr.(1983); and West (1988).

5. Little has been published about the life and work of Wertham. The most complete account thus far can be found in Reibman (1990).

6. An example of this critique of Wertham's work can be found in Lowrey and DeFleur, eds. (1983).

7. For a detailed discussion of Wertham's position, see my analysis of Wertham in Nyberg (1994).

5

❋

Criminalizing Popular Culture

JEFF FERRELL

In the United States and elsewhere, the consumption of popular culture commodities structures and symbolizes the daily experience of social life. As we move from day to day, we consume not only prepackaged food and fashion, but mediated sounds, images, and styles themselves packaged as entertainment, news, information, music, and art. As the production and consumption of popular culture lay the foundations for contemporary social life, they also become the basis for a variety of contemporary controversies. These controversies consistently incorporate conflicts over popular morality, mass media influence, and the boundaries between art and obscenity. They also regularly include attempts by politicians, legal authorities, religious leaders, and others to criminalize popular culture—that is, to recast popular culture activities and identities as criminal and to define the social effects of art, music, and media as criminogenic. This criminalization process crosses the "long front" (Alloway, 1969) of popular culture; it transcends the already battered boundaries between "high" and "low" culture and touches photographers and punk rockers, museums and music shops alike.

MOMENTS IN THE CRIMINALIZATION
OF POPULAR CULTURE

During the late 1980s and early and mid 1990s, a variety of "high culture" activities have been criminalized. Perhaps most highly publicized was the Cincinnati Contemporary Arts Center's 1990 showing of photographer Robert Mapplethorpe's works. Anticipating legal difficulties, the Center developed voluntary disclaimers, restricted admissions, and filed a preemptive lawsuit requesting legal protection for the showing. Despite this, a Cincinnati grand jury indicted the Center and its director for "pandering obscenity and for the use of a minor in materials related to the nude" (Mannheimer, 1990: 35). A Virginia Commonwealth attorney likewise charged in 1990 that a Richmond, Virginia, gallery exhibit dealing with AIDS and gay sexuality "assaulted passersby and their children," and therefore violated Virginia obscenity statutes (Scala, 1990: 13). And in San Francisco, local police and the FBI raided the home and studio of nationally known art photographer Jock Sturges, confiscating and destroying film, records, and possessions. They subsequently arrested and interrogated at length Sturges' associate, Joe Semien, and accused both men of involvement with child pornography because of a series of casual photographs Sturges had taken of friends on a nude beach in France (Atkins, 1991: 37; Shapiro, 1990).[1]

Throughout the "low culture" worlds of popular music, a variety of musicians, music retailers, and musical products have likewise been criminalized during the past couple of decades. During the 1970s, the British punk band the Sex Pistols—whose members each carried prior criminal records—came under attack by British legal authorities. The band's promotional materials were ruled obscene, record shops carrying Sex Pistols' materials were prosecuted (and vandalized), and the head of the Sex Pistols' record company was fined for obscenity. A subsequent U.S. tour was delayed when U.S. customs officials denied the Sex Pistols entry visas because of their criminal records (Hebdige, 1979; Henry, 1989; McDermott, 1987). During the 1980s, British police continued to raid record shops and to confiscate "alternative" and punk records that they considered obscene (Holden, 1993a: 12).

In 1986, California police likewise staged high-profile raids on the offices of an alternative record company and its record distributor, as well as the apartment of Jello Biafra, leader of the popular alternative/punk band Dead Kennedys. Police seized record albums, posters, and documents and subsequently charged Jello Biafra and four others with violating a California law concerning "distribution of harmful matter to minors" (Alternative Tentacles, n.d.; Holden, 1993a, 1993b). Canadian police staged a similar raid on an alternative record company in 1988, seized record albums, and charged the owner with distributing obscene matter (No More Censorship, 1990). And in 1993, California police arrested the lead singer of the punk band Insaints for "'lewd and dissolute conduct,' exposing herself, and engaging in an obscene performance" (*Arts Censorship Project Newsletter*, "Project defends punk rock performer," Fall 1993, 3: 7).

In recent years, court cases have also been brought in the United States against heavy metal groups accused of promoting Satanic worship or suicide; the heavy metal bands Metallica and Megadeth have been charged in both civil and criminal cases with precipitating the murderous actions of their listeners (Holden, 1993a; Rounds, n.d.; Woods, n.d.). Concerts by heavy metal bands have also recently been halted by police interference, or in other cases simply canceled by municipal officials (*Arts Censorship Project Newsletter*,

"Damages awarded to GWAR, fans in settlement scared of free expression in Shreveport?" Winter 1993, 2: 5). The many entanglements of punk and heavy metal music with the criminal justice system pale, though, in comparison with that most criminalized of contemporary musical forms: rap music, and especially "gangsta rap," the hard-edged, street-tough rap of Ice-T, N.W.A., Dr. Dre, and others.

Participants in all stages of rap music's production and dissemination—writers and performers, distributors, retailers—have found themselves caught not only in "one of the most sustained censorship drives in United States history" (Johnson, 1993/1994: 25) but also in expanding webs of crime and criminalization. A number of well-known rap performers, for example, have faced multiple criminal charges, and extensive media coverage in response. Tupac Shakur was first arrested in 1993 on charges of shooting two off-duty police officers during a traffic dispute, arrested a few weeks later for sexual assault, and sentenced in 1995 to 4½ years in prison on the sexual assault charges. Also in 1993, Snoop Doggy Dog was charged with two counts of being a felon in possession of a firearm, next charged with murder in a shooting incident, and later accused, along with Dr. Dre, of seizing rental vans at gunpoint. Police also arrested Flavor Flav, of the rap group Public Enemy, on charges of shooting at a neighbor.[2]

Significantly, other cases have less to do with the alleged criminal actions of individual rap artists than with the controversial content of their songs. As early as 1988, an Alabama record store owner was charged with obscenity for selling an album by the rap group 2 Live Crew. By the early 1990s, Florida's governor was publicly urging the state prosecutor to charge 2 Live Crew under racketeering statutes. A local sheriff subsequently battled the band over obscenity charges in civil court, sent undercover officers and local deputies into record shops to confiscate albums, and arrested a black record shop owner on obscenity charges. An all-white jury later convicted the shop owner of obscenity. Florida authorities also arrested the members of 2 Live Crew on obscenity charges, following a performance by the band, and in Alabama, ex-2 Live Crew leader Luther Campbell was later arrested on charges of inciting to riot.[3]

During this same period, Nebraska authorities prosecuted five businesses for selling rap music (A.C.L.U., 1992), and in Britain, Scotland Yard confiscated 24,000 copies of an N.W.A. album on grounds of obscenity (Dawtrey and Jolson-Colburn, 1991). Similar criminalization strategies emerged in response to Ice-T's song "Cop Killer," and his album *Body Count*. National, state, and local police associations, in conjunction with Vice President Dan Quayle, attempted to stop distribution of the song, staged well-publicized protests, and urged boycotts of the record's distributor, Time-Warner. Large record-store chains responded by removing the record from their shelves.[4] Police also forced the cancellation of Ice-T concerts across the country by declining to provide concert security and regularly protested outside the concerts that did occur. Virginia police arrested a record store owner for selling *Body Count*.[5]

In addition, the actions of defendants in several recent criminal cases have been publicly linked to rap music; in some cases, defendants have sought to use the lyrical content of rap music in their defense. In Texas, a young black man on trial for murdering a state trooper has argued that he was under the influence of Tupac Shakur's music; the state trooper's widow has in turn filed a $100 million dollar lawsuit against Shakur's label, Time-Warner. Also in Texas, a group of black kids imprisoned for a string of robberies has claimed in the local newspaper that they "got hyped" before the robberies on rappers Easy E and N.W.A. Four kids who shot and wounded two Las Vegas police officers are also alleged to have been motivated by Ice-T's "Cop Killer." Similarly, the judge in the trial of two kids accused of robbing and killing a motorist has claimed publicly that the kids "decided to see a movie and write their own sequel," in reference to the gang/hip hop film *Menace II Society*. In another case, *USA Today* (1994) reported that "four teen boys told authorities the movie *Menace II Society* motivated them to steal a car, wound a 19-year old, and kill James Allen Pearson, 16..."[6]

These and other cases also allude to broader confluences of rap culture, media dynamics, and criminality. The mass media, for example, report not only on *Menace II Society*'s alleged links to criminal behavior, but on the "shootings, fights, and stampedes for the exits at screenings" of films such as *Boyz N the Hood* and *New Jack City*.[7] 2 Live Crew and other rap groups go to court not only over obscenity charges but also over cases of copyright infringement stemming from their unauthorized "sampling" and parodying of previous recordings. And, increasingly, politicians, police associations, and religious and civic groups publicly condemn rap music, "gangsta rap," and the connections that they see between rap music and crime. A Baptist minister "claims there is a link between rap lyrics and murder, misogyny and promiscuity" (Saunders, 1993). A coalition of national black women's groups holds a press conference to call for a ban on "gangsta rap," claiming that "gangsta rap is plain old pornography" (Reuter, 1993b; 1994). The president of the National Association of Police Chiefs argues that the lyrics of "Cop Killer" "destabilize a democratic society by provoking civil unrest, violence, and murder" (Martin, 1993: 20). Bill Clinton, as part of his 1992 presidential campaign, attacks rapper Sister Souljah for her comments on the Los Angeles riots (A.P.: "Jackson raps Clinton for attack on singer." *Rocky Mountain News,* June 14, 1992, page 3). And in 1994, at Senate hearings investigating "gangsta rap" and "violent and demeaning imagery in popular music," senators hear testimony about "the cause-and-effect correlation between what young people hear in rap and how they act" (Simmons, 1994).

The criminalization of art photography, gallery exhibits, and punk, heavy metal, and rap music in turn exists within a cultural context that incorporates wide-ranging intersections of mediated popular culture, public concern, legal control, and crime. In a 1993 survey, for example—commissioned by the media, and in turn publicized through media channels—79 percent of those surveyed saw a connection between television violence and violence in "real life," two thirds "blamed television a 'great deal,'" and more than half supported governmental regulation (Reuter, 1993c). In this context, parents and others blame MTV cartoon characters Beavis and Butthead for inciting children to start sometimes fatal fires, and after near-daily print media coverage of the story throughout the fall of 1993, MTV agrees to move the cartoon to a later time slot and delete all references to fire.[8] Others attack the cartoon program *The Simpsons* for imparting deviant values to kids. In South Carolina, when school kids vote overwhelmingly to name their school after *The Simpsons'* fictional school, their parents vote no.[9] In reporting the case of two British boys who murdered a toddler, the *National Enquirer* headlines its story, "Horror Movie's 'Chucky' Doll Made Little Kids Murder Toddler" (Cooke, 1993); headlines in the mainstream daily press—"Boy Says Video Prompted Rape," "Officials Fear Movie Inspired Kids' Crime," "Movie Made Man Kill Clerk, Relatives Say"[10]—sketch a similar scenario.

Likewise, one teenager dies when he apparently imitates a stunt from the Disney film *The Program*—and Disney subsequently deletes the scene from the film (Hinds, 1993). A man accused of murder claims that an embarrassing televised encounter had "eaten away" at him and thus driven him to act (Taylor, 1995). The California attorney general asks video makers to remove violent scenes from video games; the FCC aggressively enforces indecency regulations on television and radio stations; a South Carolina bill aims to impose a "sex tax" on suggestive videos; and in Florida and Georgia, police stop and arrest motorists for "obscene" bumper stickers—including one that features a hand with raised middle finger and the caption, "Censor This!!"[11]

MEDIA, REPRESENTATION, AND THE
CRIMINALIZATION OF POPULAR CULTURE

What is to be made of all this—of this plethora of cases in which accusations of criminality, and often the criminal law itself, are brought against various forms of popular expression? Can we discover among these various popular culture activities and identities some common ground, some set of common circumstances leading to criminalization? And if so, do these circumstances coalesce around consensual public outrage at clearly obscene and degrading images, or around social and cultural forces somewhat more complex?

At the most fundamental level, the dynamics of the mass media themselves, and the media saturation of social and cultural life, define the context in which the contemporary criminalization of popular culture occurs. The criminalization of popular culture is, inherently, both a criminalization of particular media forms (popular music recordings and performances, television programs) and *itself* a form of media, a mediated process. Put differently, when popular culture personas and performances are criminalized, they are essentially criminalized through the mass media—through their re-presentation as criminal in the realm of sound bites, startling images, news footage, and newspaper headlines.

The public's awareness of Mapplethorpe's photographs or Ice-T's lyrics, and the public's sense of their criminality, derive less from the actions of the artists, or the criminal justice system, than from their ongoing presentation in the media.

This dialectical spiral—in which mediated popular culture forms and figures are in turn criminalized by way of the media—begins to reveal the common ground that seemingly different cases share. Within the daily swarm of mediated imagery, the boundaries blur between individual criminality and public persona, between crime reporting and cop show entertainment, and between high and low cultural forms. As headline fodder and newsshow filler, Jock Sturges and Jello Biafra, Snoop Doggy Dog the gangsta rapper, and Snoop Doggy Dog the alleged murderer share a common stage. All are not only presented through the media but constructed by the media; the public identities of these people, and the collective meaning of their actions, exist as residues of complex media processes. Thus, for example, gangsta rappers' aggressive public personas undoubtedly draw the attention of police and politicians and contribute to their criminalization in the media and on the streets, but this criminalization in turn becomes part of their public personas, legitimizes their outlaw identities for their fans, and sells more recordings. As Saunders (1993; see Blair, 1993; Scott, 1992) reports, the "outlaw image propels hard-core rap so strongly that two record company executives…joked that the longer a rapper's arrest record, the longer his record would stay on the charts."

In place of simple cause-and-effect equations—obscene acts and images precipitate criminal sanctions, public outrage provokes media response—we therefore see a complex, holistic process of presentation and re-presentation, an ongoing negotiation of mediated meaning. As we watch the criminalization of popular culture, we are watching not only images but images of images—that is, the attempts by lawyers, religious leaders, media workers, and others to craft criminalized images of the images previously presented by artists, musicians, and television and film producers. This process in turn reveals that the criminalization of popular culture incorporates far more than the simple application of criminal law to cases of art and music. As a complex cultural process, this criminalization occurs primarily within the realm of media representation, not street policing or courtroom procedure, and in this sense transcends traditional conceptions of law and justice. In many of the cases mentioned previously, accusations of criminality were publicized, but no charges filed; in other cases, charges were filed, but convictions were not obtained. Yet in each of these cases, whatever the legal niceties, criminalization can be said to have occurred, to the extent that images and personas were reconstructed publicly as criminal.

Here in this mediated spiral we can see also the inadequacy of the imitative model of crime employed by many reporters, civic and religious leaders, and politicians—and some academics as well. Underlying the attempted criminalization of art carrying "obscene" images, music incorporating violent lyrics, and television programs containing "suggestive" materials is often a deceptively simple assumption: Children and others who consume these popular culture commodities will imitate the images they contain and, thus, engage in obscene, violent crime. The media regularly focus on the sorts of alleged "copycat" crimes seen previously (*The Program* stunt, Beavis and Butthead fires), and media personalities and civic leaders decry the supposed imitative influence of popular culture personas and presentations. The president of the National Association of Police Chiefs not only condemns "Cop Killer," for example, but also asserts the "predictability of police being ambushed after such a rousing call-to-arms" (Martin, 1993: 3).

The stakes, though, are in reality much higher than this, both for those allegedly influenced by popular culture and for those who would criminalize and control it. For kids and other consumers of popular culture, the daily dose of images and ideas is unlikely to spur "copycat" crimes in any direct or causative fashion; the imitative crimes that do (allegedly) occur might be newsworthy, but they are also notable for their infrequency (Hamm and Ferrell, 1994). The steady swarm of musical lyrics and video images does, however, provide an assortment of cultural materials for constructing a sense of what is possible or desirable. The words and images help kids and others develop ways of perceiving and knowing the larger social world. In other words, mediated words and images might not "cause" particular behaviors or attitudes, but they do engage their consumers in "epistemic socialization" (Bennett and Ferrell, 1987), in an ongoing process of making sense of the world.

This broader epistemic domain of knowledge, meaning, and interpretation, rather than particular instances of imitation is actually at stake in battles over obscenity, pornography, and the criminalization and control of popular culture. In reality, conflicts over Robert Mapplethorpe, Ice-T, and Beavis and Butthead have less to do with the mimicking of mediated messages than with control of the larger epistemic framework within which such messages will be understood. Attempts at criminalizing popular culture are in this sense attempts at controlling the presentation and perception of popular images and personas. Is Mapplethorpe to be presented as photographer or pornographer? Is Ice-T in essence a rap performer, or a dangerous threat to public safety? Are Beavis and Butthead best understood as silly cartoon characters, or fiery agents provocateurs? As answers to these questions are constructed through mediated criminalization battles, so too are the contexts of knowledge and meaning by which people make sense of the popular images and symbols that illuminate their lives.

Here again we see that the criminalization of popular culture—at first glance a public response to popular culture's meanings and effects—actually helps construct these very meanings and effects. Criminalization constitutes not only a response to popular culture but an integral component in the ongoing process by which popular culture is produced and negotiated. The criminalization of popular culture is itself a popular, and cultural, enterprise; this criminalization stands in opposition to popular culture less than this criminalization participates in popular culture.

POLITICS, CONTROL, AND THE
CRIMINALIZATION OF POPULAR CULTURE

If the criminalization of popular culture moves beyond the simple application of criminal law, to incorporate mediated battles over cultural representation and control, it also includes in these battles social groups and social forces beyond the police officers, artists, and musicians seen so far. The cases previously outlined did not develop in isolation, but within broader political conflicts over cultural control and meaning. Far right politician Pat Buchanan, for example, has called for "a cultural revolution in the '90s as sweeping as the political revolution in the '80s," and vowed never to "raise a white flag in the cultural war."[12] Donald Wildmon and the fundamentalist American Family Association have likewise run a series of full-page newspaper advertisements, proclaiming that "We Are Outraged" over teen pregnancy, violence, and crime, and arguing that "it's time to put the blame where we think it belongs": on the music industry, musical recordings, music videos, television programmers, and television programs (American Family Association, 1993). Wildmon and the Association have backed this agenda with protests and boycotts against the film *The Last Temptation of Christ*, Andres Serrano's photograph "Piss Christ," pop star Madonna, and various network television programs, video stores, and bookstores (Bolton, 1990; Dubin, 1992; Vance, 1989). And, the attacks by police leaders and police associations on Ice-T and other rappers are embedded within broader attacks on popular music's promotion of "ever more vile, deviant, and sociopathic behaviors," and its "destabiliz[ing]" of social order and legal authority (Martin, 1993: 1, 3).[13]

This wider political context, and this broader battle over the perception of popular personas and images, is perhaps most evident in the controversy surrounding the criminalization of Mapplethorpe's exhibit at the Cincinnati Contemporary Arts Center. The indictment of the Center and its director on obscenity charges constituted but one episode in a larger conflict. In Cincinnati, a city with a "reputation as a blue-nose mecca," Citizens for Community Values sent 18,000 letters to community leaders "calling for action to prevent this pornographic art from being shown in our city" (Mannheimer, 1990: 33, 34), the Center suffered threatening phone calls, and the local media provided wide coverage of Mapplethorpe's homoerotic and "pornographic" images. But beyond this, the criminalization of Mapplethorpe in Cincinnati reflected a nationwide battle involving artists, the National Endowment for the Arts, and conservative political figures. Jesse Helms, Donald Wildmon, Pat Buchanan, and others attacked the NEA for funding exhibits by Mapplethorpe and Serrano, and American Family Association executive Judith Reisman argued in the *Washington Times* that Mapplethorpe worked "just as thousands of other child molesters/pornographers before and after him" (in Bolton, 1992: 57). A Mapplethorpe exhibit at Washington's Corcoran Gallery was subsequently canceled; the director of the NEA was pressured by the Bush administration, then replaced; the "NEA Four," four feminist/lesbian/gay performance artists, were denied NEA funding, as were three gay film festivals; and a "Helms amendment" preventing the NEA from funding homoerotic and other "obscene" art became law.[14]

In the pronouncements and activities of Buchanan, Wildmon, and Helms (and most recently, Robert Dole and William Bennett), and in the politics of the Mapplethorpe and NEA controversies, we thus begin to see a further pattern: When conservative activists and state authorities work to criminalize popular culture, they aim time and again at individuals and groups whose sexual and cultural politics locate them outside the constricted confines of "acceptable" society. Clearly the attacks on Mapplethorpe, the "NEA Four," and others are essential to a larger conservative agenda of marginalizing and criminalizing lesbian and gay life. As Vance (1989: 43) argues, "the desire to eliminate symbols, images, and ideas they do not like from public space is basic to the contemporary conservatives' and fundamentalists' politics about sexuality, gender, and the family." The multifaceted criminalization of punk and rap music manifests similar politics. These musical forms not only develop an alternative aesthetic (and, with rap, a powerful alternative ethnicity) but also incorporate aggressive critiques of state authority, legal injustice, and ethnic intolerance (Dyson, 1995; Hamm and Ferrell, 1994; Johnson, 1993/1994). Given this, and their frequent production and distribution by small, independent record labels, such musical forms are particularly vulnerable to the attention and the wrath of moral crusaders, police officials, and legal authorities (see Binder, 1993; Britt, 1994; Dubin, 1992).

This political battle over criminalizing popular culture is, of course, not one-sided; cultural workers who suffer criminalization fight back against it as they pursue their own popular and political agendas. In the case of the NEA, for example, Broadway composer Stephen Sondheim and Pulitzer Prize winner Wallace Stegner refused NEA awards; Beacon Press, Seattle's Artist Trust, and others turned down NEA grants, or donated them to institutions denied NEA funding; the rock band Aerosmith donated $10,000 to a gallery denied NEA monies; and artist-staffed NEA selection panels quit work (Hartigan, 1992; Kelly, 1992; Levinson, 1992; Mesce, 1992). Moreover, "guerrilla artist" Robbie Conal attacked Jesse Helms with an "Artificial Art Official" billboard and had the billboard subsequently censored by its owner, 3M (Hugo, 1990; see Conal, 1992). The "NEA Four," after receiving "moral and financial support" (Petty, 1990) from other artists and legal support from the ACLU, eventually won a $250,000 judgment against the NEA (*Arts Censorship Project Newsletter*, "'NEA Four' case settled," Summer 1993: 1, 4). In the world of popular music, publications like *ROC* (Rock Out Censorship) and *RRC* (Rock and Rap Confidential) have emerged to publicize censorship and criminalization battles and enlist support. Two of the performers under heaviest attack—Jello Biafra and Ice-T—have appeared together on stage and elsewhere as anti-censorship activists, with loud support from other musicians and consumers. They have also worked together on recorded responses to criminalization. When Ice-T was forced to pull "Cop Killer" from his *Body Count* album, he replaced it with Biafra's "Freedom of Speech" cut (Holden, 1993b; Snyder, 1992).

Clearly, then, the criminalization of popular culture exists as a key component in larger political agendas of cultural control and therefore develops also as part of an ongoing conflict between cultural conservatives and those who work outside their tight-sphinctered circles of conformity. As such, the criminalization of popular culture disproportionately marginalizes people and groups whose various configurations of ethnicity, sexuality, and politics identify them as threats to particular cultural and political perspectives. To the extent that legal and political agents participate directly in this criminalization process, the process also expands legal and state authority over cultural alternatives. And, as a process conducted largely through mediated presentation and representation, the criminalization of popular culture in turn undergirds broader crime control policies by contributing to popular perceptions and panics over crime and violence. It shapes a sort of social discomfort that reflects off the shiny face of popular culture and back onto the politics of daily life.

TOWARD A CRIMINOLOGY OF CRIMINALIZED POPULAR CULTURE

As a process that intertwines media dynamics, political conflict, and legal authority, the criminalization of popular culture resurrects and recontextualizes some old issues for criminology and raises a number of new ones as well. To begin with, many of those who work to criminalize popular culture clearly fit the mold of the "moral entrepreneurs" or "moral crusaders" whom Becker (1963) first described some 30 years ago. Just as clearly, these individuals and associations use their mediated criminalization campaigns to create "moral panic" (Cohen, 1972) around the allegedly criminogenic effects of cultural images and personas and work to reconstruct gay and lesbian artists, minority musicians, and others as popular "folk devils" (Cohen, 1972) responsible for crime and criminality. In so doing, these moral entrepreneurs stage a mediated "dramatization of evil" (Tannenbaum, 1938) meant to promote and publicize moral outrage, and, by equating artists and musicians with child molesters and pornographers, engage them in mediated "degradation ceremonies" (Garfinkel, 1956) designed to deflate status and legitimacy.

The nature of this process means that criminologists must pay particular attention to media dynamics and mediated politics if they are to make sense of criminalized popular culture and other forms of crime and criminalization as well. The increasing confluence and complexity of media channels have provided moral entrepreneurs and political authorities with ever more sophisticated symbolic tools and accelerated the production and dissemination of moral panics. More and more, politics are constructed and played out in the media, in a swirl of symbolism, imagery, and meaning. This image universe has become the turf on which clashes over social class, ethnicity, and sexuality are conducted, and the medium through which alternative groups and ideologies are often stigmatized and criminalized. It must therefore also be the focus of criminologists who want to unravel the politics of crime and criminalization.

Embedded also in this mediated process are emerging forms of state authority and state censorship (Barak, 1991; Tunnell, 1993). As the cases considered here show, not only moral crusaders are involved in the criminalization of popular culture—district attorneys, deputy sheriffs, state prosecutors, and police officers are involved as well. In criminalizing art and music, these groups lay the groundwork for the egregious expansion of state control over the operations of popular culture. They also engage in a form of state censorship, a "theft of legitimacy of dissent" (Caulfield, 1991), accomplished through the withdrawal of cultural resources and the degradation of alternative voices. Thus, for example, when a local theater staged a play dealing with gay and lesbian issues, officials in Cobb County, Georgia, withdrew the county's entire arts budget and instead earmarked the money for police dogs and police car video cameras (Britt, 1994). And in the fallout from police attacks on Ice-T's "Cop Killer," major record labels forced rap artists to delete songs from upcoming releases, canceled album releases, and in some cases voided contracts with rap groups[15]; a large record store chain that stopped selling the album containing "Cop Killer" did so because of "complaints from police, religious groups, and Alabama's governor" ("Rap song rapped," *Rocky Mountain News* June 18, 1992, page 2). Increasingly, these and other cases exist not as epiphenomenal echoes of the "real" conflict between state authority and alternative politics, but as the essence of this conflict; through these sorts of cultural channels, state authority is constructed, legal control is expanded, and alternative politics are quieted (Ferrell, 1991, 1993; Ferrell and Sanders, 1995).

The predominance of this mediated universe means that criminologists must also widen their notion of criminalization to include more than the simple creation or application of criminal law. Indeed, the dynamics of media operations and mediated moral crusades seem today to define the process of criminalization and to determine its targets, as much as the inner workings of the criminal law and the criminal justice system. As the many contemporary cases of criminalized popular culture show, this *cultural criminalization* reconstructs the epistemic framework through which artists, musicians, and others are understood (see Ferrell and Sanders, 1995). Cultural criminalization shapes new identities and remakes artists as criminals and cultural events as criminal endeavors. In some cases, this cultural criminalization stands as an end in itself; moral entrepreneurs and others succeed in publicly dehumanizing and delegitimating their enemies, though no specific legal charges are brought against them. In other cases, by redefining artists and others as dangerous "folk devils," this cultural criminalization helps construct a perceptual context in which direct criminal charges can later be brought (Cohen, 1972; Ferrell, 1993). In either case, though, news conferences and press releases, moral entrepreneurship, and media savvy drive this process of criminalization.

The criminalization of popular culture thus calls criminologists to expand their analytic focus, to widen their gaze to take in not just "crime" as such, but also the interwoven dynamics of media operations, legal authority, cultural politics, and criminalization. This sort of holistic approach carries criminology beyond the study of crime as narrowly defined and toward the analysis of crime and criminalization as complex cultural processes. As an essential component in larger legal and political conflicts, cultural criminalization—the mediated re-presentation of popular culture as criminal, with or without charges filed or convictions gained—merits the attention and analysis of criminologists.

DISCUSSION QUESTIONS

1. What does Ferrell mean when he asserts that popular culture is being "criminalized"? Explain why you agree or disagree.

2. According to Ferrell, how has this criminalization process taken place? What are the roles played in the process by interest groups, politicians, and the mass media? Can you think of other examples of this process?

3. What impact does Ferrell believe efforts to criminalize popular culture are having on various forms of popular expression? Explain why you agree or disagree with Ferrell's assertion that "criminologists must also widen their notions of criminalization."

NOTES

1. A 1988 case similar to the Jock Sturges raid is reported in Atkins (1991: 36). See also Gilkerson (1990) and the *Arts Censorship Project Newsletter* ("Censorship of Michigan exhibit illustrates dangers of MacKinnon Theories," Winter 1993, 2: 1, 6) on art censorship cases at the Universities of South Carolina and Michigan. British authorities have also impounded a book whose cover features an Andres Serrano photograph; see Dubin (1995).

2. See the following articles from the *Rocky Mountain News*: A.P., "Rappers accused in seizing of vans at gunpoint after concert," September 18, 1993, page 48A; A.P., "Rap star held in New York shooting," November 2, 1993, page 20A; A.P., "Rapper gets 4½ years in sex case," February 8, 1995, page 3; T. Hays, "Police arrest rapper again," November 20, 1993, page 38A; "Singer fined for lewdness," February 27, 1993, page 98; "Police apologize to black singers," October 14, 1993, page 93; "Rapper held in cops' shooting," November 1, 1993, page 20A; "Rapper charged with murder," November 20, 1993, page 38A.

3. See the following articles from the *Rocky Mountain News*: "Luther Campbell, dancers arrested," August 23, 1994, page 62A; and A.P.: "Shop owner takes rap on rap album," October 4, 1990, page 2. Also see *Entertainment Weekly*, 1990; Holden, 1993a; and Santoro, 1990.

4. See the following articles from the *Rocky Mountain News*: "Rap song rapped," June 18, 1992, page 2; "Police look to stop 'Cop Killer,'" June 18, 1992, page 86; and "Ice-T pleased album makes cops nervous," June 19, 1992, page 116.

5. See O'Brien, 1992, and the following articles from the *Arts Censorship Project Newsletter*: "Attacks on rap music continue," Winter 1993, page 4; and "Police force cancellation of Ice-T concerts; Madonna's *Sex* steams anti-porn groups," Spring 1993, page 7.

6. See Campbell, 1989; *Cincinnati Post*, 1994; Holden, 1993a; Martin, 1993; Woods, n.d. and the following article in the *Rocky Mountain News*: "Teen slayers sentenced," December 17, 1993, page 44A.

7. See the following articles from the *Rocky Mountain News*: "'New Jack City' movie sparks fatal shooting, theater violence," March 11, 1991, page 28; and "Theatergoers nervous but attending film," July 15, 1991, page 31.

8. See Graham 1993; Ostrow, 1993; and the following articles from the A.P. in the *Rocky Mountain News*: "Mom blames MTV cartoon for fire," October 9, 1993, page 30A; and "Beavis and Butt-head blamed for another fire," November 17, 1993, page 34A.

9. See the following article from the *Rocky Mountain News*: "Students like what's in TV name," January 24, 1994, page 50A.

   Similarly, a convicted German bomber and extortionist is alleged to have drawn inspiration and ideas from Disney duck cartoons; see the following articles from the *Rocky Mountain News*: A.P., "German bomber linked to cartoons," January 31, 1994, page 28A; and "German 'Scrooge McDuck' crook given 7 years in bombing scheme," March 15, 1995, page 38A.

10. See Foster, 1995, and the following articles from the *Rocky Mountain News*: A.P.: "Movie made man kill clerk, relative says," May 12, 1994, page 14A; and "Boy says video prompted rape," May 25, 1995, page 34A.

11. See Jolson-Colburn, 1993; A.P., "Video game companies asked to cut violence," *Rocky Mountain News,* November 23, 1993, page 70; and the following articles from the *Arts Censorship Project Newsletter*: "Florida's road censors," Fall 1993, 3, page 4; and "ACLU affiliate news," Winter 1994, 3, page 4.

12. See Vance, 1989: 41; and the following A.P. article from the *Rocky Mountain News*: "2,000 Christian conservatives cheer anti-abortion speech," September 12, 1993, page 34A.

13. Under the leadership of Tipper Gore (1987) and other "Washington Wives," the Parents' Music Resource Center (PMRC) has, of course, also led well-publicized campaigns against popular culture images and messages.

14. See Bolton, 1992; Bronski, 1989; Dubin, 1993; Parachini, 1993; Reuter, 1993a; and Vance, 1989; and the following articles: "Report from the trenches," *Arts Censorship Project Newsletter*, Spring 1995, page 3; and "Senate OKs art subsidies," *Rocky Mountain News*, September 16, 1993, page 37A.

15. See Holden, 1993a; Morris, 1992; and the following article from the *Arts Censorship Project Newsletter*: "Attacks on rap music continue," Winter 1993, page 4.

PART III

✳

Everyday Journalism

For many people an issue does not exist until it appears in the news media.

MICHAEL PARENTI, *INVENTING REALITY* (1986: IX)

In *Journalism and Popular Culture*, co-editor Peter Dahlgren writes, "the application of popular culture perspectives offer new prisms through which to view and better understand journalism" (1992: 3). He notes, "with cultural studies we witness more ambitious and systematic theoretical efforts to examine the nature of journalism" (3). The need to examine the nature of journalism becomes more pressing if we accept this assertion by Lichter, Lichter, and Rothman: "News used to be the first rough draft of history. Now it is the first of a Hollywood screen play" (1994: 6). This observation is in keeping with the exchange between Ted Koppell, the respected anchor of the late-night newsshow *Nightline*, and a member of a round table discussion about crime, violence, and TV news. After admitting that it was "an inflammatory term to use when we're talking about issues like violence in the streets," Koppell then asked Jeff Wald, news director of a Los Angeles television station, to "talk about the entertainment value of those stories and also how easy they are to cover relative to perhaps more benign stories that take a little more work" (Koppell, 1993).

Although television news can trace its antecedents to radio news and cinema newsreels and documentaries, Carroll points out that modern news programs are "still a 'show' as all television programs are 'shows.'" News programs have formats as predictable as any regularly scheduled dramatic series (1985: 214, 223). And, like other television offerings, news programs are crafted to attract as large an audience as possible.

But according to recent reports, network news is no longer as powerful as it once was. Auletta finds "networks news audiences are dwindling and news-division profits are shriveling" (1991: 5). A recent study by the Pew Research Center for People and Press concludes, "Television news is in trouble with the American public" (cited in Thomas, 1996). Media critics charge that in their efforts to improve their slipping ratings, network news programs are becoming more like "syndicated tabloid" programs such as *A Current Affair* and *Hard Copy* (Caldwell, 1995: 226–229). This kind of accusation of sensationalism is one with which print journalism (newspapers) are familiar. Long before the late nineteenth century—when charges of "yellow journalism" were leveled at rival publishers Hearst and Pulitzer—editors and reporters had faced this charge from their critics (for example, Dabney, 1987; Starker, 1989).

Aside from this matter of sensationalism in the media, a matter of some interest to scholars is the process by which an event (or "non-event") becomes news. This is particularly salient when taken with the related issue of what is not reported by the news media. For example, in the aftermath of the Los Angeles riots, media critic Howard Kurtz commented, "Still, one had to ask: Where had the press been all along?" (1993: 70) That is, why had the press not been reporting on the tensions and problems of inner-city Los Angeles before the riots? This question is a contemporary version of the concern expressed by the Kerner Commission during its investigation of urban riots in the 1960s.

Clearly, a number of issues surround media coverage of both "routine" news and more sensational events. In the five chapters that follow, the contributors offer some insight into the creation of the news.

6

❊

Police, Courts, and Corrections in the Media*

STEVEN M. CHERMAK

C rime is an important news topic. Historically, news organizations have tried to increase circulation by capitalizing on the public's fascination with crime, deviance, and justice (Chibnall, 1977; Grabosky and Wilson, 1989; Sherizen, 1978). News media provide prominent space for violent, sexy, and sensational crimes to entertain and attract as many consumers as possible. Murders are preferred, but assaults, rapes, and child molestations will be presented when they are the most serious crimes available (Chermak, 1995).

It is important to understand the messages presented as news content because of the public's heavy reliance on various news media. Newspapers, television stations, and radios are among the most influential sources used by the public to develop opinions about crime and the criminal justice system, and the frequent presentation of crime in entertainment sources, such as movies, television programs, and comic books, increases the importance of understanding the media images presented to the public. Most of the public receives its daily dose of crime vicariously through these media sources because of infrequent direct contact with the types of crime in the news (Ericson, Baranek, and Chan, 1987; Graber 1980; Hall, Critcher, Jefferson, Clarke, and Roberts, 1978; Surette, 1992).

The amount of research examining the presentation of crime in the news media has increased dramatically (Marsh, 1989) and established some standard

*A version of this paper was delivered at the annual meeting of the Academy of Criminal Justice Sciences, Chicago, 1994.

findings. First, existing research indicates that crime is an important news topic. An examination of Chicago media, for example, indicated that crime news accounted for about 25 percent of the total news space in local newspaper reports and 20 percent of stories on local television (Graber, 1980: 26). Second, research indicates that news media distort the crime problem by focusing on serious crimes that are least likely to occur (Ericson, Baranek, and Chan, 1991; Graber, 1980; Humphries, 1981; Marsh, 1988; Morash and Hale, 1987; Sheley and Ashkins, 1981). News organizations, concerned with attracting a local audience, concentrate on the most serious crimes that occur in their immediate area (Chermak, 1995).

I address two limitations in the existing content research. First, content research has not examined the presentation of the component parts of the criminal justice system, including the stages of the process discussed, whether the news media evaluate criminal justice effectiveness, and how often the news media present innovative programs. Second, existing research has neglected the sources cited within crime stories (Voumvakis and Ericson, 1984). An important consideration is how the use of criminal justice sources affects the presentation of each component of the criminal justice system. Which criminal justice sources are used most frequently? Why? How does the involvement of these sources affect the presentation of the criminal justice system?

This chapter examines how the primary components of the criminal justice system are presented in the news media. In particular, the central theme is that the news media's reliance on criminal justice sources determines what gets presented to the public about the criminal justice system. I examine the general relationship between personnel working for news media and criminal justice organizations and link these relationships to how the reliance on criminal justice sources affects the presentation of the criminal justice system.

RESEARCH METHODOLOGY

This research combines three different research methodologies (for a complete discussion of the methodology, see Chermak, 1995). First, content data from more than 2,500 crime stories were collected from two newspapers and one television station located in cities with frightening rates of crime (Dallas, Detroit), two newspapers and one television station from cities with significant crime rates (Cleveland, San Francisco), and two newspapers and one television station from cities with average rates of crime (Albany, Buffalo). Thirty-six days of newspaper and 56 days of television content were coded.

A problem with relying solely on content data to draw substantive conclusions is that the rationale for presenting particular stories is inferred. The intentions, ideology, and values of a media organization can be easily misunderstood (Ericson, Baranek, and Chan, 1987). This research overcomes this limitation by combining content results with ethnographic observations (second research methodology).

Third, field work was completed in two news organizations located in a large city. The newspaper observed will be referred to as the *Midwest Tribune*. I observed the activities of police and court beat reporters, general assignment reporters, editors, and criminal justice sources whenever possible. Similarly, I observed a television organization I call the *Midwest Nightly*, observing the behavior of reporters, editors, and producers. These content and observational data were supplemented with extensive interview data.

REPORTERS AND CRIMINAL JUSTICE SOURCES

Most news media have numerous crime stories available for two reasons. First, a steady supply of new crime events occur daily. Second, other crimes, which might have been presented previously, can be recycled as news while a case makes progress into the criminal justice system. If a crime is presented when first discovered, other stories can be produced when the suspect is arrested, arraigned, tried, and sentenced. All new and recycled crime events cannot be presented because news space is limited, forcing news media to select those events that are the most "newsworthy." News organizations "routinize" a process to make selection decisions efficiently (Tuchman, 1978). The primary participants involved in this process are news and criminal justice personnel.

Reporters rely heavily on criminal justice sources for story information to standardize the unexpected nature of crime news (Gans, 1979; Tuchman, 1978). This reliance influences the structure of news organizations and the news production process used to generate stories about crime. News media obtain story information from criminal justice sources because they are conveniently accessible, establishing police beats in police headquarters and court beats in county courthouses to increase accessibility to news. Reporters use these beats to cultivate relationships with sources and obtain access to documents.

This reliance, in turn, can influence how crime gets presented to the public. Criminal justice organizations have a vested interest in how the public perceives their organization. This interest motivates them to try to control the selection and production of news images presented by participating in the news process. This front- and back-end control of the news production process largely determines what gets presented to the public about crime.

NEWS COVERAGE OF POLICE

Police departments have become increasingly aggressive at attempting to control public perceptions, protecting their image by determining the amount and type of crimes provided to news organizations (Ericson, Baranek, and Chan, 1989). News media allow police to influence the images presented because their access to the department helps them fulfill daily story demands with minimum complications. Police take advantage of this reliance by limiting media access to working areas of the department.

News media are constrained not to sacrifice their relationship with police because they fear losing information access, and reporters must weigh these costs when making presentation decisions. An example from the ethnographic analysis illustrates how reporters are adversely affected by pushing a particular issue when evaluating source performance. A reporter discussed a story he had done about several officers involved in a ticket fixing scam. These officers accepted money from business owners to not ticket cars parked outside their business. After the story was aired, the reporter could no longer use his contacts in the police department because of the negative publicity generated from this story. Most reporters weigh these costs carefully, unwilling to risk criticizing the police because of the threat of losing access to information.

Reporters use their access to various levels of the police hierarchy for story selection possibilities. Patrol officers, sergeants, detectives, or commanders might supply news stories. For example, the location of the *Midwest Tribune's* police beat at police headquarters provided reporters with easy access to police sources. Two police reporters compiled stories during the day and another came in during the evening, using this easy access to produce between four and six police stories daily. Reporters also could peruse police documents, such as arrest logs and blotter reports, which provided additional story possibilities.

The primary police source used by television and newspaper reporters to clarify the newsworthiness of an event was a departmental spokesperson or public relations officer. This public information specialist released news to media organizations and answered questions about ongoing investigations, acting as an image control agent for the department. This source understood the intricacies of news production, was trained to be an effective advocate, and used insider knowledge to answer questions asked by reporters. For example, I spent an afternoon with a television reporter who discussed the spokesperson's media savvy. She discussed how he was almost always willing to go on camera and was skilled in how he provided information. The spokesperson kept his quotes short and to the point, making it easy for the reporter to include them in a story.

The heavy reliance on the police for story information is also reflected by the frequent reference to them as sources within crime stories. Table 6-1 presents data on the presentation of sources in crime stories. These data indicate that police representatives are the primary source cited by reporters in news stories, providing almost 30 percent of the information cited. Police sources are frequently cited because they can be easily contacted because they are available 24 hours a day and 7 days a week, and police are accustomed to the daily intrusions of the media asking questions. Moreover, police are motivated to participate. Reporters give sources status and power because they are presented as the "authorized knowers" in society, establishing a hierarchy of credibility based on the placement of their comments in the news (Ericson, Baranek, and Chan, 1987).

**Table 6-1 Sources Used
for Comment by Type
of Source**

Type of source[a]	Percent
Police	29.4 %
Court	25.3
Defendant	8.9
Not specific[b]	6.9
Victim acquaintance	3.7
Documents[c]	3.7
Victim	3.6
Witness/juror	3.6
Politician	3.0
Citizen	2.6
Media	2.1
Other[d]	1.9
School/church	1.4
Defendant acquaintance	1.3
Hospital[e]	0.9
Expert	0.9
Corrections	0.8

[a]Presented by rank order.

[b]Sources cited as "sources say," "officials say," "authorities say."

[c]Police or court documents.

[d]Highway spokesman, community groups, weather service, and so on.

[e]Includes doctors cited, emergency medical service, and coroner.

The selection and production input by police departments results in the frequent presentation of the police in the news. More than 38 percent of the crime stories analyzed covered activities by the police. Table 6-2 presents the percentage of crime stories by stage of the criminal justice process. Discovery of a crime incident, usually when a citizen reports a crime to the police, is the most frequent stage presented. Reporters are typically first exposed to these incidents when perusing police documents. Crimes that are not reported to the police are excluded from consideration, and police officials have the power to eliminate reported crimes by not making certain police reports available to reporters.

Police input into the selection and production of news stories also directly affects how the stories are presented to the public. Indeed, most crime stories reflect positively on police performance as an organization. The police benefit from their presentation generally because they are portrayed as fighting crime, receiving awards for achievements, and using innovations to respond to crime. Police use their relationship with reporters to accomplish deterrence objectives, solve crimes, and divert attention from instances of negative performance.

Table 6-2 Crime Stories by Stage of Criminal Justice Process[a]

Stage of process	Percent of cases
Discovery of crime	18.7 %
Investigation	4.2
Arrest	15.4
Arraignment	13.3
Pretrial motions	3.7
Plea agreement	2.7
Trial	9.1
Jury deliberation	0.4
Verdict	3.9
Sentence	7.3
Appeal	2.3
Supreme Court decision	0.8
Probation behavior	0.1
Commitment to prison	0.4
Parole behavior	1.8
Pardon request	0.3
Release from prison	1.1
Execution	0.5
Follow-ups[b]	12.7
Other[c]	1.4
	N=1979

[a]These results include only those stories where the focus was on a crime incident. Other crime stories, such as statistical stories, editorials, and program stories, were excluded.

[b]These are either victim, defendant, or crime follow-ups, for example, a story about the impact that a crime has had on a victim's family.

[c]Includes other court settlements.

Most crime stories cover specific incidents (that is, stories involving a suspect committing a crime). These incidents emphasize the dangers of police work, supporting the cultural myth that police are in the business of fighting crime. Police are presented as the first responders in the fight against crime, conducting investigations and responding to citizens' calls for help. Time constraints force reporters to react to crime news, reporting events long after they have transpired.

Other news stories about the police inform the public about important activities and awards received by police officers. When individual police officers receive awards, police departments request coverage of the ceremonies and provide reporters with news releases to increase efficiency in the story production. Because police sources already have an established relationship with reporters, they can encourage coverage. News coverage of these police events occur despite disinterest in award ceremonies. For example, the departmental spokesperson requested coverage of an award ceremony acknowledging the promotion of four officers. On the day of the event, the spokesperson dropped off the press release to a reporter at the *Tribune*'s police beat, noting the time of the ceremony. The news release was passed between the reporters because no one wanted to attend. The reporter who produced the story was in attendance for about ten minutes. He wrote a story, which appeared on the second page of the region section, from the information provided in the press release. Police departments also request, and news organizations cover, certain incidents to deter law violators from committing crimes. For example, police request coverage of weekend sobriety checkpoints and holiday speed traps to deter individuals from driving drunk or speeding (Ericson, 1991). Reporters follow up on the productiveness of these police tools by discussing their effectiveness. Police also accomplish deterrence goals by allowing reporters to ride with officers "on the job."

Similarly, police also use the news media to accomplish investigation goals. Police request coverage of unsolved crimes, asking reporters to include sketches of possible suspects so that someone might identify the suspect or provide leads. Or, police use the news media to warn residents of increased amounts of crime in a particular section of the city. For example, a police source asked a reporter at the *Midwest Nightly* to do a story on a number of rapes that occurred so that women who walked through that neighborhood at night would take special precautions or avoid the area.

Finally, news media are unlikely to critically evaluate police because of the benefits of having access to police information. Results from the current content analysis revealed that police effectiveness was evaluated in less than 4 percent of the total number of stories, substantiating results from other research (Graber, 1980). Moreover, even when the police are evaluated, the media evaluate their performance in specific instances. Problems are likely to be discussed as isolated and not institutional—caused by a "rotten apple."

This is not to imply that the police are never criticized by the news media. Police department corruption, scandal, and officers who break the law are priority news items. Indeed, the threat of such negative publicity has forced police departments to be actively involved in the news process.

NEWS COVERAGE OF THE COURTS

Courtrooms are symbols of dignity, respect, and custom—arenas where adversaries, representing two conflicting sides, struggle to find the "truth." Defendants receive constitutional protections from governmental intervention, and a neutral magistrate ensures that issues are resolved fairly and in accordance with the law. It would seem that the involvement of judicial and legal personnel in the news production process, attempting to use the media to mobilize public opinion and influence the outcome of a case, would oppose these traditions. Court personnel are, however, standard sources used by news personnel.

News organizations are structured to take advantage of the willingness of court sources to provide story information. For example, the *Tribune* had two separate newsbeats that produced court news. One newsbeat was located at the federal courthouse and was staffed by one reporter who covered newsworthy federal court cases and appellate decisions. The majority of daily court stories came from the other court beat, located on the first floor of the county courthouse. This beat was staffed regularly during courthouse hours by two reporters who produced between three and five stories each day.

The television organization I observed also expended considerable resources to cover court news. Since the Supreme Court has ruled that having cameras in courtrooms does not violate a defendant's right to fair trial (*Chandler v. Florida*, 1981), television coverage of courtroom activities, by all broadcast organizations, has increased dramatically. The *Midwest Nightly* took advantage of video access to courtrooms, sending a reporter and cameraperson to the courthouse almost every morning. The cameraperson would record testimony from newsworthy cases and the reporter would contact sources for on-camera comments. Most television news stories are short (30–60 seconds), so *Nightly* reporters could produce two or three court stories with minimal effort.

The location of newspaper court beats, and television access to courtrooms, provided reporters with access to various resources to make news selection decisions. *Tribune* reporters began each day by checking the court calendar for newsworthy cases. They also perused a variety of court documents, including indictments, motions filed, returned search warrants, and appellate decisions, pursuing crimes when they recognized a prominent figure listed or when a crime was serious. Moreover, these reporters were meticulous in their record keeping for upcoming cases. Court reporters also had extensive access to court proceedings, recording the testimony provided to be used in news stories. Finally, reporters cultivated relationships with potential courtroom sources when riding on elevators, when walking down hallways, or when waiting for a proceeding to start. These relationships were invaluable to reporters in their search for newsworthy cases.

There were limitations on the information provided in court stories because reporters were restricted from specific proceedings. Reporters were allowed to mingle with attorneys or judges when they were in open areas of the courthouse; however, access to decisions made in chambers or negotiations that occurred behind closed doors were restricted. Judges could also prevent television cameras from recording testimony in courtrooms. When a judge decided to prohibit cameras, television news stations could not produce a story, making it less likely that it would be presented.

The primary participants in courtroom activities (judge, prosecutor, defense attorney) are frequently asked to comment on the status of a court case. Most comments from judges included in news stories are taken from courtroom discourse. Judges do, however, use the news media to garner positive publicity by contacting reporters through their clerks, suggesting which cases might be worthy of news coverage, giving extensive courtroom access, and providing special privileges when courtrooms are overcrowded with spectators.

Reporters frequently rely on prosecuting attorneys for court information, which allows these attorneys to develop a general understanding of the type of information considered newsworthy. Various prosecutors frequented the court beat to inform reporters about the status of cases. Reporters and prosecutors discussed how the case could be presented, and the attorney informed them when their most interesting witnesses were to testify. This limited the amount of time the reporter had to spend in the courtroom.

Reporters might know the defense attorney involved, but reporters are less likely to have established relationships with defense attorneys because a larger variety of attorneys are involved in the cases presented in the news. Moreover, the motivation for defense attorneys to participate as sources, in many cases, is not as powerful as is the prosecutor's motivation because of the possibility of damaging defense tactics. A limited amount of sympathetic information is provided about defendants in court stories because of the limited use of sources knowledgeable about their perspective.

Although court reporters are more likely to use comments from prosecutors within news stories, they also have the luxury of choosing the most newsworthy quotes available from participants. Various aspects of a particular case are more easily displayed in court stories because of the dense concentration of sources in courthouses. If police beat reporters need information about an investigation, they have to find someone from the police organization to comment. When a police source refuses to comment, the reporter has a difficult time producing the story. Conversely, court reporters can turn to any of the previously mentioned sources to provide the information they need. Court reporters are more willing to provide sensitive information because of the adversarial nature of the court system. Sources realize that if they refuse to provide information about a case, a reporter could rely solely on an opposing viewpoint. The competing interests involved among members of the courtroom workgroup increases the likelihood that these sources will participate when asked by reporters.

What is presented about the court system in the news is also limited because of the need of news organizations to present stories in a manner that is attractive, and understandable, to their audiences. Legal discourse does not get presented because it has to compete against the news organization's need to satisfy news discourse (Ericson, Baranek, and Chan, 1989). Legal technicalities, such as rules of evidence, interpretation of precedent, and jury instructions, are inconsistent with the types of news preferred. Although these important issues affect the outcome of a case, they are complicated and not easy to condense into the format requirements of news discourse.

Nearly 45 percent of the stories examined by content analysis were court stories. Table 6-2 indicates that definitive stages, such as arraignments, trials, and sentencing hearings, are the most frequently presented court stages. The court process is arduous, so news media have opportunities to constantly update the public about ongoing cases. For example, if a crime was presented when originally discovered, court reporters discussed how they thought they were obligated to do a follow-up if a suspect was arraigned to demonstrate that a particular individual was off the streets. Moreover, as a case progressed through each stage of the system, reporters presented its movement as a "new" event.

News media covered trials frequently (9.1 percent of specific incident stories). The frequent presentation of trials occurs because they can span a number of days, weeks, or months. A high-profile crime trial provides reporters the opportunity to consistently update the public on the case's progress. Public interest has already been piqued, so reporters can attend the trial at their convenience to produce a story based on whichever witness testifies when the reporter is attending. Reporters can also establish relationships with the primary participants in a case and attempt to parlay this relationship into a willingness to comment.

High-profile stories remain in the news because court reporters have several opportunities to produce stories about an incident. For example, while I was observing the *Tribune*, a prominent doctor was on trial for writing illegal prescriptions. The *Tribune* reporter attended his trial each day, writing stories on the opening arguments, key prosecution witnesses, expert testimony, defense rebuttal witnesses, concluding remarks, the verdict, and his sentence. More than 15 stories were presented because the trial lasted longer than three weeks. Some stories were presented on the front page of the region section, although others were relegated to the back section. The placement of each story depended on the quality of testimony provided.

Most court stories presented are major felonies tried in courts of general jurisdiction. Appellate and civil decisions are rarely presented because of their complexity. When television court stories are presented, testimony is recorded and reporters select what is most interesting. When defendants are presented, their backs will be to the camera. Judges are frequently presented on camera, providing instructions, overseeing the proceedings, or directly addressing the courtroom.

NEWS COVERAGE OF CORRECTIONS

Only 17 percent of the crime stories covered correctional institutions. Most stories covering a specific crime incident examined how a case progressed through a police or court stage. Specific incident stories about corrections were occasionally presented to conclude an event after it had been in the news for a long time and discussed the defendant's commitment to prison, behavior on parole, or execution. News stories that discuss the daily operation of prison, how inmates adapt to the conditions of incarceration, and the violence that occurs inside are rare.

Several factors contribute to the infrequent presentation of news about corrections. First, news personnel do not think a defendant's correctional behavior is interesting to the public. The public is satisfied once defendants are sentenced to long prison sentences, assuming they are getting what they deserve (Grabosky and Wilson, 1989). Editors and reporters provide stories to the public in response to their primary concerns; the majority cover local in-cidents. Stories about the behavior of inmates, located many hundreds of miles away from a local news audience, are rarely considered newsworthy because consumers are not interested. Defendants sentenced to other correctional pro-grams, located closer to the local audience, are not frequently presented be-cause those prisoners have committed less serious crimes.

Second, corrections stories are difficult to produce because news media have only limited access to correction sources. News media do not have a cor-rections' beat that fulfills the same function as a police or court beat. Correc-tions stories are produced generally by police and court beat reporters. These stories are time consuming because news media do not have a structured beat system.

Reporters do not have relationships with officials from correctional orga-nizations. These officials were the least likely of all sources considered in Table 6-1 to be presented as providing comments in news stories, accounting for less than one percent of the total number of sources mentioned. Correction officials do not make an effort to legitimize their activities because public in-terest is limited. The police, however, have to expend resources to control the images because of public exposure. The closed environment of correctional programs shields officials from scrutiny.

In addition, correctional sources have greater opportunities to control news images because media access to inmates is limited by law. For example, if a prison warden is asked to provide comment for a story on the apparent suicide of an inmate, reporters would have a difficult time validating the warden's conclusions because access to other sources, such as other inmates, is con-strained by the policies and procedures of the Department of Corrections. News media have challenged these policies and procedures as unconstitution-ally constraining First Amendment rights, but the Supreme Court has sup-ported the officials' decisions to limit access, upholding their argument that uninhibited access pose significant safety risks.

When presented in the news, these stories typically discuss a significant problem or focus on policy issues. Most police and court stories focus on spe-cific incidents. The release of inmates on parole, escapes, and riots are news-worthy because the danger can be highlighted. Table 6-2 indicates that release from prison accounted for 1.1 percent of the total number of stories. These stories are presented to increase public awareness. Prison escapes are presented for similar reasons, and officials are willing to cooperate with news media, seeking public assistance to capture the escaped inmate(s).

Prison riots receive national news coverage. These stories are important because they are rare and can heighten public awareness and encourage prison reform. The significance of these stories is exacerbated because of the large amount of space provided while a riot is in progress. News stories detail the inmates' demands, official interpretations of the riot, and how officials plan to respond to concerns. Experts are contacted to comment about what might have caused the disturbance. News organizations capitalize on the public's fas-cination with violence, describing the number of deaths, injuries, and the structural damages to the prison. After order is restored, follow-up stories on the recovery of the prison are produced.

The death penalty gets substantial news coverage because of the frequent updates on the status of individual cases. Stories are presented as the case progresses through the state and federal appellate systems, when last minute appeals are made, when there is evidence that might indicate innocence, and when the execution is carried out. In addition, the death penalty as policy is frequently debated in the news. The racial composition of death row, the execution of juveniles and mentally retarded offenders, the deterrent or brutalization effect of an execution, and the moral implications around this issue are constantly analyzed by reporters in support of both sides of this controversial issue.

Finally, some program stories are presented. These stories are presented as direct solicitations of support by legislators or officials, seeking approval for their innovative correctional responses. For example, intermediate sanctions such as shock incarceration and electronic monitoring programs are presented. Descriptions of how these programs function, successes, budgets, and whether there are plans to expand these programs are presented to inform the public and gain support.

CONCLUSION

The presentation of the components of the criminal justice system in the news varies because of differences in criminal justice source involvement in the news production process. Police officers have a significant stake in what is presented about their organization because of direct public scrutiny. Officers have daily and frequent interaction with the public and are most likely to be criticized for the system's inability to reduce crime. When crime rates appear out of control, the public blames the police for their inability to respond effectively. Police organizations expend resources to promote their organizations favorably in the news, hiring media consultants, assigning officers to full-time public relations, and training officers to interact with the media. Most crime stories presented support the police because of the departments' efforts to promote themselves. Media allow the police to have a significant amount of control of these news images because reliance increases news efficiency.

Similarly, because the news media have virtually unlimited access to courtrooms, court sources have a stake in what is presented in the news. Prosecutors cultivate relationships with reporters and rely on them to further case goals as well as individual goals. Judges encourage reporters to cover their activities to assist in reelection bids. Defense attorneys, although the relationship is not as strong, make themselves available to control public hostility directed toward their clients. These relationships influence news selection and production decisions. Reporters attend court hearings and selectively choose the most newsworthy elements of testimony.

Correctional organizations are closed to public and media scrutiny. It is difficult for media organizations to gain access to sources that can provide different perspectives on correctional topics. Moreover, reporters are not motivated to develop relationships with correctional sources because there is little public interest in these types of stories, which are thus infrequently presented.

The crime stories presented in the news media are one source of information that the public uses to develop opinions about the criminal justice system. These images are limited because they rely heavily on police and court sources. This dependence allows news media to produce numerous crime stories in an efficient manner but also makes critical scrutiny of these images less likely. News media allow these sources to influence when and how a crime is presented to the public. For these same reasons, public understanding of corrections is extraordinarily narrow because these stories are less likely to be presented in the news.

DISCUSSION QUESTIONS

1. According to Chermak, what sources are routinely used by reporters? Are some sources considered more reliable than others? How might the sources used by a reporter affect how a story is written?

2. For news organizations, what makes one story more "newsworthy" than another? Do you think the criteria used to determine the "newsworthiness" of stories serves the best interest of the public? Why or why not?

3. According to the author, how does the way news organizations are structured affect how events are covered or whether they are covered at all? What consequences might result from the lack of coverage of certain events?

7

❀

The Role of the Media in the Creation of Public Police Violence*

JEFFREY IAN ROSS

INTRODUCTION

The process by which incidents of police violence[1] come to public, governmental, and police attention, and the reactions by various actors in these groups, consists of a complex web of responses, reactions, consequences, effects, and implications, hereafter labeled "outcomes."[2] Central to this process is the role of the mass media. Police violence can be thought of as similar to Freud's characterization of the mental process whereby 10 percent is conscious or above the surface, and 90 percent is unconscious or below the surface. The majority of police violence takes place beyond the knowledge of the public; only a small percentage of such activities become public knowledge.

Through a review of the literature and series of interviews conducted with police and crime reporters,[3] editors and producers, police public affairs personnel, and other actors in the criminal justice system in Denver, New York City, and Toronto, I developed a model of the process by which information on police violence is transformed into articles in the press and stories that are broadcast on radio and television.[4]

* An earlier version of this chapter was presented at the annual meeting of the Academy of Criminal Justice Sciences, Chicago, March 10, 1994. Special thanks to Paul Bond, Natasha J. Cabrera, and Ted Robert Gurr for comments. The points of view are those of the author and do not necessarily represent those of the National Institute of Justice nor the U.S. Department of Justice.

LITERATURE REVIEW

A series of studies have been conducted on the media. A smaller subset of that research examines the process by which media organizations make decisions about the types of stories they research, write about, and print or broadcast (for example, Chermak, 1994b; Chibnall, 1977, 1981; Ericson, Baranek, and Chan, 1987, 1989; Fishman, 1980; Gans, 1979; Glasgow University Media Group, 1980; Kasinsky, 1994; Rock, 1981). Although many researchers have investigated the way news media operate, few specifically look at the police-media relationship. Even fewer examine the media's treatment of police alleged or real deviance. A paucity of this literature analyzes the process by which the media research, write, and print or broadcast stories about police violence. This lack of coverage is unfortunate given that "because [police] are in the media spotlight constantly, [they] are especially vulnerable to having their procedural strays focused upon and controlled through the pressure of publicity" (Ericson, Baranek, and Chan, 1989: 97).[5] This gap in the literature prevents us from understanding how certain types of police violence receive the publicity and the chain reaction of events that police violence causes.

METHODOLOGY

Since I first started this research in 1988, I have conducted 55 semi-structured face-to-face interviews with reporters, editors, police public relations personnel, and lawyers representing clients who claimed to have suffered or were actually victims of police violence in Denver, New York City, and Toronto.[6] Individuals selected to be interviewed were culled from newspaper and magazine articles on police violence or through referrals. In other words, I obtained a snowball sample, and I make no pretenses or claims about having a representative sample of all individuals who work for or have contact with the media and police.

REVIEW OF THE MODEL

Publicization of incidents of police violence depends on a series of factors related to the operation of media organizations. Of paramount importance to media reporting of police violence is the working relationship between police and journalists. This can affect the number and type of stories. In addition, the "dynamics of the news production system" (that is, bureaucratic, normative, and economic), must be considered as factors that affect the printing or broadcast of stories (Fishman, 1980: 141-152).

I use the cover term *media initiation* to describe the series of events that lead to an incident of police violence coming to the attention of news organizations and the decision-making process to communicate it to the public, government, and police department. The media are seen as the primary agenda setters (for example, Gitlin, 1980). In this policy sphere, social problem, and political relationship, the media occupy a central ground for conflict management (that is, expansion and resolution). The media also serve an educational function both inside and outside the police department. For instance, the media might reveal information that can help police managers improve service delivery and might be another method of monitoring police employees. Besides their effects on the police, news media can inform politicians and activists about problems arising in police-citizen relationships.

In the long run, "newsmaking is a fluid and equivocal process yet highly structured and severely circumscribed by organization, knowledge, and capacity to communicate" (Ericson, Baranek, and Chan, 1987: 178). Media initiation, in the form of articles or broadcasts disclosing police violence, is hypothesized to depend on a composite of 10 interacting factors endemic to reporters, sources, and news organizations. These variables are ranked in increasing order of predicted importance: gender of reporter(s), experience of reporter(s), number of media outlets in a city, number of reporters, status of reporter(s), source of the report, type of reporters or beats writing or reporting about police violence, kind of news organization, type of medium, and editorial decisions and traditions.[7] (See Figure 7-1)

Gender of Reporter(s)

Gender of reporter can affect the type of information that he or she gathers or has access to. Following extensive interviews with police reporters, some trends emerged. Female police reporters are often treated differently than male police reporters are; they have more difficulty developing sources and take longer to do so than male reporters do.[9] Many male police officers are paternalistic toward female reporters and, despite the increased numbers of policewomen on forces, consider the female reporters to be "potential dates." This is not the experience of all women reporters. According to Virginia Byrne, police reporter of four-and-a-half years with the Associated Press, most sources "are interested in brightness, integrity, and the ability of the reporters to use their information judiciously"[10] and not the gender of the reporter. In addition to these problems encountered with male police officers, female police reporters also experience discrimination from male reporters that can hamper the free flow of information.

Experience of the Reporter(s)

The greater reporters' experience in the field and with their editors or producers, the higher the likelihood they will uncover stories on police violence and convince their editors to publish or air these stories. Journalists take a long time to master their working environment, develop expertise in researching and writing, and develop a sense of trust with their sources. Reporters gain experience during their formal and informal training as well as by exposure to different beats. Most reporters are trained on the job and get accustomed to

FIGURE 7-1 Media Initiation[8]

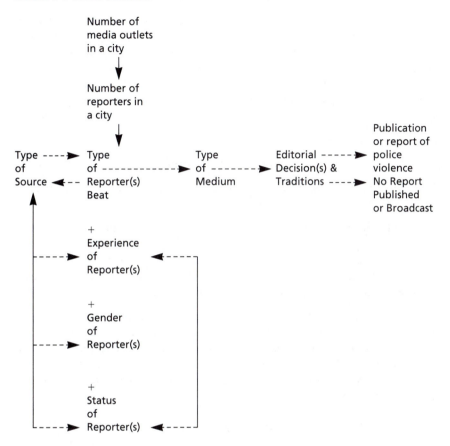

their beats through making a series of rounds to bureaucratically oriented sources (Fishman, 1980: Chapter 2). Experienced reporters are more likely to be able to negotiate with their editors and producers, extract information from sources, determine the amount of time and energy to expend in collecting information for a story, and better predict the probability of a final product (that is, article or broadcast) than are novice reporters.

Number of Media Outlets

The more media (that is, newspapers and radio and television stations) that exist in a city, the greater the competition (for example, Ericson, Baranek, and Chan, 1987: 177). Also, the greater the number of news outlets of the same type (for example, newspapers), the higher the level of competition is. If reporters feel pressured to find the most sensationalistic information, then it is reasonable to assume that some of those stories will concern police violence. This competitive spirit can also contribute to reporting police violence that is not necessarily excessive.

Number of Reporters

The greater the number of reporters and the higher the competition, the more information will be uncovered. Not only is there external competition (among media outlets), but there might also be internal competition (among reporters inside the same media organization).[11] These processes in combination increase the likelihood that reporters will uncover incidents of police violence. Large amounts of information, however, do not necessarily translate into printed or broadcast stories because of editorial constraints that I will discuss shortly.

Status of Reporter(s)

News organizations have their own pecking order for whose "copy" (story) they prefer. According to Tuchman,

> The news net is a hierarchical system of information gatherers, and so the status of reporters in the news net may determine whose information is identified as news. Editors prefer stories by salaried reporters to those by stringers, paid less well and on a piecework basis, simply because the news organization has a financial investment in the salaried reporter. (1978: 24)

Closely connected to the reporters' status is their experience because status is usually, but not always, achieved through experience. Although newcomers must go through a painful initiation process, columnists, especially those with a celebrity status, have a greater chance of having their articles published on a regular basis. Similarly, high-status journalists often have easier access to difficult-to-reach sources.

Source of Report

News of police violence comes to reporters through a variety of sources. In general, these sources mirror the typical individuals, groups, and mechanisms by which complaints are launched with police departments. Different types of reporters depend on different constellations of sources for their news stories. "Sources... [vary] as to where they are located; at what times they are available; by what means they may be tapped...; and whether the information sources can be expected to be cooperative or recalcitrant to the reporter's inquiry" (Fishman, 1980: 36). Two main types of sources, written and oral, can be structured in various ways (Ericson, Baranek, and Chan, 1987: 42).

Although sources use a variety of techniques (for example, press releases) to "can" their accounts (for example, Ericson, Baranek, and Chan, 1989: 383), the most common ways sources for stories on police violence contact reporters are by phone, mail, and fax. Generally, "sources perceive considerable variation among news organizations and respond accordingly" (1989: 393). If stories are not heard, published, or aired by the mainstream media, sources have a variety of techniques to gain publicity for their plight.[12] Sources make a variety of decisions about whether and when they will disclose information to reporters. A source's medium choice depends on a complex array of factors including speed of transmission and impact as well as knowledge of which media outlets and reporters are more sympathetic to the source's plight.

Type of Reporters and Beats

Media reports of police violence come to public attention and are sustained in the public eye primarily by the following types of reporters (in increasing order of importance): legislature, court, city hall, or police and crime. Different working conditions or beats also determine the reporters' access to sources, the type of relationship (for example, degree of autonomy) reporters have with their editors, competition among news outlets, and decisions concerning the investigation, writing, and timing of publication or broadcast of articles or segments on police violence (Fishman, 1980; Ericson, Baranek, and Chan, 1989).

If an incident of police violence has not reached the press through the police, city hall, or court reporters, then the incident is likely to be exposed or sustained through the activities of state or provincial legislative reporters, (also known as the press gallery), particularly if the issue concerns a department or ministry such as the attorney (solicitor) general or home office.

Usually, more reporters are assigned to cover the police than the courts; however, court reporters are also important as gatekeepers in the production of articles and stories on police violence (Ericson, Baranek, and Chan, 1989: 35). If a police reporter could not report the incident of police violence either because of legal complications (for example, a ban on publication) or because he or she was protecting, or feared "burning" or alienating his or her source(s), the court reporters are less likely to feel these limitations because of less conflict with their beats. Not surprisingly, most news stories emanating from the court beat are criminal cases (Ericson, Baranek, and Chan, 1989: 40; Rock, 1981) and only a minority pertain to police violence. Occasionally, however, during a major criminal trial, police violence against defendants, as a by-product of a police investigation or arrest, is emphasized by the defense's lawyer, thus stimulating a media report on real or alleged police violence.

Although not all police departments are under municipal jurisdiction, city hall and urban affairs reporters occasionally write stories that cover policing.[13] Often these stories emanate from the police department itself, or come to city hall reporters through sources that they monitor in various other agencies or departments of city hall. In the experience of many of the sources I interviewed, the city hall reporter was formerly a police reporter, which increased the likelihood that he or she would have access to police sources and would write stories on this subject.

The bulk of stories on police violence are covered by police reporters who get the material for these articles and broadcasts through a variety of different means and sources. The most common ways are community meetings, telephone calls, news conferences, and police occurrence reports. The initial sources for stories on police violence are either internal or external to the police force. The internal source can be individual police officers, including insiders, "informants," or "whistle blowers" in the police department[14]; police radio or scanner; police complaints division; public affairs; and the chief's office. Some organizational and individual sources outside the police department include the police union or association; police commission members; other reporters; other media outlets; offices of the commissioner of public complaints, coroner, and public prosecutors; governmental agencies; concerned members of the community; legal institutions; witnesses at inquiries; established ad hoc protest groups; witnesses to police violence; independent groups that monitor the police; elected representatives; prominent community leaders; lawyers for victims or their families; the alleged victims'[15] relatives or friends; and, more important, the victims themselves when possible.

A major determinant of whether or not reporters have access to information from the police is the unique working relationship between reporters and police departments. The academic literature points to two major types of police reporters: those in the inner circle and those on the outside.[16] Much of the research on this subject suggests that the inner circle works out of "the police newsroom," maintains "close affinities with police officers," and seeks "stories sympathetic to the police viewpoint" (Ericson, Baranek, and Chan, 1989: 105). Consequently, inner-circle sources are very limited in the type of articles they produce or are biased. Predictably, inner-circle reporters serve as sources of information for each other. Thus inner-circle police reporters are less likely to report information critical of the police department (1989: 106).

The outer-circle reporters, in contrast, are more likely to report police deviance; less inclined to use the police newsroom, working instead from their media organization's offices; are more detached from police sources; and have a conflictual and tense relationship with the police (Ericson, Baranek, and Chan, 1989: 104-112). This type of reporting encourages police accountability and reform. In general, outer circle reporters receive their stories "from their assignment editors" (1987) and "used a wide variety of police sources and units. When they had burned one person or unit, and were denied further access in consequence, they moved on to other persons or units to further their purpose" (1989: 130).[17]

Information gathered from interviews that I conducted with a variety of actors, especially police reporters and public information officers of big city police departments, shows that there is either a complete absence of the insider-outsider distinctions among reporters or that this arrangement varies from one news organization or reporter to another. Although the insider-outsider categorization might have been an accurate description of the state of police reporting, during the 1980s economic considerations seem to have changed the number of police reporters newsrooms can hire and consequently the number of roles they can assume. Moreover, typically police reporters now cover a variety of stories, in addition to those that focus solely on police and crime, and consequently, the reporters are in the field more. There is also a difference between Ericson's view and mine about how beats are constructed from newspaper to newspaper and from one type of media to another. For example, even though "so-called" inner-circle police reporters are provided with a newsroom by the police department, they are rarely physically present. Most of their time is spent out in the field collecting information from officers, victims, and witnesses.

Type of News Organization

Researchers also distinguish between popular (for example, tabloid) versus quality news outlets (for example, broadsheet). As Ericson, Baranek, and Chan, (1989: 118-119) pointed out, "popular news outlets were oriented to crime-incident reports and primary and tertiary understanding, whereas quality news outlets gave emphasis to policing the police." Further,

> Popular media are particularly noted for their emphasis on sensational crime, violence, sexual aberrations, major fires, disasters, and other tales of the unexpected that titillate and entertain. 'Quality' news outlets, on the other hand, disavow attention to such matters, but this is usually a matter of degree rather than kind. (Voumvakis and Ericson, 1984, as cited in Ericson, Baranek, and Chan, 1987: 48)

Finally, there is also a difference between mainstream and alternative media. Although the former with mass circulations publish frequently and are accessible by the general public, the latter cater to a small and select audience and do not publish as often. Alternative media are more likely to report stories on police deviance than the mainstream press because of political and market segmenting agendas.

Type of Medium

Although some writers have suggested that there is little difference among mediums (for example, Schlesinger, 1978; Tuchman, 1978), others disagree (Glasgow University Media Group, 1976; Graber, 1980; Sheley and Ashkins, 1981). Ericson, Baranek, and Chan, (1987: 76) say that this discrepancy exists because both groups of researchers have different foci of study. Regardless, medium type affects how reports of police violence are portrayed (that is, amount of sensationalism, comprehensiveness, and so on) and the public's perception of credibility.

Newspapers are the most comprehensive for numbers of stories on police violence, leave a relatively easily retrievable record (generally microfilm or indexes), and cover the story in greater depth. Radio and television, though leaving a permanent record of audio and video tapes, are the most difficult to access archivally. The broadcast media, however, are the most effective vehicles for sustaining the personalization and dramatization of the story (Ericson, Baranek, and Chan, 1989: 214). Yet broadcast media are also more cautious than their counterparts because their licenses can be revoked by the government for minor violations of federal communications laws.

Moreover, newspapers are potentially more comprehensive because they have more reporters in the field than do the broadcast media. This situation often leads to broadcast media producing secondary reports based on the primary research of the newspapers. And, as with different types of organizations, each source type is attracted to different mediums. Despite these differences, every newsmaking organization can marshal different resources to cover a particular story.

The popular and quality distinction determines the medium's emphasis on news originating from different beats. In the past, popular formats gave the most attention to police beat stories, but there is some indication that broadcast news are increasingly seeking out these types of stories. The court beat is primarily print-oriented, and the popular/quality distinction is a secondary consideration. In contrast, for the legislature, neither medium is preferred; rather, sources prefer outlets with large circulations or audiences (Ericson, Baranek, and Chan, 1989: 393-394).

Finally, "television journalists...rely heavily on predictable sources of stories in particular bureaucratic settings" whereas

> Newspaper [reporters] ha[ve] more resources, including a greater number of journalists. These resources allow the newspaper to set up a more decentralized system for routine news work, including a larger number and more diverse range of topic and beat specialists...newspaper time and space constraints are less severe... (Ericson, Baranek, and Chan, 1987: 354-355)

Editorial Decisions and Traditions

In addition to the relationship between reporters and sources, a complex understanding exists between reporters and their various editors and producers. This interaction affects the assignment, writing, editing, and printing or broadcasting articles or stories about police violence. Many of these decisions take place in newspaper, radio, and television newsrooms, reflecting their unique agendas and economic constraints.

In deciding if, how, and when a story will be run, most editors and producers (as do reporters) make decisions about the reliability and "abnormality" of the story, its sources, other competing newsworthy stories, and, other stories that are on schedule, or were written or shot for that day's news. Also of concern are the ramifications of the story as well as the predicted resources it will take to substantiate its claims and complete it. Some of these decisions evolve from editors' and journalists' self censorship (that is, an avoidance of controversial stories). Many of these editorial decisions are involved with what is generally referred to as aspects of occupational newsroom culture.

These decisions are made in two contexts (where editors exercise control): before a story is written or shot, and once the story is written or shot (for example, Burns, 1979; Ericson, Baranek, and Chan, 1987: Chapter 6; 1989; Fishman, 1980: Chapter 1; GUMG, 1976, 1980; Schlesinger, 1978; Tuchman, 1978: 31-38).

Editorial decisions will ultimately determine whether a segment is broadcast or article is published that mentions police violence and, in turn, will also affect the tone or treatment of that report. The publication or broadcast of a police violence report will generally lead to public, governmental, and police arousal. The media simply act as the catalyst and filter through which competing definitions and interpretations of the act(s) of police violence are channeled.

CONCLUSION

Unmistakably, these factors interact with each other in the specified causal order to facilitate the publication or broadcast of stories on police violence. In general, this process structures the type and number of articles and stories printed or broadcast on police violence. To test the strength of as many of the propositions of this model as possible, each factor should be operationalized, relationships among factors should be clearly specified, and an appropriate empirical method should be selected (for example, surveys) to assess how newspaper, radio, and television station personnel and organizations conform to the media initiation process. This will allow researchers, policymakers, and even the media to better understand how information on police violence makes its way into the public domain.

Causal modeling of the type developed here is an iterative task. First generation causal models in a field of inquiry such as the connection between the media and the police, which is descriptively rich but analytically barren, will provide the foundation for future and more complex models. More sophisticated models of media initiation should be developed in different markets (size of cities) and include psychological and rational choice theories on the causes of this process.

DISCUSSION QUESTIONS

1. According to Ross, what are some factors that determine whether or not incidents of police violence or alleged police violence will become news stories?

2. What role does the author suggest that individual factors such as gender, status, and experience of the reporter play in the news gathering and dissemination process? Does Ross's model suggest that a rookie (inexperienced) female reporter would necessarily be at a disadvantage in gathering news about police violence? Why or why not?

3. According to the author, how do police reporters generally acquire the information used in preparing stories about police violence? Does this influence what is reported?

NOTES

1. Police violence has been defined in various ways. "Most definitions, however, treat it as a type of misconduct and deviance. The term is used to cover a wide range of phenomena. Depending on the context, violent police behaviors are variously referred to as police abuse, assaults, brutality, riots, extra-legal or excessive force, deadly force, shootings, death squad activity, and torture committed by police officers" (Ross, 1995a: 223).

2. For a description of the later stages of this model, see Ross, 1995b.

3. All further references to police and crime reporters will be covered by the label "police reporters." It also must be understood that general assignment reporters can, from time to time, cover the police. Big (geographically dispersed) or complex incidents are covered by a team of these reporters. The newspapers, in particular, depend on a pool of general assignment reporters to cover a story from a variety of angles.

4. For a review of modeling in the social sciences, see, for example, Brodbeck (1959), Diesing (1971: Chapter 7), Pindyck and Rubinfeld (1981), Stogdill (1970), and in the criminal justice field, see, for instance, Bohigian (1977). This study is limited to big-city police departments and the local media that cover them.

5. Although field work by Ericson, Baranek, and Chan (1987) applies to specific news organizations in Toronto, it is not entirely generalizable to news agencies in other cities. Moreover, it neglects the newsrooms and personnel of radio stations. "In Britain, Canada, and the United States, their [media] influence is enormous. Police forces consider carefully the impact of their actions on public opinion. Sometimes, of course, this leads them to take strenuous action to mislead the public..." (Bayley, 1985: 166-167).

6. These cities were chosen based on proximity, familiarity, and comparability.

7. These factors and processes will not be explored in this model. Race was omitted from the media initiation portion of this model. This did not appear as a factor both in the literature I reviewed and the people I interviewed, most of whom were not visibly minorities.

8. This model is a modification of the one used by Ericson, Baranek, and Chan, (1987: 41), which in turn is adapted from those used by McQuail and Windal (1981).

9. According to Anne Murray, police reporter with the *New York Post*. Personal interview with author, August 26, 1991.

10. According to interview with author August 27, 1991.

11. In 1991, New York *Newsday*, for example, had five full-time police reporters.

12. See Ericson, Baranek, and Chan,(1989: 313-338) for a more detailed overview of these alternative methods.

13. For a cursory understanding of how this beat functions, see Bancroft (1967), Gieber and Johnson (1961), and Lovell (1983: Chapter 4).

14. Sometimes this is racially motivated. During the 1960s, "tensions created by blacks objecting to the treatment white officers were giving citizens...led to black and white cops pulling guns on each other in Detroit and Chicago" (Stark, 1972: 65). At other times it is a way of making another officer or officers look bad for office politics reasons.

15. All subsequent references to victims will include the understanding that they can be alleged victims.

16. This is also referred to as the good guy/bad guy reporter strategy.

17. By the same token, police organizations can use a variety of techniques to effectively control the flow of information coming to reporters (for example, Ericson, Baranek, and Chan, 1989: 140).

8

❅

Reflections on Crime, Criminals, and Control in Newsmagazine Television Programs*

KENNETH D. TUNNELL

Media crime reporting often is criticized, and rightly so, because of the selection and dissemination of skewed depictions of crime to the public. Research indicates that media coverage of crime consistently overrepresents, indeed, exaggerates particularly violent, random crimes; neglects to report that 55 percent of all murders occur between acquaintances; fails to report that about 93 percent of all crimes are property crimes; presents crime as entertainment; and groundlessly fuels viewers' perceptions that threats to them and their safety are growing even during times when crime rates have remained stable or declined (Bureau of Justice Statistics, 1991; MacGillis and ABC News, 1983). As a result, researchers conclude that crime in the media "bears little resemblance" to reality (Sheley and Ashkins, 1984: 137).

As the media overemphasize violent crime stories, the public's belief about the frequency of violent crimes has become incongruent with official crime rates. Heavy viewers of television crime and news programs are most likely to become "criminophobic," to distort the reality of violent crime from internalizing an image of a crime-filled world (Sheley and Ashkins, 1984) as they soak up crime depictions with "a can of beer in one hand, a can of mace in the other" (Rosenberg, 1995: 110). Furthermore, most Americans learn of crime and criminals only through the media, and television is *the* central medium disseminating stories of crime and criminals (for example, Barak, 1994a: 3). A

---

*An earlier version of this chapter was presented to the annual meeting of the Academy of Criminal Justice Sciences, Chicago, March, 1994.

recent National Crime Survey reports that 96 percent of the respondents relied on the news media to learn about crime and criminals (Flanagan and McGarrell, 1986) and that 49 percent of those surveyed believed the media gave the right amount of attention to stories about crime. At that time, more than 50 percent of news stories were of violent crime whereas only 6 percent of actual crimes involved some form of violence. It is not surprising, then, that 88 percent of people surveyed overestimated the number of crimes they believed involved violence (Flanagan and McGarrell, 1986).

Beyond finding these distorted images of crime in the United States, researchers have found relationships between viewing television crime stories and ideologies of crime and criminals. Viewers, for example, believe that criminals are psychological and social deviants; formal punishment deters crime; capital punishment is appropriate for contemporary U.S. society; prisons are rather lenient places of confinement; and that the U.S. criminal justice system is becoming "softer" on crime (Sheley and Ashkins, 1984). In part, the media are to blame for the less-than-real depictions of crime, criminals, and justice and are complicitous in fostering the dominant, albeit simplistic and individualistic explanations of criminal behavior (Barrile, 1984; Surette, 1984). Critics contend that such characterizations of crime and criminals groundlessly increase the public's fear of crime, do not depict those populations most often victimized, and focus on psychological rather than social explanations for criminal behavior (Surette, 1984). Although individuals' perceptions of crime are formed, in part, by their informal social networks and personal experiences with crime and victimization, the public's conceptualizations and their tendency to overestimate the pervasiveness of violent crime apparently are interrelated with the media's depiction of crime, criminals, and victimization and the public's increasing fetish for things criminal, including television characterizations (Tunnell, 1992).

A specific breed of television show, reflecting current trends in the commodification of crime, has emerged. The newsmagazine, a television program typified by its journalist-celebrities, usually devotes several minutes of coverage to a single contemporary and often controversial social event. In just a few short years, as if spawning, we have witnessed a plethora of such shows, and today each major television network airs its own version, which have only negligible differences between them. It appears that once the formula for the successful (read "income-producing") program was worked out, networks simply laid the blueprint for success in place and, voilá, produced their own newsmagazine clone (Rosenberg, 1995). Financially this makes sense. Newsmagazines are relatively inexpensive to produce. Each typically costs about half that of a dramatic or action program, even with such salary-commanding celebrity-journalist hosts as Dan Rather, Tom Brokaw, and Barbara Walters (Brodie, 1993).

The original newsmagazine program *60 Minutes*, which for years received the highest ratings of any weekly television show, celebrated its twenty-fifth anniversary during the fall 1993 television season and devoted an entire program to the reporters, their lives, and a sampling of stories from those broadcast across the years. This special program alone highlighted a fundamental criticism of this type of programming—the life of the newsmagazine journalist, apart from news, is treated as newsworthy. The success of *60 Minutes* undoubtedly left indelible impressions on the minds of programming and accounting executives because today, the newsmagazine is considered a vital part of the television entertainment industry.

Although newsmagazine programs typically present stories within a newslike presentation, their shows often are characterized as "infotainment," a term that describes the reality of this new breed of television show—part information (although the social relevance and selection processes are questionable) and part entertainment—in a contemporary, slick, sensationalist presentation.

Although a vast assortment of topics with varying degrees of social relevance are given coverage in the newsmagazine format, here I focus exclusively on those newsmagazine segments relevant to issues of criminalization, crime, criminals, and social control—that is, crime-related topics. In this chapter, I describe crime-pertinent stories presented in the various newsmagazine television programs—more specifically, (1) the types of crime, (2) the spokespersons, and (3) the dominant images of crime, criminals, and justice as presented through the interpretations and explanations of such spokespersons. To this end, the following newsmagazine television programs were viewed, whenever crime news was featured, during the 1993–1994 television season: *Day One* (ABC), *Prime Time Live* (ABC), *20/20* (ABC), *48 Hours* (CBS), *Eye to Eye* (CBS), *60 Minutes* (CBS), *Dateline NBC* (NBC), *Now* (NBC), and *Front Page* (FOX).[1] A total of 15 shows that dealt with crime-pertinent issues were viewed and are discussed in this chapter.[2]

The crime-related newsmagazine programs in this sample presented topical stories that I have categorized as: (1) high-profile and sensational crimes and criminals, (2) white-collar crimes and criminals, (3) crime control industry workers, and (4) crime control policy. These categories are explained in the following sections.

HIGH-PROFILE AND SENSATIONAL
CRIMES AND CRIMINALS

The vast majority of all crime-specific newsmagazine programs depicted high-profile crimes and criminals. Among this sample, nine (60 percent) were of the high-profile or sensationalist variety. Featured stories ranged from the beating death of a young Liverpudlian boy to the random abduction and murder of California's Polly Klaas, from the Menendez brothers to Florida's wave of random robberies and murders of international tourists, and from the New York City commuter train killings to female violent gangs. Other sensational accounts focused on such divergent issues as random child abduction-murders and a modern day Don Juan who knowingly infected his lovers with the HIV virus. Thus here, in this media format, as in media depictions of crime generally, we see an overrepresentation of sensational, exceptional, and violent crimes.

These stories, and others of the sensationalist variety, receive considerable coverage in the mass media and especially television (they are, after all, high profile) and receive the most coverage in the newsmagazine format. On one hand, it might appear odd that after news consumers have been inundated with media coverage about one particular exceptional story that newsmagazine programs would further expose viewers to yet another re-hash of the same account. Yet, on the other hand, because these stories have already been pre-tested on news-consumers, so to speak, newsmagazine producers and those in decision-making positions might recognize that they are risk-free and likely profitable. These might represent stories that are financially "safe" for newsmagazines, given that they have already sold well in media formats other than the newsmagazine. Thus, it is not all that surprising that corporate news decision-makers, recognizing the passing consumer interest in such stories, "strike while the iron is hot" and cash in on a particular crime while consumer interest is at its peak.

WHITE-COLLAR CRIME

White-collar crime undoubtedly played a part in the origination of the first newsmagazine television show—*60 Minutes*. Episodes of 20 years ago often featured governmental or corporate wrongdoing, although most analyses were individually centered. Now, even with the recent deluge of newsmagazine television programs, white-collar crime received little coverage among the newsmagazines viewed. Corporate media's tangential coverage of white-collar crime is not unusual because news in general pays little attention to white-collar crimes, especially compared with high-profile, sensationalist, violent offenses. This is partly because consumers have difficulty understanding and sustaining interest in white-collar crime stories; white-collar crime cases typically are not as sexy as violent, random one-on-one stories; and random, shocking crime depictions simply sell better than the do complexities specific to most white-collar crimes (for example, compare the O.J. Simpson case with the S&L scandal) (Friedrichs, 1996: 20).

Among those newsmagazine programs viewed for this study, three (20 percent) presented white-collar crimes. One story featured a form of professional white-collar crime by focusing specifically on an individual medical doctor who had made serious diagnostic and surgical errors with impunity as he successfully avoided censures from state licensure agencies. The second story dealt with corporations that falsely market and sell diluted orange juice to school children as pure juice. The third white-collar issue dealt with a governmental moral transgression rather than a crime per se. This program revealed that the U.S. government's reforestation program had hired illegal immigrant laborers and had provided shelter in labor camps that violate every human rights standard of proper and decent housing. Although these three stories were presented as white-collar crimes, those words were not used and, in the final analysis, were reduced to the wrongdoings of specific individuals rather than the result of potentially systemic or industrywide transgressions.

CRIME CONTROL INDUSTRY WORKERS

The second most common crime-related newsmagazine segment focused on employees of the growing "crime control industry" (Christie, 1993). Among the programs in this sample, five (33 percent) featured specific individuals and their crime control occupations. Two programs focused solely on individual police officers and their jobs or beats, and a third profiled a Palestinian police force that was to assume policing responsibilities in Gaza. The fourth program featured an individual entrepreneur of the growing private sector within the crime control industry—a bounty hunter of sorts who locates and initiates legal proceedings against "dead beat dads"—all for a 20 percent fee. The fifth program featured a Cuban-American and former Drug Enforcement Administration informant who claims the DEA reneged on its promises to compensate him monetarily and to provide other material and nonmaterial benefits. Except for this final story, none were critical of the criminal justice system and contemporary crime control industries. Most of these newsmagazine programs actually elevated crime control workers and presented their occupations as laudable, courageous, and functional, in a crime-filled, dysfunctional America. Because individual workers of the system are featured in such positive lights, little in the way of systemic criticism of such occupations, policies, or current crime control strategies emerged among these programs.

CRIME CONTROL POLICY

Three newsmagazine stories (20 percent) of this sample featured crime control policy issues, two of which focused on gun control. One program presented issues relevant to the Brady Bill, and another raised questions about the prospects of a handgun ban for juveniles. The Brady Bill segment aired one week after the bill's passage in the House during the period when the politics of gun control were at a peak. The handgun banning program featured the pros and cons of gun control, debated by a politician and a National Rifle Association spokesman, neither of whom made compellingly convincing arguments. The third policy-relevant story profiled aging, male prisoners and featured a university professor (the only academic appearing in this sample) who had implemented a program for evaluating and releasing "safe," older convicts. This story offered some insights about the "threat" that older criminals pose to society, the swelling populations of incarcerated men in America, and the need for making the best use of available prison space. Indeed, the professor participated, in part, in debunking popularly held images of crime, the limited threats posed by older criminals, the social and personal dysfunctions resulting from lengthier prison sentences, and empirical explanations for the swelling prison populations in the United States.

The next sections detail the coverage given to these crimes, criminals, and victims by focusing especially on dominant images and explanations and by describing who is doing the explaining.

CRIMES, CRIMINALS, AND VICTIMS

When we rob these people, they ain't broke. They still got more money than we do.

A FLORIDA SNATCH 'N GRAB ROBBER[3]

By far, most newsmagazine programs viewed for this study presented individual-based crimes— 80 percent of the stories presented individual-centered, random, stranger-on-stranger acts of violence. This finding is similar to claims made generally that "ordinary crime is not news. The news media present exceptional, unusual, and violent crimes" (Chermak, 1994b: 99). Those crimes that dominate Americans' thoughts largely because of media depictions are "not common crimes but the rarest ones" (Surette, 1995b: 131). Other than three stories (the Brady Bill, diluted orange juice, and governmental crimes dealing with immigrant reforestation workers), no attention was given to organizational crimes, social explanations for crime in contemporary America, or discussions of anything remotely resembling progressive crime control policies.

One component that emerges from such personal, individual, random criminal acts is the televised image of the criminal and victim. Not only did these newsmagazines describe the situational context of victim-offender relationships, but both victims and offenders typically appeared on these programs and were given extensive coverage.

The programs in this sample presented 19 criminals, 8 victims, and 8 family members of victims. The criminals comprised 5 black males, 3 black females, 8 white males, 1 Hispanic male, and 2 Hispanic females. Interestingly, 50 percent of the white males shown were white-collar criminals whereas 60 percent of the black males were violent offenders. In addition, of those featured, 25 percent of the white male violent offenders, compared with none of the black male offenders, were accused of killing for justifiable reasons or in self defense. Such images further perpetuate the dominant belief that young black males represent random violent offenders, and white males represent nonviolent, benign white-collar criminals. Furthermore, all the black female, Hispanic male, and Hispanic female criminals presented in these programs had engaged in violent crimes, further contributing to the perception that violent crime in America is overwhelmingly attributable to minority individuals.

EXPLANATIONS AND EXPLAINERS

Perhaps most important to an analysis of crime-related newsmagazine programs is unveiling explanations presented for crimes and, by logical extension, describing who is doing the explaining. Among the programs in this sample, three types of spokespersons were found—crime control industry workers, miscellaneous experts unaffiliated with the crime control industry, and federal government bureaucrats. In total, 56 spokespersons were featured in the sample's programs. Of those 56 spokespersons, 33 (59 percent) were directly connected to the crime control industry, 20 (35.7 percent) were experts of one sort or another but external to the crime control industry, and 3 (5.3 percent) were federal government bureaucrats who spoke in behalf of federal programs. Each type of spokesperson is described later.

CRIME CONTROL INDUSTRY
SPOKESPERSONS

They were freaks. This was evil torture. They killed that boy because they enjoyed it.

LIVERPUDLIAN DETECTIVE[4]

A trial is a production, not a search for the truth.

PROSECUTOR IN THE MENENDEZ BROTHERS CASE[5]

Perhaps it is not surprising that of the 33 spokespersons directly connected to crime control, the largest single group represented was police officers. Ten officers (30.3 percent of criminal justice spokespersons and 17.8 percent of all spokespersons) were featured as experts on various crime problems. Nine described conditions in the United States, and the tenth described conditions elsewhere. The nine consisted of six white males, two black males, and one white female. This overrepresentation of police officers has been observed by others in crime news construction as police consistently have been the primary sources of crime news and as they provide information "partial to their own interests and particular to their own version of crime" (Chermak, 1994b: 98; Fishman, 1981). Furthermore, although they might possess expertise in their narrowly defined occupations—law enforcement—they do not necessarily represent experts in the broader issues of crime trends, causation, justice, and crime control.

The second most represented group in the crime control industry was prosecutors. Seven prosecutors were featured (21.2 percent of criminal justice spokespersons and 12.5 percent of the total spokespersons) five of which were white males, the sixth was an Asian male and the seventh was a white female. The third group most often shown was judges. Three (9 percent of crime control and 5.3 percent of total spokespersons) were presented among those programs included in this sample. Each was male, two white and one black. Also depicted were two parole officers (6 percent of criminal justice spokespersons and 3.5 percent of total spokespersons)—one white female and one black female.

Included in this category, and equally affiliated with the crime control industry though not involved in crime control per se, were defense attorneys, jurors, and modern day bounty hunters. Four defense attorneys (12.1 percent) (one of which was a public defender) were featured on these programs. Of those, the public defender was a white male, two of the three private defense attorneys were white males, and the remaining defense attorney was a white female. Four jurors (12.1 percent) were also depicted; each was connected to the same trial, however—the Menendez brothers case. All the jurors interviewed were female, three white and one black. Lastly, three bounty hunters (9 percent) who search for "dead beat dads" were depicted—a white female, a black male, and a white male.

NONSYSTEM SPOKESPERSONS

That gun was bought in California after a 15-day check. So, even after all that, there are still problems in America.

TOM BROKAW, REFLECTING ON THE NEW YORK SUBWAY KILLER[6]

Twenty spokespersons who were not directly connected to the crime control industry were featured. Ironically, but reflecting perhaps the incestuous nature of media presentations of crime, the single most often appearing "expert" on crime was news journalist. Four journalists (22.2 percent of nonsystem spokespersons) appeared—one white female and three white males, one of whom is the host of the widely popular crime infotainment television program, *America's Most Wanted*, and who advocated Federal legislation ensuring that "predators of children...should never, ever be let back into society." A variety of other spokespersons appeared, each espousing his or her interpretation and explanation of crime, criminals, and justice. The various experts included one black male psychologist, one white male offender profile specialist, two white male chemists, two white male medical doctors, Jim and Sarah Brady (both white) speaking on behalf of the Brady Bill, one white female movie star, one Hispanic female AIDS worker, one white female planned parenthood worker, one Arab male peace negotiator, two white male National Rifle Association spokesmen, one white male governor, and—pertinent to recent calls for greater academic participation in newsmaking criminology, yet reflecting the lack of input in media dialogues of crime—a grand total of one professor, a white male (Barak, 1988; 1995; Tunnell, 1995b).

The remaining spokespersons were three federal bureaucrats—two white males and one white female. The males were high-ranking authorities in the

Drug Enforcement Administration and the U.S. Drug Administration, and the female was the vice director of the Food and Drug Administration.

CRIME, COMMODIFICATION, AND CULTURE

These newsmagazine programs, their symbolic communications, and their spokespersons are criticized on three grounds: First, the programs represent the increasing commodification of crime and crime-related consumables at the expense of escalating racial divisions and escalating fears of crime. Second, they symbolize, as they embody, cultural attributes and assumptions about crimes and criminals that nearly always are simplistic and individualistic. Third, they exclude social scientists' participation in newsmaking criminology and leave explanations primarily to crime control systems workers and journalists. The absence of knowledgeable criminologists, and especially critical criminologists, is striking for interpretations of crime: criminals and control are almost solely unidimensional. These three criticisms are developed in the remainder of this chapter.

These programs represent the further commodification of crime. Commodity exchange, or the process of buying and selling, which is unique to capitalist economics, operates by its own laws of competition.

> Commodity production, like all other forms of production, has its own laws which are inherent in and inseparable from it. These laws are manifested in the sole form of social relationships which continue to exist, in exchange, and enforce themselves on the individual producers as compulsory laws of competition (Engels, 1939: 297).

The motor of capitalism, of commodity exchange, is compulsory competition—competition that necessitates the creation of new needs, new consumer goods, and new commodities. In other words, commodity production does more than simply respond to consumer needs; it creates them (for example, Galbraith, 1978). Furthermore, commodity exchange depends on generating increasing numbers of consumer goods for buying and selling.

> And, in the course of seeking to accumulate more and more capital, capitalists have sought to commodify more and more. Since capitalism is a self-regarding process, it follows that no social transaction has been intrinsically exempt from possible inclusion. That is why we may say that the historical development of capitalism has involved the thrust towards the commodification of everything (Wallerstein, 1983: 16).

Thus, in this system that depends on increasing accumulations of capital, everything, including crime, is transposed into a commodity. As commodity production seeks new objects for buying and selling as well as new markets, the various dimensions of crime—as a threat, as imagery, as entertainment, as news, and as a challenge to defend against—increasingly are included in the production process and transformed into consumer goods, resulting today in the greatest variety of crime-related commodities in America's history. One indication among many of this new commodification of crime and criminals is evident in television networks' weekly scheduling and particularly the proliferation of newsmagazines.

Network crime programs as commodities are privately produced and sold; profits are expropriated from those laboring in their production (for example, Engels, 1906; Marx, 1939). But the new breed of television crime programs and the insurgence of crime-related consumer goods have further exploitative power than "traditional commodities." Not only are workers exploited during the production of these goods, but the very nature of crime newsmagazine programs further erodes social relationships and alienates the underclass and minorities because the majority of crimes depicted on those programs and that are, hence, in the forefront of Americans' minds, are violent street crimes committed by poor, inner-city, minority, young men.

Not only does the logic of capital and the commodification of crime explain recent increases in newsmagazine programs as well as the substantive content of these shows, but dominant cultural values found in the United States illuminate this phenomenon. American culture encourages competition rather than cooperation and community; America's dominant cultural philosophy is based on individualism and personal success (for example, Laur, 1989). Among the general public (and many politicians) street criminals are considered individual failures, and, as a result, serve as scapegoats for those offering simple, individualist explanations for the social problem of crime (for example, Sennett and Cobb, 1972). Such a perspective of criminal behavior, though focusing solely on individuals, leaves societal obligations unquestioned. As Reiman (1990: 124) succinctly expresses, such a focus "puts forth half the problem of justice as if it were the whole problem. To look only at individual responsibility is to look away from social responsibility." Not only do citizens, politicians, and the media focus on individuals and their criminality, but the crime control industry itself has such a focus and in effect "acquits the existing social order of any charge of injustice" (Reiman, 1990: 124). Americans historically have been intolerant of criminals and the poor, from which the vast majority of known street criminals are found. Few Americans believe that poverty or economic social problems (that is, those beyond the control of individuals) are reasonable explanations for crime. Criminal involvement, drug abuse, and economic problems such as unemployment typically are reduced to explanations of individual decisions rather than explanations that address the relationships between social forces and their effects on individuals' lives. The nature of these social problems typically is overshadowed by the assumption that individuals are responsible for their economic destiny and their contacts with the crime control industry (for example, Reiman, 1990; Tunnell, 1992).

Such simple, yet dominant interpretations of crime and criminals (which represent those among newsmagazines) also can reflect recent social and cultural changes in the United States. For example, during the past decade or so, widespread sociopolitical ideology has become increasingly conservative;

welfare and social service programs have come under increasing criticism; politicians "tough on crime" have become increasingly popular; and racism and racial intolerance have reemerged as minorities are blamed for the crime problem (Muir, 1984; 1991). These changes, coupled with the American philosophy of individual responsibility for crime, hinder the emergence of structural explanations that situate crime within larger systemic changes and explanations that would materialize if social scientists, and especially critical criminologists and sociologists, had greater access to the mass media and, particularly, the newsmagazine television program.

These types of newsmagazine programs, in light of the dominant cultural and social constructions of crime, represent

> The worst news, especially if one believes in communications theory which argues that attitudes and beliefs develop gradually in response to significant trends in media representation. Making these shows particularly dangerous is the absence of commentary by informed criminologists and other students of justice and social control (Barak, 1994a: 23).

Given such, criminologists, and particularly critical criminologists perhaps represent those voices needed at this time, but they have made little headway in gaining access to the media because, after all, crime control industry workers and news journalists dominate the analyses proffered in the newsmagazine format. Furthermore, within newsmagazines, fundamental questions are rarely raised regarding the drastically increasing numbers of prisoners in America, homelessness, poverty, the increasing militarization of the police, or any other crime- and justice-related issue. In short, critical criminologists' analyses, unlike crime control industry workers and news journalists, are heard rarely in mass media and especially in *the* medium—television.

The media—and as a result, most Americans—evidently dismiss progressive criminologists when they might be just those academics best equipped to explain various social phenomena and especially crime, by departing from solely behavioral interpretations. Working toward overcoming media bias and exclusion from public debates is certainly a starting place. But, this is no easy task, because opposition abounds in both criminologists' academic and social milieu and in the larger structural impasse of apparent media bias. In the newsmagazine format, critically fundamental questions are rarely raised and social problems are rarely explained from alternative perspectives. Newsmaking criminology encourages such and calls for greater participation in the propagation of more enlightened, sociological analyses within the mass media and especially within television portrayals of crime, criminals, and control.

DISCUSSION QUESTIONS

1. How does the author account for the proliferation of newsmagazine programs on television? Do you think the newsmagazine will eventually become less popular with television audiences?

2. Tunnell concludes that the segments about crime and justice on television news magazines do not portray the true picture of crime and justice. What distortions does he find in these segments? Based on your own viewing of newsmagazines, have you noted similar distortions in what is presented?

3. Who are the spokespersons, experts, and others who Tunnell finds are typically interviewed in news magazine segments? What impact does he believe this has on what is presented? Who would he like to see included among those interviewed? Do you agree or disagree with Tunnell about the need for "newsmaking criminology"?

NOTES

1. Public Television airs *Front Line*, *The Crusaders* appears on the Disney Channel. Neither was used in this study because they are not seen by the great numbers of people as the programs appearing on the four major networks (including FOX) are. Also, for a time ABC aired *Turning Point*, which was not included in this sample because it made its debut in January 1994.

2. This research, based on a nonprobability and conveniently selected sample, offers an exploratory examination of the newsmagazine program. The programs selected for this research were viewed during only one television season. The sample was compiled conveniently—when time and schedules permitted viewing primetime television. The programs might not be representative of newsmagazine shows during that one season, and furthermore, might not accurately reflect the newsmagazine format generally. Thus, drawing inferences from this sample to the population of newsmagazine programs is not advisable. Nonetheless, this sample is useful in generating limited explanations of the newsmagazine program and its media-generated assumptions about crime, criminals, and their treatment.

3. *Day One*, ABC, September 27, 1993.

4. *Day One*, ABC, November 29, 1993.

5. *Dateline*, NBC, February 1, 1994.

6. *NOW*, NBC, December 8, 1993.

9

✳

Forensic Journalism as Patriarchal Ideology:

The Newspaper Construction of Homicide-Suicide*

NEIL WEBSDALE AND ALEXANDER ALVAREZ

INTRODUCTION

Newspaper reports of crime constitute one of the many ways that culture is reproduced and transformed. Among these reports, articles on violent crime are the most widely read by the general public (Antunes and Hurley, 1977; Ditton and Duffy, 1983; Gorelick, 1989; Sherizen, 1978;). This cultural fascination with violent crime has deep historical roots, although its portrayal through the corporate print media is a relatively recent phenomenon (Surette, 1992: 51–52). The decisions of newspaper editors and reporters to cover certain forms of crime rather than others and to report those crimes within discernible stylistic parameters provide a rich substrate for sociological analysis. These parameters offer clues about the wider processes involved in the social construction of reality and, in particular, how popular understandings of crime become enshrined in individualistic and astructural explanations.

We begin with a definition of homicide-suicide and situate the reporting of homicide-suicide within the broader framework of the media discourse on violent crime. We analyze the content of 153 articles on homicide-suicide events from the *Arizona Republic*. Our analysis is enhanced by an interpretive exploration of crime stories. We conclude with a discussion of the ways in which what we call "forensic journalism" creates a discourse on homicide-suicide that observes systemic violence against women in a patriarchal society.

*The authors wish to thank Melissa Hickman Barlow, Jeff Ferrell, and John Hewitt for their helpful comments on earlier drafts of this article.

123

HOMICIDE-SUICIDE

Homicide-suicides are homicides that are closely followed by the suicide of the perpetrator. They occur relatively infrequently compared with homicides and suicides, and their rare and unusual nature renders them a particularly newsworthy form of violent crime. Typical homicide-suicides are perpetrated by enraged males, and the recent separation or estrangement of the spouses or lovers is a prominent precipitating factor. (Marzuk, Tardiff, and Hirsch, 1992: 3180). Their relationship was often characterized by physical or emotional abuse or both. Marzuk, Tardiff, and Hirsch comment,

> While some murder-suicides occur shortly after the onset of "malignant jealousy," more often there has been a chronically chaotic relationship fraught with jealous suspicions, verbal abuse, and sublethal violence. (1992: 3180)[1]

Currens et al. concur with Marzuk, Tardiff, and Hirsch and note,

> In 15 (41%) of the 37 cases in which the current husband was the perpetrator, the couple had previously filed for divorce (12) or was separated (3). In 7 of these 15, the wife had obtained a domestic violence protective order or restraining order from a court. (1991: 2063).

THE REPORTING OF CRIME

The News Appeal of Violence

In the United States, crime is a highly charged social issue that serves as both a lightning rod for political debate and a major source of social fear. As Chermak points out, the potency of crime has not been lost on newspapers (Chermak, 1994b: 95). According to Surette, articles on crime in newspapers are read consistently by a greater percentage of subscribers (24-26 percent) than other news topics (1992: 63). The least common forms of crime are reported most. Rarer forms of crime are newsworthy in part because of their rarity, but also because they lend themselves to graphic and sensationalistic reporting, which sells newspapers. Esterle (1986: 5) notes that murder, the rarest form of violent crime, is reported most often. In a similar vein, Graber (1980: 39–40) stresses that although murder constitutes only 0.2 percent of crime known to the police, fully 26.2 percent of crime news covers murders.

The Routinized Production of Crime News

According to Ericson (1991), the media enjoys a relative autonomy from its material owners (see also Hall, Critcher, Jefferson, Clarke, and Roberts, 1978: 57), but is strongly influenced by a production schedule that requires stories be easily constructed. The newspaper reporting of crime is therefore "routinized." To minimize production costs and maximize profits from advertising, newspapers engage in the factory-type production of crime news. For example, newspaper reporters often rely on readily accessible and low-cost official sources to confirm stories. This routinized relationship between the print media and criminal justice sources is well documented (Ericson, Baranek, and Chan, 1987, 1989; Fishman, 1978, 1980; Gans, 1979; Hall et al., 1978; Sanders and Lyon, 1995; Tuchman, 1973; Voumvakis and Ericson, 1984). This synergistic relationship serves the interests of newspapers and source agencies. Reporters acquire up-to-date information on crime that can be cheaply and readily parlayed into crime stories. In return, criminal justice and governmental agencies that supply information benefit from being portrayed as credible and professional sources and from having their notions of crime and crime control placed on the public agenda. As Cohen and Young (1981) point out, this type of relationship between media and sources results in news items that are primarily informative and that support the source agencies.

Media as Dominant Ideology

Several studies illustrate how crime news is a nonconspiratorial source of dominant ideology (Barlow, Barlow, and Chiricos, 1995; Chibnall, 1975; Hall et al., 1978; Fishman, 1978, 1980; Gorelick, 1989; Humphries, 1981). For example, Hall et al. (1978) deconstruct the media panic about "mugging" that developed in England between August 1972 and August 1973. During this period newspaper reporting of mugging emerged and became increasingly sensationalistic. The newspaper panic about mugging led to the construction of the young black male as the archetypal mugger who came to symbolize why British capitalism was in decline. In short, the mugger became a scapegoat or, to use Stanley Cohen's term, a "folk devil" (see Cohen, 1980).

Soothill and Walby's (1991) analysis of the reporting of sex crime in England also emphasizes the reproduction of dominant values by the media. These authors show that the newspaper representation of sex crimes adopts individualistic explanations that ignore or de-emphasize the importance of wider social structural patterns of disadvantage. The sex offender is presented sensationalistically as a monster or a freak. In addition, news articles about rape only report so called "stranger" rape and serial rapists. Readers are left with the impression that sex crimes against women are aberrant features of social life rather than criminal events endemic to patriarchal society. In addition, newspapers rarely contextualize the reporting of sex crimes against the systematic knowledge of academe. In particular, certain voices, such as those of the Women's Movement, are marginalized in the debate. The suggested solution to the "problem" of sex crimes is an increased "law and order" effort, rather than a battery of social reforms that empower women vis-à-vis men.

Crime texts relay information concerning death, bodily injury, and the forces of good and evil, so they offer "emotional hooks" for a large number of readers. "Emotional hooks" refer to those experiences that readers can relate to at some deep level and perhaps even project themselves into. Such projection, if it occurs, might result in readers being considerably relieved that their own lives were not taken or jeopardized. At a subliminal level, crime texts tend to convey the sense that crime and social disorder can be understood and explained at an individual rather than a social structural level.

DEVELOPING THE NOTION
OF FORENSIC JOURNALISM

As we will show, the reporting of homicide-suicide takes a different form from reports of muggers and sex fiends. Perpetrators of homicide-suicide are not portrayed as folk devils. We use the term "tainting" to describe the occasional process of "discrediting" or "compromising" the persona of the perpetrator of homicide-suicide. Tainting refers to the way in which negative aspects of the perpetrator's past are presented to sully his or her image. Tainted offenders differ from labeled sex fiends or what Goffman once called "stigmatized" (deeply discredited) individuals because of the much lower level of intensity of the media attribution. Although the reports of the events are somewhat sensational, they do not consistently contain the kinds of lurid detail noted by Soothill and Walby (1991) or the kind of factual exaggeration noted by Hall et al. (1978) and Cohen (1980).

The reporting of homicide-suicide follows a certain routinized formula that does, we contend, constitute a form of patriarchal ideology. The ideological impact of this style of journalism stems from its obfuscation of systemic patterns of violence against women. We employ the term "forensic journalism" to describe that routinized style of crime reporting that focuses on the details of individual crimes and the immediate situational dynamics within which the crime takes place. In the final analysis, forensic journalism tells readers more and more about less and less. The sharper the focus and the more details we know, the less we learn about larger issues and patterns. It is worth pausing to lay out some broader qualities of forensic journalism.

Crudely defined, forensic science refers to the application of the scientific method to the solution of legal or criminal problems. We use the term "forensic journalism" very specifically here. Our use of the term should not be taken to refer to the reporting of crime or criminologically oriented stories. Rather, our use of the term refers to a style of newspaper reporting that focuses on the minutiae of the crime scene rather than on the social context in which the crime is embedded. By analogy, we employ the term "forensic journalism" to refer to that stylistic coverage of violent crime that relies heavily on a pseudo-scientific ethos. That ethos explains violent crime "objectively" by describing the situational details of the crime scene. This "objectivity," informed as it is with the "irrefutable" logic and meticulousness of forensic science, imparts a powerful credibility to crime reporting. Just as forensic science relies on agents of the state to confirm scientifically the nature of the crime scene, so too does forensic journalism draw upon official explanations of violent crime. The accounts given by police officials figure prominently in these explanations (see Chermak, 1994b:110).

Police accounts of crime are "factual" and confined to the immediacy of the crime scene itself. Reports of violent crime will typically include details about the age, sex, and race of the offender and victim(s) and the relationship between the parties. Forensic journalism is imbued with an "investigative motif" or an "ethic of detection" that feeds off details such as who killed who and when, the location of corpses, and so on. The entire report is written in the language of perpetration and victimization. This linguistic style tends to anchor the explanation of the violence to the level of the individual participants. Reporters select material from police sources, but they do not select the conceptual framework within which the information is presented to them. In other words, reporters might decide what "fact" to publish and when and how to publish it, but they do not decide (without seriously disrupting their own routinized production schedules) to eschew the forensic frames within which facts are routinely presented to them. Hence reports of violent crime, as we have seen from our review of the literature, focus more frequently on individual offenders and virtually never on structural contexts (Barlow, Barlow, and Chiricos, 1995; Humphries, 1981).

On further reflection, we can discern three interrelated characteristics of forensic journalism: "situationally based explanations," "situationally based dramaturgical representations," and "internal myopia." "Situationally based explanations" refer to the routinized newspaper manufacture of violent crime stories that includes a common core of facts about the participants with which the readership can easily identify. We learn details about age, sex, relationship types, weaponry, and so on. Consequently, forensic journalism reports the details of individual offenders and the crime scene, but not social structural contexts.

"Situationally based dramaturgical representations" are central to forensic journalism. That this dramatic imagery often emanates from police sources gives it an extra edge of legitimacy. Imbued with the aura of forensic analysis (even if forensic science is only marginally used in the case in question), the dramaturgical details are elevated (blood, gore, and all) to a position of prominence. Forensic journalism tends not to "demonize" offenders or construct them as "folk devils." Rather it occasionally resorts to tainting them, if the appropriate information required for tainting is available. The sensationalism resorted to in forensic journalism is more constrained and routinized. The legitimacy of constrained sensationalism stems partly from its association with police sources and partly from the way forensic journalism conveys facts that for the most part are irrefutable. We might argue about the appropriateness of including details about how a murder victim was shot in the face with a 12-gauge shotgun, but it is difficult to argue with the fact that this was how the victim was killed. Once these gory details are in circulation, it is difficult if not impossible for either the press or the audience to discuss structural contexts without seeming to lessen the individual responsibility of the "guilty" party.

The third quality of forensic journalism that is worth noting is its "internal myopia." Although media portrayals of crime largely ignore structural explanations, they also ignore, or fail to explore fully, the implications of the patterns evident in their own history of reporting a particular crime phenomenon. For example, when newspapers write stories about violent crime, they consistently ignore structural patterns that are discernible in their own prior reports. The ignoring of these patterns might reflect the pressures of adhering to a routinized news production schedule. As we will show, however, the failure to explore patterns of gendered asymmetry of the homicide-suicide perpetrator-victim relationships that are evident in prior reports might also reflect the patriarchal imperatives of news production.

It is in the daily rhythms of forensic journalism with its language of perpetration, its pseudoscientific logic, and its occasional tainting of perpetrators, that we see a most insidious and nonconspiratorial deployment of power. Amidst the seeming objectivity, situational explanations, and dramatic representations of crime and criminals, systemic patterns of violence and their structural causes are marginalized or disappear altogether.

METHODOLOGY

We conducted a content analysis of 153 *Arizona Republic* newspaper stories on homicide-suicide events. These 153 articles represent an exhaustive listing of every news story printed about homicide-suicide in the paper from 1987 through 1994. Most of these stories concerned homicide-suicide events in Arizona, although occasionally national stories were covered. In 84 percent of the 153 *Arizona Republic* articles, the police were the major source of confirmation for the case facts. The majority of articles reported distinct cases, although within our sample were a number of repeat articles. These repeat articles covered the same case two or more times. Our focus is on the media portrayal of homicide-suicide, so we have treated the repeats as separate units of media analysis even though they refer to a case already reported.

DISCURSIVE PATTERNS

Table 9-1 shows the reported relationship of the victim to the perpetrator. Of the *Arizona Republic* reports of homicide-suicide, 79.1 percent of the events occur between spouses, lovers, parents, children, and siblings. This is consistent with the literature on homicide-suicides, which indicates that familial homicide-suicides constitute the overwhelming majority of cases. Within the "familial" category we find that interspousal relationships compose the single largest group of perpetrator-victim dyads (36.2 percent), followed by lovers (27.1 percent). Put differently, intimates (men and women in intimate relationships such as marriage, common-law partners, ex-husbands, boyfriends,

Table 9-1 Reported Relationship between Victim and Perpetrator in Homicide-Suicide Articles, *Arizona Republic*, 1987–1994

Reported Relationship		Total	%	Total %
Familial	Spouse Kills Spouse	64	36.2	
	Lover Kills Lover	48	27.1	
	Child Kills Parent	4	2.3	
	Parent Kills Child	20	11.3	
	Sibling Kills Sibling	4	2.3	79.1
Nonfamilial	Stranger Kills Stranger	4	2.3	
	Acquaintance Kills Acquaintance	5	2.8	5.1
Unknown[b]		23	12.9	12.9
Other[c]		5	2.8	2.8
	Total	177[a]	100	100

[a]Total exceeds *n* of sample (153) because some homicide-suicide cases have more than 1 victim and each victim is listed separately.

[b]"Unknown" refers to articles in which the relationship between victim and offender was not specified within the article.

[c]"Other" refers to cases such as cult killings in which the victims and offenders were both familial and nonfamilial.

and girlfriends) constitute the most common group of perpetrator-victim dyads (63.3 percent of all reported homicide-suicides and 80 percent of reported familial cases). These findings are consistent with the previous research about homicide-suicide (see Allen 1983; Berman 1979; Palmer and Humphrey 1980; Santoro, Dawood, and Ayral 1985; Selkin 1976; West 1967; Wolfgang 1958). Of the remaining familial homicide-suicide events, we find that 11.3 percent consisted of a parent killing a child, 2.3 percent consisted of children killing their parents, and the remaining 2.3 percent consisted of a sibling killing a sibling. Reported cases of nonfamilial homicide-suicide constitute only 5.1 percent of the all reported cases (2.3 percent are perpetrated by strangers, and 2.8 percent by acquaintances).

Given that the majority of homicide-suicide reports refer to intrafamilial killings, we examined "familial" cases more closely. Table 9-2 reports on the sex makeup of the perpetrator-victim relationship in reported cases of familial homicide-suicide. Fully 87 percent of all these intrafamilial perpetrators were adult males. In 7 percent of familial cases, the perpetrators were adult females and in 5.8 percent, they were children. In not one reported case did a female intimate kill her male intimate and then kill herself.

Table 9-2 powerfully illustrates the reported sexual asymmetry between perpetrators and victims present in this type of killing. The sexual asymmetry evident from our analysis of the *Arizona Republic* articles is consistent with the actual sexual asymmetry reported in the research literature.[2]

Of the entire 119 reports of familial homicide-suicide, only 8 (7 percent of total) reported a female perpetrator. In all 8 cases, the female killed her children. Child perpetrated homicide-suicides were just as rare in the *Arizona Republic* reports, constituting only 5.8 percent of all familial cases.

Table 9-2 Sex of Perpetrators and Reported Relationship between Perpetrator and Victim(s) in Familial Homicide-Suicide Articles, *Arizona Republic*, 1987–1994

Familial Perpetrator	Perpetrator & Victim Relationship	Total	%	Total %
Male	Male Kills Partner	96	81	
	Male Kills Partner and Child	7	6	
	Male Kills Child	1	.8	87
Female	Female Kills Partner	0	0	
	Female Kills Partner and Child	0	0	
	Female Kills Child	8	7	7
Child[a]	Child Kills Mother	0	0	
	Child Kills Father	2	1	
	Child Kills Mother and Father	1	.8	
	Child Kills Child	4	3	5.8
	Total	119	100%	100%

[a]Child refers to the young or adult offspring of the victim or perpetrator or both

Rather than use the language of domestic violence, or, more rarely, the term "woman abuse," the *Arizona Republic* reports are significantly more likely to refer to divorce, separation, estrangement, or breakups as antecedents to homicide-suicide events. Table 9-4 displays the reported antecedents to the homicide-suicide event and shows that 16.3 percent of stories referred to the couple being divorced, separated, estranged, or recently broken up.[3] The greater tendency to use the language of divorce and so forth to allude to relationship breakdown or dissolution may reflect that it is easier and cheaper for newspapers to learn of divorce, and so on than it is to include details of domestic violence or woman abuse. This tendency may also reflect the fact that this language of divorce, separation, estrangement, and breakup (as opposed to domestic violence or woman abuse) is more supportive of the myth of harmonious heterosexual relationships that has been well documented by feminist scholars. In other words, rather than just being a product of routinized crime story manufacture, this choice of language may also be a source of patriarchal ideology. We will return to this possibility later.

Marzuk, Tardiff, and Hirsch (1992) and Currens et al. (1991) show that many familial homicide-suicides are preceded by a history of domestic violence. Consequently, we examined the reports of homicide-suicide for reference to or evidence of a prior history of domestic violence, woman abuse, or other forms of relationship breakdown. The antecedents "prior history of domestic violence specified" and "no prior history of domestic violence specified," tell us whether or not the newspaper article mentioned or contextualized the event within the framework of violence within the family. Most of these cases (79 percent of our sample) were reported to be familial in nature, so we were interested in whether or not the reporting of these homicide-

Table 9-3 Reported Weapon Use by Year in Homicide-Suicide Articles, *Arizona Republic*, 1987–1994

Weapon Used	Total	%
Firearm	145	86
Sharp Object	4	2.4
Blunt Object	1	0.6
Other[b]	7	4.2
Unknown[c]	11	6.5
Total	168[a]	100%

[a]Total exceeds *n* of sample (153) because in several cases more than one weapon was used and each was coded separately.

[b]"Other" includes killings by such things as fire, poison, and vehicles.

[c]"Unknown" includes articles in which the weapon was not specified in the article.

Table 9-3 shows that in 86 percent of reports of homicide-suicide, firearms were used in the killing. This heavy reliance on firearms in homicide-suicides significantly exceeds the level of firearm use in the commission of both homicides and suicides.

suicides demonstrates the broader context of domestic violence. Only 15 articles (9.8 percent of the total articles, and 12.7 percent of the familial articles) referred to a history of domestic violence. In only 5 articles (3.3 percent of the total articles, and 4.2 percent of the familial articles) did the report specifically indicate there had not been a history of previous violence between the offender and victim(s).

From the extant research literature and the reported perpetrator-victim relationships in the *Arizona Republic* articles, it is clear that homicide-suicides are mostly perpetrated by men. Numerous studies also show that violence between intimates is mostly perpetrated by men against women and that when women are killed by men, it is usually the endpoint in an abusive relationship of long standing (see Dobash, Dobash, Wilson, and Daly, 1992). Given these facts on the sexual asymmetry of intrafamilial homicide, homicide-suicide and domestic violence,[4] we felt it was important to examine how many homicide-suicide stories reported a specific history of "woman abuse." Our intent was to determine to what extent the *Arizona Republic* reports captured, or at least alluded to, the sexual asymmetry of intimate violence.

Although we have no way of determining the proportion of reported familial homicide-suicides that were preceded by domestic violence or more specifically woman abuse, it is reasonable to suggest, given the aforementioned studies, that the majority of cases may have been preceded by domestic violence, most of which probably took the form of woman abuse.[5] However, as

Table 9-4 Reported Antecedents to the Homicide-Suicide Event, *Arizona Republic,* 1987–1994

Reported Antecedents	Total	% of Total Articles (153)	% Familial Articles (119)
Divorce/Separation/ Estrangement/Breakup	25	16.3	21.0
Problems/Arguments[a]	15	9.8	12.6
Prior History of Domestic Violence Specified	15	9.8	12.6
No Prior History of Domestic Violence Specified	5	3.3	4.2
Abuse of Woman Specified	5	3.3	4.2
Medical/Health Problems	22	14.4	18.5

[a]This category refers to articles in which it was stated, for example, that the couple had been having some problems in the relationship, had been seeing a counselor, or had an argument just before the killing. These relationship problems preceding the homicide-suicide event are not the same as reported domestic violence or woman abuse.

Table 9-4 shows, 9.8 percent of stories report a prior history of domestic violence and only 3.3 percent reveal that woman abuse had occurred.

The reported antecedent "medical or health problems" refers to those categories in which the article indicated or suggested that the homicide-suicide event was precipitated by some type of chronic, terminal, or painful medical condition. As Table 9-4 illustrates, 22 articles (14.4 percent of the total number of articles) referred to a medical or health problem that preceded and may have influenced the decision to commit homicide-suicide. We cannot assume that these medical cases did not involve domestic violence or woman abuse. Of these 22 cases, 82 percent involved a male perpetrator and only 14 percent a female. In the remaining 4 percent of cases, the perpetrator was unknown. With this small number, it is risky to make too much of the perpetrator-victim relationship. However, that men continue to be the perpetrators in these cases is notable. Likewise, it is important to note that in the three cases where women perpetrated medical homicide-suicides, they killed their children before killing themselves. In no cases did women kill their male partners before killing themselves.

In Table 9-5, we identify six components of forensic journalism that, when combined, give the homicide-suicide reports a sensational and astructural flavor. We found that 80 articles (52 percent of the total) described the weapon in detail. For example, we found that if the weapon involved was a firearm (as in 86 percent of the articles), the article often specified whether it was a handgun, rifle, or shotgun. If it was a handgun, the article often specified the make and model, caliber, and whether it was a revolver or semiautomatic. Even in cases where the details of the firearm were not provided, the newspaper still discussed firearms. For example, regarding a homicide-suicide in Algona,

Table 9-5 Elements of Situationally Based Dramaturgical Depictions of Homicide-Suicide Events, *Arizona Republic*, 1987–1994

Dramaturgical Elements	Elements	Total %
Specifics of Weapon(s)[a]	80	52.3
Location of Wound(s)	59	38.6
Location/Position of Corpses[b]	60	39.2
Horrific Portrayals of "Last Moments"[c]	56	36.6
Tainting[d]	24	15.7
Construction of Innocence and Tragedy[e]	26	16.9

[a]This category refers to the specifics of weapons, such as caliber and make of gun.

[b]This category refers to the specific location of the bodies within or outside of a residence and the relative positioning of the corpses.

[c]This category refers to the dramatic portrayal of the last interactions between participants, for example, screams, violence, and so forth.

[d]This refers to language that discredits the perpetrator.

[e]This refers to the portrayal of the innocence and worth of the victims and the tragedy of their deaths.

Iowa, the county attorney declined to speculate on the nature of the weapons used. However, one crime story noted,

> Sporting goods stores in the area were being questioned about recent purchases of .223-caliber ammunition, the type used in M-16 rifles. (AR, December, 31, 1987: A1)

The minutiae of the weaponry provides readers with the opportunity to reconstruct, in lurid detail, the heinousness of the injuries sustained in the incident. Including specific details of the weapon dovetails neatly with several other discursive themes of forensic journalism. Fatal wounds are brought to life through the imagery of weapon types. In a homicide-suicide in Mesa, Arizona, Elmer Lee Dean shot his wife in their backyard and then killed himself. For the readers' edification we learn that,

> Both were shot in the face with a 12-gauge shotgun. (AR, December 30, 1988: B5)

In another story about the same case, we learn that Pete Bowen, who lived next door,

> Heard some loud voices and then the thud of what sounded like wood falling to the ground. (AR, December 29, 1988: B1)

Taken together, news of the 12-gauge, the location of where they were shot and the thudding sound of wood falling, conjure up a lurid crime scene.

In about 39 percent of the stories (56 articles), the location of the injuries were specified. If there was more than one wound, very often each was described. As in the Elmer Lee Dean case, we must remember that the imagery created by describing the wound site is enhanced when combined with the other themes of forensic journalism.

"After finding each other amid Manhattan's tangle of disconnected lives," (AR, April 9, 1994: A2) Rick Varela killed Sarah Auerbach after she broke off her relationship with him. Both were financial executives. The language of forensic journalism situates the location of the wound amid a number of themes including the cunning of the perpetrator, the gruesome nature of the homicide-suicide, and the irony of the perpetrator's fall from success.

> Varela donned a disguise, followed Auerbach into a dry cleaning shop and pumped six bullets into her head in front of several customers. Sometime later, Varela shot himself in the head.
>
> Varela's body was found . . . on a park bench in the elegant Brooklyn Heights section, along a promenade offering a striking view of the Wall Street world where Auerbach had prospered. (AR, April 9, 1994: A2)

The location of the corpse can galvanize the attention of the readers and summon up vivid images of the homicide-suicide scene. In 60 of the articles (39 percent of the total articles) the location or position of the bodies was described. Such descriptions include references to whether the corpses were lying inside or outside of a dwelling and where the corpses were found in relation to one another. Vivid imagery was constructed through reference to the position of the corpses in a Mesa, Arizona, homicide-suicide case. Penny Marie Roberts was found by her parents in the bedroom of an apartment she shared with her boyfriend, William Ashby. Ashby killed Roberts then hung himself. The crime text reports that,

> Ashby was found hanging from a ceiling fan in the bedroom. (AR, June 16, 1992: CL10)

It is almost as if the reader is invited into the bedroom to gaze at the way in which the corpse of the perpetrator is still surveying the corpse of the victim. Again, in the lurid architecture of death, we find the geometry of domination that recreates or enlivens the crime scene. Forensic journalism is imbued with an "investigative motif" or an "ethic of detection" that feeds off minute details such as the location of corpses. The reader, in the space of few lines, is introduced to the hard (and mostly undisputed) "facts" of the case. In other words, the descriptions of the locus of the corpse, contribute more factual information that reaffirms both the accuracy and, more important, the authenticity of this way of understanding the violent event. The effect of such reporting is an astructural appreciation or representation of violent crime.[6]

In 56 articles (37 percent of the total), we find a heightened fascination with the "horrific" final moments in the lives of the perpetrators and victims. Reporters engage in a dramatic reconstruction of the interactions between the offender, victim, and possible witnesses and bystanders. This reconstruction furnishes the readership with yet more emotional hooks to draw them into the immediate "reality" of the situation.

Robert Mosley shot and killed his estranged girlfriend, Gloria Procela, and then killed himself. One news story of this incident reported the event through observations of eyewitness and friend of the estranged couple, Larry Jacquez. Jacquez provides rich and horrific detail about the crime scene and in particular the last moments of the victim.

> "She had her (car) window almost rolled up, and then he shot her," Jacquez said. He said Mosley shot her twice, then put the gun to his head and shot himself . . . Jacquez immediately ran across the street...Jacquez said Procela was alive for about two minutes after he got there. "She was moaning and breathing rapidly," he said. (AR, June 28, 1990: B1)

Horrific portrayals of the last moments crystallize most dramatically if they are conveyed through the eyes of a survivor who was also terrorized at the scene of the homicide-suicide. We witness such a portrayal in the case of Jose Delapena, who shot and killed his girlfriend, Ellen Bergsman, in the head and then took his own life. The crime story reads,

> Delapena . . . forced his way into Bergsman's home and ordered Blanche Cutlap, a female friend and co-worker, into a bathroom at gunpoint. Cutlap said she heard Bergsman begging not to be harmed and then heard two shots. (AR, August 17, 1994: A8)

The frequency with which the articles "taint" the perpetrators of homicide-suicide in some way (15.7 percent) is roughly the same as the frequency with which the articles convey a general sense of tragedy or selectively reconstruct the persona of the victims to emphasize their innocence or their essential goodness (17 percent). It is important to note that "tainting" is not juxtaposed alongside the "construction of innocence." In other words, there appears to be no systematic theme whereby tainting and the construction of tragedy or innocence appear in the same article. Where the two occur together they clearly reinforce each other. This reinforcement allows for the emergence of a stronger sense of good versus evil. However, the number of articles that show signs of both tainting and the construction of tragedy or innocence is small.

Greg McDonald Larrabee killed his common law wife, Portia Caton, and their son, Greg Michael Larrabee, in a murder-suicide at their home in Phoenix, Arizona. According to some neighbors, Greg McDonald Larrabee had

> Seemed a little disoriented at times. Nancy Horton said Larrabee once told her that he believed people were shooting gamma rays at his home and that the CIA was after him. She said she saw him on top of his roof about two months ago yelling about the rays. (AR, July 27, 1993: B1)

Another neighbor by the name of Wilburn is reported as saying,

> The dad thought aliens were coming into his home. (AR, July 27, 1993: B1)

This case typifies the tainting of perpetrators. In the Larrabee case, the discrediting of the perpetrator is mild. He is not portrayed as a fiend or monster or as a serious threat to the social fabric. The use of the language of tragedy and the construction of the victims as innocent or laudable individuals or both provides yet another potential emotional hook to lure readers into the spirit of forensic journalism. In a homicide-suicide in Phoenix, four people including two children were found dead. Their neighbor described the two young daughters in the following way:

> "I saw the girls all the time. They were always smiling and laughing and playing house in the back yard." (AR, January 20, 1989)

Our point here is not that the daughters did not play happily but that the article, and many others like it, selectively reconstructs the persona of victims, perhaps to evoke a sense of loss.

In the case of George P. Smith who murdered his ex-girlfriend Kerryn O'Neill, there is no mention of how these killings typically involve men killing women (often in the context of relationship breakdowns). However, there is a detailed portrayal of O'Neill:

> Everyone loved Kerryn O'Neill, the outgoing track star with the candy jar kept filled on her desk. Six months after leaving the U.S. Naval Academy with honors, the young engineer was restlessly reassessing her future. (AR, December 5, 1993: A28)

According to her grandfather O'Neill was "heaven." He went on to comment,

> She was always with a smile, smart as a whip. (AR, December 5, 1993: A28)

We also learn of her athletic prowess and her feminine beauty.

> She was about 5 feet, 5 inches tall and slim. After work, she commonly ran up to 12 miles each day, her long, dark hair pulled back off her face. (AR, December 5, 1993: A28)

In the space of these few lines we learn of Kerryn's "candy jar" youthfulness, her physical fitness, and her intelligence. In many ways she was the embodiment of success, and we also learn that she was "restlessly reassessing" her future. The article conveys a sense of her immense human potential and so amplifies the tragedy's impact. The emotional hooks go deep in this article because they emerge out of the multiple themes that culminate in the loss of a life with rich human potential.

In sum, a significant number of articles stress the dramaturgical nature of the homicide-suicide event, rather than social structural patterns within which they are imbedded. This is a defining characteristic of forensic journalism. Disguised as a simple recitation of the event, the articles in reality highlight those specific aspects of homicide-suicide that titillate, horrify, and appeal to our voyeuristic and baser desires.

HOMICIDE-SUICIDE REPORTS AS PATRIARCHAL IDEOLOGY

Feminist perspectives argue that women have been and still are systematically disadvantaged vis-à-vis men. Some feminists have explained the subordinate position of women in terms of the structure of patriarchy. Walby defines patriarchy as a

> System of social structures and practices in which men dominate, oppress and exploit women. (1990: 20)

It lies beyond the scope of this article to discuss the plethora of empirical studies that support the notion that women are systemically disadvantaged vis-à-vis men (see for example Walby, 1990), our main concern here is with patriarchal ideology, namely, that system of beliefs and ideas that justify or legitimate the power of men over women. These beliefs and ideas present existing patterns of gender relations as natural and inevitable. Patriarchal ideology operates in a number of ways in a number of different social arenas. For example, Ann Oakley (1981) identifies the way functionalist social scientists assume that the roles of men and women are natural, inevitable, and functional for "society" (in reality, men). More specifically, Cynthia Cockburn (1983) identifies the ideology of the "natural weakness" of women, as a means of excluding women from jobs as compositors in the print industry.

Our interest lies in identifying the ways in which the *Arizona Republic*'s reporting of homicide-suicide constitutes a form of patriarchal ideology. We do not argue that the representational processes of forensic journalism can be reduced to their effects in reproducing patriarchal relations. Neither do we argue that forensic journalism constitutes a form of patriarchal ideology that works independently of the wider routines of newspaper reporting or the material conditions within which those routines are embedded. Rather, we contend that one important effect of forensic journalism is that it conveys a misleading picture of homicide-suicide by framing those events in astructural ways that ignore systemic violence against women. To better understand this process of distortion, we must revisit our empirical findings in the light of the concept of forensic journalism.

Our analysis shows that the majority of homicide-suicide reports refer to familial homicide-suicides. In the majority of familial cases, the reports indicate that a male spouse or partner kills his female spouse or partner before killing himself. These findings from the newspaper reports closely correspond to the actual frequencies of homicide-suicide, which clearly show it to be a largely intrafamilial offense perpetrated by men. This correspondence also holds true in cases where medical or health reasons were reported as significant antecedents to the killing. Even in medical or health cases, we find men to be the perpetrators and women to be the victims of the homicide. However, the newspaper reports fail to acknowledge or even notice that perpetrators of homicide-suicide, especially the intrafamilial forms, are nearly always men. This is not surprising given the internal myopia of forensic journalism, which ignores past reports of homicide-suicide that clearly show a pattern of sexual asymmetry in the perpetrator-victim relationship. It is important to note here that we are not suggesting that newspaper reporters have Ph.D.s in Sociology but, rather, that they pay closer attention to their own patterns of reporting.

Familial homicide-suicides are often preceded by a history of domestic violence. Newspaper reports only occasionally allude to this history (9.8 percent in our sample) and rarely to a history of woman abuse (3.3 percent in our sample). Significantly, in only 3.3 percent of cases did reporters inform readers that there was no history of domestic violence. Although in many familial cases of homicide-suicide, domestic violence is a major antecedent, the press reports attach relatively little importance to it in their accounts of the event. In those cases where conflict in the relationship is reported, it is more often reported in terms of divorce, separation, estrangement, or breakup of the parties.

Although failing to indicate the sexual asymmetry of the perpetrator-victim relationship and the possible role of domestic violence or woman abuse as a significant antecedent to homicide-suicide, the newspaper reports nevertheless were consistent in their use of somewhat sensational language to describe the crime scene. This usage included a hyper-fascination with weaponry and references to the location of wounds, the relative position of corpses, and reconstructing the final horrific moments before death. At times newspaper accounts also "tainted" the perpetrator; constructed victims as vulnerable, innocent, and undeserving of their fate; and portrayed the entire event as dramatic tragedy.

We do not argue that press reports of homicide-suicide represent a deliberate attempt to ignore or obscure the wider power relations of gender. Rather, it seems reasonable to suggest that, as the state's premier newspaper with an average circulation of 365,544 (Monday through Saturday) and 573,497 (Sundays), the *Arizona Republic* is an influential source of information for its readers. Given the prominence of crime stories and the way newspaper readers consume these stories enthusiastically, it is also reasonable to argue that the forensic journalism of the *Arizona Republic* plays an important role in shaping the parameters within which many readers actively make sense of the world of violence and crime. Herein lies the power of the *Arizona Republic* to contribute to the social construction of reality. By using forensic journalism, the social reality of homicide-suicide is framed through the immediacy of the crime scene including the relationships between the individuals involved ("situationally based explanations"), the deployment of the language of drama ("situationally based dramaturgical representations"), and a failure to discern structural patterns of the offense in their own journalistic coverage of the past cases of homicide-suicide ("internal myopia").

Nevertheless, we cannot attribute the astructural substance of homicide-suicide reports solely to the institutional practices of newspapers. Within newspaper institutions, human agency is also exercised, and choices about what to publish are based not only on the financial exigencies of news production but also on the political orientation of reporters, editors, and newspaper owners. Our research therefore begs a number of important questions about the reporting of homicide-suicide. Is the "tainting" rather than outright stigmatization or demonization of perpetrators because the offense is rare and therefore not sufficiently amenable to press hysteria? Or, alternatively is it because the perpetrators of homicide-suicide are "family" men whose victims are usually wives, partners, or ex-partners, that the offense is not defined in heinous terms? Is it likely that we will ever see the same kind of hysteria about perpetrators of homicide-suicide that Jenkins (1994) has noted in connection with serial killers, even though there are more homicide-suicides than there are serial killings?

We must weigh the ideological imperatives of forensic journalism and its reporting of homicide-suicide against the agency of the audience. We cannot assume readers accept the individualistic or astructural explanations of homicide-suicide presented to them and assimilate them into their world view. In the absence of audience studies, it would be most inappropriate to suggest that the ideological imperatives of the homicide-suicide reports are monolithic. Such a suggestion would deny the complexity of ideology and ignore the fact that newspaper audiences are not homogeneous. It seems to us, however, that the representational outcome of forensic journalism is to convey an explanatory matrix, which in and of itself obfuscates systemic violence against women. Whether such an outcome is intended is an empirical question that warrants more research. In the meantime, in the spirit of what Gregg Barak (1994b) has recently called "newsmaking criminology," we recommend that press coverage of homicide-suicide incorporate more of the social structural context of systemic violence against women that are clearly identified in the *Arizona Republic's* past reports of homicide-suicide. Such a process of incorporation would transcend forensic journalism, debunk its objectivist and patriarchal posturing, and confront the internal myopia that characterizes the homicide-suicide discourse.

SUMMARY

We began by stating that violent crime is highly newsworthy. The reporting of violent crime is influenced by both the routines of newspaper production in general and the imperatives of certain ideological positions. From the extant literature on the reporting of crime we developed the concept of "forensic journalism." Forensic journalism refers to that style of reporting that stresses sensational crime scene minutiae over the social structural context within which that violence occurs. Newspaper accounts suffer from what we call "internal myopia" because they fail to look at and report social structural patterns evident in their own patterns of reporting crime. Using the notion of forensic journalism we explored 153 newspaper accounts of homicide-suicide appearing in the *Arizona Republic* (1987 through 1994). These accounts consistently fail to highlight the gendered nature of the perpetrator-victim relationships, especially the fact that men are nearly always the killers. Likewise, the reports fail to mention the well-documented role of domestic violence, or more accurately "woman battering," as a crucially important situational antecedent to the homicide-suicide. Juxtaposed alongside these failures is the hyper fascination of journalists with weapons, wounds, and the horrific last moments before death. Finally, we note that the perpetrators of homicide-suicide are rarely vilified in the way that serial killers are, even through there are more homicide-suicides than there are serial killings. We ask whether the "tainting" of perpetrators of homicide-suicide, as opposed to the "demonization" of serial killers, results from homicide-suicide being exemplified by the killing of family members, whereas serial killers murder strangers.

Finally, our analysis is based on our content analysis of newspaper accounts. We read ideology into the text. This approach is limited insofar as it ignores the agency of the audience in interpreting text. We recommend that more research be conducted about how readers of newspaper accounts of violence interpret them before more solid statements can be made about the extent to which newspapers espouse certain forms of ideology.

DISCUSSION QUESTIONS

1. What do Websdale and Alvarez mean when they refer to crime news as a "nonconspiratorial source of dominant ideology"? Explain why you agree or disagree with this characterization of crime news.

2. According to the authors, what formula is routinely followed in reporting homicide-suicide cases? Why do they term this "forensic journalism"?

3. How do the newspaper articles about homicide-suicide analyzed by the authors reflect "patriarchal ideology"? What is it that the authors say the newspaper accounts fail to relate about such cases? Do you think what is not reported in such newspaper accounts has consequences in public perceptions or public policy?

NOTES

1. Marzuk refers to the research of Allen (1983), Berman (1979), and Dorpat (1966) to support his argument. Without giving specific percentages, Allen (1983), Palermo (1994), Rosenbaum (1990), and Selkin (1976) argue that a history of dysfunction, conflict, and/or violence between intimates is a common antecedent

to homicide-suicides. Easteal's (1994) study of homicide-suicide found that 80 percent of the cases between intimates had a prior history of violence.

2. See Allen, 1983; Berman, 1979; Easteal, 1994; Palmer and Humphrey, 1980; Rosenbaum, 1990; Wolfgang, 1958, who all found males committed more than 90

percent of the homicide-suicides. Santoro, Dawood, and Ayral (1985) found males committed 78 percent, and Selkin (1976) recorded 85 percent of homicide-suicides perpetrated by males.

3. See also Easteal, 1994; Marzuk, Tardiff, and Hirsch, 1992; Rosenbaum, 1990; Santoro, Dawood, and Ayral, 1985; Selkin, 1976—who all suggest that relationship breakdown is a significant antecedent to homicide-suicide.

4. We prefer the term woman abuse to domestic violence because it unmasks the sexual asymmetry in the perpetrator-victim relationship.

5. It could be objected that the homicide-suicide cases reported in the *Arizona Republic* were somehow different and did not have the same levels of domestic violence as those reported in the wider literature. However, such a departure from the normal homicide-suicide case pattern seems unlikely. It is not our contention that newspapers maliciously underreport a history of domestic violence in cases of homicide-suicide. Although our assertion that the likely amount of domestic violence preceding homicide-suicides is underreported may seem speculative, it is a logical supposition based on the research literature. Clearly, more empirical research is needed to examine the relationship between domestic violence and homicide-suicides to determine if domestic violence is being underreported.

6. Although one possible rationale for newspapers only reporting the "facts" is that in cases of homicide-suicide, there are no involved parties left alive to tell the tale, this is never the only, or even the most important reason. Clearly, the events preceding the event can often be reconstructed through other family members, witnesses, and friends. In this sense, the reconstruction of homicide-suicides resembles the reconstruction of airplane crashes. Our point is that the reconstruction process is largely astructural in a sociological sense.

10

❀

The Role of the Media in Reintegrative Shaming: A Content Analysis*

KATHERINE BENNETT,
W. WESLEY JOHNSON,
AND RUTH TRIPLETT

INTRODUCTION

T he powerful influence of the media on the public's beliefs, attitudes, and practices is generally acknowledged. Indeed, some suggest that the media shape people's "very idea of themselves and the world" (Berger, 1990: 63). Some of those beliefs, attitudes, and practices are likewise very important to the process of reintegrative shaming theory as Braithwaite presents it in *Crime, Shame and Reintegration* (1989), a theory that includes "ceremonies to decertify deviance" (1989: 163). Criminal justice processes such as criminal trials have traditionally been considered types of formal degradation ceremonies (Garfinkel, 1956). Braithwaite (1989) expanded the notion of shaming to include informal processes of private shaming used by family members and other persons close to the offender. Recently, Benson (1990) addressed the news media's role in status degradation ceremonies of white-collar criminals. We believe that media coverage of offenders can play a role both in the ceremonial process of reintegrative shaming and its antithesis, disintegrative stigmatization or status degradation.

This study investigates current news articles about crime in an attempt to analyze the extent to which reintegrative shaming or disintegrative stigmatiza-

*An earlier version of this paper was presented by Katherine Bennett at the Academy of Criminal Justice Sciences Conference in Chicago, Illinois, on March 10, 1994. The authors wish to thank John Braithwaite for reading and commenting on that version.

tion is present in the news media. In addition, we analyze the content of news articles in an effort to define public perception of crime and criminal behavior as determined by what the public reads.

THE ROLE OF THE MEDIA IN SOCIETY

Researchers have claimed that the media have exerted "subtle influences on citizens' attitudes toward crime and justice" (Bouza, 1990: 235; Surette, 1992: 2). Surette notes that the relationship between the media and culture is reciprocal: Changes in one influence changes in the other, and the media are simultaneously affecting, reacting to, and reflecting culture and society (1992: 4–5). Gottfredson and Hirschi (1990: 35) have cited the media's emphasis on atypical and violent crimes as creating serious misperceptions about crime, both among the general public and among criminologists. News portrayals expounding social change or structural causes of crime are seldom seen (Surette, 1992: 76). Instead, the public appears to accept, and the media tend to present, portrayals of causation of crime as being rooted in individual criminals. The public and the media support a punitive approach to crime as the appropriate societal response (1992: 72, 76, 251).

Some media analysts believe that the media's role should be to provide the public with an objective representation of facts and events (Bender and Leone, 1994). However, the very mechanisms of objective reporting allow journalists to present their own biased views. Journalists can easily practice selective reporting, attributing their views to outside sources and omitting information that does not fit their slant (Bender and Leone, 1994).

Although the "power of the press" seems apparent, we also have to look at the import and power accorded to the press by society. Our focus is the importance of the media's treatment of crime. Most people learn about crime from the mass media (Graber, 1980). In her extensive study, Graber found that 95 percent of the people stated that the mass media were the primary source of their information about crime. The print medium, more than television, has been related to people's knowledge about crime and adoption of crime prevention policies (Surette, 1992: 9). Further, research suggests that print, being factual and analytical, tends to affect beliefs more than does television (1992: 96). Because the public rarely has enough information to form opinions independently on many issues, people are often at the mercy of the media, not only for information, but also for interpretation (Graber, 1980). Graber also found that media information can alter or reinforce existing stereotypes, even though people can't recall most media stories accurately (Graber, 1989).

The media and the public tend to support a punitive response to crime. One issue concerning the punitive approach is whether criminals are forgiven and reintegrated back into society. Punitive approaches are directly antithetical to recent criminological theory such as Braithwaite's (1989) reintegrative shaming theory. The next section briefly reviews Braithwaite's (1989) theory of reintegrative shaming and a possible contribution that the media can provide to this theory.

BRAITHWAITE'S THEORY OF REINTEGRATIVE SHAMING

Braithwaite describes reintegrative shaming as "shaming which is followed by efforts to reintegrate the offender back into the community of law-abiding or respectable citizens through words or gestures of forgiveness or ceremonies to decertify the offender as deviant" (1989: 100–101). Such shaming is different from stigmatization, which makes no effort to reintegrate the offender back into the community (1989: 101). Stigmatization often results from the punitive approach to crime.

Braithwaite theorizes that if shaming is stigmatizing rather than reintegrative, and if there is subcultural support for the outcast status, then there will be a rise in crime rates. The theory emphasizes the informal control processes in society that might hold criminal behavior in check. Reintegrative shaming theory "implies that punishment need be no more severe than is required to communicate the degree of community disapproval appropriate to the offense" (1989: 178). In discussing reasons why reintegrative shaming works to reduce crime, Braithwaite notes that public shaming puts pressure on parents, teachers, and others to ensure that they engage in private shaming (1989: 82).

Reintegrative shaming theory also predicts that "public shaming generalizes familiar principles to unfamiliar or new contexts" (Braithwaite, 1989: 82). In other words, new types of offenses arising from societal change are explained within familiar frameworks through public shaming. Social processes also combine individual acts of shaming into cultural processes of shaming, such as gossip and media coverage of shaming incidents, which are more or less integrative. These macro processes of shaming feed back to ensure that micro practices of shaming cover the range of crimes (1989: 104).

Western culture is characterized by Braithwaite as a culture that thrives on scandal and is unmoved by reform (1989: 163). Thus, shaming in Western society is more apt to be stigmatizing, or disintegrative shaming (1989: 101). Such a stigmatizing society, then, does "little to prevent cycles of re-offending" (Braithwaite and Mugford, 1994: 140). Braithwaite concludes that there is almost no place in Western culture for "ceremonies to decertify deviance" (1989: 163).[1]

The media are a potential source of shaming ceremonies. The media's role in degradation ceremonies that reinforce deviance through stigmatization has recently been noted. Benson, in interviews with white-collar offenders, noted that for the offenders in his study, the news media contributed to the degradation ceremony of the criminal trial partly by one-sided magnification of the criminal events (1990: 518–520). This exaggerated focus fulfills the first condition of successful degradation ceremonies: "Both event and perpetrator must be removed from the realm of everyday character and be made to stand as 'out of the ordinary'" (Benson, 1990: 520; Garfinkel, 1956: 422). Conversely, "communicative tactics"[2] can just as well be used to construct reintegrative shaming ceremonies in the media.

Shaming depends greatly on others' attitudes, perceptions, and behavior. Evidence suggests that the media can "indirectly affect the way audiences perceive, interpret, and behave toward the world" (Surette, 1992: 103). An examination of Braithwaite's theory indicates that because of the media's potential for influencing attitudes and behavior, the media as a tool for reintegrative and disintegrative shaming bear investigation.

METHODOLOGY: CONTENT ANALYSIS

Content analysis is defined as a "standard sociological technique which uses statistical techniques to make inferences about what is found in the media" (Berger, 1990: 91). This technique is usually based on categorizing groups of words in a sample of some form of communication (Weber, 1990). In our particular study, newspaper articles are analyzed and coded individually for evidence of reintegrative shaming and disintegrative stigmatization.

Babbie notes that the best approach in content analysis is to use both the manifest content and latent content. "Manifest content" means the "visible, surface content" of a communication, whereas "latent content" refers to the underlying meaning of a communication (Babbie, 1986: 272). If the coding from both methods is close in agreement, then validity and reliability are reasonably ensured (Babbie, 1986: 272). Some researchers note that a problem often encountered in content analysis involves finding a "measurable unit" (Berger, 1991: 27). One appropriate measure when doing content analysis of newspaper articles is to use column inches as the uniform standard measure (1991: 27). Such a method is inappropriate, however, for a predominantly qualitative study such as this one. Our research emphasizes the meaning of words and the nature of the articles, focusing on manifest and latent content.

We examined newspaper articles for both manifest content and latent content for indications of reintegrative shaming and disintegrative stigmatization. In analyzing the articles' manifest content, we sought verbal expressions from offenders or victims or both, victims' families, community, and offenders' families or friends that were shaming or stigmatizing in the sense that Braithwaite uses these terms. Braithwaite states that reintegrative shaming is nurturing and is more often the job of family and friends. These verbal expressions show that "even though the blow to reputation has been severe, the offender is forgiven and still accepted by her loved ones, and her loved ones are by her side to provide practical support in getting on with life" (Braithwaite, 1989: 87). Latent content was determined partly by the manifest content and was measured by a score given to each article reflecting the type of shaming in the article. The present research includes a preliminary study of a smaller sample of articles, giving us an opportunity to pretest the coding scheme for reliability. Discussion of the test of the coding scheme and some of the themes identified in the preliminary study follows. (See appendix for reintegrative and disintegrative words and phrases.)

METHODS

Preliminary Study: Testing the Code

The preliminary study, to test the coding scheme, looked at articles from one newspaper that, at the time of the study, was one of two major newspapers in the fourth largest city in the United States and the largest city in the South. The paper then had a circulation between 300,000 and 325,000.

For 14 weeks, we conducted a daily analysis of articles that were selected at random, based on a cursory overview to assure that they did concern crime and possibly more than "just the facts." The type of content for which we were looking, however, is particularly rare. Graber (1980) found that only 1.4 percent of crime news deals with the personality of the criminal or victim, whereas 56 percent of crime news deals with crime details. A search for crime news dealing with more than just details yielded 53 articles. Three individuals read and coded each of the articles separately. The articles were coded on such features as the number, gender, ethnicity, and age of offenders and victims; the type of crime covered; and the status of the offender. How ethnicity was determined was also coded, such as whether it was determined by a picture or whether ethnicity was specifically mentioned in the article.

We then met as a group to discuss our scores and to arrive at a consensus if there were discrepancies in scores. It was first necessary to clarify the code and to verify what the scale meant to each coder. We agreed on the following scale:

0: Factual, no evidence of either shaming or stigmatization

1: Strong evidence of disintegrative stigmatization

2: Some evidence of disintegrative stigmatization

3: About half and half stigmatization and reintegrative shaming

4: Some evidence of reintegrative shaming

5: Strong evidence of reintegrative shaming

Of the 53 articles, 6 articles were of such a general nature that they did not lend themselves to coding at all. Thus, a total of 47 articles were coded.

In verifying the reliability of the code, we were in majority agreement 43 out of 47 articles. Agreement was unanimous on 11 articles. Thus, the coding process appeared reliable 91 percent of the time. We disagreed on four articles. In the cases of disagreement, the articles and our reasons for particular coding were discussed. Consensus was then reached. The following discussion illustrates stigmatizing content in headlines and some content of articles that were coded as evidence of reintegrative shaming.

Several articles in the preliminary study follow the same offender and crime. The offender covered the most in this data set is parolee Raul Meza, identified in seven articles as "child-killer." Some of the headlines are particularly enlightening about the reception accorded Meza who had committed a particularly heinous crime:

"Meza: State Agrees to Allow Child-Killer to Live in Austin," October 2, 1993

"Austin Neighbors Don't Want Child-Killer Either," October 12, 1993

"Slain Child's Father Tells Town to Accept Meza," October 16, 1993

"New Round of Protest Against Meza," October 17, 1993

"Board Ends Good-Time Restoration: Would Have Prevented Early Release of Child-Killer Raul Meza," November 21, 1993

The articles recount how six Texas towns objected and demonstrated publicly against the parole division's attempts to place Meza in those towns. In addition, 270 halfway houses across the United States were contacted but rejected requests to place Meza. In a remarkable statement, the father of the child murdered by Meza said, "Let's move on and deal with the problems that allowed him to reach the point of being able to murder Kendra. . . . I want to say I hold no more grudges. I want the problem resolved. Enough is enough." ("Slain Child's Father Tells Town to Accept Meza," October 16, 1993.) In the same article, Meza referred to this statement as a "blessing." This article is one of the nine that scored a 5, "strong evidence of reintegrative shaming."

Four articles concern Katherine Ann Power, the "former fugitive and antiwar radical," charged with manslaughter and bank robbery in 1970. Three of the four articles received a score of 5, exhibiting strong evidence of reintegrative shaming. A relative of the victim suggested that Power has suffered long enough and that he was sure she had changed ("Power's Surrender Brings Closure to Sorrowful Case," September 16, 1993). Power herself remarked that she had to take responsibility for her actions ("Radical Fugitive Surrenders after Hiding 23 Years," September 16, 1993). Power also said that "in order to live with openness and truth rather than hiddenness and shame," she had to "reclaim her past" ("Fugitive Longed for Life of 'Openness and Truth,'" September 17, 1993). She received support from her friends for her surrender, who said that they admired her for "following through on her convictions" and expressed hope that she would return soon to her community ("Radical Fugitive Surrenders after Hiding 23 Years," September 16, 1993).

Sample for the Principal Study

Because of the apparent reliability of the coding scheme, a larger sample covering a complete year, January 1, 1993, through December 31, 1993, was then obtained from the other major newspaper in the same city. This newspaper has a circulation of 570,000 daily readers. Using the computer database, NEXUS, newspaper articles containing the search terms "probation" or "parole" were downloaded. In theory, institutionalization and criminal trials can be characterized as status degradation ceremonies (Braithwaite and Mugford, 1994); thus, articles about sentencing and criminal trials are apt to use more disintegrative stigmatization. Because we were particularly interested in finding evidence of reintegrative shaming in the news media, the terms "probation" or "parole" were selected, based on the supposition that reintegrative shaming occurs in the community. Thus, articles concerning offenders receiving community sanctions appeared to be the most appropriate unit of analysis. NEXUS yielded a total of 200 articles for the year under study.

Coding the Articles

In coding the articles, the original coding scheme was maintained, except one category was added, that of "N/A." This category differed from 0, or Factual, in that it pertained to articles that were about the probation or parole *process* and not about individuals on probation or parole.

For this sample, we were in majority agreement for 78 percent of the articles, or 155 articles. For the remaining 45 articles, we were able to reach consensus on all but 2 articles, thus leaving a total of 198 articles in the sample. Forty-two of these articles, or 21 percent, were coded as "N/A"; consequently, the following discussion of results concerns 156 articles.

Results of the Analysis

Table 10-1 displays the demographic characteristics of offenders and victims that could be ascertained. Both gender and age were fairly consistently identifiable. Race, another factor that could be important in the level and type of shaming, was not readily identifiable for either offenders or victims, and thus is not reported in the table. More articles mention male offenders and male victims than mention female offenders and victims. Males account for 79 percent of all offenders mentioned and 55 percent of all victims. We find that offenders' average age was 35, whereas the average age for victims was 22.

The number of female and male offenders is somewhat consistent with the actual proportion of male and female offenders. According to Uniform Crime Reports (UCR), males are arrested for crimes at a rate approximately four to five times higher than females are. Our findings show males mentioned as offenders approximately three times more than females are. On the other hand, the media are overrepresenting the amount of female victimization. According to the National Crime Victimization Survey, the estimated female victimization rate for personal crimes is 81.8 for every 1,000 compared with a male victimization rate of 101.4; for robbery, males have a victimization rate of 8.1 compared with females at 3.9; for aggravated assault males are victimized at a rate of 12.0 compared with females at 6.1. For theft, males have a victimization rate of 62.6, females a rate of 55.9. Thus, males are approximately twice as likely to be victims of violent crimes (excluding rape) than females and only slightly more likely to be the victim of property crimes. Our finding that females constitute 45 percent of the victims mentioned suggests a much higher rate of victimization than actually occurs.[3]

Table 10-2 displays the results of the presence of reintegrative and disintegrative shame in the media. More articles approached disintegrative stigmatization than reintegrative shaming: 43 percent of the articles used disintegrative stigmatizing, whereas only 12.1 percent of the articles were characterized as using reintegrative shaming. From this sample, it appears that about 45

Table 10-1 Offender (*n*=151) and Victim (*n*=101) Characteristics

Offender

	Gender		
		Male	120 (79%)
		Female	31 (21%)
	Age		Range 14–66
			Mean 35
Victim			
	Gender		
		Male	56 (55%)
		Female	45 (45%)
	Age		Range 1–74
			Mean 22

Table 10-2 Reintegrative and Disintegrative Shame in the Media

Shaming Score	Number	Percent
0: Factual	44	28.2
1: Disintegrative Stigmatization	14	9.0
2: Some Stigmatization	53	34.0
3: Half and Half	26	16.7
4: Some Reintegrative Shaming	18	11.5
5: Strong Reintegrative Shaming	1	0.6
Total Number of Articles	156	100.0%

percent of the articles were either factual or half stigmatizing and half shaming and could thus be characterized as unbiased. It could be suggested then that newspapers appear to present an evenhanded treatment in articles about crime about 45 percent of the time.

Past research has consistently shown that newspapers present an exaggerated picture of the incidence of violent crime (Chermak, 1994a; Graber, 1980), and this finding is further borne out by our present study (see Table 10-3). More than 57 percent of the articles coded concerned the crimes of murder, manslaughter, assault, or armed robbery and rape or sex crimes.

Table 10-4 shows cross-tabulations of shaming score by offenses. Of the 90 articles involving violent or sex crimes, 50 percent were characterized as using disintegrative stigmatizing, and 11 percent were seen as reintegrative shaming. The only article that showed evidence of *strong* reintegrative shaming concerned fraud; the other 18 articles in that category were classified as "some reintegrative shaming."

Table 10-3 Frequency of Types of Crime or Offense Covered

Type of Crime/Offense	Number	Percent
Violent	74	47
Rape/Sex Crimes	16	10
Fraud	18	12
Property	9	6
Drug	4	3
Other	35	22

Table 10-4 Shaming Score by Offense*

Shame Score	Violent/Sex	Property/Fraud/Drug	Other
0: Factual	16 (17.8%)	16 (51.6%)	12 (34.3%)
1: Disintegrative Stigmatization	45 (50.0%)	8 (25.8%)	14 (40.0%)
2: Reintegrative Shaming	10 (11.1%)	3 (9.7%)	6 (17.1%)
3: Half and Half	19 (21.1%)	4 (12.9%)	3 (8.6%)
Column Totals	90 (57.7%)	31 (19.9%)	35 (22.4%)

*Offense categories were collapsed into violent and sex offenses; property, fraud, and drug offenses; and other. Shame scores were also collapsed into three categories: factual, disintegrative stigmatization, and reintegrative shaming. Articles coded as N/A or related to criminal justice process were coded as missing variables.

Other cross-tabulations examined relationships of the shaming type by gender (see Table 10-5), by age of both offender and victim, and by the gender relationship between offender and victim. Although small numbers in each category prevented us from interpreting Chi-square tests of significance, several noteworthy trends emerged. Table 10-5 displays the results of type of shaming by gender of offender and shaming type by the victim's gender in 125 articles that identified sole offenders and sole victims (although not all these articles mentioned the victim). Of 57 articles characterized as disintegrative stigmatization, 86 percent involved male offenders. Ninety percent of reintegrative shaming articles *that identified the victim* had male victims; 58 percent of disintegrative stigmatizing articles identifying victims involved female victims. This finding was significant at a .04 level of significance and suggests that media coverage of criminal offenders is more likely to be stigmatizing when the victim is female. Likewise, when a reintegrative shaming approach toward offenders is taken and a victim is involved, the victim is almost always male. Again, however, thin cells limit the generalizability of these findings.

The younger the victim, the more likely that the article was characterized as disintegrative stigmatization: 62 percent of the articles coded as disintegrative stigmatization involved *victims* 18 years old and under. (Results not shown in table). On the other hand, almost all of the articles (71.2 percent) characterized as disintegrative stigmatization involved adult *offenders* (ages 19–50).

Table 10-5 Shaming Score by Gender*

Shame Score	Male Offender	Female Offender	Male Victim	Female Victim
0: Factual	26 (81%)	6 (19%)	6 (67%)	3 (33%)
1: Disintegrative Stigmatization	49 (86%)	8 (14%)	14 (42%)	19 (58%)
2: Reintegrative Shaming	11 (69%)	5 (31%)	9 (90%)	1 (10%)
3: Half and Half	14 (70%)	6 (30%)	6 (43%)	8 (57%)

* Percentages in this table are row totals rather than column totals.

Conversely, media presentations were more likely to be seen as reintegrative shaming when the offenders were either young or older than 50 years of age.

Finally, we found that when articles concerned male offenders and female victims, 59 percent of the articles were characterized as disintegrative stigmatization. This compared with 39 percent when both offender and victim were male. Once again, this is evidence that media presentations of crime are more likely to be stigmatizing when female victims are involved. Overall, these findings suggest that the media are more likely to portray criminal offenders in a stigmatizing manner when offenders are adult males and victims are female or very young. Such conclusions are tentative, however, and should be interpreted with caution given the small number of articles in this data set. Further analysis with a larger number of articles is needed.

DISCUSSION

Our study examined articles about offenders receiving probation or parole sanctions and thus is too narrow to counter Graber's (1980, 1989) assertions that most crime news in print deals with crime details only. However, the news media format might be changing. Meyrowitz (1985) notes that some examinations of media content suggest that the print media are adapting more to people's needs and the influence of television. Newspapers, according to Meyrowitz, now often imitate the type and form of information provided by television, thus describing events in manners simulating what one might have seen and heard on television. Descriptions of events in print are now more likely to include more direct quotes and accounts of individuals' appearances and demeanor. Whether these descriptions are objective, stigmatizing, or shaming remains to be seen. Our research certainly found more evidence of disintegrative stigmatization than reintegrative shaming and more of both than factual reporting.

One article in the preliminary study that seems to suggest that some tenets of reintegrative shaming are nonexistent in contemporary society discussed a 1993 study by the National Safe Workplace Institute. This study concluded that a significant dynamic in American society today is "the absence or ineffectiveness of certain social control processes," including a cultural system that promotes orderly behavior ("Workplace Violence Tied to 750 Deaths Last Year," September 4, 1993). This theme of ineffective social control processes occurs in another article, one which concerns juvenile violence and identifies a "bonding attachment deficit" in violent youths ("Violent Youths 'Would as Soon Kill You as Look at You,'" November 15, 1993). Such a deficit is attributed to the dissolving of families and communities. In this same article, a professor of social sciences, Beth Pelz, states that the country needs to reestablish the kind of bond with society and its values "so that when someone else hurts, you hurt." The theme of community responsibility is emphasized in another article on the same day, in which the Reverend James Lightfoot says that "We need to foster the old idea of community, extended families looking out for each other, and realizing the community must be responsible for its children" ("Black Leaders Say Answers Lie in Community," November 15, 1993). And on the following day, President Clinton is quoted in another article: "We have got to take more responsibility for these little kids before they grow up and start shooting each other. We have to find ways to offer hope and reconnect people" ("Armed, Dangerous, 9 Years Old," November 16, 1993).

News portrayals expounding social change or structural causes of crime are seldom seen (Surette, 1992: 76). The previous articles then are apparently not the norm but, rather, echo Braithwaite as he identifies social conditions that facilitate reintegration. Most important of these social conditions, according to Braithwaite, is a larger society that is characterized by cohesiveness, a sense of interdependency, and a strong family system (Walker, 1994: 232). Interdependency increases the effectiveness of shaming practices. In contrast, Braithwaite identifies factors that weaken interdependency, which include unemployment, breakdown of the family, and cultural diversity. Walker claims that Braithwaite has offered, "unintentionally," a "brilliant explanation of why the United States has high rates of crime and why neither punishment- nor rehabilitation-oriented programs effectively reduce criminal behavior" (1994: 232).[4] Factors that weaken interdependency apply particularly to American society, and Walker further observes that "given recent trends in American economy and race relations, social cohesion may be getting weaker rather than stronger" (1994: 232). The previous articles seem to support Walker's contention.

Graber (1980) is a proponent of change in crime coverage by the print media. She suggests that stories explore the origins of crime in greater depth, perhaps covering the home life, economic status, and work history of criminals and victims. Such coverage could provide solutions to the causes and prevention of crime. It could certainly aid in better educating the public and could use reintegrative shaming practices more fully. Braithwaite and Mugford note that in the reintegration ceremonies they have witnessed, "the more serious the delinquency of the young offender, the more likely it is to come out that she has had to endure some rather terrible life circumstances" (1994: 145). This information changes the picture of the offender to more than just a stereotype; witnesses see the offender as a "whole person" (1994: 145).

An example of what reintegrative shaming practices might look like in the criminal justice system might be the sentences imposed by Judge Ted Poe ("Doing Time in the Courtroom," September 26, 1993). This judge sentences nonviolent, first offenders to court time as one condition of their probation. The time in court is substantial: Monday through Friday, 8:30 – 4:00, for two months. The judge sees this time in court as a chance to impose structure and discipline and to teach lessons that he believes families, schools, and churches have failed to teach. One probationer, a drug dealer, sentenced to court time, remarks that he is "ashamed to be in court." Admittedly, this is one isolated comment, but that an attitude of shame was engendered in this person and reported by the person is nevertheless important because adopting the attitude of shame can be a first step in the reintegrative process.

Other articles describe programs whose policies might not signify reintegrative shaming as much as stigmatization. One such article concerns a movement on a national scale to track known sex offenders ("Experts Want National Registry to Track Known Sex Offenders," November 14, 1993). Records would be kept of where known sex offenders live, and communities would be warned when an offender moves in. Samples of DNA, blood, and saliva would be kept on file so that they could be tested for later crimes. Like Hawthorne's character Hester Prynne, such probationers carry a stigma with them wherever they go; indeed, the stigma follows their records in a manner far more intrusive than that envisioned by Hawthorne.

Recent charges of sexual abuse by priests have prompted a national outcry for the needs of the victims as opposed to reintegrating these offenders. Alleged victims have asked Catholic bishops to "change their focus from concern for abusers to concern about the needs of the abused" ("Alleged Victims of Abuse Asking Bishops to Focus on Their Plight," November 14, 1993). One bishop states that bishops see a need to be "evenhanded, offering concern and pastoral direction to victims, to priests, to all." This article, viewed in the context of reintegrative shaming, illustrates some of the difficulties with applying reintegrative shaming when competing interests are involved. Braithwaite and Mugford emphasize, however, that "effective reintegrative shaming ceremonies are victim-centered" and also address the victim's own possible shame and fear (1994: 155). They describe reintegrative ceremonies as practices that give victims a meaningful voice and *also* reintegrate offenders back into the community, reducing recidivism (1994: 139).

CONCLUSION

The media have been credited with providing 95 percent of the information that the public receives about crime (Graber, 1980, Surette, 1992), so the way that information is portrayed bears vigilant examination. Our study supports observations by others that the media generally apply more punitive and stigmatizing approaches to crime than reintegrative shaming approaches.

Graber (1980) notes that human concerns in the media only come to the forefront in the most sensational types of crimes or when prominent criminals or victims are involved. Chermak suggests that the media's emphasis on "celebrated cases and moral panics" contributes to distorting the public's view about crime (1994a: 580). This emphasis on atypical crime is discouraging for those who believe in the tenets of reintegrative shaming. Reintegrative shaming might not be appropriate for sensational crimes, thus leaving the media with very little opportunity to provide ceremonies to decertify deviance. Although a few articles in the preliminary study did look at the role that a disintegrating, fragmented community plays in crime causation and the need for communities to become more socially cohesive, such articles were rare. The principal study focused on articles about offenders who had received community sanctions and found that significantly more of these articles used disintegrative stigmatization in their content than used reintegrative shaming approaches.

The print media currently are sources for both disintegrative stigmatization and, to a lesser extent, reintegrative shaming. They still have the potential to be powerful examples of reintegrative shaming ceremonies. Braithwaite and Mugford (1994) term those reintegration ceremonies with juvenile offenders that they have witnessed as a "practical program of communication tactics that can accomplish reintegration" (1994: 168). Such ceremonies as they describe work at the individual or micro level, serving, it is hoped, to specifically deter that offender and even possibly other family members and friends. The media can function as other communication tactics on a societal, macro level, serving the purpose of general deterrence by educating a public within a reintegrative shaming framework. Reintegrative shaming theory's significance, in fact, lies more in its potential for general deterrence rather than for specific deterrence (Braithwaite, 1989: 119–120).

Because this study was limited to news articles in one city during a limited period of time, further research is needed. The reliability of the coding scheme suggests that such research can be conducted with confidence. It would be particularly interesting to examine the content of newspapers in countries with low crime rates such as Japan, a country and culture that does practice reintegrative shaming ceremonies (Braithwaite, 1989: 61–65). A replication of the current research using newspapers from smaller communities in the United States could also be particularly illuminating. The power of the media and their symbiotic relationship with society attests to the need for this and similar research.

APPENDIX

In coding articles as reintegrative shaming or disintegrative stigmatizing, the following evidence was sought. Words from the offender which were characterized as reintegrative were

embarrassment	regret	shame	sorry
guilt		remorse	sorrow

Words from victims, victims' families, persons in the community, offenders' families and friends included the following:

accept	harmless	pity	sympathy
empathy	love	rehabilitate	tolerance
forgiveness	nurture	reintegrate	understanding

Reintegrative phrases expressed by the victim, victim's family, offender's family, or the community were also sought. These phrases were

paid her/his debt to society

acceptance back into the community

welcome back into community

contributing member of community

hope for future (may be expressed by offender)

forgiveness by victim/victim's family/community

has problems enough without being punished more

has been punished enough

time to get on with life

Disintegrative or stigmatizing words were

fear	punish/punishment	shun
dangerous	reject	threat
hate/hatred	revenge	unforgiving

Disintegrative phrases included phrases that signified a rejection by family, friends and peers, or the community. Other phrases or expressions were

victim's/victim's family's fear for safety

others' fear for safety

not punished enough

threats by victim/community toward offender

desire for revenge by victim/victim's family/community

DISCUSSION QUESTIONS

1. What is "reintegrative shaming"? What is "disintegrative stigmatization"? What is the relevance of these concepts to criminal justice?

2. What conclusions do the authors reach about reintegrative shaming in media crime stories?

3. How do Bennett, Johnson, and Triplett suggest the criminal justice system might be modified to better achieve reintegrative goals? What function do they suggest the media might play in this process? Can you think of incentives for the media to focus more on the reintegrative process in reporting crime stories?

NOTES

1. An anonymous reviewer of this book alludes to religious activity in the United States as a form of a deviance-decertifying ceremony. Although acknowledging research addressing success of the repentant sinner model in Alcoholics Anonymous programs, Braithwaite observes that "the sacrament of penance, confession, baptism as a rite during which the sinner is reborn and washed clean of past sins, and other cultural apparatus which routinize the repentant role have withered or disappeared in the West" (1989: 162).

2. Garfinkel defines a status degradation ceremony as "any communicative work between persons, whereby the public identity of an actor is transformed into something looked on as lower in the local scheme of social types" (1956: 420).

3. One anonymous reviewer suggested excluding rape and sex crimes from the analysis and then comparing the male/female victimization ratio. When articles regarding sex and rape crimes were excluded, 52 males and 33 females remained in the sample, with females accounting for 39 percent of victims mentioned. As the reviewer noted, news coverage might be biased toward the presentation of rape and sex crimes, thus leading to an overrepresentation of female victims in the media.

4. Support for the concept of reintegration does come from stigmatic societies. Although public opinion surveys show persons to be "punitive and supportive of degradation ceremonies," the closer people are to individual cases, the more receptive they are to the offender's "signs of remorse and willingness to reform" (Braithwaite and Mugford, 1994:149). This finding does little to strengthen reintegrative shaming's place in the media given that media accounts are distant contacts.

PART IV

❋

Popular Images

During the first half of the twentieth century, real-life police women were few in number. But in 1946 to 1947, Phillips H. Lord (the producer of such radio crime programs as *G-Men*, *Gangbusters*, and *Mr. District Attorney*) presented, in conjunction with "America's crusade against crime," a program called *Policewoman*. The series concerned events in the career of Sergeant Mary Sullivan, who offered "personal comments at the end of each show" (MacDonald, 1979: 168). Sullivan was one of what MacDonald (1979) describes as the "realistic" detectives of crime radio. Elsewhere in the real world, another female law enforcement officer, Sheriff Lillian Holley of Crown Point, Indiana, gained her place in history when John Dillinger was lodged in her "escape-proof" jail (Nash and Offen, 1970: 18). Newsreel cameramen and photographers persuaded Sheriff Holley and Prosecutor Estill to pose with the gangster (Toland, 1963: 196). However, Sheriff Holley—who was serving out her murdered husband's term of office—took her duties seriously. The sheriff "buttressed the defenses [of her jail] with armed members of the local Farmers' Protective Association and a squad of National Guardsmen" (Toland, 1963: 209). Still Dillinger managed to escape. He drove away in the sheriff's stolen Ford (Toland, 1963: 216), leaving Sheriff Holley to explain what had gone wrong.

But for the most part, the careers of female police officers did not attract public or media attention. Not until the 1970s did women as law enforcement officers became a more visible presence both in real-life police forces and in popular culture. On television, female police officers evolved over two decades from *Mod Squad*'s Julie (the sixties' "flower child" recruited as an undercover operative) to *Cagney and Lacey*'s Chris and Mary Beth (detectives, partners, capable professionals). In the 1990s, female police officers are a taken-for-granted presence on television crime shows. In films, they have not fared as well.

The female police officer has her counterpart in the female attorney. Spring (1992) describes a 1907 film, *Down With Women*, in which the misogynistic protagonist encounters women in a variety of occupations, including an attorney who defends him in court (14). Despite this early appearance of this female advocate, no female equivalent of the brilliant trial attorney Perry Mason or of the dignified and virtuous Atticus Finch (as played by Gregory Peck in the film version of *To Kill a Mockingbird*, 1962) followed. On television in recent years, we have seen *The Trials of Rosie O'Neil*, *Sweet Justice*, *Equal Justice*, and, of course, the women of *L.A. Law*. Today's female lawyers on television are found as members of the ensemble cast of crime shows such as *NYPD Blue*, *Law & Order*, and *Walker, Texas Ranger*. Depictions of female attorneys in movies have been more problematic.

The first two chapters in this section focus on female police officers and on female attorneys. The last two chapters are about prisons and popular culture. Americans don't spend a lot of time thinking about prisons. Occasionally an event such as a prison riot or a film such as *Dead Man Walking* (1996)—about capital punishment—will focus public attention on prisons and what happens in them. Changes in penal policy also elicit passing interest. For example, a recent segment of the newsmagazine *20/20* dealt with Alabama's decision to reinstate the chain gang. But for the most part, unless we happen to live in a town where a correctional institution is located or have a family member or friend working or serving time in one, most of us tend not to know—or perhaps care—a great deal about the day-to-day routine of prisons. Munro-Bjorklund (1991) asserts that for many of us, our ideas about prisons have been shaped by events such as the Attica Riot (1971) or the politicalization of Willie Horton (see later). We might have also learned much of what we think we know about men in prison from movies such as *I Am a Fugitive from a Chain Gang* (1932), *Birdman of Alcatraz* (1962), *The Longest Yard* (1974), *Brubaker* (1980), and, more recently, *The Shawshank Redemption* (1994).

When it comes to women in prison, we have at one end of the spectrum Susan Haywood's Academy Award winning performance in *I Want to Live* (1958) and at the other end "sexploitation" films such as *Chained Heat* (1983) and *The Big Bird Cage* (1972). Faith (1993) writes,

> The one cinematic arena in which the stereotypes are thoroughly entrenched with little sign of changing is that of the low-budget women's prison movies. Prison movies have been predominately about men, and the stock characters in female prison films are borrowed from the male genre . . . (55)

In 1996, Sharon Stone starred in a movie (*Last Dance*) about a woman on death row. Unfortunately, it seemed a pale echo of *Dead Man Walking*, which had premiered earlier that year.

In the essays that follow, the contributors examine the neglected or distorted popular culture depictions of women as criminal justice professionals (police officers and lawyers) and of prisons, prisoners, and correctional officers.

11

✹

Keeping Women
in Their Place:

An Analysis of Policewomen
in Videos, 1972 to 1996

DONNA C. HALE

INTRODUCTION

From 1910 until 1972, women were hired by municipal police departments to handle cases pertaining to women and children. They were not permitted to handle patrol or criminal investigation activities. In 1972, women gained entry to sworn police officer positions by the extension of Title VII of the Civil Rights Act. Unfortunately over the 25 years since Title VII's passage, the percentage of women as municipal police officers has grown only to 9.5 percent (U.S. Department of Justice 1994: 294).

Why have the numbers of sworn women officers consistently remained low? Research on the performance of women patrol officers indicates that they are successful at accomplishing the duties of patrol (Abrecht. 1976; Bloch and Anderson. 1974; Charles, 1981; 1982; Grennan, 1987; Milton, Abramowitz, Crites, Gates, Mintz, and Sandler, 1974). Currently three explanations describe the slow growth of women as sworn police officers: myths, stereotypes, and the organizational culture of police departments. Balkin (1988), Bell (1982), and Van Wormer (1981), relate that myths and stereotypes—particularly those pertaining to the female officer's smaller physical size and lack of muscular strength—are used as justifications for why women can not accomplish the duties of a sworn police officer.

Police literature describes police work as a "man's club" (Charles, 1982; Jones, 1986; Milton, 1978; Remmington, 1983). Hale and Bennett (1995) indicate that the organizational culture of police work as "man's work" began in nineteenth-century United States; men were considered the most capable to serve as police officers because of their physical size. During that time, it was felt that only men could deal with the potential danger of street fighting associated with the nativism riots. The potential use of gunfire was a second justification for hiring men because gunfire was part of the fighting in the streets. Ultimately, the uniform, the badge, the baton, the bullet, and later handcuffs became the primary symbols associated with police work.

Over the decades, police work became synonymous with masculinity. The role of women as "policewomen" was defined in the early twentieth century to provide assistance to women and children who came into contact with the criminal justice system. The policewoman's role over time became synonymous with femininity and implied not fighting but nurturing and caretaking. Until 1972, the only positions for women included clerical, dispatch, traffic, parking enforcement ("meter maids"), or juvenile officers. As needed, women could be reassigned to work undercover in vice (gambling/drugs) or serve as decoys in prostitution operations.

Consequently, women were effectively excluded from sworn police positions because of stereotypes that women were not authoritative, aggressive, or physically strong enough to handle the duties of policing (Bell, 1982; Pogrebin, 1986). Once allowed to go on patrol in the early 1970s, women experienced various forms of overt sexual discrimination, including verbal (language, jokes, put-downs) and sexual harassment (see Fletcher, 1995).

Unfortunately, the myths and stereotypes regarding women as sworn officers is not just indigenous to policemen. These misconceptions are also prevalent in our society through the media, especially movies and videos. Macdonald (1995: 13) concluded that the media play an important role in "setting stereotypes and promoting a limited number of role models" for women (1995: 2).

My purpose in this chapter is to discuss how policewomen have been portrayed in videos produced from the 1970s until 1996. The films examined are those in which a woman has a predominant role in the story's plot. The basic premise of this research is that videos insidiously place women (and men) in their "proper" societal roles—that is, men as crime fighters and women as nurturers and caretakers.

ORGANIZATIONAL AND POPULAR
CULTURE: CONCEPTS AND APPLICATION

Strati defines organizational culture as

> The symbols, beliefs, and patterns of behavior learned, produced, and created by the people who devote their energies and labour to the life of an organization. It is expressed in the design of the organization and of work, in the artifacts and services that the organization produces, in the

architecture of its premises, in the technologies that it employs, in its ceremonials of encounter and meeting, in the temporal structuring of organizational courses of action, in the quality and conditions of its working life, in the ideologies of work, in the corporate philosophy, in the jargon, lifestyle and physical appearance of the organization's members (in Gherardi, 1994, 593).

Symbols are useful in gender study (Gherardi, 1994: 598) and apply to the study of policewomen in film. For example, the length of the policewoman's hair can symbolize either "masculinity" or "femininity" of the officer. Importantly, the police woman's use of weapons (guns, batons), physical fighting (kick boxing or karate), or her clothing (form fitting versus traditional male uniform) are all symbols of the policewoman's proficiency in accomplishing her official duties.

The predominant symbol associated with men and police is the gun. Weibel, in her discussion about why women had such minimal roles in television Westerns and crime dramas, suggests that many people might have considered it a "travesty of [a woman's] femininity" just to hold a gun (1977: 83). The women who became heroines in crime dramas did so without guns and used special skills of martial arts. Other women relied on their "feminine wiles," that is, their powers of persuasion and deception (Weibel, 1977: 88).

Gherardi (1994) notes that the use of sarcasm is important in gender studies. Symbolically, sarcasm by a policewoman is a way to counter sexist comments or attitudes of male officers. "Conventional femininity," according to Gherardi (1994) is a condition of subordination. Women, Gherardi continues, are "expected to be more personable, to display more emotion and to contribute, constantly to the power and status of others (1994: 604–605)."

The "male gaze" (van Zoonen, 1994: 870) is a another way to examine how women are presented in movies and videos—as a curiosity to be looked at by a male audience. This emerged out of recent psychoanalytic, structuralist, and semiotic theories (Kaplan, 1983, 2). The male gaze is the patriarchal domination of women to control and repress them through the male's controlling power over female discourse and female desire (Kaplan, 1983: 1–2). Kaplan claims that the male gaze "defines and dominates the woman as an erotic object," repressing the woman in her place as Mother (1983: 2).

Mulvey used psychoanalysis as a process to view films and concluded that "classic American film gives priority to male perspectives, both narratively, by giving male stars the more interesting roles, and visually, by making women the object of a dominant male gaze" (in Macdonald, 1995, 26–27). Mulvey further concluded that the female characters are filmed in a way that emphasizes their "to-be-looked-at-ness, and point of view shots within the frame are predominantly from a male perspective" (in Macdonald, 1995, 26–27).

But, Mulvey remarked,

> The visually stunning woman threatens to activate castration anxiety in the male viewer. Two strategies are used in American film to prevent this from destroying his pleasure. The woman is . . . turned into a fetish,

thereby distracting attention from her fatal lack of a penis. This might be achieved by draping her in furs or figure-hugging silk or, more dramatically, by placing a phallic weapon in her hand. The second tactic is to ensure that the plot narratively restores the threatening woman to her due place in the patriarchal order by the end of the film either by punishing her or by reintegrating her into a romantic relationship with a man (in Macdonald, 1995, 27).

Gamman indicates that when a film has an underlying theme that portrays the policewoman as independent and isolated in the male world of policing, the women are defined as unique rather than introducing themes of sexual discrimination (1989: 11). Her comment is especially important when observing films where the policewoman is either the senior officer in charge of an investigation, or is the only police officer. When policewomen are equal in rank with their partners, they become subordinate in their roles.

Gamman agrees with Williams (cited in Gamman, 1989: 19) that it is unusual for women characters to have roles as detectives that portray them as "'thinking' and pursuing 'knowledge' without overdetermined reference to their physical competence or conventional 'attractiveness.'" This occurs because this "type of plain straightforward and honest character (particularly in formulas that depend on excitement, movement, and conflict)" are often written out of the script.

Deputy Chief Inspector Jane Tennison in the *Prime Suspect* television series is an exception to Gamman's archetype. She is portrayed as a plain, straightforward, and honest character who does think and pursue knowledge. Inspector Tennison is the antithesis of the 1970s television policewomen including Angie Dickinson's *Police Woman* and former policewomen turned PIs *Charlie's Angels*. These highly sexualized or overfeminized television cops subverted the seriousness of police work and made it difficult for other policewomen struggling against sexual stereotyping (Clark, 1990: 132).

TIME FRAME ANALYSIS

In this chapter, I use Farganis' (1994) three-part time period developed to discuss the development of feminist theory. Her time frame conveniently parallels events that led to the eventual employment of women as police officers.

Because Farganis emphasizes that the three phases are related to each other and "that none is distinct and none abruptly ends and another begins" (1994: 25), I have extended the third phase to 1996. The period from 1993 to 1996 includes 55 films. Farganis' description of the third phase as focusing on cultural diversity, multiculturalism, and tribalism" (1994: 25) still pertains to the movies produced in this period.

According to Farganis (1994), the first period (1963 to 1973) begins with the publication of Betty Friedan's *The Feminine Mystique*, parallels the Civil Rights Movement and also was a time when the Women's Movement agenda was "to achieve gender equity through antidiscriminatory legislation" (Farganis,

1994: 23, 25). In 1972, Title VII of the Civil Rights Act of 1964 was extended to cover state and local governments and their agencies. This extension gave women the legal standing to enter policing as sworn officers.

Farganis' second period (1973 to 1983) "was a shift away from the talk of rights and analyses of legal discrimination and toward an examination of women's experiences, emotions, and feelings," or "seeing the world through a woman's eyes" (1994: 23). The women's movement encouraged women to take possession of their own sexuality (Kaplan, 1983: 7). Farganis emphasizes that the second period focused on gender traits.

The third phase—1983 to 1993—concentrates on the diversity and variety of women's lives (Farganis, 1994: 24). This period deals with "cultural diversity, multiculturalism, and tribalism" (1994: 25).

METHODOLOGY

Three classes of undergraduate students (two freshman introduction to criminal justice classes and one upper class police operations and management class) were assigned to go to local video stores and locate films about women as police officers, not as private investigators. Students were told to locate these films by reading the backs of the video boxes for descriptions. The titles of the videos were compared with a list of videos that I had compiled by perusing the video guide books, as well as through snowball sampling whereby local video employees informed the author about videos that they either received as previews or that they knew portrayed women as police officers.

From this procedure, 121 films (see Appendix) were located. The year of production and respective genres of the film were verified in Martin and Porter's *Video Movie Guide 1996.*

Each student was assigned a video and asked to view the film and to complete a 7-page coding instrument. I also viewed and coded the same videos. Comparison between the two instruments showed strong agreement about the way the videos were viewed.

This chapter provides an overview of how videos illustrate women's roles in policing and also explains, through examples from representative videos, how myths and stereotypes relegate policewomen to traditional roles or places. This is accomplished in the videos by (1) the manner in which the woman is dressed (conservatively or in silks and furs); (2) the length of her hair; (3) the policewoman's misuse of a weapon, usually the gun; and, (4) in the final scene the police woman is either involved romantically with her partner, is injured, or slain in the line of duty.

Film Analysis

For Period I, 1963 to 1973, only one video, *Fuzz*, (1972) that featured a woman in policing was located. This movie starred Raquel Welch as Detective Eileen McHenry who played a decoy in a rape investigation. This role would not have been perceived unusual for policewomen because during this period television audiences were accustomed to the role of policewomen as decoys and assistants to male officers (Rose, 1985). This portrayal also supports Haskell's observation that the films of the 1960s and the early 1970s reflected "a steady deterioration of the role of women on screen, until eventually, in some films, women disappear altogether" (Fishburn, 1982: 140).

For the second period, 1973 to 1983, only nine videos were located. These films include *Cleopatra Jones and the Casino of Gold* (1975), *The Enforcer* (1976), *No Mercy* (1977), and *The Black Marble* (1980). Weibel reports that the roles of women as police officers during this time period was "subsidiary, and they were shown doing much less real police work than their counterparts on television" (1988: 88).

Cleopatra Jones and the Casino of Gold (1975) is a sequel to *Cleopatra Jones* (1973) that again stars Tamara Dobson as a U.S. Special Agent sent to close down a drug empire run by another woman. Cleopatra Jones is especially notable because she is 6' 2" tall and is noted for her physical prowess.

The Enforcer (1976) stars Tyne Daly as Inspector Kate Moore who is the partner of Harry Callahan in the third of the *Dirty Harry* series. This movie is the first to introduce a woman who is promoted to an Inspector after serving nine years in the personnel and records division (civilian duties). This film vividly portrays sexual harassment of a woman who is a police officer. She is also put in her place because she dies in a shoot-out at the end of the movie after she warns Harry that he is about to be shot. She apologizes as she dies. Her death makes her acceptable as a police officer: She risked her life to save her partner's.

No Mercy (1977) stars Michele Pfeiffer as Officer Samantha Jensen who is portrayed as a "side-kick" to two male police officers. She wears civilian clothes (generally pink), and has long blond hair. She is referred to as "Tater-Pie" "Babe," "Honey," and "Sunshine." Her responsibilities include answering the telephone, working as a dispatcher and making arrangements for the captain's wife's car to be washed. At the end, she is shown laughing with her two "side-kicks."

The Black Marble (1980) is based on a Joseph Wambaugh novel in which a male homicide detective, Valnacoff, who has a drinking problem, is assigned a new female partner, Natalie, by the department. She was primarily reassigned to look out for him while on duty. Eventually, she sleeps with him and the movie ends with them kissing.

Police Academy (1984) is similar to *The Enforcer* (1976) because in the very beginning of both movies it is stated that women and minorities are entering police work because of affirmative action legislation. In *Police Academy*, minorities and women, as well as small and large men, and men and women in instructor roles in the academy are clearly evident, illustrating the impact of Title VII's passage.

Forty-six percent (56 of 121) of the videos showing policewomen were produced in the third period—1983–1993. During this period comedies including *Police Academy* (1984), *Night Patrol* (1985), and *Vice Academy* (1988) lampooned the role of women as police officers. They were clearly "put in their place" by their depictions as either scatter-brained, naive, or sex objects presented for the male gaze.

During Period III several films were produced that many individuals still recall. *RoboCop* (1987), *Kindergarten Cop* (1990), *Blue Steel* (1990), *Internal Affairs* (1990), and *Silence of the Lambs* (1991) have all become part of the popular culture of video audiences.

The last period (1993 to 1996) covers four years during which 45 percent of our total sample of videos was produced—similar in quantity (46 percent) to the 10-year span of Period III (1983 to 1993). Undoubtedly, the two most popular films of this last period are *In the Line of Fire* (1993) and *Copycat* (1995). Several films were produced in 1996, including *Fargo*, *Sabotage*, and *Broken Arrow*.[1]

The chapter appendix identifies the movies by title, year of production, and rating. The next section highlights films that illustrate women's roles in policing.

Women as Patrol Officers

Jamie Lee Curtis stars as Megan Turner in *Blue Steel* (1990). She is a New York City police rookie who intervenes in a grocery store robbery and, during the apprehension, shoots the robber who refuses to drop his gun. She empties her gun into his body, and his gun flies across the room, landing on the floor by a male customer, Eugene, who has been ordered to the floor by the robber. Eugene slips the gun into his jacket and does not turn it in during the investigation of the robbery by the police department. Because the robber's gun was not found, Turner's supervisor puts her on indefinite suspension because of her questionable use of deadly force. Later when victims are found shot with bullets from the missing robber's gun, Detective Nick Mann (note his surname "Mann") of Homicide is temporarily assigned to be her supervisor. The police department believes this action will give her high visibility and protection from whoever is killing individuals with the missing gun. The department is concerned because each one of the bullets found in the victims' bodies has "Megan Turner" etched on it.

Blue Steel (1990) portrays Turner as an attractive young woman with short hair who makes a mistake when she intervenes in the robbery without backup, almost gets her supervisor Nick Mann killed, and later ends up in a sexual relationship with him. At the end, she once again makes a decision to shoot that will undoubtedly place her on suspension again while yet another investigation is conducted.

The Ambulance (1993) is also set in the New York City Police Department with patrol officer Sandra Malloy. She first appears in the blue uniform with tight pants, blue shirt sleeves rolled up, tie, badge, but with no gun on her hip. Her long red hair is pulled back and braided. When asked by the main character, a civilian named Eric Roberts, why an attractive woman like her wants to be a police officer, she responds that with "a badge and a gun you don't feel like a victim anymore." Once she decides to help him in his search for a missing woman, she appears in street clothes with her hair loose on her shoulders. On one occasion, he asks her where she keeps her gun in that outfit.

Officer Malloy is shown early in the movie as a nurturing, caring individual. She has assumed personal responsibility to assist the lieutenant who has had a nervous breakdown by reminding him of his dental appointment and insurance due date. She also decides to help Roberts, who comes to the police to report the abduction of a young girl from the street by men in an unidentified ambulance. Malloy does use a gun in the club/bar called The Vintage. She is informed by the department that she will lose her badge for discharging her gun in a crowded room. She discovers the young woman and others in a room above The Vintage. After these individuals are rescued, Malloy is complimented by another officer for making the discovery. Later she is grabbed from behind by one of the ambulance criminals who is dressed as a police officer. Although she does use physical force to escape from the man who has her by the neck, her physical agility is marred by the intervention of an old man who hits the suspect with a bed pan and saves her.

In the closing scene, Malloy and Roberts are going back to his apartment to "get between the sheets" where he will recuperate, and she will save him from future attacks. The "mad doctor" returns in the ambulance, runs over her, and Roberts (a civilian) saves the day by leading the ambulance into a pit. At the end, both are injured and in the ambulance trying to kiss. He says to her, "you are beautiful."

This movie parallels *Taking the Heat* (1993), which portrays a black policewoman who is a uniformed officer in the first scene, but has been promoted in the next scene. Much to her disdain she is assigned by her superior to protect a witness who is testifying against an organized crime figure in a homicide case. The police officer and the civilian spend most of the movie avoiding the criminals who want to kill him before he gets to the courthouse. Similar to the situation in *The Ambulance*, the civilian man takes charge and directs the woman officer about how to get away from the "bad guys." At the end of the movie, the policewoman and the civilian are in bed together.

Also paralleling these two videos is the comedy *Exit to Eden* (1994) where the undercover male and female team are investigating a sex spa. This movie is very stereotypical. The women have very strong roles and are in positions of "authority" over men. At the end, the woman police officer tells the viewing audience that the man who had been her "slave" at the health spa is someone she is now dating. The second strong woman, the dominatrix, also leaves her profession to get married.

These three movies each portray women in stereotypical fashion with each policewoman having her position as a police officer diminished by her romantic involvement with a man at the end of the movie. In these three movies, the men that the policewomen become involved with are civilians rather than police officers. Except for *Exit to Eden*, these movies portray men as protecting the policewomen—the chivalry factor.

Women as Police Detectives

Above the Law (1988) stars Pam Grier as Delores "Jacks" Jackson. She and her partner are assigned to vice. Similarly to Officer Kate Moore in *The Enforcer*, Jacks saves her partner's life when she sees a shooter and calls out warning her partner, thus saving his life. Her partner, Nikko, is very protective of her and at times tells her to stay in the car while he goes out to pursue incidents. On the first occasion, Jacks says to him "I'm not a rookie; I'll do what I have to do." On a second occasion when he tells her, "In no circumstances come out of the car, just stay here," she looks uncomfortable but stays in the car in the alley until she hears shots. Then she gets out of the car and gets shot in a stairwell. But she survives because she was wearing a bullet-proof vest. At the hospital, her major concern is wondering where Nikko is. At the end of the movie, he receives a commendation for his police work, and she is seated in the audience with her arm in a sling.

Jacks is portrayed as a member of her partner's immediate family. He is very protective of her throughout the movie. Although she ignores his instructions to stay in the car and is shot, she survives. Unlike the policewomen in other films, there are few stereotypical images of her. She is a recent law school graduate, and we learn at the beginning of the movie that in eight days she will begin working for the local district attorney's office. She is not put in her proper place by myths, stereotypes, and the male gaze because she is leaving policing.

Another movie produced in 1988 was *L.A. Crackdown 2* featuring Pamela Dixon as Officer Karen Shore. In the beginning she is portrayed as a patrol officer in uniform with badge and gun, and she has a female partner. She is later reassigned to a new partner, Jamie, so they can pose as undercover dance girls. Karen pursues the criminal, Michael, up to the roof where she confronts and shoots him. The police arrive and place her under arrest because she shot an unarmed man. Karen physically fights off the arresting officers and kicks Michael off the roof to his death. At the end, she is led off in cuffs.

L.A. Crackdown 2 begins stereotypically: women officers are working undercover as dance girls to learn the identity of a serial killer. Both police officers are portrayed very negatively at the end of the movie. They are punished for their use of force against men: Jamie is murdered by Michael. Karen faces either losing her job, or going to prison for killing Michael who, although a criminal, was unarmed when she killed him.

Unlike Karen in *L.A. Crackdown 2*, who failed to deal justice to a criminal, Sybil Danning as "Ruger" in *L.A. Bounty* (1989) is successful at making the world a safer place to live. Ruger is a bounty hunter but was formerly a cop. She got fired for "going way out of bounds" on a drug case. She drives a camouflage car; eats hamburgers for breakfast; guzzles beer; smokes little cigars; wears a black leather jacket, jeans, turtle neck, and boots; has blond hair; and uses massive guns. She is very masculine (portrayed as "hard looking"), and says or speaks little. After she rescues the mayoral candidate's wife, the wife says to Ruger "you're real "macho" and then corrects herself "macha" to feminize the term macho to describe Ruger. Although Ruger is referred to as "bitch" and "honey," she does kill all the criminals single-handedly. The final scene shows many police cars and officers responding to the crime scene, but they are oblivious to Ruger as she walks away from the burning warehouse.

Ruger single-handedly decides how she is going to accomplish the task of bringing criminals to justice. She is not portrayed as an erotic object of the male gaze, presented maternally, or placed in a romantic relationship with a man.

Traci Lords stars in *Laser Moon* (1992) as policewoman Barbara Fleck. At the beginning of the film she is reassigned to work with Detective Musso of Homicide who is having a difficult time apprehending a serial killer of women. On her first day she shows up dressed in a black mini skirt suit; she has long blond hair. She is referred to by her new partner as "Barbie Doll." On another occasion he quips "Bring the car around, Barbie" to which she politely requests that he use her name, *not* "Barbie," if he wants her to get the car.

When she tells Musso that she has a four-year degree in police science, he retorts that the police department is no place for college girls. Later Fleck makes the connection that the serial killer murders on the full moon. Therefore, on the night of the full moon Fleck and Musso stakeout the radio station because they suspect the disc jockey is the killer. Musso gets out of the car to relieve himself. At that moment, Fleck realizes that the disc jockey is not in the station because the disc jockey's voice becomes incoherent on the car radio. She realizes that it is not a live broadcast, but that he has taped it. Musso is still out of the car, so Fleck goes to the disc jockey's estranged wife's home where she (Fleck) suspects he has gone. She arrives just in time to kill him after yelling "freeze." The last scene is of Fleck comforting the victim, that is, the wife.

Officer Fleck's physical appearance and dress is very sensual; however, she is assertive and stands up for herself in all her interactions with Detective Musso. She realizes the identity of the murderer, and she rescues the victim.

Rachel Ticotin stars as Detective Sandra Tores in *Falling Down* (1993). She is Hispanic and a young, fresh-faced, attractive woman with dark brown, shoulder-length hair. She has a badge and handcuffs both prominently displayed on her skirt belt. Similarly to Officer Malloy in *The Ambulance*, she is portrayed as nurturing and caring toward retiring robbery detective Prendergast. Prendergast tells her that unlike his wife, who had only her youthful beauty that has now faded, Tores has a career. During the investigation to discover who is committing crimes in Venice, California, an army supply store owner asks Tores if the police department has "officeresses." She replies that "a police officer is a police officer." Tores gets shot when she and Prendergast go to the suspect's former wife's home. Prendergast tells her to cover the back door. The suspect goes out the back door and shoots Tores. However, at the end of the movie she is taken out on a stretcher, and the ambulance paramedic states that she'll be all right.

Tores is concerned about Prendergast who is retiring after this day. She is shown early in the film making arrangements to take him to lunch, and she spends a lot of time talking to him on the telephone about his concerns about work when she should be handling a complaint. She does experience sexual innuendoes from other officers, but she ignores them. She is a very nurturing, caring police officer who gets shot following her older partner's instructions to cover the back door. She is wounded, but not seriously.

Hard Target (1993) takes place in New Orleans and stars Kasi Lemmons as Detective Carmine Mitchell who is the only officer on duty at the time because the police department is on strike. She is professionally attired in plain clothes and has a gun prominently displayed at her waist. She tells a young woman, Nat, who comes into the station to report her father missing that she can not help unless the young woman can provide more information about her father. They meet again when Nat returns to the police department after being notified that her father is dead. Mitchell orders a new autopsy after she suspects that the dead man was murdered. She is portrayed as very authoritarian when ordering the pathologist to conduct a new autopsy; she throws the deceased man's autopsy folder at the pathologist indicating that it was worthless for the investigation. She tells him to do the autopsy again, or she will get a formal order. The pathologist relates this incident to the criminals who ask if she can be bought. He replies, "No."

The final scene depicting Detective Mitchell is when she is killed during gunfire. She appears on the scene driving a patrol car with Nat and Nat's friend Chance in the back seat. She hears something and tells them to get down. She jumps out of the car firing her gun; gets shot, but keeps shooting. She is shot a second time, and Chance takes over. She dies from her injuries at the end of this scene. Chance says to Nat "Come on . . . she's dead" and proceeds to "save the day."

Criminal Passion (1994) stars Joan Severance as a police detective who is a loner, spending her off-duty time driving around the city streets, looking for what she does not know. She has a partner, but she decides that the best way to investigate a serial killer is to become intimately involved with the suspect. It is obvious to the audience that she is attracted to the suspect sexually, and no one is surprised when she becomes another of his many sex partners. She is told by her supervisor that she is violating her position; she ignores him. She is seductively portrayed with wavy hair to her shoulders, face makeup, and clothes that are silky and clingy. In the end, she kills the suspect. The audience is left wondering whether she killed him because he said he was only intimate with her because she was a cop. She shoots him one time for each of the women he killed. The movie ends as it begins—with her driving the streets late at night.

Throughout the movie, the detective is the object of the male gaze because of the silk clothing she wears that clings to her body, her makeup, and her wavy hair. She is very sensuous and desired by both the officers and the suspect. She fits Mulvey's description of the female characters filmed in a manner that emphasizes their "to-be-looked-at-ness."

Internal Affairs (1990) stars Laura Metcalf as Sergeant Amy Wallace who is the supervisor of a new trainee portrayed by Andy Garcia. This movie is one of two (*Arizona Heat* is the second one) in which other police officers refer to the woman officer as a "dyke." At the end of the movie, she gets shot by a corrupt police officer. When Garcia finds her, she apologizes for getting shot. We do not know for certain what happens to her; however, it appears she will survive because the doctor states that if she's a fighter she stands a good chance. The movie ends with Garcia killing the corrupt police officer. Throughout the movie, Wallace is presented as Garcia's equal, rather than as his superior training officer. Oftentimes during the movie, Garcia's character gives the instructions. Wallace is never presented as threatening to the male gaze. The officers perceive her as a "dyke," consequently, she does not threaten their masculinity.

Lethal Weapon 3 (1992) stars Rene Russo as Lorna Cole, assigned to the Internal Affairs Division of the police department. She is first introduced to the audience when she and two officers are in the elevator. One of them, Martin Riggs (Mel Gibson) concocts a story about embezzlement just to get her attention. He later attempts to embarrass her by asking her to step into his office which is really the men's room. She remains unruffled by this incident and proceeds to wash her hands. She is portrayed as an effective kick-boxer and drives a get-away truck at high speeds. In a scene in her apartment, after the encounter with the criminals that led to the high-speed truck chase, Riggs asks her for something for his head. When she does not respond sympathetically to his slight wound, he asks her "I thought you were going to get tender and maternal with me." This comment leads to them comparing scars they received in the line of duty. The scene ends with them in a sexual encounter that she in fact initiates. He kisses her and she throws him to the floor. The audience can surmise that she behaves in a more masculine manner (that is, a "tom-boy") because of her comment that she was raised with four brothers.

In a later scene she gets shot but survives because she was wearing a vest. As she is taken away in the ambulance, a romantic scene occurs: Riggs tells her that he wants to grow old with her. In the last scene Riggs comments to his partner that he is picking up Cole at the hospital. The audience is left to wonder whether or not she will be returning to her job as a police officer.

To Protect and Serve (1992) stars Lezlie Deane as Detective Harriet McCallister. She has long hair and is professionally dressed. Her captain refers to her as "a great cop" and praises her for both her toughness and intelligence. Detective McCallister is reassigned to work with Detective Philip Egan—considered a "loose cannon" by the captain. McCallister and Egan are investigating a series of police killings. When they go to the first crime scene, one officer on the scene asked Egan, "Who's the lady?" Egan responds "That's no lady—that's my partner."

Later, when Egan and McCallister go to question a witness to one of the crimes, Egan hears a gun being cocked behind the door. He pushes her away from the door. She says she will call for backup; he tells her to go around back. She apprehends a man running from the scene, and tells him to drop the gun; instead he aims the gun at her. Egan arrives at that moment and tackles the criminal. McCallister tells him her procedure of holding the suspect at gun point was fine. He disagrees, saying he refuses to get shot just to obey her procedure.

Both Lorna Cole and Harriet McCallister are presented early in the films as effective police officers. They are portrayed as confident and assertive in their roles as police officers. This confidence threatens the masculinities of Riggs and Egan. Cole ends up injured and in the hospital with Riggs' commitment of love ever after.

In the final scene of *To Protect and Serve*, McCallister is pushed to the ground in a shuffle with the captain who is the killer. As a result, she twists her ankle. Egan pursues him on foot through the warehouse. She limps over and sits down, takes off her shoe, rubs her ankle, and waits huddled against the wall for the outcome. She hears shots, she pulls out her gun, she sees Egan coming. They smile, she looks at him with hurt in her eyes. He rubs the cut on her face. He says, "Let's go home." She replies, "I'd like that." They exit walking with their arms wrapped around each other. Similarly to *Lethal Weapon 3*, the audience is not certain about her future in police work.

In *Copycat* (1995), Holly Hunter plays Inspector Mary Jane Monahan who, along with her male partner Inspector Ruben Goetz, is investigating a series of serial killings in San Francisco. Goetz has not been on the job very long and refers to himself as an "intuitive cop." Monahan is diminutive and is dressed conservatively with her hair pulled back at all times.

Later in the film when she is rescuing Dr. Helen Hudson, Monahan fails to realize that the serial killer is posing as the dead officer on the bathroom floor. He shoots her twice in the chest; however, she is able to rescue Hudson from the rooftop later because she had on a vest (similar to Cole in *Lethal Weapon 3*).

In *Copycat*, there are few stereotypes surrounding the character of Monahan. Although she is petite, she is presented as both confident and competent at her job. She dresses professionally and is never portrayed in provocative clothing. She is not in a sexual relationship with any of the officers in her department.

Women as Police Supervisors

In the comedy *Stop! Or My Mom Will Shoot* (1992), it is no secret to any of the officers that Lieutenant Gwen Harper of the Los Angeles Police Department is romantically involved with one of the detectives in her unit. In an early scene, she calls the detective into her office demanding to know why he did not call the night before; she was worried. She wants to talk to him about "feeling and responsibility." She remarks that "me being a lieutenant makes everything worse." He walks out of her office, and she yells after him ordering him to come back. He does not respond to this direct order from his superior officer. Later, when she receives an office full of flowers, she gives him a huge kiss in the office crowded with police officers. When she learns the flowers were sent by his mother, she gives him a big punch in front of the officers. At the end of the movie, she is sporting a huge diamond on her hand, but the male detective chases the fugitive in the airport. This movie is very stereo-typical: he does not want to get married; his mother wants him to; mother gets him the girl; and he, rather than the female officer who is admiring her ring, pursues the criminal.

Unlike Lieutenant Harper, Sean Young's portrayal of Lieutenant Lois Ein-horn in *Ace Ventura: Pet Detective* (1994) is a strong portrayal of a woman as a police officer. The audience's first view of Lieutenant Einhorn is by a camera frame beginning with her shoes, legs, and on up to her head. She has wavy, dark hair to her shoulders. She is also very authoritarian, and her badge is al-ways prominently displayed, either on her belt or pocket.

We find out later that Lieutenant Einhorn is a man posing as a woman. After a physical confrontation with her, Ace attempts to prove to the group of officers present that she is a man by tearing her clothes off. Once we realize that she is a man, it diminishes all the positive characteristics of her role as a police officer because *she* is a *he*. Once it is revealed that the lieutenant is a man, nothing else is indicated about his fate.

Women as Federal Police Officers

The Silence of the Lambs (1991) starring Jodi Foster begins very similarly to *Rush* (1991)— both women are selected for assignment while still in training. FBI trainee Clarice Starling reports to her superior officer Jack Campbell. He tells her he has "more of an errand than a job" for her to complete. Her as-signment is to interview serial killer Hannibal Lecter who has not been coop-erative in past attempts to interview him; maybe Starling can get his cooperation.

Agent Starling arrives at the prison in Baltimore where she is told by Dr. Chilton that many detectives have been to the institution, but none as attrac-tive as she. It is obvious that she is flustered; however, she handles this com-ment and his invitation to sightsee with diplomacy.

In a later scene, when Campbell and Starling have gone to view a body re-cently recovered, Campbell says to the Sheriff that he needs to discuss this sex crime with him in private. They depart leaving Starling alone in a room with male officers who stare at her making her feel uncomfortable. Later when she and Campbell are alone, he asked her if she was "burned" when he told the sheriff he needed to discuss the case in private. She replies "cops look at you to see how to act." By this, Starling means that it is his responsibility to lead by example.

Starling is very professional and is the first one to see something in the vic-tim's throat when looking at a photo of the murdered woman. Starling follows leads, tracks, and kills "Buffalo Bill." The conclusion of the film is very posi-tive with Starling being congratulated by her superior Jack Campbell. It is evident that she has gained his respect and that her career has started well.

Starling is similar to FBI supervisor Brenda Chandler in *Desperate Hours* (1990) who is also depicted as a female officer without a partner. Agent Chan-dler is very authoritarian and reminds other male agents that she is in charge.

Even when wounded, she continues to carry out her duties. Agents Chandler and Starling are different from the female Secret Service agent in *In the Line of Fire* (1993) who is romantically involved with a much older man at the end of the movie.

DISCUSSION

In this chapter, I used content analysis to explore several concepts about myths and stereotypes regarding gender and the organizational culture of policing. Van Zoonen points out that "content analysis is an invaluable" tool to use to convince "decision and program makers of the necessity for a diverse portrayal of women and men" (1994, 73). If content analysis is used "within a solid theoretical framework, [it] can shed light on social and cultural matters of representation" (73).

From the movies discussed in this chapter, it is evident that out-of-date myths of femininity still exist in movies about women in policing. The only films that portray women as effective police officers are those where the women are either the superior officer (Brenda Chandler in *Desperate Hours*, 1990); FBI trainees (including Clarice Starling in *The Silence of the Lambs*, 1991 and DeWitt and Zuckerman in *Feds*, 1988); or detectives or inspectors (Inspector Mary Jane Monahan in *Copycat*, 1995 and Detective Chief Inspector Jane Tennison of the *Prime Suspect* series, 1990, 1992, and 1993).

In 1996, *Fargo* is the first portrayal of a police woman as a chief of police. Although her role is a very positive portrayal of a woman as a competent investigator, it is also very stereotypical. Chief Marge Gunderson is employed full time; her husband is an artist who stays home working on his painting for a U.S. postal stamp competition. Throughout the film Norm is portrayed as taking care of his pregnant wife, for example, fixing her breakfast, jump starting her car, bringing her lunch to the office, and being concerned when she drives to the "twin cities" to conduct part of the murder investigation. *Fargo*, similarly to *Exit to Eden*, uses role reversal of the male and female characters. Similarly, at the end of *Fargo*, the final scene depicts Marge and Norm in bed talking about his 3-cent stamp painting of "The Mallard" winning the competition. She complements and reassures him that his stamp is just as important as the 29-cent stamp and concludes with "I'm so proud of you, Norm." Her support of him is admirable. But, there is never any acknowledgment by Norm that she had just solved a major crime, apprehended and arrested the male suspect, and *that* he is proud of her. As in *Taking the Heat*, *The Ambulance*, and *Exit to Eden*, the final scenes depict policewomen in their stereotypical positions (supportive, caring, and "my job is not as important as yours or as you are to me") roles.

A reexamination of Farganis' third phase (1983 to 1993), and my extension of it into a fourth period (1993 to 1996), shows that in a four-year period, 55 videos have been produced (N=56 for the third period).

Unfortunately, the total films for these two periods (111 of 121 or 92 percent) do not represent a diversity and variety of policewomen's lives as far as cultural diversity and multiculturalism (Farganis, 1994).

For example in Period III, only 4 of 56 videos (.07 percent) represent women as minority police officers (*Johnnie Mae Gibson: FBI* (1986); *Fatal Beauty* (1987); *Catch the Heat* (1987); and *Above the Law* (1988). In *One Good Cop* (1991), there are two roles for policewomen in peripheral or marginal roles within the movie's plot. The percentages are not much better for Period IV. Only 5 of 55 (.09 percent) of those produced show women as minority police officers, including *Hard Target* (1993), *Taking the Heat* (1993), *Vampire in Brooklyn* (1994), *Timecop* (1994), and *Ballistic* (1995). Two peripheral roles were as an FBI agent near the end of the comedy *Dumb and Dumber* (1994) and as an Hispanic policewoman in *Falling Down* (1993).

The four time periods applied to this video analysis do not show any differences regarding the policewoman's marital status. It makes little difference what type of police officer the women portray (federal, state, sheriff, or municipal), they are predominately cast as single women.

The women who serve as federal agents are portrayed more favorably than the women police in the other categories. None of the female agents die, less than 1 percent are injured (*Desperate Hours*, 1990), and 19 percent (3 of 16) are romantically involved at the end of the movies.[2] The more positive portrayal of women federal police agents might be a reflection of the popular culture of the federal police, and especially the FBI, as more professional and highly respected by the public.

Ironically, few videos currently portray policewomen as patrol officers in municipal departments. To date, only six videos have been produced depicting women as patrol officers. *Police Academy* (1984) is a comedy about police recruits. Another comedy is *Night Patrol* (1985) where the women are highly sexualized and spoofed. The four remaining films are a true story about a policewoman who posed for a *Playboy* centerfold (*Police Woman: Centerfold*, 1983), *Blue Steel* (1990), *The Ambulance* (1993), and *The Ladies Club* (1987).

When we examine the videos, we see that policewomen are kept "in their place" (die at end of movie, injured, or romantically involved). For example, in videos where women detectives have equal rank, two die at the end (*Breaking Point*, 1993 and *Probable Cause*, 1994); two are romantically involved (*Zipperface*, 1992 and *Vampire in Brooklyn*, 1994); and one police detective is both injured and romantically involved (*To Protect and Serve*, 1992). Both female internal affairs officers (*Lethal Weapon 3* and *Internal Affairs*) are injured, and one, Lorna Cole from *Lethal Weapon 3*, is romantically involved with another police officer.

For women serving as vice officers, a similar pattern emerges. Two of the four films depict vice policewomen with ranks equal to their male counterparts. One policewoman is injured (*Above the Law*, 1988), and two are romantically involved (*Ballistic*, 1995 and *Catch the Heat*, 1987). Interestingly, all three films depict minority policewomen. Further examination of the policewoman detective in *Above the Law* and the policewoman detective in *Taking the Heat*

(1993), finds these two African-American policewomen kept in their place (either by injury or romantic involvement) at the end of the movie.

Concomitantly, women police who have lower ranks than their male partners are kept in their places as well. The policewoman detective dies at the end of *The Enforcer* (1976) after saving her male partner's life; the African-American policewoman detective dies in *Hard Target* (1993); the Hispanic female officer is injured at the end of *Falling Down* (1993) because she followed her superior's order "to go around back." The African-American woman detective in *Fatal Beauty* (1987) is romantically involved with a Caucasian male security officer at the end of the movie. The undercover policewoman in *Impulse* (1990) is romantically involved at the end. The Hispanic female police officer serving as an undercover officer in *One Good Cop* (1991) is injured at the end of the movie after saving a male officer's life.

The future world of policing is not much brighter for women police officers. In three of the four futuristic movies where the women have lesser ranks than the male officers, two are romantically involved by the end (*Demolition Man*, 1993 and *Judge Dredd*, 1995) and one is injured (*Timecop*, 1994).

CONCLUSION

It is important to remember that although Title VII extended the legal standing for women to enter police work as sworn officers, the videos produced during the past 25 years still show policewomen in the stereotypical roles ascribed to women. Primarily, women are shown as leaving police work either because of their emotions or their inability to perform police officer duties.

This is what the videos are depicting but this might not be the actual reality of women's roles in police work. The research that has been completed on the performance of women as police must be made available to video producers. The role of researcher and consultant is important to break these myths and stereotypes by producing films that show women are successful in accomplishing the police work duties.

APPENDIX: POLICEWOMEN IN FILMS

Period I: 1963–1973

Fuzz	1972, Comedy, Parental Guidance

Period II: 1973–1983

Cleopatra Jones	1973, Action/Adventure, Parental Guidance
Cleopatra Jones and the Casino of Gold	1975, Action/Adventure, Restricted
The Enforcer	1976, Action/Adventure, Restricted
Behind the Badge	1977, Originally made for TV, TV Not Rated
No Mercy	1977, Unknown Type, Unknown Rating

Period II: 1973–1983 *(continued)*

Dear Detective	1979, Mystery/Suspense, Unrated
The Black Marble	1980, Drama, Parental Guidance
The Fan	1981, Mystery/Suspense, Restricted
Endangered Species	1982, Science Fiction/Fantasy, Restricted

Period III: 1983–1993

Utilities	1983, Comedy, Parental Guidance
Policewoman Centerfold	1983, Drama, Not Rated
Police Academy	1984, Comedy, Restricted
Runaway	1984, Science Fiction/Fantasy, PG-13
Night Patrol	1985, Comedy, Restricted
Johnnie Mae Gibson: FBI	1986, Not Rated Film, Not Rated Rating
Silk	1986, Action/Adventure, Restricted
Black Widow	1987, Mystery/Suspense, Restricted
Catch the Heat	1987, Action/Adventure, Restricted
Caribe	1987, Action/Adventure, Restricted
Code Name: Dancer	1987, Action/Adventure, Unknown Rating
Commando Squad	1987, Action/Adventure, Restricted
Fatal Beauty	1987, Action/Adventure, Restricted
Ladies Club	1987, Action/Adventure, Restricted
RoboCop	1987, Science Fiction/Fantasy, Restricted
Stripped to Kill	1987, Action/Adventure, Restricted
Above the Law	1988, Action/Adventure, Restricted
Arizona Heat	1988, Action/Adventure, Restricted
Betrayed	1988, Mystery/Suspense, Restricted
Doin' Time on Planet Earth	1988, Comedy, Parental Guidance
Feds	1988, Comedy, PG-13
L.A. Crackdown	1988, Action/Adventure, Restricted
L.A. Crackdown 2	1988, Action/Adventure, Unrated
Vice Academy	1988, Comedy, Restricted
L.A. Bounty	1989, Action/Adventure, Restricted
Silk II	1989, Action/Adventure, Restricted
Blue Steel	1990, Action/Adventure, Restricted
China O'Brien	1990, Action/Adventure, Restricted
Desperate Hours	1990, Action/Adventure, Restricted
Impulse	1990, Mystery/Suspense, Restricted
Internal Affairs	1990, Action/Adventure, Restricted
Kindergarten Cop	1990, Comedy, PG-13
Martial Law	1990, Action/Adventure, Restricted
Prime Suspect I	1990, Mystery/Suspense, Unknown Rating
RoboCop 2	1990, Science Fiction/Fantasy , Restricted
The Rookie	1990, Action/Adventure, Restricted
Vice Academy II	1990, Comedy, Restricted
China O'Brien 2	1991, Action/Adventure, Restricted
The Killing Mind	1991, Mystery/Suspense, Not Rated

Naked Gun 2 1/2	1991, Comedy, PG-13
One Good Cop	1991, Drama, Restricted
Rush	1991, Drama, Restricted
The Silence of the Lambs	1991, Mystery/Suspense, Restricted
Striking Distance	1991, Action/Adventure, Restricted
Vice Academy III	1991, Comedy, Restricted
A Stranger Among Us	1992, Mystery/Suspense, PG-13
Hit Woman: The Double Edge	1992, Action/Adventure, Restricted
Honor And Glory	1992, Action/Adventure, Unrated
Ladykiller	1992, Mystery/Suspense, Unrated
Laser Moon	1992, Mystery/Suspense, Unrated
Lethal Weapon 3	1992, Action/Adventure, Restricted
Prime Suspect II	1992, Mystery/Suspense, Unknown Rating
Rage and Honor II: Hostile Takeover	1992, Action/Adventure, Restricted
To Protect and Serve	1992, Action/Adventure, Restricted
Stop Or My Mom Will Shoot	1992, Comedy, Parental Guidance
Zipperface	1992, Mystery/Suspense, Unrated

Period IV: 1993–1996

The Ambulance	1993, Mystery/Suspense, Restricted
Angel Fist	1993, Action/Adventure, Restricted
Breaking Point	1993, Mystery/Suspense, Restricted
Demolition Man	1993, Science Fiction/Fantasy, Restricted
Eliminator Woman	1993, Action, Restricted
Falling Down	1993, Action/Adventure, Restricted
Full Eclipse	1993, Horror, Restricted
Guardian Angel	1993, Action/Adventure, Restricted
Hard Target	1993, Action/Adventure, Restricted
In the Line of Fire	1993, Action, Adventure, Restricted
Prime Suspect III	1993, Mystery/Suspense, Unknown Rating
Red Sun Rising	1993, Action/Adventure, Restricted
Snapdragon	1993, Mystery/Suspense, Restricted
Striking Distance	1993, Action/Adventure, Restricted
Taking the Heat	1993, Drama, Restricted
When the Bough Breaks	1993, Mystery/Suspense, Unknown Rating
Ace Ventura: Pet Detective	1994, Comedy, PG-13
Bodily Harm	1994, Mystery/Suspense, Restricted
Criminal Passion	1994, Mystery/Suspense, Restricted
The Crow	1994, Horror, Restricted
Dumb and Dumber	1994, Comedy, PG-13
Exit to Eden	1994, Comedy, Restricted
Police Academy: Mission to Moscow	1994, Comedy, Parental Guidance
Probable Cause	1994, Mystery/Suspense, Restricted
Serial Mom	1994, Comedy, Restricted
The Haunting of Seacliff Inn	1994, Mystery/Suspense, Unrated
Soft Deceit	1994, Mystery/Suspense, Restricted

Period IV: 1993–1996 (continued)

Timecop	1994, Science Fiction/Fantasy, Restricted
Undercover	1994, Erotic Thriller, Unrated
Vampire in Brooklyn	1994, Comedy & Horror, Restricted
Bad Boys	1995, Action/Adventure, Restricted
Bad Company	1995, Mystery/Suspense, Restricted
Ballistic	1995, Action/Adventure, Restricted
Black Scorpion	1995, Science Fiction, Restricted
Copycat	1995, Action/Adventure, Restricted
Cover Me	1995, Action/Adventure, Restricted
Die Hard With A Vengeance	1995, Action/Adventure, Restricted
Deadly Love	1995, Mystery/Suspense, Restricted
Dream Man	1995, Mystery/Suspense, Restricted
The Final Cut	1995, Unknown Type, Unknown Rating
Frame by Frame	1995, Mystery/Suspense, Restricted
Hollow Point	1995, Action/Adventure, Restricted
Indictment	1995, Drama, Not Rated
Jade	1995, Drama, Restricted
Judge Dredd	1995, Science Fiction/Fantasy, Restricted
Silk Stalkings: Natural Selection	1995, Mystery/Suspense, Parental Guidance
The Glass Shield	1995, Drama, PG-13
Tunnel Vision	1995, Mystery/Suspense, Restricted
Under Lock and Key	1995, Action/Adventure, Restricted
Black Scorpion II	1996, Action/Adventure, Restricted
Breach of Trust	1996, Action/Adventure, Restricted
Broken Arrow	1996, Action/Adventure, Restricted
Fargo	1996, Drama, Restricted
Madame Savant	1996, Adult, Restricted
Sabotage	1996, Mystery/Suspense, Restricted

DISCUSSION QUESTIONS

1. According to Hale, what three explanations can be offered for the slow growth of the number of women who are sworn police officers? What is Title VII and what impact did it have on the entry of women into policing? Do you agree or disagree that women police officers are now generally accepted by the public? Explain.

2. Hale discusses the symbolic ways in which women in films are "kept in their place"? What mechanisms are used to present women as subordinate to men in films?

3. What conclusions does Hale reach about the film depictions of female police officers during the periods she examined? How do these portrayals relate to real-life issues concerning women as police officers?

NOTES

1. Although 1996 had ended by the time this chapter went to production (December, 1996), films produced during 1996 were just beginning to appear both on video stores' shelves and in television (generally cable) listings during this period. Undoubtedly, more videos depicting women as police officers will appear in the first six months of 1997.

2. Sixteen videos depict a female federal agent. These include *Cleopatra Jones* (1973), *Cleopatra Jones and the Casino of Gold* (1975), *Johnnie Mae Gibson: FBI* (1986), *Commando Squad* (1987), *Betrayed* (1988), *Feds* (1988), *Desperate Hours* (1990), *The Silence of the Lambs* (1991), *Hit Women: The Double Edge* (1992), *Honor and Glory* (1992), *Rage and Honor II: Hostile Takeover* (1992), *In the Line of Fire* (1993), *Dumb and Dumber* (1994), *Under Lock and Key* (1995), *Broken Arrow* (1996), and *Sabotage* (1996).

The three films in which the female agent is romantically involved with her partner at the end of the movie are *Broken Arrow* (1996), *Commando Squad* (1987), and *In the Line of Fire* (1993).

12

❁

The Best Defense: Images
of Female Attorneys
in Popular Films

FRANKIE Y. BAILEY,
JOYCELYN M. POLLOCK,
AND SHERRY SCHROEDER

INTRODUCTION

He kidnaps her, keeps her a prisoner, and strips away her defenses. And
she ends up falling in love with this master seducer.

The preceding scenario reads like a cover blurb for a type of romance
novel known as a "bodice ripper." It is actually the description given by
director Lizzie Borden of the relationship between the principal characters in her film *Love Crimes* (1992). In the movie, an assistant D.A. (played by
Sean Young) falls prey to the serial rapist she has been pursuing. According to
Borden, the photographer and rapist (played by Patrick Bergen, the sadistic
husband in *Sleeping with the Enemy*) is "not a stone-cold rapist; he assaults
women by confusing them. It's very, very borderline, which for me is more
interesting" (Lovell, 1992: 20).

These comments by Borden raise some fascinating questions about how
and why Hollywood filmmakers blend elements of sex and violence in their
films. Borden's comments also highlight one theme we have identified as recurring in the depiction of female attorneys in popular films. Borden says of
her film, "It plays with the idea of a strong but repressed woman who almost
needs to be humiliated to find her sexuality" (Lovell, 20). In the pages that
follow, we will argue that this "idea" is not unique to *Love Crimes* but is, instead, a common one in the subgenre of movies we call "female attorney
films." We will explore how women are depicted as lawyers in Hollywood

films and consider how these images apply to the real-life status of women in the law.

IMAGES OF PROFESSIONAL
WOMEN IN HOLLYWOOD FILMS

As Walsh notes in her study of *Women's Film and Female Experience, 1940–1950,*

> Studying artifacts such as popular film yields insight that other historical methods cannot. Popular culture explores both the surface and underside of human experience and is particularly suited to discovering historical undercurrents (1984: 4).

Since the early 1970s, Walsh and a number of other scholars (Basinger, 1993; Clover, 1992; Haskell, 1973; Mellen, 1973; Rosen, 1973) have examined female character depiction and the female experience in popular films. These studies have focused on "reading" the content of these films.

Regarding the depiction of female experience in popular films, Galerstein, in the introduction to her filmography on *Working Women on the Hollywood Screen* (1989), observes that from 1930 to 1975, American films portrayed women in diverse occupations. However, "the employed woman was in a distinct minority as compared with the great majority of women shown in non-working roles" (Galerstein: xiii). During these years, as the number of women in the real-life work force increased, the number of employed women shown in Hollywood films actually decreased. Moreover, although professional women, such as journalists and attorneys, were occasionally portrayed, the most common category of working woman was entertainers, followed by secretary or other office worker (Galerstein: xiii).

As do other scholars (Haskell, 1973; Rosen, 1973), Galerstein concludes that in these earlier films, a woman's career was perceived and presented as secondary to "finding a man." Actually, a woman's job was presented as a stop-gap en route to marriage and motherhood.

Basinger observes of professional women in films from 1930 to 1960: "When women hold these occupations, they encounter grief for being in them. They are *told* by characters in the movies that these jobs are not appropriate woman's work..." (1993: 452).

Haskell asserts, "A movie heroine could act on the same power and career drives as a man only if, at the climax, they took second place to the sacred love of a man" (1973: 4).

And finally Walsh observes concerning the lawyers, reporters, and doctors in the films of the 1930s who were women:

> These heroines face the hostility of threatened husbands, lovers, and male co-workers. While the femininity-achievement conflict creates tension,

that tension proves both positive and negative, however. These embattled superwomen seem to have far more exciting lives than their homebound sisters. However, dominant ideology—in the studios and audiences—prevailed in the (usually) conservative endings (1984: 138).

In short, in these early films, career women were presented as women who risked losing their "femininity" as they pursued achievements in male professional arenas. The "screwball comedies" of the 1930s and 1940s presented the most egalitarian images of female professional women in relationships with men. But even in these comedies, there was a quality of ambivalence and ultimate conservatism for female career women (Phillips, 1982; Sikor, 1989; Walsh, 1984).

POPULAR CULTURE IMAGES
OF LAWYERS AS PROFESSIONALS

Post asserts, "The most striking aspect of the image of the lawyer in popular culture is the intense hostility with which it is invested" (1987: 379). He goes on to note that lawyers are "simultaneously praised and blamed for the very same action" (for example, providing vigorous advocacy for their clients) (380).

Chase proposes a more complex interaction between the legal profession and popular culture. He argues that public schools and the mass culture socialize Americans to feel both cynicism and deferential respect for the law and lawyers (1986: 551). He proposes a framework for analysis of popular culture images of lawyers that focuses on three "antinomic pairs" relating to (1) virtue, (2) money or power, and (3) order. For each pair, there are both positive and negative archetypes.

These images of lawyers in relation to virtue, money or power, and order have been forged in a popular culture that until recently focused on the attorney as male. In a review of *Class Action*, Lucia asserts that Maggie, the young lawyer in the film, shares the common fate of other such female characters: "Like many of her predecessors in the new crop of female lawyer films such as *Jagged Edge*, *Music Box*, and *The Big Easy*, Maggie is caught within a web of deception constructed by the male characters surrounding her"(1990: 49).

Lucia argues that Maggie "by virtue of being a woman in a nontraditional role" is a threat to the men around her, and in the end Maggie's powers are neutralized by her opponent (who is also her father, hence a true "patriarch") (1990: 49).

In analyzing this subgenre of films, we considered how female attorneys were presented as professionals and the challenges they faced as "career women" in a traditionally male profession. Were they presented as virtuous and powerful defenders? Did the images of female attorneys reflect stereotypes about lawyers in general or were they more specific gender-based stereotypes?

But before turning to our analysis of these films and to the comments of real-life attorneys about them, we should seek sociohistorical perspective by looking briefly at the life and times of women in the legal profession.

WOMEN IN THE LAW

In 1917, Grace Humiston, a female attorney who had become known for her investigative skills, was described by the *New York Times* as "the woman who shamed the police in the Ruth Cruger Murder Case" (McCarl, 1978: 89). During her brief period of celebrity (before a later fall from grace), Mrs. Humiston was known in the media as "Mrs. Sherlock Holmes" (McCarl: 75, 89).

Grace Humiston's public fame was not typical of female attorneys during the period. Historically, women who practiced the law did not receive praise from the media, the public, or their male colleagues—they found it difficult to enter the profession at all. In 1880, there were about 200 women attorneys in the United States (Morello, 1986). Resistance to women was grounded in a belief that they were innately unsuitable for this "masculine" profession because of their sensitive natures and delicate constitutions. In *Bradwell v. Illinois*, 83 U.S. 130, 140 (1873), the Supreme Court echoed these beliefs in its holding that women did not have a fundamental privilege under the federal constitution to engage in any and every profession, occupation, or employment in civil life, and that the law was no place for a "lady." Law was considered the work of the mind, not the heart (Drachman, 1992: 44), and women were deemed unable to perform in the same manner as men because they were said to operate under the influence of their emotions and sentimental nature. They needed to be protected from a profession that "has essentially and habitually to do with all that is selfish and malicious, knavish and criminal, coarse, and brutal, repulsive, and obscene in human life" (In re Goodnell, 39 Wis. 232, 242 [1875]).

By 1900, 34 states had admitted women to the practice of law, and by 1920 all states allowed women to be admitted (Wiseman, 1991). Even though women attorneys now could be admitted to the bar, their roles continued to be supportive to the primary advocate role of the male attorney. Very few women did any trial work at all; if they did spend any time in the courtroom, they usually practiced in the newly emerging juvenile courts and the so-called "women's courts" founded in cities such as Los Angeles and New York (Drachman, 1992).

Even after admission to the bar was allowed, women continued to have difficulty obtaining their credentials. For many years, apprenticeships or clerking were the prerequisites for bar eligibility, and it was a rare attorney indeed who would take on a female clerk, unless she was his wife or daughter. When a law school degree gradually became the requirement for admission to the bar, most law schools barred women from admission. In 1869, Washington University in St. Louis, Missouri, became the first law school to admit women

(Bernat, 1992). Not until 1950, however, did Harvard finally admit women (Morello, 1986).

Today, though almost half of all students are women, they still represent a minuscule proportion of law school faculty and administrators. In the late 1980s, only 10 percent of tenured faculty were women, and only 6 percent of deans were women (Wald, 1988). Women report that the law school experience is still rife with evidence that law is a male world. Studies show that women tend to participate less and less over time in law school classes (Wald, 1988). There is evidence that more women than men perceive the experience as alienating and hostile (Banks, 1988).

Although women comprise 50 percent of entering enrollments to law schools, they still face lower pay and fewer occupational choices once they enter the workplace. The percentage of female practicing attorneys is still relatively small at only 21 percent, and the percentage of partners in firms is tiny at 8 percent (Wald, 1988). Some evidence indicates that women are more likely than their male counterparts to leave the profession (Wald, 1988). There is mixed evidence related to the relative earning power of men and women. Although some studies report that women earn 40 percent less than men 10 years after graduation (Wald, 1988), in at least one study done on graduates admitted to the bar during 1979 and 1987, earnings were comparable given the same job type (that is, government attorney versus private practice, associate versus partner, and so on) (Caplow and Scheindlin, 1990). Because the area of law or type of practice is heavily influenced by gender, there is really no inconsistency between these findings. Women do tend to cluster in public interest law, are more likely to have a solo or small practice rather than work in a large firm, and are less likely to make partner status.

Female attorneys perceive more discrimination than their male associates perceive (Hanson, 1992). About 25 percent in one survey reported being the victim of sexual harassment on the job (Caplow and Scheindlin, 1990). They report that they have less desirable work assignments, are subject to higher performance expectations, are less valued by clients, and receive less respect from opposing counsel (Cook and Spanhel, 1991). Twice as many women as men indicated they were unhappy with the profession in one survey (Wald, 1988). Not "fitting in" to the associate subculture is reported by many female attorneys. Mentors among partners are more difficult to cultivate or are misinterpreted as sexual partners if they exist. Women suffer from a lack of "rainmaking" ability because of their absence from the social world of business clubs and golf courses. Finally, women find it difficult to meet the demands of the legal profession, which include an extremely large number of hours per working week, travel, and commitment to extend working relationships to one's social life. Maternity leaves are not very common and, even when available, usually result in being diverted to the "mommy track" of less exciting assignments and reduced opportunities for advancement.

Women have, by choice or necessity, tended to move into governmental agencies after law school. Numbers of women are found in paid legal services, public defender programs, prosecutors offices, and government agencies such as offices of the Attorney General. One of the more interesting results of this trend is women's presence in criminal law—both as defense attorneys and as prosecutors. Criminal law is trial work, so this is contrary to the trend of women avoiding (or being excluded from) trial work. Only subjective accounts of female's performance in these roles is available. Some believe that women tend to have a less aggressive style than their male counterparts, which sometimes can work to their advantage. Women might be better listeners and as such better cross-examiners. They can suffer from patronizing attitudes from judges and other lawyers but also might be able to use these things to their advantage in trial tactics (Pollock and Ramirez. 1994).

The practice of law still bears the legacy of its history of female exclusion. The law itself is primarily male oriented in its language, priorities, and interpretations of what is important. The "reasonable person" endemic to all legal analysis is still inevitably male. It is unclear whether women have made any impact at all on the legal world or whether the legal world has molded those women who have chosen to enter into some semblance of conformity to a traditional male model of attorney-professional.

One question we wanted to answer was whether or not Hollywood films reflect these realities of the work and personal lives of female attorneys.

WOMEN LAWYERS IN HOLLYWOOD FILMS

Methodology

A list of 55 films in which female attorneys are featured was generated using a combination of methods: (1) systematic search of two movie video guides (Martin and Porter, 1992; Scheuer, 1992), (2) use of Galerstein's filmography, and (3) use of informants who had seen films in which they recalled female attorneys.

From this list of 55 movies available on video, 25 (see Appendix) were located and viewed. The authors believe that these 25 films are representative of the films featuring female attorneys that are most often seen by the audience for popular films. The original list of 55 films included several made-for-television movies that are available on video; however, these films were not readily available at the video store. Therefore, the final list comprises theatrical releases that are now on video.

In the final sample of 25 films, movies made in the 1980s and 1990s predominate. This too reflects the current availability of films on video. Although Galerstein identifies 28 films featuring female attorneys (and at least four additional films under the heading "law enforcement" featuring female judges) as made between 1930 and 1975, only two of these films were found on video. These two films, *Adam's Rib* (1949) and *The Bachelor and the Bobby-Soxer* (1947), are both classic "screwball comedies" and, therefore, have been preserved and made available to a modern audience.

The instrument used in this analysis was designed to (1) provide information that would allow comparison of film images of female attorneys with their real-life counterparts, and (2) allow detection of the presence of gender stereotypes in popular films.

The content analysis was done by two coders. One of us watched all 25 films. A second coder, as a check of the reliability of the principle coder, watched a subsample (eight) of the films. The two coders were in complete agreement about how these eight films should be coded. The third researcher had seen the more popular of the films in the sample but did not participate in the coding.

Because of plot conventions that place more emphasis on action than exposition, some information we had hoped to obtain about fictional female lawyers was not routinely provided. Also, in at least one area (the attire of the female characters), the visual images were too complex to lend themselves neatly to coding categories. These aspects of our findings will be discussed later.

Findings

Galerstein (1989) observes about the Hollywood films of 1930 through 1975: "Women lawyers are as scarce...as they were in the law firms and courtrooms of America during that period...Most films tend to treat such professional women as smart women but rare birds" (1989: 227). Galerstein identifies at least 18 films featuring female lawyers or judges as having been made between 1930 and 1946. Unfortunately, we were unable to find these films. Most were apparently "B-movies" that disappeared from circulation. The two earliest films in our sample are the "screwball comedies" already mentioned: *The Bachelor and the Bobby-Soxer* (1947) and *Adam's Rib* (1949), starring, respectively, Myrna Loy and Katharine Hepburn. Although a handful of additional films featuring female attorneys were made after *Adam's Rib*, not until 1976 with *Lipstick* did another popular film enjoy a wide audience and continued distribution. It should be noted, however, that at least in made-for-television movies, the modern female attorney put in an appearance as early as 1971. *Ransom for a Dead Man* starred Lee Grant as a brilliant attorney who matches wits with Peter Falk's Lt. Columbo. And by the 1980s, female attorneys had again achieved some limited visibility in Hollywood feature films.

In our film sample, we found that the majority of the women were European American. In fact, in only three of the films, *The Big Easy* (1987), *Reversal of Fortune* (1990), and *Music Box* (1989), did we spot a nonwhite female legal professional. In *The Big Easy*, an African-American female judge presides at an arraignment. In *Reversal of Fortune*, several female law students of color appear. In *Music Box*, Glenn Close is assisted in preparing her case by her friend, an African American woman, whose status is not clear, but who appears to be a paralegal. In all the films in the sample, the primary female role is played by a European American.

The female attorneys portrayed were usually young. Although the exact age of the characters was provided in only two of the movies (*The Pelican Brief* and *The Accused*), other characters were placed within an age range. That breakdown is shown here:

Age Range	Number of Characters
24	1
25–30	3
31–35	11
36–40	6
41–45	4

The youngest character was the law student played by Julia Roberts in the *Pelican Brief*. (In *Reversal of Fortune*, we used the age of the primary female attorney on the case, who was no longer in law school). Although several veteran actors portrayed lawyers in these films, most women appeared to be younger than 35.

Most of the women (16 of 25) were single. Six were divorced. Three were married. However, the marital status of the women was not always immediately clear. One of the more confusing films (for a coder) is the comedy *Bird on a Wire* (1990) in which corporate attorney Goldie Hawn has been married, is now divorced, has one present lover and one lover from the past, and at various times tells Mel Gibson (lover from the past) several misleading stories about her present status. Equally confusing initially is *Hanna K.* (1983), a French-made film starring Jill Clayburgh, in which an American-born woman living in Israel has apparently abandoned (but not divorced) her French husband. She is referred to as "Mrs." but not by her husband's name or by that of her Israeli lover. In other films, we identified the women as single (that is, never married) based on the story line.

For our purposes, little information was provided about the characters' educational background or career path. In four cases a law school was identified:

Adam's Rib—Yale Law

Pelican Brief—Tulane

The Client—Memphis State

Reversal of Fortune—Harvard

In *Hanna K.*, the woman had moved to Jerusalem to attend law school. In *Defenseless* (1991), the character had a sterling undergraduate record, having graduated Phi Beta Kappa from Smith. But we are told little else about the educational backgrounds of these characters. Even less information is presented about their career paths. As the films begin, three of the women are in solo practice; seven are members of law firms. In a distinct departure from real life, during the course of these films 21 of the 25 fictional attorneys become involved in a criminal case as a prosecutor or defense attorney (public or private). One character is a judge. One is involved in a civil suit. One is a student who investigates an assassination conspiracy following the murder of her professor/lover. One is a corporate attorney who spends much of the film fleeing with her hunted ex-lover.

We do learn that the female attorney who is the murder victim in *Presumed Innocent* (1989) was a probation officer before becoming an assistant district attorney. In *Lipstick* (1976), the prosecutor resigns her position so that she can act as defense attorney for the female heroine. In *Guilty as Sin* (1993), the attorney has been both a paralegal and a law clerk. She is now in private practice. And, we can assume that before becoming a judge in *The Bachelor and the Bobby-Soxer* (1947), the judge (who comes from a family of lawyers and judges) did duty as an attorney. But in most cases, we must make assumptions about the career path of the attorney.

It should be noted, however, that this lack of information has less to do with the gender of the characters than with the conventions of moviemaking. As in most popular films, we join these characters when they are faced with a dilemma (whether comic or dramatic). As with male characters, background information about the female characters is provided as needed and only in passing.

Enough information is provided so that it is possible to discuss some issues faced by fictional attorneys. Common to all of these films is what Walsh (1984) refers to as the "femininity-achievement conflict." Often the fulfillment of their "traditional" roles (daughter, lover, wife, or mother) is presented as being in direct conflict with the decisions and choices they must make as effective attorneys. For example, in *Class Action* (1991), the young attorney finds herself opposing her father in court. In *Hanna K.*, the character's first assignment as a court-appointed attorney pits her against her lover, who is the prosecutor. And, in the classic comedy *Adam's Rib* (1949), defense attorney Katharine Hepburn faces prosecutor Spencer Tracy in a battle that rages from the courtroom to their marital bedroom.

These interpersonal conflicts with loved ones are complicated because, in 15 of 25 films, the female attorney finds herself in physical danger (assault, kidnapping, attempted murder). In 2 of the films, *Presumed Innocent* (1989) and *Perfect Witness* (1989), the attorney is dead or dies. This physical jeopardy is sometimes the direct result of the error in judgment the woman has displayed in her choice of sexual partner or lover. In *Presumed Innocent*, the attorney (who we see only in flashbacks) has pursued (among others) her married colleague, Harrison Ford. She is murdered by his wife. In *Jagged Edge* (1985), Glenn Close is drawn into an affair with her client who might have murdered his wife.[1] When she finds the evidence to prove his crime, he tries to kill her. In *Defenseless* (1991), attorney Barbara Hershey is taken in by her client/lover who turns out not only to be married to her friend from college but also to be a pornographer and incestuous father. When he is murdered, she finds herself in both physical and professional jeopardy.

We admit that in popular films, male characters also suffer the consequences of misguided love or lust. This is true in both classic *film noir* (for example, *Double Indemnity*) and recent films such as *Body Heat*, *Fatal Attraction*, and *Basic Instinct*. The difference here seems to be the degree to which female characters are defined by their sexuality. This is best exemplified in several films in the sample in which the changes in the woman's feelings about her sexual identity are "signaled" by changes in her outward appearance. In *Ultimate Desires* (1991), the repressed young attorney is drawn into the life of her murdered friend, a call girl. As she goes "undercover" to investigate the murder, she discovers her own sensuality and begins to enjoy wearing the silk underwear, make-up, and tight, short dresses that are a part of her "disguise." At the end of the film, her disillusionment when she discovers she has been used and betrayed by the man she has met is indicated by her rejection of adornment. Clad in her suit, glasses back in place, hair up, she drops her lipstick into her desk drawer. And in *Love Crimes* (1991), the assistant district attorney who sets out to trap a photographer/con man/rapist is trapped by him and forced to face her traumatic childhood. Her discovery of her sexual self is signaled by the short red dress she wears when she goes to meet him in a bar and the seductive way she dances with a stranger at his request. We have found no such commonly used and equivalent signals of sexual awareness and availability in films in which male characters are presented as criminal justice system professionals. Does an open shirt collar displayed by a male character indicate he has suddenly realized he is "a man"?

Related to this is a coding problem we encountered. Although we had thought female attire would be significant as we examined gender stereotypes, what we had not anticipated was the complexity of answering a question such as whether the attorney ever appears in "sexy" or "provocative" dress. Although a checklist of examples of such dress was used, the problem was that the actual items of clothing worn was only a part of the story. For example, in *Guilty as Sin* (1993), Rebecca De Mornay appears in court in a simple beige dress and pearls. But, De Mornay's physique and her body language might well be perceived as "sexy" by an audience viewing the movie. And, in fact, when she has completed her competent cross-examination of a witness, the opposing attorney quips "Say, Counselor, what would it take to keep you on retainer?" It is not clear whether he is complimenting her on her skills as an attorney or making a crude pass. (Her response is "A lot.")

But although this character and the other women are generally presented as competent attorneys, their competence is sometimes not well received. In the classic *Adam's Rib*, Tracy accuses Hepburn of having turned the courtroom into "a circus" to win her case. These two eventually reach an amicable and loving, if slightly ambiguous resolution of their "battle of the sexes." But in the modern films we viewed, some men seem to handle female commitment to job and client with less finesse and greater sense of threat than did Tracy in 1949. For example, in *Physical Evidence* (1989), the attorney's lover described her as "obsessed" with her job. In *Guilty as Sin* (1993), De Mornay's lover is disturbed by her new client and not only wonders briefly about her fidelity but also questions her involvement in criminal law.

When the woman's sexual partner is also her boss, the question is implicitly or sometimes explicitly raised about the woman's motives for the involvement. Is she "sleeping her way" into a promotion or a partnership? This is presented as clearly the case in *Presumed Innocent* (1990), but the character is already dead, so we don't hear her side of the story. In other films, even when the woman is presented as less manipulative, there is the question of whether a smart woman would find herself in this situation. Such involvement also can create ethical dilemmas that go beyond the relationship. In *Class Action* (1991), the attorney discovers her boss/lover has covered up their client's culpability and failed to provide the opposing counsel with documents that should have been delivered during discovery. In *Perfect Witness* (1989), Stockard Channing must decide whether to stand by the legal but immoral determination by her boss/lover to make a witness testify by keeping him in jail until he "cracks."

In these films, ethical dilemmas are particularly difficult for the women because of the emotional involvement they seem to have not only with sexual partners and relatives but also with the other characters. As scholars of women in film have observed, women often relate to other characters not only in sexual terms but also as nurturers and caregivers (Walsh, 1984). This is most obvious in *The Client* (1994) in which Susan Sarandon—deprived of her own children—becomes a surrogate mother to her young client. This type of emotional involvement is also evident in *The Accused* (1988) in which the young D.A. defies her boss to obtain some measure of justice for a gang rape victim. In this film, as in *Lipstick* (1976), the attorney's behavior also reflects a form of female solidarity (Clover, 1992). And in *A Few Good Men* (1992), attorney Demi Moore cajoles and browbeats Tom Cruise into doing the right thing and taking their case to trial. But she is equally concerned that he not be harmed by his vigorous defense of their clients. In a conversation in which she is as much mother or sister (and would be lover?) as colleague or superior officer, she advises him to back down if he feels their courtroom strategy could fail.

These are some of the more dramatic situations faced by female attorneys in films. But even more common in these movies are the sexual innuendoes by male colleagues, clients, witnesses, police officers, and others. These comments range from lame jokes (to which the female attorney often responds with a quip or a groan) to heavy-handed verbal aggression. And there are other job-related issues. For example, in *Suspect* (1989), the attorney is an overworked public defender with no time for the personal life she would like to have. In *Physical Evidence* (1989), the public defender (with vocal support from her female colleagues) expresses her annoyance over case assignment to her boss: "My last three cases have been a postman bitten by a poodle, some first-time grass smokers, and a derelict knocking quarters out of a parking meter."

But in the films of the 1980s and 1990s, unlike the career woman films of the 1930s and 1940s, the female attorney does not give up her career for a man. This does not mean that she is not "punished" for her ambition or her occupation. The physical jeopardy she must face seems often to be a form of punishment. And her sometimes "manless" state at the close of the film can be read as another statement about the choices she has made. The most striking example of this is in the film *Hanna K.*, in which the attorney angrily sends both her estranged husband and her discarded lover (who is also the father of her child *and* the prosecuting attorney) away. In the final scene, she hears a knock and rushes to the door thinking her lover/client (a suspected terrorist) has returned. Clad in a bathrobe, she finds herself facing dozens of armed and helmeted police officers who have come to arrest her client—and perhaps her as well? A melodramatic plot, but striking in its final comment about the fate of a woman who rejects two "good" men because she wants her independence. The movie also presents a subtle comment that this woman has achieved professional status and monetary reward by virtue of her chance assignment to a client in what turns out to be a high-profile, political case.

Finally, these attorneys occasionally apply what might best be described as "situational ethics" in deciding how to resolve their problems. In *Defenseless* (1991), Barbara Hershey lies to the police about her involvement with her client and her presence in his office just before he was murdered because she needs time to find the real killer. In *Guilty as Sin* (1993), Rebecca De Mornay is manipulated and blackmailed into defending Don Johnson, who might best be described as "the client from hell." She decides that it is "him or me" and "plants" the physical evidence that she hopes will prove his guilt. In *Class Action* (1991), the attorney betrays both the client and her own firm when she realizes both are guilty of wrong-doing and will avoid punishment unless she provides the plaintiff's attorney (her father) with the name of a witness crucial to the case. Of course, such moral dilemmas are common to popular films and do not reflect the gender of the characters. And, as a group, the female attorneys are often heard to challenge the ethical sidestepping and professional pragmatism of their male colleagues.

In the next section of the chapter, we examine the responses of real-life female attorneys to their fictional counterparts.

TELEPHONE INTERVIEWS
WITH FEMALE ATTORNEYS

In a random telephone sample of female attorneys (obtained from the phone book in a medium-sized city), respondents were asked their opinions about the portrayal of female attorneys in films and other media. We employed a survey instrument. Although the sample of 26 women was small, it was fairly representative of female attorneys. Most were in general practice (31 percent), or some type of litigation work, which includes personal injury or criminal defense (23 percent). Only 19 percent of the sample had a family practice, although those who specified a general practice indicated that they did family work as well. Only 6 percent were in agency work, and the remainder were in varied fields such as immigration and employment law. Most had been in practice between 6 and 15 years (53 percent) with smaller numbers reporting a practice of 5 years or less (19 percent) or of more than 15 years (23 percent). Most were married (58 percent). Most were white (58 percent), although the sample also included Hispanics (25 percent), blacks (7 percent), and Asians (7 percent). Most were between the ages of 35 and 49 (58 percent) with 23 percent younger than 35 and 15 percent older than 50. Most watched movies or videos at least three times a month (77 percent); however, those who were mothers and worked as attorneys reported they "didn't have time to do anything."

Most felt that the portrayal of female attorneys in popular films was somewhat or largely unrealistic (70 percent). We asked whether they had seen some of the films in our sample. The most watched film turned out to be *A Few Good Men* and the least watched film was *Music Box*. There were roughly equal numbers who had either seen or not seen the remaining movies.

A sizable minority of the female respondents did not feel any aspect of the portrayals of female attorneys was offensive or objectionable, but their reasoning was typically that neither male nor female attorneys were portrayed realistically, that movies were not real life, or that they didn't take movies seriously anyway. Some indicated that they tended to avoid movies about lawyers in general, finding them ridiculous or unrealistic.

If they did find some aspects of movies objectionable or disturbing, the most common factor was that the female attorney was portrayed as "bitchy" if successful or, more often cited, seductive or unrealistically glamorous. They noted that skirts tended to be too tight and too short, and the persona of the female character was more "sexual" than "intellectual." Another factor noted was the unrealistic portrayal of relationships with clients that often went way beyond the bounds of professional ethics. Even though most respondents liked *The Client*, they noted that it probably wasn't coincidental that the character was a woman, because the intensive involvement with a client was very unrealistic of the profession as a whole. One respondent noted that all female attorneys in films tended to be completely wrapped up with work; they were never shown as mothers or wives or involved in family or other interests. Another respondent echoed the belief that successful female attorneys were shown as "hard" and "bitchy," but that wasn't inevitable in real life. She pointed out that female attorneys could be polite and respectful and even nice and still be successful as attorneys. A few respondents noted the supportive roles females tended to play, even if professionals themselves. The film cited as an example was *A Few Good Men* where the character played by Demi Moore was portrayed in the opening scenes as a consummate professional, yet later with the entry of the younger, brasher character played by Tom Cruise, she was relegated to "briefcase carrier."

When asked if there were aspects of the portrayal of women that were positive or praiseworthy, most respondents noted that it was nice to be represented at all in films, that at least today there is recognition of the existence of female attorneys. Many noted that the women attorneys were portrayed as intelligent and professional (or powerful). Some cited the glamorous nature of female film roles as a positive rather than a negative aspect of the portrayal. Another group of respondents noted that females tended to be portrayed as more caring than males. One interesting observation repeated a couple of times was that females tended to be portrayed as more ethical than male attorneys, that often the female role acted as the conscience in the film.

Although *The Client* was cited as the most realistic portrayal of women in film, respondents hastened to add it wasn't because the female attorney was an alcoholic, but rather because she was older, was not a "sexpot," and because she was portrayed in a more three-dimensional fashion than most characters. A few respondents, interestingly, cited this same movie as the most unrealistic because her involvement with her client was extremely unrealistic. Many respondents could not think of one single realistic portrayal. In some cases only one aspect of the portrayal was described as realistic, for instance, the age and full life of the lawyer in *The Client*, even though other parts of the movie were very unrealistic. Others mentioned the role of the prosecutor in *The Accused* as somewhat realistic. At least one respondent mentioned *Suspect*, insofar as it portrayed the public defender's job as one where overwork, crummy conditions, and no respect was common. Most of our respondents (62 percent) believed that these film portrayals had some or a great deal of impact on how the public viewed female attorneys.

Those expressing opinions about how women attorneys were portrayed on television pointed out that the television roles tended to show attorneys as hardworking—a realistic element of the true life of an attorney. They also mentioned that television attorneys tended to be less glamorous and more three-dimensional than film attorneys. The most common opinion was that television portrayed all attorneys and the practice of law in general in a very unrealistic light, specifically courtroom and investigative tactics that were ridiculous, the length of time it took to get a case to trial was incredibly and unrealistically short, and that practicing law was not as exciting as television or movies portray it to be.

CONCLUSIONS

In this chapter, we have examined how female attorneys have been depicted in popular films from the 1940s through 1990s. We conclude that the images of female attorneys in films have been true to life to the extent that they reflected (1) the scarce representation of women in the law, (2) the gender-based attitudes toward women as lawyers, and (3) the "femininity-achievement conflict" faced by attorneys. But as we (and the female attorneys surveyed) have observed, these films offer a distorted image of female attorneys to the extent that (1) the emphasis is placed on the woman's sexuality rather than her professionalism; (2) young, glamorous, single, and childless characters are overrepresented among fictional attorneys; and (3) the dangerous and more sensational aspects of the profession are overemphasized, specifically the predominance of these fictional characters in criminal law. Moreover, even though film attorneys are no longer forced to choose between career and personal relationships, this seems to happen almost by default in many of the films in our sample. Only in films such as *Legal Eagles*, *Bird on a Wire*, and *The Big Easy*, which are arguably "throwbacks" to the romantic films of an earlier era, is the attorney-heroine allowed a happy ending in which she gets her man and keeps her career. In both *Lipstick* and *The Accused*, the endings are upbeat in that each attorney wins her respective case. But also the raped and battered female victim has won, and the emphasis is on the system having finally given the victim the justice she should have received in the first place. And what has gone before arguably has been so disturbing for both victim and attorney that the moment of triumph is bittersweet.

So perhaps modern films send at best a mixed message to audiences. Even as these fictional female attorneys take their places in law offices and courtrooms, they continue to play "traditional" roles in their relationships with men. The issues facing real-life female attorneys are raised, but often the treatment of these issues is slick and stereotypical. As several of the real-life attorneys note, fictional female attorneys are generally presented as competent and capable lawyers. Unfortunately, in these films, a woman who is competent and capable is sometimes perceived and described by other characters as obsessed with her job, overly aggressive, emasculating, or unwomanly. This film dilemma both reflects and exaggerates a real-life dilemma faced by career women.[2]

DISCUSSION QUESTIONS

1. What is the "femininity-achievement conflict" the authors discuss? Do you agree or disagree that this conflict is one that real-life women have faced (continue to face) in their professional lives?

2. Historically, why was there resistance to women practicing law?

3. What conclusions do the authors reach about how female attorneys are portrayed in popular films? How do the real life attorneys who were interviewed feel about these films? If you have seen any of these films, do you agree or disagree with the assessments offered by the authors and by the real-life attorneys?

APPENDIX: FILMS VIEWED

The Bachelor and the Bobby-Soxer (1947)

Adam's Rib (1949)

Lipstick (1976)

Hanna K. (1984)

Jagged Edge (1985)

Legal Eagles (1986)

The Big Easy (1987)

Suspect (1987)

The Accused (1988)

Music Box (1989)

Perfect Witness (1989)

Physical Evidence (1989)

Bird on a Wire (1990)

Criminal Justice (1990)

Presumed Innocent (1990)

Reversal of Fortune (1990)

Class Action (1991)

Defenseless (1991)

Love Crimes (1991)

Ultimate Desires (1991)

A Few Good Men (1992)

Another Stakeout (1993)

Guilty As Sin (1993)

The Pelican Brief (1993)

The Client (1994)

NOTES

1. Film critic Michael Wilmington (1995: 297) notes that *Jagged Edge* is an "erotic thriller"—the name given to the new subgenre that blends violence and sex. And though it seems primarily a post-1980 phenomenon—with movies like *Fatal Attraction, Basic Instinct, Unlawful Entry, Internal Affairs, Jagged Edge*, and numerous other examples—the primal source is Hitchcock's 1960 *Psycho*.

2. Since this research was completed, several films featuring female attorneys in significant roles have premiered in theaters. These films include *Primal Fear* (1996) and *A Time to Kill* (1996). Although these films are not included in our video sample, we have seen them and would like to make several passing observations. In *Primal Fear*, female attorneys are well-represented, occupying the second chairs at both tables, defense and prosecution. The prosecuting attorney is a woman, and although she has had a prior romantic involvement with the male defense attorney (Richard Gere), she declines his overtures to resume the rela-

tionship. In this film, the presiding judge—a tough no-nonsense type—is an African American woman (Alfre Woodard). *A Time to Kill* reminded us of an earlier film, *The Pelican Brief*. Both films are based on novels by John Grisham, and in *A Time to Kill*, again a brilliant, young female law student (Sandra Bullock) finds herself in jeopardy. After offering the handsome, young defense attorney (who happens to be married) both her legal services and herself and being turned down on both counts, Bullock is kidnapped and abused by the Ku Klux Klan. Left tied to a tree in the swamp, she is rescued by an undercover operative. She is last seen when the defense attorney visits her in the hospital. What the portrayal of female attorneys in recent films would seem to suggest is that their presence in movie courtrooms is becoming somewhat commonplace. However, the female attorney's (or law student's) credibility as a professional still might be rendered problematic by focusing on her sexuality.

13

❈

Public Perception and Corrections:

Correctional Officers as Smug Hacks

ROBERT M. FREEMAN

C orrections is the third major element of any criminal justice system. The role of corrections in American society is

> To protect the public from criminal offenders through a system of incarceration and supervision which securely segregates offenders from society, assures offenders of their Constitutional rights, and maintains programs to enhance the success of the offender's reentry into society. (Mission statement of the Illinois Department of Corrections as cited in Houston, 1995: 69)

Accomplishing this mission statement is the responsibility of correctional staff, the most visible of which are the correctional officers charged with the specific responsibility of providing the supervision necessary for the safe and humane management of 1.6 million incarcerated offenders, many of them violent, in a stressful environment of total confinement. Accomplishing the corrections mission is critical. Many correctional professionals believe that although corrections does accomplish its mission, the public perception of the correctional officers responsible for that accomplishment is overwhelmingly negative.

Dr. Jeffrey A. Schwartz, president of LETRA, Inc., a nonprofit probation and parole research and training organization in California, reports that

> Many corrections workers believe the public image of the corrections field is quite bad. Actually, it is nowhere that good . . . The public view of

corrections in this country is, frankly, terrible. The major stories that reach the public about corrections are almost universally negative (Schwartz, 1989: 38).

M. Wayne Huggins, director of the National Institute of Corrections, states, "I believe no profession has been more unfairly, inaccurately, or intentionally distorted than ours" (Huggins, 1992: 58). Dr. Jack Kamerman of the Department of Sociology, Anthropology, and Social Work at Kean College in New Jersey begins an article on correctional officer suicide with

> It is not exactly revelatory to say that correctional work is stressful and that part of that stress comes from the fact that the work of correctional officers is neither understood nor appreciated by the public at large. (Kamerman, 1996: 23)

Is there empirical support for this belief that the public has a negative perception of corrections? Doris Graber (1979), in a study of the influence of the print media on public opinion about the criminal justice system, surveyed four panels randomly drawn from a sample of registered voters in Illinois, Indiana, and New Hampshire. Survey participants were asked to rate the performance of police, courts, and corrections on a scale of good, fair, and poor. The rating for police performance was 57 percent good and 43 percent fair. The courts had a rating of 11 percent good; 47 percent fair and 42 percent poor. The rating for corrections was 15 percent good, 20 percent fair, and 65 percent poor.

What could account for such an unfavorable public perception of corrections? Ken Kerle, managing editor of the American Jail Association, believes that the media coverage of corrections has created a type of stereotyping ("gratuitous vilification") that presents correctional staff as

> A bunch of noncaring, selfish, greedy, corrupt individuals. Many institutions, people on the outside will be surprised to learn, are staffed by concerned, caring individuals. (Kerle, 1996)

What are the stereotypes involved in "gratuitous vilification?" The most obvious stereotype is that category of correctional officer known as the "smug hack" (Klofas and Toch, 1982: 238–254): an officer characterized by brutality, incompetence, low intelligence, indifference to human suffering, and obsession with routine. The following inmate description of a speech given by a Texas "guard" with unblinking icy-blue eyes set in a heavily tanned, weathered face is typical:

> "I'm gonna tell ya'll one time, and one time alone how I'm gonna deal. First off, if airy one uv you tries to run off, I'm gonna kill ya. If airy one uv you 'sputes my word, I'm gonna kill ya. If airy one uv you don' do lak I tell ya, I'm gonna kill ya. If you lay th' hammer down under me [refuse to work], I'm gonna kill ya. And if I jes take a notion to, I'm gonna kill ya." (Crouch and Marquart, 1989: 59)

There was a time in the history of corrections when smug hacks were accepted and appreciated:

> There is much about the history of corrections in America that reflects cruelty and an organized policy of breaking the human spirit. The state prison flogging, for example . . . (Freeman, 1996a: 12)

But many individuals, inside and outside of corrections, argue that corrections, and the correctional officer, have changed since the rehabilitation goal was formally introduced into corrections during the early 1960s:

> An issue commonly agreed upon by conservative, liberal, and radical penologists is that guards need and deserve continuing professionalization. . . . The objective of professionalization is to upgrade the staff in ways that promote more humane and professional management of inmates. (Welch, 1996: 145)

Correctional administrators report that they now require "guards" to be correctional officers, that is, skilled human service workers who use their authority to help inmates adjust to the deprivations of prison life, minimize custodial repression, and apply skill and ingenuity to humanizing the prison environment. Correctional staff training programs currently being conducted throughout the nation reflect this emphasis on professionalism (Silverman and Vega, 1996: 298–301). Yet,

> The image of the subhuman and senselessly brutal custodian lives on, as if the modern prison were frozen in time as a relic of . . . the Big House." (Johnson, 1996: 199)

John DiIulio, in *Governing Prisons*, notes that popular stereotypes continue to portray correctional staff as

> Stupid ogres and inmates as their victims . . . underplay the difficulty of their work and portray those who work in prisons as sadistic or subhuman. (DiIulio, 1987: 254)

The stereotype of the correctional officer as a smug hack presents the imagery of an officer who can be classified as

> Possibly the lowest imaginable form of humanoid life, a species somewhere about the level of the gorilla and often rather easily mistaken for one. (Schroeder, 1976: 151–152)

Anecdotal material and research, although limited because of the general lack of empirical study, does appear to suggest a negative public perception of correctional staff, particularly correctional officers. My basic premise is that this negative public perception can be best understood by examining the interaction of three critical elements: the sociological literature concerning corrections; the media (Hollywood, television news, and print news) coverage of corrections; and current correctional behavior.

THE SOCIOLOGICAL LITERATURE

Historically, the primary contributors to the formal study of corrections have been sociologists interested in the study of inmates as a group (Houston, 1995: 6). Sociologists have traditionally paid little attention to correctional staff, preferring to focus on inmate experiences within the correctional system and inmate perceptions of that system:

> Beginning in the 1960s much of the sociological writing on prisons became informed by countercultural assumptions, chief among them that prisons are the oppressive instruments of an oppressive, racially discriminatory, and vengeful society. (DiIulio, 1987: 19)

In sociological writings, the correctional officer is often described in stereotypical terms:

> A harsh (if not sadistic), power-hungry illiterate—an ignorant, rigid, authoritarian, individual who is vigorous only when demanding inmate compliance, when opposing inmate's rights, when criticizing management policies or when scuttling rehabilitation programs . . . thugs . . . clones or zombies . . . uniformed automatons performing routine, mundane, and mindless tasks which anyone could do, which permit no individual excellence, and require no notable skills. (Ross, 1981: 3)

In his landmark work, *Prisons in Turmoil*, John Irwin writes, "I hate prisons; that is, I hate what happens to convicts in prison (my people, I suppose)" (Irwin, 1980: xxiii). This hatred is apparently based, in part, on Irwin's opinion that correctional officers are poorly educated racists:

> Guards are more racially prejudiced than the average citizen. . . . Guards' racism takes three forms. First, they do not like, and in fact often hate, nonwhites. . . . Moreover, most white guards believe that nonwhites are inferior. . . . Finally, the guard force, with a rural background and poor education, misunderstand the perspectives of subcultures of most prisoners. (Irwin, 1980: 125)

It could be argued that this kind of negative imagery does not reach beyond the classroom to the general public. But these negative images do reach beyond the classroom. For 50 years they have provided the foundation for "the conventional wisdom of numerous legislators, judges, prison reformers, journalists, prison administrators, inmates, academics in other fields, and others" (DiIulio, 1987: 14).

THE MEDIA

The "others" noted in the previous quote would logically include Hollywood writers, producers, directors, actors, newspaper and television newscast editors, publishers, bureau chiefs, and reporters. These individuals play a most important role in the public perception of corrections because

> In modern societies, the media often play a more crucial role than personal social networks in constructing social reality because knowledge of many social phenomenon is obtained solely from the media. Because few people have direct experience with crime and because the media are a primary source of crime-related information, the process of social construction of reality and the role of the media have been proposed as particularly important for crime and justice. (Surette, 1995a: 357)

If the smug hack of sociological literature has been the primary exposure for media personnel, then it can become the template that is used to provide the base-line imagery necessary for public construction of the social reality of corrections and the correctional officer:

> Most of the public's knowledge of corrections comes from what it sees on television and reads in the newspapers. If all the information is negative . . . public perception of corrections can be negative . . . the perpetuation of the stereotype that correctional officers and administrators are "disgruntled, alienated hacks prone to violence under pressure" misleads the public, giving it an unrealistic view of the corrections profession. (Zaner, 1989: 65)

Hollywood

In her exploration of the impact of Hollywood movies on the public perception of correctional staff, Laura Zaner reviews 14 movies, two of which are especially important in the discussion of correctional officers as smug hacks because of the popularity of the actors.

Cool Hand Luke (1967). Paul Newman is the lovable petty criminal Luke confined to a Southern prison work camp for cutting the tops off of parking meters while drunk. He is a devil-may-care rebel who immediately engages the affection of the audience. George Kennedy is his best inmate buddy—not too bright, but he cares about Luke. Strother Martin, as the sadistic captain of the work camp, utters the famous line, "What we got here is a failure to communicate," after Luke has been beaten by guards and rolled into a ditch. Subject to the unemotional sadism of the "Boss" who wears reflecting sunglasses, and rarely speaks, Luke escapes three times, is captured each time, and is finally murdered.

The Longest Yard (1974). Burt Reynolds is an ex-pro quarterback in prison for stealing his nagging girlfriend's car. A nice guy, Reynolds is beaten by the brutal captain of the guards and forced into fielding an inmate football team to play the guards' team. Eddie Albert is a sadistic warden so sleazy that by the end of the movie, the captain of the guards, won over by Reynold's refusal to surrender his dignity, refuses the warden's order to shoot Reynolds in the back as he casually walks to retrieve the game ball.

Zaner observes that the importance of movies like *Cool Hand Luke* and *The Longest Yard* is that "the bad rap corrections takes in the movies may translate into a lack of public support for real-life correctional institutions" (Zaner, 1989: 64).

In 1994, the popular *The Shawshank Redemption* was released. Tim Robbins plays the innocent man framed for murder. His first night in prison, the guards beat a new inmate (fat and terrified of prison life) to death because he is crying for his mother, a show of emotion that annoys the captain of the guard. The warden is grossly corrupt and orders the murder of the inmate who can prove Robbins is innocent. Robbins escapes and exposes the warden's corruption, an act that drives the warden to suicide by revolver. In the theaters, audiences cheered at two points in the movie—when Robbins escapes and when the warden commits suicide:

> What's really bad . . . is that the inmates often end up as more sympathetic characters than the officers. The pervasive attitude is that the crowd should be rooting for the kept, not the keepers. (Zaner, 1989: 65)

Occasionally a movie portrays a correctional officer or administrator in a positive light. In the 1970s, Robert Redford starred in *Brubaker* as the new warden of an Arkansas prison. A man of morality, compassion, and sincerity, Redford battles a system where injured inmates have to bribe an incompetent doctor to treat them; inmates are routinely murdered and buried in unmarked graves; political corruption is rampant; and the new warden is fired on in his own home, probably by disgruntled guards. The positive portrayal of the warden makes more pronounced the brutality and moral corruption of the staff.

Smug hack imagery is not limited to the theater. In an October 1995 episode of the popular *The X-Files* television series, a story set in a maximum security prison has the warden (on two separate occasions) *personally* beat to death a Death Row inmate in a shower room while an indifferent guard ignores celled inmates begging the warden to "leave him (the inmate) alone."

But do movies and television series really influence the public perception of correctional officers? *Cool Hand Luke*, *The Longest Yard*, and *The Shawshank Redemption* are just movies. *Shawshank*, in particular, was a period piece set in the 1940s. And *The X-Files* deals with aliens and government conspiracy.

In examining this question, we remember that the imagery supplied by Hollywood is useful for

> Shaping the individual and collective consciousness organizing and circulating the knowledge which people have of their own everyday life and of the more remote contexts of their lives. (McQuail, 1972: 13)

For most Americans, corrections is not a part of daily life. Because the work of correctional officers is routinely hidden from public view, carried out behind walls and fences and a policy of rigidly enforced limited public access to the prison, the public perception of these officers can not be based on personal experience or knowledge. For most people corrections is indeed a "remote context." The more remote the context, the more likely public perception is to be shaped by the imagery presented by Hollywood:

> The degree of media contribution to the individual's construction of subjective reality is a function of one's direct experience with various phenomena and consequent dependence on the media for information about these phenomenon. (Adoni and Mane, 1984: 327)

If personal knowledge about corrections is absent, Hollywood's smug hack can create a viewer perception of 1990s corrections that is framed in pre-1960s terms.

The News Media

Many correctional professionals accuse the visual and print news media of reinforcing Hollywood stereotypes by sensationalizing its coverage of unpleasant events and failing to report explanatory or positive information. If media reporting is biased, or sensationalized, observes Commissioner Koehler of the New York Department of Correction, "the public will often view you and your organization as a bunch of buffoons . . . " (Koehler, 1989: 16).

Television News

The kind of sensational television news coverage often cited by correctional staff as an example of deliberate media bias occurred in Michigan. Following a series of escapes, a television news crew was permitted to interview prison officials and shoot film. The escapes had involved minimum security facility "walkaways": low-risk inmates assigned to outside work details who had simply walked away. Instead of reporting this fact, the reporters filmed the forbidding walls of a maximum-security prison where no escapes had occurred and

> Presented an alarmist view of how prison officials were failing to protect the public. The reporters could have done a public service by conveying accurate and pertinent information that would truly inform the public, benefit the agency, and assuage the community's unjustified fears about escaped felons. Instead, they miscast the department's record and heightened public excitement. (DiIulio, 1987: 254)

But what about those reporters who attempt to present correctional news in an objective, professional manner?

Sensational stories about prison disturbances and hostage takings are not the only source of bad publicity. There's also the regular occurrence of bureaucratic snafus and administrative failures that reinforce the public's negative view of corrections (Meddis, 1989: 26).

The Print Media

The print media reports the behavior of both inmates and staff. Does the specific behavior being reported reinforce, or challenge, the perception of correctional officers as smug hacks? To examine this question more thoroughly, Freeman (1996b) analyzed the content of 1,546 newspaper articles concerning corrections that appeared throughout the United States between September 8, 1994, and November 24, 1995. Duplicated stories (and there were numerous instances in which a story was picked up by a variety of newspapers or formed the basis of ongoing coverage over a period of days or weeks) were counted only once. The articles were provided by a news clipping service and the material received for analysis was either in the form of the complete article, if it was short enough, or in the form of a summary. In both cases, the behavior of the subject(s) of the article was readily identifiable.

First the Numbers

After preliminary review of the data, 11 categories of negative behavior and 4 categories of positive behavior were established and a frequency distribution of 105 staff and 222 inmate behaviors developed. Negative behavior was defined as behavior that could be reasonably expected to create a negative impression in the reader's mind. Positive behavior was defined as behavior that could reasonably be expected to create a positive impression in the reader's mind. Most articles (85.4 percent) referenced adult correctional institutions. The results of this analysis are presented in Table 13-1.

The surveyed news articles appear to provide a degree of support for Hollywood's smug hack and *Cool Hand Luke*. Inmates engaged in 53 positive behaviors; staff engaged in only 42 positive behaviors (35 of which involved being the recipient of an Employee of the Month award). Inmates engaged in 169 negative behaviors; staff engaged in 63 negative behaviors.

A note of caution in interpretation is needed at this point. Seventy-four of the inmate negative behaviors were escapes. A strong argument could be made, however, that a successful inmate escape might be perceived by the public as an example of negative staff behavior, that is, if the officers were doing their job, the escape could not have occurred. The escapee might actually be seen as more intelligent, competent, and skilled than the officers who failed to prevent the escape.

Now the Quality

This study involves more than the numbers. The quality and nature of the behavior are also an issue. How much will a reasonable reader admire or respect or approve or identify with a specific behavior? In this area a clear trend emerges. The 53 positive inmate behaviors reported in the articles included a variety of activities with which the reasonable reader could identify or perceive as being beneficial to the community:

1. Earning a GED or college diploma
2. Participating in community art programs
3. Organizing runathons to collect contributions to aid victims of multiple sclerosis, Big Brothers and Big Sisters, and other community groups

**Table 13-1 Print News Coverage of
Inmate and Correctional Staff Behavior**

N = 327	Correctional Staff	Inmates
Negative Behaviors	**N = 63**	**N = 169**
Assault	15	47
Sexual Assault	4	12
Sexual Harassment	2	2
Corruption	9	0
Theft	3	3
Fraud	3	3
Negligence	11	0
Drug Violations	8	19
Abuse	5	0
Contraband	3	9
Escapes	—	74
Positive Behaviors	**N = 42**	**N = 53**
Self-Improvement	0	34
Assisting the Community	2	17
Heroic Actions	5	2
Employee of the Month	35	—

4. Participating in parenting classes

5. Making Christmas toys for needy children

6. Playing Santa Claus in the prison visiting room

7. Giving hand-painted handkerchiefs with Christmas themes to sick children in a children's hospital

8. Engaging in charity work to help the physically disabled and the elderly

9. Performing voluntary community services such as renovating and repairing government-owned vehicles.

10. Educating public school students about the evils of crime or drugs and crime

11. Translating books into Braille for blind children

12. Building homes for the needy

13. Advocating education as a solution to gang membership

14. Performing heroic deeds such as rescuing a civilian trapped in a construction ditch cave-in and capturing a kidnapper and rescuing the child victim

Positive inmate behaviors of the type identified in the articles surveyed can arguably create a sense of approval and identification between reader and inmate that gives the *Cool Hand Luke* image credibility.

What about positive staff behaviors? Forty of the behaviors were work-related (35 involving the rationale for being selected Employee of the Month).

The two nonwork behaviors involved (1) a prison food service supervisor devoting a day off to cooking for the elderly at a picnic and (2) a father-and-son karate team. Positive inmate behavior was not only reported slightly more frequently than positive staff behavior was, it was also more community-oriented.

Although inferences can be drawn from these results, appropriate empirical follow-up is needed to determine what specific influence, if any, positive news stories about inmate behavior have on the public perception of both inmates and correctional officers.

The Language of the Media

The language used by the print media can reinforce the imagery of the smug hack. For example, in the December 12, 1994 issue of *Time*, the career of Tim Allen, star of the popular television show *Home Improvement*, is examined in an article titled "Tim at the Top." While discussing the two years Allen served in a federal penitentiary on drug charges, the article notes:

> Allen found humor useful in prison. He made the *meanest guard* (italics mine) laugh by putting pictures of Richard Nixon in the peephole of his cell when they made their rounds. Later he staged comedy shows for the other inmates. Once, while riding a bus to another prison, he managed to slip out of his hand-cuffs. The only thing he could think to do was to bum a cigarette off the old bank robber sitting in front of him (Zoglin, 1994: 80).

The language in this article can be interpreted as reinforcement of the smug hack imagery presented by Hollywood. "Guards" are both mean and incompetent. The officers transporting Allen could not even manage the simple task of making certain that inmates have properly secured handcuffs.

Is It Just Bad Public Relations or Is It a Deeper Problem?

Richard J. Koehler, commissioner of the New York Department of Correction, argues that corrections has a serious public relations problem (Koehler, 1989: 16–17). If the issue of negative perception of correctional staff is one of bad public relations, then corrections should be able to address the issue with a strategy of positive public relations:

> The basic problem of public relations involves doing whatever is necessary to create and maintain good relations and to avoid or remove bad relations. If bad relations are due to ignorance or misunderstanding by the public concerned, an education or informational campaign may be indicated. (Brody, 1992: 355)

In an effort to create positive public relations, correctional administrators employ public information officers (PIOs). Although much of what PIOs do is reactive (response to routine and crisis-generated requests for information from the media), many administrators encourage their PIOs to be proactive in dealing with the media (Houston, 1995: 60–65). A favorite proactive activity designed to present a positive public image is the Employee of the Month Award, a plaque or certificate presented to a staff member in an official ceremony. The question now becomes, "If correctional administrators engage in proactive public relations, and the work of correctional officers is indeed positive and valuable, why doesn't the public appreciate their contribution to society?" Is this an issue of media indifference to the reality of corrections, or is the issue deeper than that?

THE ROLE OF CORRECTIONS IN
PROMOTING SMUG HACK IMAGERY

The answer appears to be that the issue of the negative public perception of correctional officers goes beyond the media. The value of attempts at proactive publicity, such as Employee of the Month awards, in influencing public perception is arguably questionable because of three variables: the intensity of image created by correctional officer misconduct, officer machismo, and the silence of correctional administrators.

Intensity of Image of Staff Misconduct

A typical PIO press release about an Employee of the Month Award recipient is as follows:

> Sgt. Robert A. McMillan, a correctional officer at SCI Mahanoy in Mahanoy Twp., was named the facility's employee of the month for October. McMillan transferred to SCI Mahanoy from SCI Retreat 15 months ago and has been employed for nearly five years with the state DOC (Hazelton Standard Speaker, 1994).

This type of news release is sterile, arouses no emotion, and has no reader impact because there is no imagery worthy of the reader's interest. Now read the factual article concerning a correctional officer tried on six counts of aggravated indecent sexual assault and official oppression of a female inmate:

> At age 15, her father forced her to have sex with men for money. A year later, she was arrested for killing a fellow teen-ager and sentenced to life in prison . . . Now she's 22, and her words have sent shock waves through Georgia's legal community and the state's Corrections Department. . . . "The prison guards have taken this little girl, whose daddy put her in a prostitution ring, and abused her much worse in prison than the truckers and bikers she had sex with every night," says Robert W. Cullen, director of Georgia Legal Services. (Curriden, 1993)

This article has an emotional impact, the images presented are vivid and disturbing and reinforce the imagery of numerous B-grade movies in which guards have raped female inmates. How many readers, especially women, will be able to relate to the victim? What value does the Employee of the Month Award press release have in comparison? The misconduct of correctional staff speaks so loudly that no one can hear what correctional managers and PIOs are trying to say in mission statements and press releases. Sterile press releases lack the power to counteract the powerful imagery of staff misconduct.

Correctional Officer Machismo

Many correctional officers, especially males, relish the image of a tough officer doing a dangerous job in an environment few individuals are qualified to handle. They enjoy telling war stories that demonstrate their physical toughness and ability to control others. In telling these war stories, officers tend to exaggerate by overstating the personal dangers to which they are exposed. For example, witness this statement by a male correctional officer protesting the hiring of female officers:

> A lot of things can happen to you in here—guards get killed every day. When I go into a dangerous situation, I want to know that my partner is going to be there to help me. You just can't count on a woman. And even if you can, what is she going to do? Is she going to be able to pull an inmate off my throat before he has the chance to kill me? No way in hell! (Zimmer, 1986: 55)

Too often, the image conveyed to the public by war stories and pronouncements of danger is that of the smug hack.

Correctional Administrator Silence

During the 1988 presidential campaign, the country was bombarded with campaign ads about Willie Horton, an African American lifer who committed rape and assault while on furlough from a Massachusetts prison. Factual articles about Willie Horton were used to promote campaign rhetoric about getting tough on crime by eliminating community-based corrections programs. Many correctional professionals believe that community-based programs

> Are among the more progressive directions in corrections. They recognized that closing these release valves could have catastrophic consequences for population levels within our institutions. Finally, most correctional professionals quickly recognized the broad emotional attack on furlough programs would have a long-term negative effect on the field of corrections as a whole. What, then, was the response from the corrections field? A deafening silence! (Schwartz, 1989: 38).

Freeman (1996b), in his content analysis of 1,546 newspaper articles, also examined the issue of correctional administrator silence. A total of 224 articles on the death penalty, sex offender community notification laws, get tough on crime legislation, parole effectiveness, three strikes legislation, crime prevention, and the economic benefits of prisons were examined to determine the discussants of each issue. Each issue has important policy implications for corrections. Yet, the distribution of discussants was as follows: citizens, 80; politicians, 75; media representatives, 54; and correctional administrators, 15. And administrators were most likely to be discussants only when the issue was the positive economic benefits to the community of prison construction.

Why are correctional administrators not taking part in the public discussion of critical criminal justice issues?

> Historically, "fortress corrections" has been both a mentality and a philosophy in the field. Prisons . . . were built far from populated areas partly because those places wanted no more public scrutiny than absolutely necessary. Too many staff . . . do not understand the public's right to know or disagree with the concept and work actively to thwart efforts to open up corrections to the public. (Schwartz, 1989: 40)

Given this, it appears safe to conclude that the Hollywood imagery of the smug hack is alive and well in American culture. This imagery is reinforced by news media coverage conducted in a vacuum of correctional silence that provides the public with no alternative basis for the social construction of correctional reality. The public perception of the correctional officer as smug hack will undoubtedly continue to exist for some time.

DISCUSSION QUESTIONS

1. Freeman uses the term "smug hacks" to describe one popular image of correctional officers. What does he mean? According to the author, what factors explain the existence of this image? Do you agree or disagree that this is the predominant Hollywood image of the correctional officer in the prison movies that you have seen?

2. Why does the author believe efforts by public information officers (PIOs) to create positive images of corrections have been ineffective?

3. Based on his research, what does Freeman conclude about the coverage of corrections by the media. Do you agree or disagree that the media should provide more vigorous coverage of corrections?

14

✸

Prison Movies:

Films About Adult, Male, Civilian Prisons: 1929–1995

DERRAL CHEATWOOD

> You know . . . people see movies about prison life, but until you've actually spent a little time here you can't get the real flavor. I think more Americans should spend some time behind bars.
>
> GENE WILDER'S CHARACTER IN *STIR CRAZY* (1980)

THE ENTERTAINMENT MEDIA
AND CORRECTIONS

The impact of popular film is not just something of casual interest to corrections, nor merely an academic footnote to the real concerns of the field. The motion picture audience forms the constituency of the elected legislatures of the states, and the legislature is the direct source of the funding necessary for any change or improvement in the correctional system. Each legislator is necessarily concerned with the attitudes of his or her constituents toward the funding, design, and implementation of correctional programs within the state. The assumed perceptions of this vague, often unspecified and unorganized voting mass constitute the foundations on which our correctional structures are built.

Most people in the general public have formed their images of what prison life is "actually" like from the mass media. Television has produced few "prison" series that lasted beyond one season. Indeed, even since the advent of cable television, dedicated movie channels, and made-for-TV movies, most presentations of prison life on television have been via the movie format rather than the series format. Books and magazines are not only less widely employed for entertainment by the general public than is television, but they lack the visual impact of either television or the movies as well. This leaves motion pictures as the primary medium that has created and supported popular images of what incarceration is, and this is a role motion pictures have filled since their inception.

As products in a competitive high-risk market, the goal of motion pictures is to make money—not to educate, to deliver messages, or to present realistic portraits of prison life. If these things are done, they are by-products of the primary demand for financial return. As products for a mass audience, these films present society's baseline attitudes about corrections at specific times and places, undisguised by academic jargon or political rhetoric. As such, they are almost pure "morality plays" that allow us to see the optimism or pessimism society holds toward the "system" and toward "individuals" at that time. The very characteristics that allow us to characterize these films as unrealistic, then, are those that help make such films more abstractly pure and valuable for an investigation of general public attitudes.

These films (focusing on films about adult, male, civilian prisons for reasons I will discuss later) divide into four identifiable eras: Depression Era films, 1929 to 1942; Rehabilitation Era films, 1943 to 1962; Confinement Era films, 1963 to 1980; and Administrative Era films, 1981 to present. Prison films—and my analysis—revolve around the themes of confinement, justice, authority, and release. These components, as defined later, enable us to see how our theories and public positions are translated and presented to the public.

In this chapter, I attempt a systematic analysis of commercial films on men's prisons based largely on objective data. My goal is to develop a typology of those films based on their content and to consider how that typology corresponds to the academic criminology and pragmatic correctional operations that existed during the same era.

MEDIA, CRIMINAL JUSTICE, AND PUBLIC PERCEPTIONS

Little previous literature about the relationship of mass media and the correctional system exists. Almost no one has considered the effect of media presentations of prison life on the public's perception of corrections, or the related process by which general public attitudes toward corrections become crystallized through the influence of these presentations. Further, much of the research that does exist is highly impressionistic or treats only one film, one national event, or one limited time period. Anthony Travisono concluded, "movies and television dramas come and go without much impact on the public . . . Hollywood and the television writers continue to portray the vilest aspects of prison life, and the public is led to believe that nothing can be accomplished because that's 'the way it is' with the system" (1980: 1). However, he also concluded, "the movie viewing public need not become hopeless about efforts to reform the prison system" (1980: 1).

His discussion is rather optimistic regarding the history of the films' impact on the public's perceptions of corrections and the role of those films in promoting or supporting ongoing change in corrections. A more troublesome point, however, is his implication that Hollywood has no interest in motivating people to act and, therefore, that the movies have no effect on the public because nothing happens. Quite probably, both ideas are overly naive and optimistic. Hollywood makes pictures to make money, and the effect of pictures on the public is more subtle than an immediate cause-and-effect sequence. People see pictures that support their established and currently held views of the world, and films can only gradually reshape or crystallize amorphous visions, perceptions, or ideas that the viewing public holds. A film analysis provides us only with a clearer and closer look at the problem symptoms, perhaps indicating conditions of which we were previously unaware. We cannot solve the problem through manipulation of those media.

THE STUDY OF PRISON FILMS

From the inception of sound in 1929 until 1995, more than 100 American films about prisons and incarceration have appeared. These have varied from military prison escape films to musicals about maximum security institutions. To establish a workable group of films relevant to American corrections, I limited my sample to films whose predominant subject was incarceration in a male, adult, civilian correctional facility. There are several pragmatic reasons for this limitation. In the public, the "prison problem" tends to be identified with adult, male, civilian facilities. So few "probation or parole" films exist that they do not constitute a genre at all. Although there are quite a few films about women's prisons, many are sexploitation films of the "Kittens Behind Bars" genre. Although these concerns—women and juvenile prisons—are legitimate both in pragmatic corrections and as film types, and as such are deserving of analysis, they are simply beyond the scope of my analysis in this chapter.

Determining which films were to be considered as prison films was not as difficult as it might seem, primarily because prison films are so clearly focused around that theme. I used the following specifications for "theme." First, a film was considered a prison film if a significant portion of the action, measured by actual screen time, occurs in and around the prison. I was not interested in films that employed a shot, a scene, or a sequence of action inside a prison if the major action and theme of the film was outside of the institution. Second, to be considered a prison film, the actual prison setting (including the adjunct of the prison road camp) and the action occurring within the prison were a virtual necessity for the film. Specifically, many gangster genre films have some prison scenes in them, but the film could have been shot without those scenes or with other scenes in their place. For prison films, on the other hand, such substitutions would be impossible. Finally, to be considered a prison film, the motion picture had to specifically address the prison experience and had to be based on that experience or components of that experience. This latter feature is admittedly more impressionistic than the first two. Fortunately, the distinction between prison films and even their closest cousins, the gangster films, was so clear that there were extremely few films that were at all questionable.[1]

To determine which motion pictures met these criteria for analysis, I initially employed a filmography of prison films developed by Querry (1973). I updated this through a review of titles of films produced since the publication of his filmography, using published synopses to clarify whether a film with an unclear title should be considered for analysis. My final universe, then, consisted of all films since 1929 that dealt with adult, male, civilian correctional facilities. I found 101 such films. The total number of films dealing with adult male corrections represents a rather surprising 1 percent of all commercial motion pictures made in the United States over this 66-year period. This percentage is unexpectedly high given the rather limited notice given to the prison film as anything more than a subgenre of the gangster film in either the social science or the film criticism literature.

Some of these motion pictures, particularly the more recent, I was able to view in theaters or on commercial television. The film collection of the Library of Congress provided viewing opportunities for some films, a National Endowment for the Humanities project at the Maryland Penitentiary allowed me to view others, and I rented a few films from film distribution companies. Even with these resources, however, it proved to be impossible to obtain all the films. Through all the resources available, I was able to obtain a sample of 56 of these films (see Appendix A). This is not a random sample because I could not control the factors operating to make some films unobtainable. However, I have not attempted any statistical analyses that would assume randomization in my analysis, and the categories of films I developed do not seem to display any obvious bias. In any case, this sample limitation should be kept in mind.

To guarantee that reliable and comparable data would be available across the range of films studied, I devised an instrument similar to a regular interviewing form (see Appendix B). Many questions were specific and objective, and the criteria used to establish the film eras were based on these objective data. I recorded, for example, whether the film specified the crime for which the offender (or hero) was incarcerated, the period of time for which he was incarcerated, whether eventual release was obtained, and how such release was obtained. Whether these facts were presented at all in the film, and what the nature of these facts were, were significant factors in separating the eras.

Other questions required some researcher evaluation, so that some sections required an evaluation of the film's attitude toward inmates, administrative staff, guards, or professional staff. On the negative side, these latter questions should have been ranked by a number of respondents and the results compared for inter-rater reliability. Unfortunately, when dealing with more than 50 films with an average length of one-and-a-half to two hours, many of which are available only through specialized film libraries or accessible only on the late-late show on television, such a luxury as multiple raters was unobtainable. On the positive side, motion pictures are not a particularly subtle medium, especially in their early years and especially in the action-film mode to which many prison films belong. The attitudes the film portrayed toward administrators and guards was usually quite clear and pronounced and was seldom balanced or equivocal. The films usually either failed to consider professional staff at all or were as clear about their messages as about administrators and staff. Commonly, the attitude toward inmates was mixed, recognizing the bad and the good among that population.

Without doubt, this does make conclusions drawn from these items on the film questionnaire more tentative. However, I have attempted two counterbalances to this. First, I have compared the logic of the evaluations on attitudes toward specific populations with the more objective data available. If, for example, I evaluated the film's presentation of administrative personnel as being negative, I would expect the film to result in a change of administrative staff or the release (or escape) of the hero in some way to remove him from the control of this staff. This was invariably the case (commonly both would happen; in some films only one or the other). Second, I recognized the limitations of the data and attempted to make the most conservative conclusions if I relied exclusively on this material. Also, the basic divisions of these films were obtainable through the completely objective data obtainable from the films. These checks recognize the limitations of the data drawn from these questions.

It is critical to understand that each film was observed as a self-contained universe of fiction, as a culture that was created to present a consistent reality within the confines of the film. Just as with a novel, a short story, or a television program, each fictional entity contains its own realities and can be analyzed as such. My question is not whether the film presents a true or valid picture of prison life or prison practice. My data was the reality presented on the screen. Although the "attitudes toward administration" presented in the films require a subjective evaluation, whether there is a "prisoner meets warden" scene, who—or what—the warden is, and what data are presented on the hero are not subjective. They are facts, presented within the film's reality.

THE FUNDAMENTAL STRUCTURAL
ELEMENTS OF PRISON FILMS

Four fundamental elements—confinement, justice, authority, and release—form the necessary and unique set of conventions used to analyze prison films. The objective criteria for selecting a prison film only determined which films legitimately fell with the defined genre. The more important questions had to do with the way in which these films were structured, and the basic questions they addressed. Once I determined that a film was about adult, male, civilian prisons, these four elements evolved as the features that enable us to plot changes across eras in the films. The way in which these elements are dealt with came to define the various eras.

Confinement

This might seem an obvious component because incarceration involves confinement by definition. The appeal of prison films since their inception has been their ability to make concrete things that are metaphorical in the larger society, and perhaps confinement is the most significant aspect. One fundamental theme of literature and philosophy since the inception of western thought has been the tension between individual desires and outside forces of control. These forces can be as straightforward as the commands given to Antigone, or as subtle as the pressures haunting Hamlet. In most genres, these forces are general or subtle. In prison films, these forces are direct.

For the purpose of analyzing prison films as sociohistorical documents, or to understand the genre of the prison film, the portrayal of the nature or form of confinement is informative. As with the other components of prison films, although confinement itself is a constant, its nature has shown clear and distinct changes in presentation. In the various eras of these films, we find dramatic changes in the portrayal of confinement from bars, walls, and chains through more subtle portrayals of the psychological fences in the minds of the offenders to impersonal and removed caves, islands, or cities.

Justice

In a sense, prison films begin with a statement of justice. In the early years, it was of justice denied, as an innocent or coerced man was sent to prison. In later years, it was a statement of the inevitability of justice for wrongdoing and the potential for the individual to reestablish a personal balance in the process of serving one's time. Most recently, films portray a surrealistic, malevolent, or abstracted justice that has little concern with individual lives, or is a dictatorial force that confronts the individual. The manner in which this presentation of justice has changed, and the movie maker's choice about where the sense of justice is to be perceived by the audience, is critical to understanding how society viewed corrections during any given decade.

Authority

In very pragmatic and down to earth ways, every prison film deals with the question of the ultimate moral good of the system. Characteristically, the answer presented varies significantly across the history of these films and is uniquely characteristic of the era in which the film was made. Because the prison situation is inherently confrontational—very few people actually want to be in prison—the questions of authority and the good following from the decisions of those enforcing that authority are thrown into relief against some other choice. The manner in which this conflict is presented, the manner in which it is resolved, and the role of individual and social responsibility in the resolution vary significantly by era.

All prison films address, in one form or another, the characters coming to grips with the code, or codes, of the system in which they exist. Within the physical confines of a prison, a limited number of codes can be presented, representing each of the four subgroups in the prison (administration, professionals, staff, and inmates). The manner in which the hero in prison films comes to identify with one or another of the codes presented in the film not only clarifies our perceptions of these codes but also highlights how society seems to regard the authority of each of these codes. The manner in which these competing claims to authority are resolved clarifies our belief in which is the most worthy code at any point in time. This is true whether the choice is the inmate's code of honor or the code of social optimism found in the vocabulary of rehabilitation.

Release

All prison films, either as a major or minor plot device, deal with the question of release. Of concern in an analysis of film eras is whether the film regards the question of release as important. The most obvious device of building the film around the theme of escape, for example, has changed in importance as the eras of prison films have changed.

The goal is to determine and understand the manner in which the character is released, works out his release, or reacts to his failure to be released. The changing portrayal of this theme reflects our overall view of the nature, adequacy, and promise of the prison system as we look at prison films as data for social study.

THE CHANGING NATURE OF PRISONS AND PRISON FILMS

Examining the ways in which these four elements have been portrayed in prison movies since 1929, I find four distinct eras of prison films made in this country. Within each of these eras, the treatment of distinct elements and the manner of their combination has been relatively consistent through the films produced. Further, the nature of these films displays a relationship both to the academic theories of corrections predominant in the era and to changes and events in the pragmatic operations of corrections in the nation. Thus, as an art form, these films show a process of internal growth and change, a cause-and-effect relationship existent within the film community and culture. But they also display a responsiveness to the realities of theory, practice, and public perceptions and interests, a responsiveness clearly visible in the characteristics of the central figures and structural conditions within the films.

THE DEPRESSION ERA FILMS: 1929-1942

Andrew Bergman writes,

> The motif of imprisonment and entrapment was a popular one in 1930 and 1931, and an entire cycle centering around prison life reached American screens in the post-Crash days. (1971: 93)

The films released between 1929 and 1942 can be divided into a group of films that followed the success of the film *Little Caesar* (from 1929 to 1932) and a second group from 1932 to 1942 that reflect the external reality of rising optimism for the potential of corrections to improve and the internal reality of the Hays Office on film production. In correctional practice, the period from 1929 to 1942 was the age of the Big House, a form that "emerged, spread, and prevailed, then generated images and illusions and, with considerable help from Hollywood, displayed these to the general society" (Irwin, 1980: 1). Indeed, one of the first films of the era is called *The Big House* (1930).

> *The Big House* was the source of images and illusions that continue to obscure the contemporary prison. Some of these images and illusions were created by sociologists who began investigating the prison in the 1930s and have since become the authorities on life there. (Even Hollywood, the society's leading image maker, consults sociologists when it makes a new movie about prisons.) (Irwin, 1980: 29)

There was surprising unanimity of theme and conventions among the films. These prison films followed the successes of the gangster films, and most of them followed the creation of Hays Office restrictions demanding that the bad must not triumph, which precluded guilty men getting out of prison. The impact of these facts produced very stable and consistent situations dramatized in the films.

In almost every film, the hero's confinement is a miscarriage of justice. Just as hardworking individuals found themselves in a Great Depression that they had no hand in creating, protagonists in these films find themselves in prison because of something beyond their control. The hero is either framed by some villainous force (a syndicate trying to shut up a crusading reporter in *Each Dawn I Die*, 1939) or other gangsters (*Prison Break*, 1938), or pushed into his act by some external agent (*I Am a Fugitive from a Chain Gang*, 1932) or by accident (*The Big House*, 1930). Logically, then, his release is secured (or is supposed to be secured, as in *I Am a Fugitive from a Chain Gang*) through formal channels as a realization of the mistake occurs and justice is enacted. The only exceptions are those films where the hero begins as a gangster, obviously guilty and justly sentenced, then progresses to become good and do some socially beneficial act. Even here, however, his earlier crimes are not balanced by this act, and in the end he must die at the hands of the state (*20,000 Years in Sing Sing*, 1937), in the process of a riot or escape (*Big House*, 1930; *Each Dawn I Die*, 1939; or *The Last Mile*, 1932), or at the hands of other gangsters as in *San Quentin* (1937).

Inside the facility, the individual comes to accept the authority of the inmates' code and to identify with that code as he comes to see it as a system demanding integrity and honesty among like kinds of individuals. Often, a framed protagonist comes to recognize the inmate code as it is: In *Each Dawn I Die*, James Cagney's character snarls that "Now . . . I look like a convict, I smell like a convict, I think and I hate like a convict." This code dominated *The Big House* and "could be translated into these rules: Do not inform, do not openly interact or cooperate with the guards or the administration, and do your own time" (Irwin, 1980: 12). A recurrent theme is the confrontation of the "upright" code of the inmate with the corrupt values of those in power. These films are classic "Depression Era" political morality plays, contrasting the simple code of the working man—mutated into the inmates' code—with the corruption and insensitive anonymity of big systems. The code itself recognizes the loss of individuality and self-determination, wherein "We call each other by numbers. Names don't mean anything anymore" (*The Last Mile*, 1932). The significance of the loss of a self and referent by numbers is a common theme. An inmate encapsulates the change in *20,000 Years in Sing Sing* (1933) when he tells another prisoner, "You're still news 'till that gate slams on you. Then you're just a number." The prison then, with its confined setting, is a perfect venue for this confrontation, providing a limited space in which to play out the confrontation of the single individual with the powerful and established agencies that have wronged him.

Given the corruption of the system that put him in prison in the first place, the hero seldom identifies with the authoritative system of the society until the structure is changed and the administration of corrections is replaced in the very process that eventually leads to the hero's release. Because of this, the "new warden" is a stable feature of these films. Indeed, during this era the social structure of the institution was such that "a persistent conflict prevailed, producing factions in most administrations, influencing the strategies and careers of many administrators (particularly wardens), and resulting in regular reshuffling of administrations" (Irwin, 1980: 27). These films are models of the Depression, and a New Deal is enacted in the prison just as in the society.

In the interplay of justice and authority, both the individual hero and the system per se are potentially good or moral. It is, rather, the corruption, insensitivity, and mismanagement of a few key figures that is the evil. Usually, this is exposed in the process of discovery of the truth of his situation, which then frees the hero. Everyone involved in the correctional setting seems to know something is dreadfully wrong, but no one is sure what, or precisely what to do about it. In *The Big House* (1930), the warden has the following speech:

> I warned them at the last governor's conference. We have 3,000 here, and cell accommodations for 1,800. They all want to throw people in jail, but they don't want to provide for them after they're in. You mark my words . . . someday we're going to pay for this short-sightedness.

For these films and the generation in which they were made, it was too difficult to argue that the individual was at fault. In society, the Depression had made victims of too many innocents to hold them responsible for their own troubles. In Hollywood, it was still unprofitable (and later impossible under the Hays Office) to make crime pay or to have a real criminal as a hero. As a result, these films are predominantly about innocent people. To argue that the system itself was wrong was also generally too extreme. The system is not evil in these films, and the system does not change. The warden is changed, the guards are changed, particular prison conditions from beds to food are changed and this brings better conditions overall. But through it all, the fundamental integrity of the structure and the eventual triumph of good and justice is, with very few exceptions, never challenged. Even when guilt exists, it is conditioned. A district attorney prosecutes a young man with a poor defense lawyer and confesses, "It's just a rotten break. I'd get this kid off, he'd never serve a day." Yet when this district attorney is later made the new warden at the "kid's" prison, he still acknowledges that, "A kid (the offender's victim) is dead. Somebody has to pay. It's the criminal code" (*The Criminal Code*, 1931).

Few issues that are viewed as problems in the nature of corrections and society in later eras are considered at all in these films. Coercive individual violence, rape, racism, rehabilitation, and the other problems that we now focus on within institutions are almost never addressed. Certainly they existed in these prisons, and the strict code of segregation as well as the riots that tore through these institutions in waves during 1912 to 1915, 1927 to 1931, 1939 to 1940, and 1950 to 1953 indicated the problems that were to follow (see Irwin, 1980: 9–24). But the optimism of the New Deal, expressed by the new Warden in the prison, was paramount.

As a consequence, when the sociology of the prison came of age in the early and middle 1950s, academia, the prison, and Hollywood all adopted the new approach and helped shaped the next era—that of the correctional institution in corrections and the Rehabilitation Era in film. But, as with all things, this new era carried the flawed seeds of its predecessor. As Andrew Bergman writes,

> Thirties environmentalism became . . . the basis for social action in the post-war period, its relevance rapidly diminishing. What were patent necessities—minimum wages, social security, medical and unemployment insurance, aid to education and housing—became the ends of the society, rather than prerequisites. The sixties would pay dearly for this misjudgment. (1971: 158)

THE REHABILITATION ERA: 1943–1962

From 1943 to 1962, 24 films about men's correctional facilities were released, and although the number is less than in the previous years, the percentage of these films compared with the total number of films released during this time remains roughly comparable with *The Big House* era films. Again, we find two phases within this era. Those films made from 1943 through 1955 deal generally with issues of personal responsibility and rehabilitation. A later transitional group of four films was produced from 1960 to 1962, and these represent a movement toward the Confinement Era films that follow.

These Rehabilitation Era films are the logical sequel to the Depression Era films. They present prisons now staffed with the crusading reformers of the earlier era. Not only do they form an internally consistent extension of the earlier films, then, but they also reflect these changes as they are occurring in correctional practice across the states and in academic models of corrections within the field of criminology. The characters in the films often represent these changes—and the attitudes toward them. In *Convicts Four*, an old-line guard speaks of a new guard in the following terms:

> He went to one of those colleges where they specialized in uplift. He's a do-gooder. Thieves I don't mind, and murderers, well, I can take 'em or leave 'em. But do-gooders! [He spits.]

The new guard embodies the philosophy of the era when he says "If we can find out why a man like Resko commits a crime maybe we can prevent him from committing another." And one inmate echoes both this sentiment and Quetelet when he observes that, "This society we live in, it gets the criminals it deserves."

This was the era of the correctional institution, a penal model based on the ideal of rehabilitation that began to gain prominence with the movement of like-minded professionals to California in the late 1940s (Irwin, 1980: 40–42; McKelvey, 1977). This model "spread and became the dominant type of prison in the 1950s . . . and, like Big Houses, their images live on, blurring our view of contemporary prisons" (Irwin, 1980: 37).

The almost imperceptible movement into the models of individual rehabilitation of the 1950s was a logical outgrowth of the foundation laid in the 1930s. It seemed that now that the social groundwork had been prepared, now that the proper structures of the society were in place, all that was left was to work on the individuals to ensure that they fit into the system. The implication had always been there in the academic work of the era. Social study had become scientific, and policy could now follow. It is hard to find a more explicit statement of this position than that found in George Vold's discussion of the era:

> A principal assumption as to crime causation . . . places the real difficulty within the individual in the mixed up and maladjusted personality components that are viewed as the controlling factors. Rehabilitative penology, both in theory and in practice, ignores the social conflict aspect of criminality entirely and seeks to 'do something' to change the orientation and the behavior of the individuals under its control. The prison can not change the society of which it is a part . . . hence it ignores what it cannot manipulate, and constructs its penological theory to provide suitable rationalization for what the institution hopes it may be able to do. (1986: 292–293)

The films of this era have two major themes. A lesser theme in many re-volves around violence—riots, escapes, or personal violence. The film titles indicate this focus: *Brute Force* (1947), *Riot in Cell Block 11* (1954), and *Crashout* (1955). The major theme, however, is consistently personal, psychological re-habilitation and the responsibility of the individual for his own actions. In both cases, the key feature is an understanding administration or professional staff working in a poorly budgeted and fiscally restrained institution for, and with, the inmates. The administration is the focus in films such as *Prison War-den* (1949) and *Convicted* (1950), whereas the possibility of rehabilitation through individual efforts (*Carbine Williams*, 1952) or with the help of con-cerned professionals (*San Quentin*, 1946; *My Six Convicts*, 1952; or *Convicts Four*, 1962) appears in others. Indeed, in an introduction to the film, former warden Lewis E. Lawes dedicates the movie *San Quentin* to "institutions help-ing to rehabilitate and educate their inmates."

Confinement in these films, then, is justified. The offender-hero is charac-teristically guilty of a serious crime. In contrast with the Big House films, he is not framed and was seldom coerced, although in the early films his move-ment into prison might have been abetted by incompetent legal counsel (*Con-victed*, 1950). Protagonists in the films are in prison for everything from murder (*Convicts Four*, 1962) through burglary (*San Quentin*, 1946) to tax evasion (*My Six Convicts*, 1952). As a result, there is no question of the culpability of the system in his incarceration, and the film is free to address the more central is-sues of personal responsibility and rehabilitation.

Justice in these films involves a confrontation of the individual not with the external systems of justice in the social order, but with himself. The indi-vidual is fighting himself in these films, and the laws of the society and the criminal justice system have simply gotten in the way. The hero is neither a victim of society nor a rebel against that society, the sense of balance sought has to be found within the individual. The requirement for social justice is met in the length of time served in prison by the individual, but it is impossi-ble to tell if this is a reflection of the demands of the moral order of the soci-ety, or the more pragmatic requirements of the Hays Office, requirements that were beginning to break down.

The question of authority is presented as a highly individualistic problem. The hero is forced to become personally aware of the nature of the systems of authority and the competing value codes that surround him, and to make a choice regarding them. The code of the administrator or the professional who is trying to help the inmate is portrayed as workable and morally correct, but the individual must realize this and adopt this code. The convict code—though still holding some shred of legitimacy, is now an obstruction with its demand to avoid all interaction and cooperation with authorities. The conflict between these codes is now internal, as the individual fights within himself. Indeed, the code of the inmate and authority come together in *San Quentin* (1946) in the Inmate Welfare League, where inmates come to govern them-selves. Again, this is with the help of a supportive warden who notes that "The press calls it mollycoddling prisoners. I call it treating them like human beings." In the full embodiment of the rational, scientific, rehabilitative model, an inmate asks the psychologist in *My Six Convicts*, "Whose side are you on?" And the professional answers, "I'm not on either side. I'm a scientist."

Release, then, is not obtained by exposing the faults of the system, as was so common in the earlier era. The individual is genuinely responsible for his actions, so only through the acceptance of his failing can he begin to find release. The inmate finds release through art (*Convicts Four*, 1962), craft, or engineering skills (*Carbine Williams*, 1952), or personal awareness (*My Six Convicts*, 1952). By confronting the reality of the system and by being willing to work through official procedures, the convict attains release or, in those cases where release does not come, obtains better conditions of life within the institution (*The Birdman of Alcatraz*, 1962).

Other factors were beginning to have an impact on these films as well. After a series of destructive prison riots in 1952 to 1953, a special committee formed under the auspices of the American Prison Association concluded that the underlying cause of the riots "was a lack of understanding on the part of the public as well as among the convicts of the rehabilitative functions and purposes of prisons" (McKelvey, 1977: 326). In response to this, the American Prison Association in 1954 "voted to change its name to the American Correctional Association . . . and encouraged the states to redesignate their prisons as correctional institutions" (McKelvey, 1977: 327). Hollywood followed the theme, beginning *Riot in Cell Block 11* with the documentary introduction, which states, "Riot is the result of short sighted neglect of our prisons amounting to criminal negligence." And Hollywood made big money with *Riot in Cell Block 11* (1953), *Crashout* (1955), *Bighouse USA* (1955), *The Steel Jungle* (1956), and *The House of Numbers* (1957).

These violent films are the logical counter to the "successful" rehabilitation films. In films where rehabilitation is successful, the individual rejects the demands of the inmate code, accepts his failing, and adapts to a constructive social code. In the riot films, we see the inmate who does not make the adjustment, who sticks with the inmate code, and who decides to take release into his own hands. And, of course, we see what happens to him. Even the most moralistic of these films (*Riot in Cell Block 11*) has the warden acknowledge that "65 percent [of these convicts] will break the law again." One film, *My Six Convicts*, combines the two features and accents the positive impact of rehabilitation on most of the six inmates by having the character played by Harry Morgan stay bad, only to die in a failed escape attempt.

In general, these rehabilitative era films reflect the economic boom of the 1950s, the social changes that decade began to witness, and the social optimism that followed. The American system had just won World War II. We were living in an age of prosperity, employment, stability, television, air conditioning, the conquest of polio, and a multitude of other minor and major triumphs that made all things seem possible within the system. These films embodied that optimism for the individual in the rehabilitation theme and again presented a morality play about the fate of those who resist "self awareness" and the benefits of a progressive society.

But by 1965 the bloom was fading, and films like these were no longer made. The concern for prisons and the problems of prisoners faded as the society faced its own contradictions and the failure of many grand schemes. It was not that the schemes had not made things better, for they noticeably had. But these schemes had not made things *right*, and that was the flaw in the great American myth. John Irwin points out that the stability of the correctional institution as model was "shattered by at least two developments that began in the 1950s . . . First, black prisoners were increasing in numbers and assertiveness . . . Second, many prisoners in California and other states with correctional institutions eventually soured on rehabilitation and its artifacts" (1980: 62). These groups "continued to work on a criticism of the 'system' and to spread this criticism. This eventually contributed heavily to the great disillusionment with and the eventual dismantling of the rehabilitative ideal. Racial conflict and the sense of injustice that followed this dismantling tore the correctional institution apart" (65).

THE CONFINEMENT ERA: 1963–1980

From 1963 to 1980, only about 15 Hollywood films were made about prisons, reflecting a far smaller percentage of total films that existed in the prior decades. These films share a much more pessimistic view of prisons, a view reflected in the decline of rehabilitation. There were always grumblings and dissatisfaction with the rehabilitative model from various quarters, but the publication of Robert Martinson's "What Works" in 1974 provided a springboard for these frustrations. It did not matter that the critiques initially did not provide alternatives. "Penal practice," as George Vold writes,

> Cannot wait on theory. Organized society must do something about crime . . . theory therefore often may be little more than subsequent rationalization of and justification for the practices established as a consequence of what at the time was deemed a practical necessity, and not as the result of rational deliberation and knowledge of cause and effect." (1986: 282)

The search for a new philosophy led to the "new penology," one that abandoned the rehabilitative model and argued, partly because of the absence of any other model, for deterrence, confinement, or effective administration as the only reasonable ends of corrections:

> Once in prison, the offender should have available as many rehabilitative programs as possible, but these programs should not influence his release date. The inmate could then use the programs to improve himself if he so desired, but he would have no incentive to fake it. (Vold, 1986: 411)

In short, if he wants to he can, and that is acceptable. And if he does not want to he does not have to, and that is acceptable also.

Now there is no hope drawn from either the prison system or the individual. People are hopeless, nondangerous rebels or they are individuals like anyone else, divergent only in that they are criminals legitimately confined inside a correctional institution. Inmates are "desperate men who will do anything to escape" (*Riot*, 1969). Prison is a hopeless oppressive structure. Everybody is fragile, and no identifiable person or agency is at fault, if fault is even a reasonable word to use in a considering these films. It is a society and a prison where, in perhaps the greatest line of all prison films, "What we've got here is failure to communicate" (*Cool Hand Luke*, 1967).

The codes, values, and heroes of the contemporary prison have changed from the earlier eras, and toughness and the image of the Bad Dude have replaced loyalty and the Square John as primary values. "Toughness in the new hero in the violent men's prisons means, first, being able to take care of oneself in the prison world, where people will attack others with little or no provocation. Second, it means having the guts to take from the weak" (Irwin, 1980: 193). Fear of the "tough" appears as a major theme in film, where this fear can be more destructive than the systems itself. As one character says to another in *Short Eyes* (1977), "Your fear of this place has stolen your soul."

Confinement is justified for the individuals in these films, as in the Rehabilitation Era films, but it is for more common and often less serious crimes. *Cool Hand Luke* (1967) is sent to a road gang for the utterly senseless act of cutting the heads off of parking meters, and the man who would *Escape from Alcatraz* (1979) was an armed robber. In some cases the reason for confinement is not even disclosed (*Riot*, 1969), a situation that would be unthinkable in either of the two previous eras because in those times the prison was there for a reason. In contrast, in Confinement era films the hero is simply there, as the prison is something that is simply there, neither brutally corrupt nor concerned with rehabilitation.

Justice, as one might surmise from the foregoing, is not some absolute but is a temporary negotiation among parties or is simply irrelevant. It is a concept above the rules of men and laws and can be obtained only by overcoming authority, often at a total cost to the individual involved. The films are almost existentialist in tone. They seem to seek no meaning beyond the perverse depression of the state of affairs as they are. In keeping with this, these are the first films to address the day-to-day issues of most modern prisons. For the first time, we see not only riots and escapes as plot devices, but sex (*Short Eyes*, 1977), rape (*Brubaker*, 1980), racism (*Riot*, 1969), drugs (*On the Yard*, 1979), corruption (*The Longest Yard*, 1974), and all the other facets of prison life that have become subject to big screen observation and exaggeration.

As a consequence, the location of authority is confused and often shifting. There are few real heroes. The inmates are a mixed lot, with some trustworthy individuals and some genuinely bad persons. There is a relatively consistent view of prison administrators, although not necessarily of guards, as vaguely crazy (*Escape from Alcatraz*, 1979), insensitive (*Short Eyes*, 1977), or ineffective (*Cool Hand Luke*, 1967). But, their corruption is not seen as exceptional within the system nor as serious enough to suggest the possibility of change.

Release is obtained, if it is obtained at all, by nonlegitimate means—usually escape, sometimes death, sometimes not at all. Escape, then, is the theme in *Riot* (1969) and *Escape from Alcatraz* (1979), death the culmination of *Cool Hand Luke* (1967) and *Short Eyes* (1977), and continued imprisonment the unavoidable implication left in *The Longest Yard* (1974), *On the Yard* (1979), *Penitentiary* (1979), and, in a sense, *Brubaker* (1980). Moreover, the release is not central to the film and need not achieve nor prove anything. In previous eras, release was somehow central to the morality of the film. In this era, however, the individual simply gets out, as he was simply there in the first place, and the system goes on.

There are a few successful Hollywood prison films from this era (*The Longest Yard*, 1974; *Escape from Alcatraz*, 1979; *Brubaker*, 1980; and *Stir Crazy*, 1980). There were also several films that existed on the fringe of the commercial and the underground markets. Films such as *Short Eyes* (1977) or *On the Yard* (1979) have no big stars and were relatively low budget. Yet they, with the other more accepted films, shared a common bond. In all these films, the diversity and confusion of the groups involved in corrections is presented. The general ambiguity of the setting is found in a group counseling scene in *On the Yard* (1979), when one inmate tells another, "If you're reduced to telling the truth, you'll never get out of here." The disagreements within and among administration, staff, professionals, and inmates appear repeatedly. The racial conflicts existing between the inmates are a subtle underplay, and the existence of violent individual coercion and rape are exposed. At least in this regard, Hollywood moved toward capturing the reality of the new prison.

Prison films of this era deal in part with the old themes of escape, violence, and riot. But the common impression of the impossibility of real change for either the individual or the system is something that is new and unique. More important, it reflects with some accuracy the general perception of the movie-going public and implies a pessimism and stagnation within the correctional system.

THE ADMINISTRATIVE ERA:
1981–PRESENT

It is significant that the current era of prison films begins with a film unlike any other prison film ever made. *Escape from New York* (1981) is a science fiction (or at least futuristic) prison film. Before this, themes and types of films had been fairly consistent through the history of prison films. There have been escape films, death-row films, and innocent-man films in each era. Likewise, there have been comedies through the eras (*Pardon Me*, 1931, to *Ernest Goes to Jail*, 1989) as well as musicals (*Hold 'Em Jail*, 1932), psychological dramas, and, obviously, adventure dramas. Before 1981, there had not been (to the best of my knowledge) a science fiction prison film. Yet between 1981 and 1994, at least four science fiction films and one horror film have appeared in the prison genre. In all, 20 to 25 prison films have appeared since 1981. It becomes more difficult to count accurately during this time because of questions about whether prison "films" made exclusively for television or for video should be counted. To maintain consistency in my evaluations, I am counting those films that saw some theatrical circulation, even if they were better known in video stores.

Beginning with this era, the questions of confinement, authority, and justice take on dimensions that simply have not existed before. From the beginning of the growth of professional corrections and scientific social science around 1930, in both academic theory and correctional practice, there has been an assumption that prisons "did" something, that prisons had some function. As a result, if a prison is supposed to fulfill some function, it is reasonable to find films presenting the moral aspects of questions surrounding our sense of justice in society and our sense of proper authority. When prisons are not necessarily to do anything besides hold people, or possibly to satisfy some moral balance, then authority becomes an abstraction measured by the quality of the administrative organization. An example of this is telling. Almost all prison films have a "meet the warden" scene. It is one of the most basic conventions that sets the tone for the confrontations of authority that follow. The warden can be an incompetent speaking to an innocent man, characteristic of the Big House era films, or he can be a well-intentioned administrator seeking to help the justifiably convicted inmate as in the Rehabilitation era films. In the Administrative Era, however, the meeting becomes increasingly abstract. In *Lock Up* (1989), the warden is certifiably crazy (and is so certified at the end); in *The Fortress* (1992), one warden is part machine; and in the film *No Escape* (1994), the warden is a holographic projection.

Similarly, the questions of justice and the propriety of the inmate's confinement are also confused. In *Deadlock* (1992), the hero is legitimately a criminal, but is framed by his partners to "take the fall" nonetheless, and in *The Fortress* (1992), the hero and his wife are in a futuristic prison for the crime of having a child. In short, prison films in this new era have taken on a dimension—or have branched off in a direction—that does not lend itself to clear analysis.

Film makers and film goers seem to be dealing with the same ambiguities that are affecting practitioners and scholars. The clear need for the professionalism that drove the early experts and found itself manifested in Big House films is no longer present, the synthesis of philosophy and purpose that was provided by the rehabilitative philosophy is missing, and even the demand for more and tougher prisons that came with the conservatism of the Confinement era is missing.

One feature that defines the new penology in corrections and the Administrative Era in films is the expectation of a rational, cost effective administration. Ironically, the warden in a film made in 1979, just two years before the dates given this era puts the "point" of the Administrative Era most directly.

In the "meet-the-warden" scene in *Escape From Alcatraz* (1979), the warden says, "We don't make good citizens. But we make good prisoners." The warden as computer or as machine is the extreme outgrowth of this model. The loss of a single unifying purpose in corrections is evident in real-world correctional practice, where we find chain gangs being resurrected in some states and a return to rehabilitative models in others. By the same token, in *No Escape* (1994), the inmate is simply dropped on an island and left to fend for himself in a primal social setting, but in *Deadlock* (1992), men and women live in a pleasant, nonsmoking prison named Camp Holiday.

Logically, then, there is no predictable or expected mode of release. The "hero" usually manages to get out, but he is released (*The Shawshank Redemption*, 1995) or escapes (*No Escape*, 1994) or virtually destroys the prison (*The Fortress*, 1992). If there is no logical model of justice and authority, then there is no expected—or demanded—manner in which an individual must obtain release. A voice-over in the film initiating this age, *Escape from New York* (1981), sets the tone:

> The rules are simple. Once you go in you don't come out.

The very philosophy of the prison film becomes confused, and the morality play has no set of morals to work with.

In short, the current era of prison films is like no other. Although the same themes are still being presented—an innocent man in *An Innocent Man*, or the possibility of rehabilitation in *Weeds*—there is a degree of abstraction not seen in previous eras. Not only do we see an unusually wide diversity of models of confinement, authority, and justice, but the films are distanced from reality. It is telling, then, that at the point in time when there are more prisons and prisoners than ever before in our history, and when prisons are the largest growth segment of government, films about prisons have taken off into flights of futurism and science fiction.

It is somehow fitting to conclude with an anomaly. The most successful commercial and critical prison film in a decade or more was *The Shawshank Redemption*, released in 1995. This film, at first glance, does not seem to fit into the current era, nor neatly into any era. One lead character is innocent, the warden is corrupt, and the guards are brutal, all of which would place it firmly in the Big House era. Significantly, the film's setting is a classic Big House of stone walls, barred doors, and guard towers. The other lead character is guilty of his crime and, although he rejects the label of rehabilitation, eventually confronts himself and recognizes what he has done wrong. That, of course, is a key feature of the Rehabilitation era. Yet much of the action and theme of the film revolves around the brutal individual violence of the prison, including rape and murder, which began to appear as a significant motif only in the Confinement era. *Shawshank* is a difficult film to categorize, either by era or by theme.

Nonetheless, two aspects of the film make it important for understanding its place in this current era. First, the very confusion itself, the overlap of themes, and conventional presentations represents the confusion and lack of a single direction that characterize modern correctional theory and practice. Second, the action in the film stretches from 1947 to 1967, which means that the film is not set in a modern prison but, in common with the science fiction films, looks to a time other than the present.

In short, it is likely that the film was a critical success and will continue to be a well-regarded prison film precisely because it is "timeless," in the sense of not being locked into the stereotype of a period.

CONCLUSION

I have argued that prison films tell us a great deal about the nature of our society, our prisons, and our theorization about prisons at any point in time. We found four distinct eras of prison films, which corresponded in time and in content with similar eras of correctional philosophy and practice. Prison films are morality plays, in which the tension between individual wants and social needs is made direct and physical through the convention of the physical prison setting. Confinement, the physical restriction of the individual's freedom, is used to examine our models of justice at that time in the society, and those agents or agencies of authority that the society holds in regard at that time. Release becomes the convention by which these tensions are resolved.

Yet movies are first and foremost money-making ventures, and their concern is not in presenting morality plays, but in making money. They are not abstracted academic debates but are straightforward presentations to a very diverse public that has political and social concerns of its own. As such, movies represent the broad feeling of the era and put into layman's language those ideas that scholars are attempting to formulate and practitioners are attempting to carry out. Probably the best that can be said about modern prison films, and what they tell us about modern prisons and theory, is that they are accurate representations of the state of ambiguity or confusion we currently hold about corrections.

APPENDIX A: FILMS USED IN THE ANALYSIS BY ERA

The Depression Era: 1929–1942

The Big House

Numbered Men

Up the River

The Criminal Code

Pardon Me

Hold 'Em Jail

The Depression Era: 1929–1942 (continued)

I Am a Fugitive from a Chain Gang

The Last Mile

20,000 Years in Sing Sing

The Last Gangster

San Quentin (1937)

Prison Break

Blackwell's Island

Each Dawn I Die

You Can't Get Away with Murder

Castle on the Hudson

Millionaires in Prison

The Rehabilitation Era: 1943–1962

San Quentin (1946)

Brute Force

Convicted

Carbine Williams

My Six Convicts

Duffy of San Quentin

Crashout

Riot in Cell Block 11

Prison Warden

Birdman of Alcatraz

Convicts 4

The Confinement Era: 1963–1980

Cool Hand Luke

Riot

Take the Money and Run

Fortune and Men's Eyes

The Glass House

The Longest Yard

Short Eyes

Escape from Alcatraz

On the Yard

Penitentiary

Brubaker

Alcatraz: The Whole Shocking Story

Stir Crazy

I Escaped from Devil's Island

Brothers

The Administrative Era: 1981 to Present

Escape from New York

Off the Wall

Six Against the Rock

Ernest Goes to jail

Doing Life

Prison

Lock Up

Deadlock

The Fortress

No Escape

Dead Man Out

Weeds

An Innocent Man

The Shawshank Redemption

APPENDIX B: CODESHEET
FOR VIEWING PRISON FILMS

The codesheet for the prison films obtained the following information. Note that data on items 1, 2, 5, 7, 9, and 10 are objective and obtainable from the information presented in the film. Items 6 and 8 require some subjective evaluation, but only items 3, 4, and 5b are completely subjective. On each relevant item space was left for additional comments, quotes, and so forth.

1. Motion picture name, year, producer, stars, and studio.

2. a. Is the hero in for a long time, and is the amount of time specified?
   b. Is he in for a specified crime?
   c. Is justification for the crime presented? What is it?
   d. Does he express remorse?
   e. Was the hero framed?
   f. Additional comments:

3. a. What are the attitudes, by group [administration, staff, professionals, inmates] toward rehabilitation, deterrence, confinement, and retribution. [This was coded on a 5-point scale from Very Negative to Very Positive, with a Not Shown option.]

4. a. What is the attitude presented in the movie toward administration, staff, professionals, and inmates. [This was coded on a 5-point scale from Basically Bad to Basically Good, with a Not Shown option.]

5. a. Which of the following activities or characteristics are shown in the movie?
   Industry, drugs, yard activities (other than escape talk), arts, cell activity, eating, escape, race, riot, sex, additional activities.

   b. If presented, what are the attitudes of groups involved or the movie toward each of these activities? (for example, is industry seen as rehabilitative or demeaning?)

6. In the movie, do "prison conditions" and administration: improve significantly, improve, stay the same, worsen, or worsen significantly?

7. What is the resolution? (How does the movie end; how does the hero get out?)

8. What is the overall theme? Note particularly personal biography of inmate or staff, action (riot or escape), prison conditions, others.

9. Time span covered in the movie (exact years if possible). Also note major changes in the prison's administration, staff, or inmates and indicate approximate dates if possible.

10. Prisons or actual persons presented in the movie.

11. Additional comments, notes, or significant quotes from the movie.

DISCUSSION QUESTIONS

1. What four themes (fundamental elements) of prison films does the author identify? The author asserts "prison films begin with a statement of justice." Discuss this assertion.

2. What four eras of prison films does the author identify? What changes does he detect in prison films from 1929 to 1995? Does the author believe social changes and changes in penological theory and practice have had an effect on Hollywood's depiction of adult, male, civilian prisons?

3. Why do you think a large number of the films about women's prisons have been "sexploitation films"? What, if anything, does this suggest about societal attitudes or penological theory and practice regarding women prisoners?

NOTE

1. The films *Weeds* and *Deadlock* are examples where a larger amount of screen time is not in a prison, but in both cases the films are so completely concerned with the prison experience that they were included. *Weeds* is devoted to a troupe from a prison giving plays about a prison, and *Deadlock* is about an escape from a prison, including ubiquitous exploding prison neckbands.

✳

Epilogue

FRANKIE Y. BAILEY
AND
DONNA C. HALE

R ay Surette observes in the prologue to this volume that we often interact with popular culture casually, almost without thought. We wake up
to music on the radio; we watch the morning news on television as we
dress and have breakfast. Popular culture is with us throughout the day as the
background noise of our lives. As Cottle observes regarding television, television both reflects and helps us "to constitute those temporal rhythms, routines, and rituals of modern existence" (1993: 3). The same is true of other
mediums. And when media are not present, we might feel their absence. Snow
notes that media can soothe social situations, but

> The absence of media may also heighten self-consciousness, particularly
> when alone in public places and sensitivity to scrutiny from others be-
> comes exaggerated. . . . In these situations media may be used to divert
> one's attention from unwanted attention by strangers, to an engagement
> with a medium as a surrogate other. (1995: 87–88)

If for no other reasons than because of how we use media and the possible
impact of such uses on social interaction, media should merit our attention.
But specifically regarding crime and justice, as Ericson (1995: xi) asserts, "The
centrality of crime and law enforcement and the mass media results in an om-
nipresent public discourse about disorder and decline." As citizens of a mass-
mediated society, we are participants in an ongoing discourse about such
matters as the social location of crime and the possibility of achieving "justice
for all" in a heterogeneous society.

As the chapters in this book illustrate, there are many topics to which we might turn our attention as we study popular culture, crime, and justice. For example, in their chapter on the role of media in reintegrative shaming, Bennett, Johnson, and Alvarez consider the media as "a potential source of shaming ceremonies." Manning asserts, "'talk shows' weave together scandal, shaming, and degradation ceremonies." So perhaps, although we might have little interest in scandal, if we are interested in the process by which offenders ("transgressors") are reintegrated into a community, we should be watching talk shows to learn a thing or two from Sally, Jenny, and their audiences. This suggestion might sound frivolous; however, it is important to take even "throwaway," "low-brow" popular culture seriously if it has a significant and receptive audience. That audience is obviously receiving some form of gratification. And in the process of being entertained or informed, the audience also might be forming beliefs and attitudes about crime and justice.

Surette writes, "The belief in individual responsibility and individual-based explanations for crime is the primary image reflected in our popular culture and has significant impact on crime and justice policies." If that is the case, then social scientists and others concerned with issues of crime and justice should be giving more attention to the explanations of crime causation available to consumers of popular culture and to their acceptance or rejection of these explanations.

There are other related topics that we think also merit more attention. For example,

1. The function played by popular culture (mass media) in the lives of youth, particularly adolescents growing up in impoverished and neglected inner-city communities and in other environments in which the images of middle-class success that they see in the media have little to do with their daily lives.

2. The influence—from fashion and slang to images and attitudes—of so-called "criminal" and "deviant" subcultures on "mainstream" culture.

3. The role of popular culture images in shaping public attitudes toward and responses to criminal justice system professionals (for example, police officers and lawyers) and in shaping the feelings of those professionals about themselves and their jobs.

4. The long-term effect of being the object of intense media scrutiny on the lives of those who are caught in the criminal justice system as suspects in criminal cases (for example, Robert Jewell in the Atlanta Olympic park bombing), defendants (for example, the McMartin family charged with the sexual abuse of children in their daycare center), crime victims (for example, the victims in rape or harassment cases involving "celebrity" offenders), or grieving relatives (for example, the parents of murdered children).

5. The treatment given different types of crimes and different types of offenders by the media. For example, Benedict (1992) has found stereotyping and sensationalism in "how the press covers sex crimes."

6. The role(s) played by media as conveyors of information about the people comprising the various communities in urban areas. Do the media still merit low marks for how they cover poor and minority communities? Does media reporting have an impact on relations between the residents of these communities and local criminal justice agencies?

As should be clear from the essays in this volume, some scholars are already engaged in examining various aspects of these topics. But we believe more systematic research is needed.

At the same time, regarding the pedagogical uses of popular culture, we believe popular culture can be a starting point for enlightening and informative classroom discussions. For example, Giroux asserts, "teachers and students should engage popular films seriously as legitimate forms of social knowledge that reveal different sets of struggles among youth within diverse cultural sites" (1996: 45). We suggest both teachers and students should explore the usefulness of popular culture documents such as "true crime novels." Although works such as Truman Capote's *In Cold Blood* and Norman Mailer's *The Executioner's Song* are not standard criminal justice texts, when carefully questioned and probed, they can yield valuable insights. Katz warns, "Academic social scientists will either learn to think intelligently about using the genre of nonfiction novels about murders or they will leave this part of our social life, and whatever these crimes might reveal about us more generally, to journalists, politicians, and literary critics" (1988: 280–281).

We believe it is important to use books and films and other mass media products as teaching—and learning—tools as we bring our "sociological imagination" to focus on popular culture, crime, and justice.

References

A.C.L.U. (1992) "The Arts Censorship Project." (pamphlet) New York: A.C.L.U.

Abrecht, M. (1976) *The Making of a Woman Cop.* New York: Morrow.

Acland, C.R. (1995) *Youth, Murder, Spectacle: The Cultural Politics of "Youth in Crisis."* Boulder, CO: Westview.

Adoni, H. and S. Mane (1984) "Media and the social construction of reality: Toward an integration of theory and research." *Communication Research,* 11(3) (July): 323–340.

Allen, D. and D. Chacko, eds. (1974) *Detective Fiction (Crime and Compromise).* New York: Harcourt Brace Jovanovich.

Allen, N.H. (1983) "Homicide followed by suicide: Los Angeles, 1970–1979." *Suicide and Life Threatening Behavior,* 13(3) 155–165.

Alloway, L. (1969) "The long front of culture." Pp. 41–43 in John Russell and Suzi Gablik (eds.), *Pop Art Redefined.* London: Thames and Hudson.

Alternative Tentacles Records (no date) "Welcome to 1984 . . ." (informational flier).

Altheide, D. (1986) *Creating Reality.* Beverly Hills, CA: Sage.

Altheide, D. (1992) "Gonzo justice." *Symbolic Interaction,* 15 (1): 69–86.

Altheide, D.L. (1984) "TV news and the social construction of justice: Research issues and policy." In R. Surette (ed.), 292–304. *Justice and the Media: Issues and Research.* Springfield, IL: Charles C. Thomas.

Altheide, D.L. and R.P. Snow (1994) *Media Worlds in the Postjournalism Era.* Hawthorne, NY: Aldine.

American Family Association (1993) "We are outraged!" *Rocky Mountain News* (October 31): no page number.

Anderson, C. and C.M. Ford (1987) "Affect of the game player: Short term effects of highly and mildly aggressive video games." *Personality and Social Psychology Bulletin,* 12 (4) Dec.: 390–402.

Antunes, G.E. and P.A. Hurley (1977) The representation of criminal events in Houston's two daily newspapers. *Journalism Quarterly*, 54: 756–760.

Atkins, R. (1991) "A censorship time line." *The Art Journal* (Fall): 33–37.

Auletta, K. (1991) "Is network news crumbling?" *TV Guide*, November 9–15: 4–7.

Babbie, E. (1986) *The Practice of Social Research* (4th ed.), Belmont, CA: Wadsworth.

Bailey, F. (1993, Summer) "Real life vigilantism and vigilantism in popular films." *Justice Professional* 8(1): 33–51.

Balkin, J. (1988) "Why policemen don't like policewomen." *Journal of Police Science and Administration 16*, 29–38.

Ball, M. (1981) *The Promise of American Law*. Athens: University of Georgia Press.

Bancroft, R. (1967) *City Hall and the Press*. Washington, D.C.: National League of Cities.

Bandura, A. (1973) *Aggression: A Social Learning Analysis*. Englewood Cliffs, NJ: Prentice-Hall.

Banks, T. (1988) "Gender bias in the classroom." *Journal of Legal Education* 38: 137.

Barak, G. (1988) "Newsmaking criminology: Reflections on the media, intellectuals, and crime." *Justice Quarterly* 5: 565–587.

Barak, G. (1993) "Crime, criminology and human rights: Toward an understanding of state criminality." Pp. 207–230 in Kenneth D. Tunnell (ed.), *Political Crime in Contemporary America*. New York: Garland.

Barak, G., ed. (1991) *Crimes by the Capitalist State*. Albany: State University of New York Press.

Barak, G. (1994a) *Media, Process and the Social Construction of Crime: Studies in Newsmaking Criminology*. New York: Garland.

Barak, G. (1994b) "Newsmaking criminology: Reflections on the media, intellectuals, and crime." In G. Barak (ed.), *Media, Process, and the Social Construction of Crime: Studies in Newsmaking Criminology*. New York: Garland.

Barak, G. (1995) "Media, crime, and justice: A case for constitutive criminology." Pp. 142–166 in Jeff Ferrell and Clinton R. Sanders (eds.), *Cultural Criminology*. Boston: Northeastern University Press.

Barlow, M.H., D.E. Barlow, and T.G. Chiricos (1995) "Economic conditions and ideologies of crime in the media: A content analysis of crime news." *Crime and Delinquency*, 41: 3–19.

Barrile, L. (1984) "Television and attitudes about crime: Do heavy viewers distort criminality and support retributive justice?" Pp. 141–158 in R. Surette (ed.), *Justice and the Media: Issues and Research*. Springfield, IL: Charles C. Thomas.

Basinger, J. (1993) *A Woman's View: How Hollywood Spoke to Women, 1930–1960*. New York: Knopf.

Bayley, D. (1985) *Patterns of Policing: A Comparative International Analysis*. New Brunswick, NJ: Rutgers University Press.

Baxandall, M. (1972) *Painting and Experience in Fifteenth Century Italy*. Oxford: Oxford University Press.

Becker, H. S. (1963) *Outsiders*. New York: Free Press.

Bell, D. (1982) "Policewomen—Myths and reality." *Journal of Police Science and Administration* 10, 110–120.

Bender, D. and B. Leone, eds. (1994) *Mass Media: Opposing Viewpoints*. San Diego, CA: Greenhaven.

Benedict, Helen (1992) *Virgin or Vamp: How the Press Covers Sex Crimes*. New York: Oxford University Press.

Benjamin, W. (1964) *Illuminations*. New York: Schocken.

Bennett, H. Stith and J. Ferrell (1987) "Music videos and epistemic socialization." *Youth and Society* 18: 344–362.

Benson, M. (1990) "Emotions and adjudication: Status degradation among white-collar criminals." *Justice Quarterly* 7(3):515–528.

Benton, M. (1993) *Crime Comics: The Illustrated History*. Dallas, TX: Taylor.

Berger, A. (1990) *Media Analysis Techniques*. Newbury Park, CA: Sage.

Berger, A. (1991) *Media Research Techniques*. Newbury Park, CA: Sage.

Berger, A.A. (1992). *Popular Culture Genres*. Newbury Park, CA.: Sage.

Bergman, A. (1971) *We're in the Money*. New York: Harper & Row.

Berman, A.L. (1979) "Dyadic death: Murder-suicide." *Suicide and Life Threatening Behavior*, 9(1): 15–23.

Bernat, F. (1992) "Women in the legal profession." Pp. 307–321 in Imogene Moyer (ed.), *The Changing Roles of Women in the Criminal Justice System*. Prospect Heights, IL: Waveland.

Best, J. (1991) *Images of Issues: Typifying Contemporary Social Problems*. New York: Aldine de Gruyter.

Best. J. and G.T. Horiuchi (1995) "The razor blade in the apple: The social construction of urban legends." Pp. 203–214 in Richard V. Ericson (ed.), *Crime and the Media*. Aldershot, England: Dartmouth.

Bettelheim, B. (1976) *The Uses of Enchantment: The Meaning and Importance of Fairy Tales*. New York: Knopf.

Binder, A. (1993) "Constructing racial rhetoric: Media depictions of harm in heavy metal and rap music." *American Sociological Review* 58: 753–767.

Binyon, T.J. (1989, 1990) *'Murder Will Out': The Detective in Fiction*. New York: Oxford University Press.

Biskind, P. (1983) *Seeing is Believing: How Hollywood Taught Us to Stop Worrying and Love the Fifties*. New York: Pantheon.

Blair, M.E. (1993) "Commercialization of the rap music youth subculture." *Journal of Popular Culture* 27: 21–33.

Bloch, P.B. and D. Anderson (1974) *Policewomen on Patrol: Final Report*. Washington, D.C.: Police Foundation.

Bohigian, H. (1977) "What is a model?." Pp. 15–28 in Stuart S. Nagel (ed.), *Modeling the Criminal Justice System*, Beverly Hills: Sage.

Bolton, R., ed. (1992) *Culture Wars: Documents from the Recent Controversies in the Arts*. New York: New Press.

Bolton, R. (1990) "The cultural contradictions of conservatism." *New Art Examiner* 17: 24–29, 72.

Bouza, A. (1990) *The Police Mystique*. New York: Plenum.

Bowers, W. (1988) "Violent pornography." *The Humanist*, 48 (January, 22–23).

Braithwaite, J. (1989) *Crime, Shame, and Reintegration*. Cambridge: Cambridge University Press.

Braithwaite, J. and S. Mugford (1994) "Conditions of successful reintegration ceremonies: Dealing with juvenile offenders." *British Journal of Criminology* 34:139–171.

Brandon, C. (1986) *Murder in the Adirondacks: An American Tragedy Revisited*. Utica, NY: North Country Books.

Briggs, Joe Bob (1996, Dec. 12), Commentary on *Friday the 13th*. On TNT's *Monster Vision*.

Britt, B. (1994) "State of the arts in Cobb County." *The Nation* 258: 196–198.

Brodbeck, M. (1959) "Models, meaning and theories," Pp. 373–403 in Llewellyn Gross (ed.), *Symposium on Sociological Theory*. New York: Harper and Row.

Brodie, J. (1993) "The truth squads." *Mother Jones*. September/October: 21–25.

Brody, E.W. (1992) "The domain of public relations." *Public Relations Review*, 18(4): 349–363.

Bronski, M. (1989) "It's not the flesh, it's the flowers: The 'art wars' rage on." *Radical America* 23: 46–55.

Brown, R.H., ed. (1995) *Postmodern Representation: Truth, Power, and Mimesis in the Human Sciences and Public Culture*. Urbana: University of Illinois Press.

Brunsdon, C. (1982, September–October) "A subject for the seventies." *Screen*, 23(3–4): 20–29.

Bullah, R., R. Madsen, W. Sullivan, A. Swidler, and S. Tipton (1985) *Habits of the Heart*. Los Angeles: University of California Press.

Bureau of Justice Statistics (1991, March) "Violent crime in the United States." Washington, D.C.: U.S. Department of Justice.

Burns, T. (1979) "The organization of public opinion," Pp. 44–69 in James Curran, Michael Gurevich, Janet Woolacott et al. (eds.), *Mass Communication and Society*. Beverly Hills, CA: Sage.

Caldwell, J.T. (1995) *Televisuality: Style, Crisis, and Authority in America Television*. New Brunswick, NJ: Rutgers University Press.

Campbell, R. (1989) "Prison life dims glory days." *Fort Worth Star-Telegram* (December 24): 1, 10.

Caplow, S. and S. Scheindlin (1990) "Portrait of a lady": The woman lawyer in the 1980s." *New York School Law Review* 35: 391–428.

Carroll, R.L. (1985) "Television news." Pp. 213–236 in Brian Rose (ed.), *TV Genres: A Handbook and Reference Guide*. Westport, CT: Greenwood.

Cater, D. (1975) *TV Violence and the Child: The Evolution and Fate of the Surgeon General's Report*. New York: Russell Sage Foundation.

Caulfield, S.L. (1991) "Subcultures as crime: The theft of legitimacy of dissent in the United States." In Gregg Barak (ed.), *Crimes by the Capitalist State*. Albany: State University of New York Press.

Cavender, G. and L. Bond-Maupin (1995) "Fear and loathing on reality television: An analysis of *America's Most Wanted* and *Unsolved Mysteries*." In Richard V. Ericson (ed.), *Crime and the Media*. Aldershot, England: Dartmouth.

Cavender, G. and M. Fishman (forthcoming) *Reality Programming: The New Crime News*.

Cawelti, J.G. (1976) *Adventure, Mystery, and Romance (Formula Stories as Art and Popular Culture)*. Chicago: University of Chicago Press.

Chambliss, W.J. and M. Mankoff, eds. (1976) *Whose Law? What Order? A Conflict Approach to Criminology*. New York: Wiley.

Chandler, R. (1934) "The simple art of murder: An essay," Pp. 1–21 in *The Simple Art of Murder*. New York: Ballantine.

Charles, M.T. (1981) "The performance and socialization of female recruits in the Michigan State Police Training Academy." *Journal of Police Science and Administration* 9: 209–223.

Charles, M.T. (1982) "Women in policing: The physical aspect." *Journal of Police Science and Administration* 102: 194–205.

Chase, A. (1986) "Toward a legal theory of popular culture." *Wisconsin Law Review*, 1986(3): 527–568.

Chermak, S. (1994a) "Body count news: How crime is presented in the news media." *Justice Quarterly* 11(4): 561–582.

Chermak, S. (1994b) "Crime in the news media: A refined understanding of how crime becomes news," Pp. 95–129 in G. Barak (ed.), *Media, Process, and the Social Construction of Crime: Studies in Newsmaking Criminology*. New York: Garland.

Chermak, S. (1995) *Victims in the News: Crime in American News Media*. Boulder, CO: Westview.

Chibnall, S. (1975) "The crime reporter: A study in the production of commercial knowledge." *Sociology*, 9: 49–66.

Chibnall, S. (1977) *Law-and-Order News*. London: Tavistock.

Chibnall, S. (1981) "The production of knowledge by crime reporters," Pp. 75–97 in Stanley Cohen and Jock Young (eds.), *The Manufacture of News* Beverly Hills: Sage.

Christie, N. (1993) *Crime Control as Industry*. London: Routledge.

Christopher Commission (1991) *Report on the Los Angeles Police Department*. Los Angeles.

Cincinnati Post (1994) "4 teens charged in spree." (January 27): 12A.

Clarens, C. (1980) *Crime Movies: An Illustrated History*. New York: Norton.

Clark, D. (1990) "Cagney & Lacey: Feminist strategies of detection." Pp. 117–133 in Mary Ellen Brown (ed.), *Television and Women's Culture: The Politics of the Popular*. Newbury Park, CA: Sage.

Clover, C.J. (1992) *Men, Women, and Chain Saws: Gender in the Modern Horror Film*. Princeton, NJ: Princeton University Press.

Cockburn, C. (1983) *Brothers: Male Dominance and Technological Change*. London: Pluto.

Coffin, T.P. (1975) *The Female Hero in Folklore and Legend*. New York: Seabury.

Cohen, D.A. (1993) *Pillars of Salt, Monuments of Grace: New England Crime Literature and the Origins of American Popular Culture, 1674–1860*. New York: Oxford University Press.

Cohen, S. (1972) *Folk Devils and Moral Panics*. London: Macgibbon and Kee.

Cohen, S. (1980) *Folk Devils and Moral Panics*. London: Martin Roberson.

Cohen, S. and J. Young (1981) *The Manufacture of News: Deviance, Social Problems and the Mass Media*. London: Constable.

Comics Magazine Association of America, files (1970) Minutes of the Board of Directors Meeting, 9 June, New York, NY.

Comics Magazine Association of America (1971) Code of the Comics Magazine Association of America, Inc.

Comstock, A. (1884) *Traps for the Young*. New York: Funk and Wagnalls.

Conal, R. (1992) *Art Attack*. New York: HarperCollins.

Cook, L. and C. Spanhel (1991) "Attorney perceptions of gender inequality in the workplace." *Texas Bar Journal* (October): 971.

Cooke, J. (1993) "Horror Movie's 'Chucky' doll made little kids murder toddler." *National Enquirer* (December 14): 10.

Cooper, J. and D. Mackie (1986) "Video Games and Aggression in Children." *Journal of Applied Social Psychology*, 16(8): 726–744.

"Cops" (1993) *Parade Magazine*. (June 22): 3–5.

Cottle, S. (1993) *TV News, Urban Conflict and the Inner City*. Leicester, London: Leicester University Press.

Cowan, G. (1979) *See No Evil: The Backstage Battle Over Sex and Violence on Television*. New York: Simon and Schuster.

Crane, J.L. (1995) *Terror in Everyday Life*. California: Sage.

Crenson, M. (1996) "Doctor theorizes rabies, not liquor, killed author Poe." *USA Today*, 9/12/96, 8A.

Crouch, B.M. and J.W. Marquart (1989) *An Appeal to Justice*. Austin: University of Texas Press.

Culler, J.(1996) "Semiotics." Entry in *The 1996 Grolier Multimedia Encyclopedia*.

Currens, S. et al. (1991) "Homicide followed by suicide—Kentucky, 1985–1990." *Journal of the American Medical Association*, 266(15): 2062–2063.

Curriden, M. (1993) "Prison scandal in Georgia: Guards traded favors for sex." *National Law Journal*, (16(3): 8.

Dabney, V. (1987) *Pistols and Pointed Pens: The Dueling Editors of Old Virginia*. Chapel Hill, NC: Algonquin.

D'Acci, J. (1994) *Defining Women: Television and the Case of Cagney & Lacey*. Chapel Hill: University of North Carolina Press.

Dahlgren, P. and C. Sparks, eds. (1992) *Journalism and Popular Culture*. London: Sage.

Dance, D.C. (1987) *Long Gone: The Mecklenburg Six and the Theme of Escape in Black Folklore.* Knoxville: University of Tennessee Press.

Dawtrey, A. and J. Jolson-Colburn (1991) "Scotland Yard confiscates rap albums." *Rocky Mountain News* (June 7): 111.

Dayan, D. and E. Katz (1993) *Media Events.* Cambridge: Harvard University Press.

Debord, G. (1983) *Society as Spectacle.* Detroit: Red and Black Books.

deGrazia, E. and R.K. Newman (1982) *Banned Films: Movies, Censors and the First Amendment.* New York: Bowker.

Denzin, N.K. (1986) "Postmodern social theory." *Sociological Theory,* 4: 194–204.

Denzin, N.K. (1995) *The Cinematic Society.* London: Sage.

Department of Justice (1990) *Crime in the United States.* Washington, D.C.: FBI.

Department of Justice (1991) *Crime in the United States.* Washington, D.C.: FBI.

Diesing, P. (1971) *Patterns of Discovery in the Social Sciences.* New York: Aldine.

DiIulio, J.J. Jr. (1987). *Governing Prisons.* New York: Free Press.

Ditton, J. and J. Duffy (1983) "Bias in the newspaper reporting of crime news." *British Journal of Criminology,* 23: 159–165.

Dobash, R.P., R.E. Dobash, M. Wilson, and M. Daly (1992) "The myth of sexual symmetry in marital violence." *Social Problems,* 39(1): 71–91.

Dominick, J. (1973) "Crime and law enforcement on primetime television." *Public Opinion Quarterly,* 37: 241–250.

Dorpat, T.L. (1966) "Suicide in Murderers." *Psychiatry Digest,* 7: 51–55.

Dove, G.N. (1982) *The Police Procedural.* Bowling Green, OH: Bowling Green State University Popular Press.

Dowell, P. (1988) "Sex makes a comeback," *Psychology Today,* 24 (Sept.): 64–65.

Drachman, V. (1992) "Entering the male domain: Women lawyers in the courtroom in modern American history." *Massachusetts Law Review* 77: 44–50.

Dubin, S. (1992) *Arresting Images: Impolitic Art and Uncivil Actions.* London: Routledge.

Dubin, S. (1995) "Poisoned pens and rattled sabers." *New Art Examiner* 22: 26–29.

Dubin, S. (1993) "Tongue untied." *The Nation* 257: 72–74.

Dyson, M.E. (1995) "Gangsta rap." Pp. 46–54 in Carol Becker and Ann Wiens (eds.), *The Artist in Society.* Chicago: New Art Examiner.

Easteal, P. (1994) "Homicide-suicides between adult sexual intimates: An Australian study." *Suicide and Life Threatening Behavior,* 24(2): 140–150.

Eco, U. (1986) *Travels in Hyperreality.* New York: Harcourt, Brace and Jovanovich.

Edelman, M. (1988) *Society as a Spectacle.* Chicago: University of Chicago Press.

Elliott, P. and P. Golding (1979) *Making the News.* London: Longman.

Engels, F. (1939) *Anti-Duhring.* New York: International (originally published 1878).

Entertainment Weekly (1990) "Do the rights thing." (March 30): 38–39.

Epstein, E. (1974) *News From Nowhere.* New York: Vintage.

Ericson, R., ed. (1995) *Crime and the Media.* Aldershot, England: Dartmouth.

Ericson, R.V. (1991) "Mass media, crime, law and justice: An institutional approach." *The British Journal of Criminology,* 31(3): 219–249.

Ericson, R.V., P.M. Baranek, and J.B.L. Chan (1987) *Visualizing Deviance: A Study of News Organization.* Toronto: University of Toronto Press.

Ericson, R.V., P.M. Baranek, and J.B.L. Chan (1989) *Negotiating Control: A Study of News Sources.* Toronto: University of Toronto Press.

Ericson, R.V., P.M. Baranek, and J.B.L. Chan (1991) *Representing Order: Crime, Law, and Justice in the News Media.* Toronto: University of Toronto Press.

Esterle, J. (1986) "Crime and the media." *Jericho*, 41:5, 7.

Faith, Karlene (1993) "Gendered imaginations: Female crime and prison movies." *The Justice Professional*, 8(1): 53–69.

Faludi, S. (1991) *Backlash: The Undeclared War Against American Women.* New York: Anchor.

Farganis, S. (1994) *Situating Feminism: From Thought to Action.* Thousand Oaks, CA: Sage.

Ferrell, J. (1991) "The brotherhood of timber workers and the culture of conflict." *Journal of Folklore Research* 28: 163–177.

Ferrell, J. (1993) *Crimes of Style: Urban Graffiti and the Politics of Criminality.* New York and London: Garland.

Ferrell, J. and C.R. Sanders, eds. (1995) *Cultural Criminology.* Boston: Northeastern.

Fishburn, K. (1982) *Women in Popular Culture: A Reference Guide.* Westport, CT: Greenwood.

Fishman, M. (1978) "Crime waves as ideology." *Social Problems*, 25: 531–543.

Fishman, M. (1980) *Manufacturing the News.* Austin: University of Texas Press.

Fishman, M. (1981) "Police news: Constructing an image of crime." *Urban Life*, 9: 371–394.

Fiske, J. (1994) *Media Matters.* Minneapolis: University of Minnesota Press.

Fiske, J. (1987) *Television Culture.* London: Methuen.

Flanagan, T. and E.F. McGarrell (1986) *Sourcebook of Criminal Justice Statistics 1985.* Washington, D.C.: U.S. Department of Justice.

Fletcher, C. (1995) *Breaking & Entering: Women Cops Talk about Life in the Ultimate Men's Club.* NY: HarperCollins.

Foster, D. (1995) "Officials fear movie inspired kids' crime." *Rocky Mountain News* (March 17): 8A.

Franklin, H.B. (1978) *The Victim as Criminal and Artist: Literature from the American Prison.* New York: Oxford University Press.

Freeman, R.M. (1996a) "Correctional staff as the villain and the inmate as hero: The problem is bigger than Hollywood." *American Jails*, 10(3): 9, 11–13, 16.

Freeman, R.M. (1996b) *The Correctional Officer as Villain and the Inmate as Hero: How the Print Media and Corrections Perpetuate Hollywood Stereotyping.* Paper presented at the March 1996 annual meeting of the Academy of Criminal Justice Sciences in Las Vegas, Nevada.

Friedman, L.M. (1993) *Crime and Punishment in American History.* New York: Basic Books.

Friedrichs, D.O. (1996) *Trusted Criminals.* Belmont, CA: Wadsworth.

Frye, C.A. (1980) "The bad man be stylin' for days: The symposium overview." Pp. 2–11 in C.A. Frye (ed.), *Values in Conflict: Blacks and the American Ambivalence Toward Violence.* Washington, D.C.: University Press of America.

Galbraith, J.K. (1978) *The New Industrial State* (3rd ed.). Boston: Houghton Mifflin.

Galerstein, C. (1989) *Working Women on the Hollywood Screen.* New York: Garland.

Gamman, L. (1989) "Watching the detectives: The enigma of the female gaze." Pp. 8–26 in Lorraine Gamman and Margaret Marshment (eds.), *The Female Gaze: Women as Viewers of Popular Culture.* Seattle: Real Comet.

Gans, H. (1988) *Middle American Individualism.* New York: Free Press.

Gans, H.J. (1979) *Deciding What's News: A Study of CBS Evening News, Newsweek and Time.* New York: Pantheon.

Gardiner, H.C. and S.J. (1958) *Catholic Viewpoint on Censorship.* Garden City, NY: Hanover House.

Garfinkel, H. (1956) "Conditions of successful status degradation ceremonies." *American Journal of Sociology* 61: 420–424.

Gates, D. (1993) *Chief: My Life in the LAPD*. New York: Bantam.

Gerda, S. (1985) *Accounting for Aggression*. London: Allen and Unwin.

Gergen, K. (1991) *The Saturated Self*. New York: Basic Books.

Gherardi, S. (1994) "The gender we think, the gender we do in our everyday organizational lives." *Human Relations* 47(6): 591–610.

Gibson, J.W. (1994) *Warrior Dreams: Paramilitary Culture in Post-Vietnam America*. New York: Hill and Wang.

Gidley, M. (1976) "Elements of the detective story in William Faulkner's fiction. Pp. 228–246 in Larry N. Landrum, Pat Browne, and Ray B. Browne (eds.), *Dimensions of Detective Fiction*. Bowling Green, OH: Popular Press.

Gieber, W. and W. Johnson (1961) "The city hall 'beat': A study of reporter and source roles," *Journalism Quarterly*, 38: 289–297.

Gilbert, J. (1986) *A Cycle of Outrage: America's Reaction to the Juvenile Delinquent in the 1950s*. New York: Oxford University Press.

Gilkerson, M. (1990) "USC administrators post disclaimer on student art exhibit." *New Art Examiner* 17: 72.

Girard, R. (1972) *Violence and the Sacred*. Baltimore: Johns Hopkins University Press.

Giroux, H.A. (1996) *Fugitive Cultures: Race, Violence, and Youth*. New York: Routledge.

Gitlin, T. (1980) *The Whole World is Watching*. Berkeley: University of California Press.

Gitlin, T. (1986) *Inside Prime Time*. New York: Pantheon.

Glasgow University Media Group (1976) *Bad News*. London: Routledge and Kegan Paul.

Glasgow University Media Group (1980) *More Bad News*. London: Routledge and Kegan Paul.

Goldwater, J. (1964) *Americana in Four Colors: A Decade of Self Regulation by the Comics Magazine Industry*. New York: Comics Magazine Association of America.

Gooding-Williams, R. ed. (1993) *Reading Rodney King*. London: Routledge, Kegan, Paul.

Goodwin, C. (1995) "Professional Vision." *American Anthropologist*, 96: 606–633.

Gore, T. (1987) *Raising PG Kids in an X-Rated Society*. Nashville: Abingdon.

Gorelick, S. (1989) "Join our war: The construction of ideology in a newspaper crime-fighting campaign." *Crime and Delinquency*, 35: 421–436.

Goffman, E. (1974) *Frame Analysis*. New York: Basic Books.

Gottfredson, M. and T. Hirschi (1990) *A General Theory of Crime*. Stanford, CA: Stanford University Press.

Graber, D. (1979) "Evaluating crime-fighting policies: Media images and public perspective." Pp. 179–199 in Ralph Baker and Fred A. Meyer, Jr. (eds.), *Evaluating Alternative Law Enforcement Policies*. Lexington, MA: D.C. Heath.

Graber, D. (1980) *Crime News and the Public*. New York: Praeger.

Graber, D. (1989) *Mass Media and American Politics* (3rd ed.). Washington, D.C.: Congressional Quarterly Press.

Grabosky, P. and P. Wilson (1989) *Journalism and Justice: How Crime is Reported*. Leichhardt, AUS: Pluto.

Graham, R. (1993) "Death of Ohio girl spurs criticism of MTV show." *Rocky Mountain News* (October 31): 76A–77A.

Grant, J. (1992) "Prime time crime: Television portrayals of law enforcement," *Journal of Popular Culture*, 15(1, Spring): 57–68.

Graziano, F. (1992) *Divine Violence : Spectacle, Psychosexuality, and Radical Christianity in the Argentine "Dirty War."* Boulder, CO: Westview.

Grennan, S. (1987) "Findings on the role of officer gender in violent encounters with citizens." *Journal of Police Science and Administration* 15: 78–85.

Hale, D.C. and C.L. Bennett (1995) "Realities of women in policing: An organizational cultural perspective." Pp. 41–54 in Alida V. Merlo and Joycelyn M. Pollock (eds.), *Women, Law, and Social Control.* Boston: Allyn and Bacon.

Hall, S., C. Critcher, T. Jefferson, J. Clarke, and B. Roberts (1978) *Policing the Crisis.* London: Macmillan.

Hallett, M. and D. Powell (1995) "Backstage with Cops." *American Journal of Police,* 14(1): 101–129.

Hamm, M. and J. Ferrell (1994) "Rap, cops, and crime: Clarifying the 'cop killer' controversy." *ACJS Today* 13: 1, 3, 29.

Hans, V. and J. Dee (1991) "Media coverage of law: Its impact on juries and the public." *American Behavioral Scientist,* 2(35): 136–149.

Hansen, M. (1992, November) "Ninth circuit studies gender bias," *American Bar Association Journal* 78: 30.

Harding, S., ed. (1987) *Feminism and Methodology: Social Science Issues.* Bloomington: Indiana University Press.

Harris Poll (1994) November 28, p. 2. Los Angeles: Creators Syndicate. Adapted by *SOURCEBOOK of Criminal Justice Statistics,* 1994, Table 2.25, "Attitudes toward reasons why the U.S. has more homicides and violent deaths than other countries."

Hartigan, P. (1992) "NEA in limelight again as panel challenges decisions on grants." *Rocky Mountain News* (August 8): 75.

Haskell, M. (1973) *From Reverence to Rape: The Treatment of Women in the Movies.* New York: Holt, Rinehart and Winston.

Hawes, J.M. (1971) *Children in Urban Society, Juvenile Delinquency in Nineteenth Century America.* New York: Oxford University Press.

Hazelton Standard Speaker (1994) "Sergeant honored." (October 12) 7.

Hebdige, D. (1979) *Subculture: The Meaning of Style.* London: Methuen.

Henry, T. (1989) *Break All Rules!* Ann Arbor: UMI Research Press.

Herbert, S. (1997) *Policing Space: Territoriality and the Los Angeles Police Department.* Minneapolis: University of Minnesota Press.

Hinds, M. (1993) "3 teens lie in roads like film hero; 1 dies." *Denver Post* (October 19): 2A.

Hinson, H. (1995) "In defense of violence: Why movie murder and mayhem may not be so bad." Pp. 287–294 in Peter Keough (ed.), *Flesh and Blood: The National Society of Film Critics on Sex, Violence, and Censorship.* San Francisco: Mercury House.

Holden, D. (1993a) "Pop go the censors." *Index on Censorship* 22: 11–14.

Holden, D. (1993b) "Sayings of Chairman Jello." *Index on Censorship* 22: 15.

Houston, J. (1995) *Correctional Management: Functions, Skills, and Systems.* Chicago, Illinois: Nelson-Hall, Inc.

Huggins, M.W. (1992, April) "Changing public perception is everyone's responsibility." *Corrections Today,* 54(2): 56, 58, 60.

Hugo, J. (1990) "Smoke screen censorship." *New Art Examiner* 18: 56.

Humphries, D. (1981) "Serious crime, news coverage, and ideology: A content analysis of crime coverage in a metropolitan paper." *Crime and Delinquency,* 27(2): 191–205.

Hunt, W.R. (1990) *Front-Page Detective: William J. Burns and the Detective Profession, 1880–1930.* Bowling Green, OH: Bowling Green State University Popular Press.

Inciardi, J.A. and Dee, J.L. (1987) "From the Keystone Cops to Miami Vice: Images of policing in American popular culture. *Journal of Popular Culture,* 21(2): 84–102.

Irwin, J. (1980) *Prisons in Turmoil.* Boston: Little, Brown.

Jacobs, R. (1996, March) "Civil society and crisis: Culture, discourse and the Rodney King beating." *American Journal of Sociology*, 101: 1238–1272.

Jameson, F. (1992) *Postmodernism.* Durham, NC: Duke University Press.

Jenkins, P. (1994) *Using Murder: The Social Construction of Serial Homicide*, New York: Aldine De Gruyter.

Johnson, L. (1993/1994) "Silencing gangsta rap: Class and race agendas in the campaign against hardcore Rap lyrics." *Temple Political and Civil Rights Law Review*, 3: 25–43.

Johnson, R. (1996) *Hard Time: Understanding and Reforming the Prison* (2nd ed.). Belmont, CA: Wadsworth.

Jolson-Colburn, Jeffrey (1993) "Film, record industries to battle 'sex tax'." *Rocky Mountain News* (June 13): 67A.

Jones, Sandra (1986) "Women police: Caught in the act." *Policing* 2(2): 129-140.

Kamerman, J. (1996) "Correctional officer stress and suicide." *American Jails*, 10(3): 23, 24, 27-28.

Kaminsky, K.L. (1974) *American Film Genres: Approaches to a Critical Theory of Popular Film.* Dayton, OH: Pflaum.

Kania, R.R.E. and R.E. Tanham (1987) *The Portrayal of Police in the Visual Entertainment Media.* Paper presented at the annual meeting of the Academy of Criminal Justice Sciences, St. Louis, Missouri.

Kaplan, E.A. (1983) *Women & Film: Both Sides of the Camera.* New York: Methuen.

Kappeler, V.E., M. Blumberg, and G.W. Potter (1995) *The Mythology of Crime and Criminal Justice.* Prospect Heights, IL: Waveland.

Kappeler, V.E., M. Blumberg, and G.W. Potter (1996) *The Mythology of Crime and Criminal Justice* (2nd ed.). Prospect Heights, IL: Waveland.

Kappeler, V.E., R. Sluder, and G. Alpert (1994) *Forces of Deviance.* Prospect Heights, IL: Waveland.

Kasinsky, R.G. (1994) "Patrolling the facts: Media, cops, and crime," Pp. 203–234 in Gregg Barak (ed.), *Media, Process, and the Social Construction of Crime: Studies in Newsmaking Criminology.* New York: Garland.

Katz, J. (1988) *Seductions of Crime: Moral and Sensual Attractions in Doing Evil.* New York: Basic Books.

Kelly, D. (1992) "NEA's woes continue." *Rocky Mountain News* (May 22): 122.

Kerle, K. (1996) "The jail image and the caring factor." *American Jails*, 10(3): 5.

Klein, M. (1994) *Easterns, Westerns, and Private Eyes: American Matters, 1870–1900.* Madison: University of Wisconsin Press.

Klofas, J. and H. Toch (1982) "The guard subculture myth." *Journal of Research in Crime and Delinquency*, 19(2): 238–254

Koehler, R.J. (1989) "Like it or not: We are news." *Corrections Today*, 51(1): 16–17.

Kooistra, P. (1990) "Criminals as heroes: Linking symbol to structure." *Symbolic Interaction* 13(2): 217–239.

Koppell, T. (1993) "ABC Viewpoint: Crime, violence & TV news." Channel 10, Albany, NY, September 10.

Kunzle, D. (1973) *History of the Comic Strip*, Vol. 1. Berkeley: University of California Press.

Kurtz, H. (1993) *Media Circus: The Trouble with America's Newspapers.* New York: Random House.

Lancaster, K. (1994, Fall) "Do role-playing games promote crime, satanism and suicide among players as critics claim?" *Journal of Popular Culture*, 28.2: 67–79.

Landrum, L.N., P. Browne, and R.B. Browne, eds. (1975) *Dimensions of Detective Fiction.* Bowling Green, OH: Popular Press.

Laur, R. H. (1989) *Social Problems and the Quality of Life* (4th edition). Dubuque, IA: William C. Brown.

Lee, L. (1993) "Brian DePalma's 'Carlito's Way' joins the gangster-film pantheon," *ETC., Times Union*, Albany, New York (December. 2): 8.

Leff, L. and J. Simmons (1990) *The Dame in the Kimono: Hollywood, Censorship and the Production Code from the 1920s to the 1960s.* New York: Grove Weidenfeld.

Levi-Strauss, C. (1967) *Structural Anthropology.* New York: Anchor.

Levinson, N. (1992) "The death of art." *Index on Censorship* 7: 14–15.

Levy, E. (1991) *Small-Town America in Film: The Decline and Fall of Community.* New York: Continuum.

Leyton, E. (1990) *Hunting Humans.* New York: Pocket Books.

Lichter, S. (1988) "Media power: The influence of media on politics and business." *Florida Policy Review,* 4: 35–41.

Lichter, S.R., L.S. Lichter, and S. Rothman (1994) *Prime Time: How TV Portrays American Culture.* Washington, D.C.: Regnery.

Logan, M. (1993, October 16–22) "Return engagement," *TV Guide,* 41(42): 12–15.

Los Angeles Times Staff (1992) *Understanding the Riots: Los Angeles Before and After the Rodney King Case.* Los Angeles: *Los Angeles Times.*

Lotz, R.E. (1991) *Crime and the American Press.* New York: Praeger.

Lovell, R. (1983) *Reporting Public Affairs* Belmont, CA: Wadsworth.

Lovell, G. (1992) "Tenderness fled from the silver screen." *The Times Union (Preview)* [Albany, NY]. (February 13): 20.

Lowery, S. and M. De Fleur, (1983) "Seduction of the innocent: The great comic book scare," Pp. 233–266 in S. Lowery and M. De Fleur (eds.), *Milestones in Mass Communication Research.* New York: Longman.

Lucia, C. (1990) "Class action." *Cineaste,* 18(1): 48–49.

Lynch, M.J. and G. Newman (1987) "From feuding to terrorism: The ideology of vengeance." *Contemporary Crises,* 11: 223–247.

Lyon, D. (1994) *The Surveillance Society.* Minneapolis: University of Minnesota Press.

MacDonald, J.F. (1979) *Don't Touch that Dial!: Radio Programming in American Life, 1920–1960.* Chicago: Nelson-Hall.

Macdonald, M. (1995) *Representing Women: Myths of Femininity in the Popular Media.* London: Edward Arnold.

MacGillis, D. and ABC News (1983) *Crime in America: The ABC Report.* Radnor, PA: Chilton.

Maguire, K. and A. L. Pastore, eds. (1994) *Sourcebook of Criminal Justice Statistics 1993.* Washington, D.C.: The Hindelang Criminal Justice Research Center.

Manchel, F. (1978) *Gangsters on the Screen.* New York: Franklin Watts.

Mannheimer, S. (1990) "Cincinnati joins censorship circus." *New Art Examiner,* 17: 33–35.

Manning, P.K. (1995a, August) *Interactional Shadows.* Unpublished paper, School of Criminal Justice, Michigan State University.

Manning, P.K. (1995b, September) *Reflexions.* Unpublished paper, School of Criminal Justice, Michigan State University.

Manning, P.K. (1996) "Dramaturgy, spectacles, and the axial media event." *The Sociological Quarterly,* 37: 261–278.

Marongiu, P. and G. Newman (1987) *Vengeance: The Fight Against Injustice.* NJ: Littlefield Adams.

Marsh, H.L. (1988) *Crime and the Press: Does Newspaper Crime Coverage support Myths about Crime and Law Enforcement?* (Ph.D. Dissertation: Sam Houston State University). Ann Arbor, MI: University Microfilms International.

Marsh, H.L. (1989) "Newspaper crime coverage in the U.S.: 1893–1988." *Criminal Justice Abstracts,* 506–514.

Martin, D. (1993) "The music of murder." *ACJS Today* 12: 1, 3, 20.

Martin, M. and M. Porter (1992) *Video Movie Guide 1993.* New York: Ballantine.

Martin, M. and M. Porter (1996) *Video Movie Guide 1996*. New York: Ballantine.

Martinson, Robert (1974) "What works: Questions and answers about prison reform." *Public Interest*, 35: 22–54.

Marx, K. (1906) *Capital, Volume 1*. New York: Random House (originally published in 1867).

Marzuk, P.M., K. Tardiff, and C.S. Hirsch (1992) "The epidemiology of murder-suicide." *Journal of American Medical Association*, 267(23): 3179–3183.

Matelski, M.J. (1991) *Daytime Television Programming*. Boston: Focal.

McCarl, T. (1978) "Grace Humiston, the first woman detective." In K. Kraus (ed.), *Murder, Mischief and Mayhem: A Process for Creative Research Papers*. Urbana, IL: National Council of Teachers of English.

McDermott, C. (1987) *Street Style: British Design in the 80s*. New York: Rizzoli.

McKelvey, B. (1977) *American Prisons: A History of Good Intentions*. Monclair: Patterson Smith.

McKenna, A.J. (1991) *Violence and Difference: Girard, Derrida, and Deconstruction*. Urbana: University of Illinois Press.

McQuail, D. (1972) "Introduction." In D. McQuail (ed.), *Sociology of Mass Communications*. Harmondworth: Penquin.

McQuail, D. and S. Windal (1981) *Communication Models: For the Study of Mass Communications*. London: Longman.

Meddis, S. (1989) "A reporter's notebook: Forming partnerships with the press." *Corrections Today* 51(1): 22, 24, 26.

Medved, M. (1992) *Hollywood vs. America: Popular Culture and the War on Traditional Values*. New York: Harper-Collins.

Mellen, J. (1977) *Big Bad Wolves: Masculinity in the American Film*. NY: Pantheon.

Mellen, J. (1973) *Women and Their Sexuality in the New Film*. New York: Dell.

Mennel, R.M. (1973) *Thorns and Thistles: Juvenile Delinquency in the United States, 1925–1940*. Hanover, NH: University Press of New England.

Mesce, D. (1992) "NEA grant winner donates money to two snubbed institutions." *Rocky Mountain News* (June 4): 79.

Meyers, R. (1989) *Murder on the Air: Television's Great Mystery Series*. New York: Mysterious.

Meyrowitz, J. (1985) *No Sense of Place*. New York: Oxford University Press.

Miller, M.C. (1988) *Boxed In*. Evanston, IL: Northwestern University Press.

Milton, C. (1978) "The future of women in policing." Pp. 185–204 in Alvin W. Cohn (ed.), *The Future of Policing*. Beverly Hills, CA: Sage.

Milton, C.A., A. Abramowitz, L. Crites, M. Gates, E. Mintz, and G. Sandler (1974) *Women in Policing: A Manual*. Washington, D.C.: Police Foundation.

Mintz, L.E. (1985) "Situation comedy." Pp. 107–129 in Brian Rose (ed.), *TV Genres: A Handbook and Reference Guide*. Westport, CN: Greenwood.

Mirande, A. (1987) *Gringo Justice*. Notre Dame, IN: University of Notre Dame Press.

Mitroff, I. and W. Bennis (1993) *The Unreality Industry*. New York: Oxford University Press.

Moore, W.H. (1974) *The Kefauver Committee and the Politics of Crime, 1950–1952*. Columbia: University of Missouri Press.

Morash, M. and D. Hale (1987) "Unusual crime or crime as unusual images of corruption at the Interstate Commerce Commission." Pp. 129–149 in Timothy S. Bynum (ed.), *Organized Crime in America: Concepts and Controversies*. Monsey, NY: Criminal Justice.

Morello, K. (1986) *The Invisible Bar: The Woman Lawyer in America, 1638 to the Present*. New York: Random House.

Morris, C. (1992) "Record labels move to tone down rap songs." *Rocky Mountain News* (September 1): 33.

Muir, D.E. (1984) "Trends in integration attitudes on a deep-south campus during the first two decades of deseg-regation." *Social Forces* 62: 963–972.

Muir, D.E. (1991) "White fraternity and sorority attitudes toward blacks on a deep-south campus." *Sociological Spectrum* 11: 93–103.

Mulvey, L. (1975) "Visual pleasure and narrative cinema." *Screen* 16(3): 6–18.

Munro-Bjorklund, V. (1991) "Popular culture images of criminals and prisoners since Attica." *Social Justice*, 18(3): 48–70.

Murrell, J. (1954, August) "Annual rating of comics magazines." *Parents' Magazine*, 29: 114.

Nash, J.R. and R. Offen (1970) *Dillinger Dead or Alive?* Chicago: Henry Regnery.

National Research Council (1992) *Understanding Violence*. Washington, D.C.

Nevins, F. (1995) "Law school seminar on popular fiction and film." *Murder is Academic*, 3(3, Nov.): 5.

Newman, G. (1978) *Understanding Violence*. New York: Harper and Row.

Newman, G. (1990) "Popular culture and criminal justice: A preliminary analysis." *Journal of Criminal Justice*. 18(3): 261–274.

Newman, G. (1993) "Batman and justice: The true story." *Humanity and Society*, 17(3): 297–320.

Newman, G. and A. Bouloukos (1993, August 18). Review of "Reservoir Dogs." *Journal of Criminal Justice and Popular Culture*. 1(3): 20–23. (Available electronically on the Internet from sunycrj@uacscz.albany.edu or on bitnet from sunycrjgalbanyum1.bitnet, both at SUNY, Albany.)

Newsweek (1995, September 4): 25.

No More Censorship (1990) "Dayglo Abortions, Part II." Fact Sheet No. 4: 4.

Norden, M.F. (1985) "The detective show." Pp. 33–55 in Brian Rose (ed.), *TV Genres: A Handbook and Reference Guide*. Westport, CN: Greenwood.

Nimmo, D. and J. Combs (1983) Mediated Political Realities. New York: Longman.

Nyberg, A.K. (1994) Seal of Approval: The Origins and History of the Comics Code. Ph.D. dissertation, University of Wisconsin, Madison.

O'Brien, E. (1992) "Dallas officers plan no protest of Ice-T concert New Year's Eve." *Fort Worth Star-Telegram* (December 30): 19A, 22A.

Oakley, A. (1981) *Subject Women*. Oxford: Martin Robertson.

O'Kane, J.M. (1992) *The Crooked Ladder: Gangsters, Ethnicity and the American Dream*. New Brunswick: Transaction.

Ostrow, J. (1993) "MTV's 'B and B' ignites call for parental guidance." *Denver Post* (October 12): E1.

Owens, T. (1994) *Lying Eyes*. New York: Thunder Mouth.

Palermo, G.B. (1994) "Murder-suicide: An extended suicide." *International Journal of Offender Therapy and Comparative Criminology*, 38(3): 205–216.

Palmer, S. and J.A. Humphrey (1980) "Offender-victim relationships in criminal homicide followed by offender's suicide, North Carolina, 1972–1977. *Suicide and Life-Threatening Behavior*, 10(2): 106–118.

Panati, C. (1991) *Panati's Parade of Fads, Follies, and Manias*. New York: HarperCollins.

Panek, L.L. (1987) *An Introduction to the Detective Story*. Bowling Green, OH: Bowling Green State University Popular Press.

Papke, D.R. (1987) *Framing the Criminal: Crime, Cultural Work and the Loss of Critical Perspective, 1830–1900*. Hamden, CT: Archon.

Parachini, A. (1993) "N.E.A. story." *The Nation* 257: 197.

Parenti, M. (1986) *Inventing Reality: The Politics of the Mass Media*. New York: St. Martin's.

Petty, J. (1990) "Artists back 'NEA Four.'" *New Art Examiner* 18: 13.

Phillips, G.D. (1982) *George Cukor.* Boston: Twayne.

Pindyck, R. and D.L. Rubinfeld (1981) *Econometric Models and Economic Forecasts* (2nd ed.). Toronto: McGraw Hill.

Pogrebin, M. (1986) "The changing role of women: Female police officers' occupational problems," *Police Journal,* 59: 127–133.

Pollock, J. and B. Ramirez (1994) "Women in the legal profession." Pp. 79–97 in Alida Merlo and Joycelyn Pollock (eds.), *Women, Law and Social Control.* Boston: Allyn and Bacon.

Porsdam, H. (1994, Summer) "Law as soap opera and game show: The case of *The People's Court." Journal of Popular Culture,* 28(1): 1–15.

Post, R.C. (1987) "On the popular image of the lawyer: Reflections in a dark glass." *California Law Review,* 75(1): 379–389.

Poster, M., ed. (1990) *Jean Baudrillard.* Stanford, CA: Stanford University Press.

Powell, S.M. (1996) "Clinton accepts police group's support." *The Times Union* (Albany, NY). (September 17): A-3.

Powers, R.G. (1983) *G-Men: Hoover's FBI in American Popular Culture.* Carbondale and Edwardsville: Southern Illinois University Press.

Queen, E. (1969) *Queen's Quorum.* New York: Biblo and Tannen.

Querry, R.B. (1973) "Prison movies: An annotated filmography 1921–present," *Journal of Popular Film,* 2(2):181–197.

Quinney, R. (1970) *The Social Reality of Crime.* Boston: Little, Brown

Real, M.R. (1989) *Super Media: A Cultural Studies Approach.* Newbury Park, CA: Sage.

Reibman, J.E. (1990) "The life of Dr. Fredric Wertham," in *The Fredric Wertham Collection.* Cambridge, Mass.: Bush-Reisinger Museum, Harvard University.

Reiman, J. (1990) *The Rich Get Richer and the Poor Get Prison* (3rd ed.). New York: Macmillan.

Remmington, P. (1983) "Women in the police: Integration or separation?" *Qualitative Sociology* 6: 118–135.

Reuter (1993a) "NEA reverses decision on 3 grants." *Rocky Mountain News* (August 29): 62A.

Reuter (1993b) "Black coalition raps 'gangsta rap.' " *Rocky Mountain News* (December 18): 44A.

Reuter (1993c) "Most blame TV for real-life crime." *Rocky Mountain News* (December 21): 8D.

Reuter (1994) "Group urges ban on 'gangsta rap.' " *Rocky Mountain News* (January 7): 11D.

Rock, P. (1981) "News as Eternal Recurrence," Pp. 64–70 in Stan Cohen and Jock Young (eds.) *The Manufacture of News.* Beverly Hills, CA: Sage.

Rose, B., ed. (1985) *TV Genres: A Handbook and Reference Guide.* Westport, CT: Greenwood.

Rose, T. (1994) *Black Noise: Rap Music and Black Culture in Contemporary America.* Hanover & London: Wesleyan University Press.

Rosen, M. (1973) *Popcorn Venus: Women, Movies & The American Dream.* New York: Coward, McCann & Geoghegan.

Rosenbaum, M. (1990) "The role of depression in couples involved in murder-suicide and homicide." *American Journal of Psychiatry,* 147(8): 1036–1039.

Rosenberg, H. (1995) "Nervous in the naked city." Pp. 103–110 in Craig L. LaMay and Everette E. Dennis (eds.), *The Culture of Crime.* New Brunswick, NJ: Transaction.

Roshier, B. (1981) "The selection of crime news by the press." Pp. 40–51 in Stanley Cohen and Jock Young (eds.), *The Manufacture of News: Social Problems, Deviance and the Mass Media.* Beverly Hills, CA: Sage.

Ross, J.I. (1995a) "Violence by municipal police in Canada: 1977–1992." Pp. 223–249 in Jeffrey Ian Ross (ed.), *Violence in Canada: Sociopolitical Perspectives.* Toronto: Oxford University Press.

Ross, J.I. (1995b) "A process model of public police violence in advanced industrialized democracies," *Criminal Justice Policy Review*, 7(1): 67–90.

Ross, R.R. (1981). "Introduction." Pp. 1–5 in R.R. Ross (ed.), *Prison Guard/Correctional Officer*. Canada: Butterworth.

Rounds, V. (no date) "Heavy metal and satan: Are they to blame?" *Rock Out Censorship* 13: 3.

Rowland, Jr., W. D. (1983) *The Politics of TV Violence: Policy Uses of Communication Research*. Beverly Hills, CA: Sage.

Rushkoff, D. (1994) *Media Virus: Hidden Agendas in Popular Culture*. New York: Ballantine.

Russell, D.E.H., ed. (1993) *Making Violence Sexy: Feminist Views on Pornography*. New York: Teachers College Press.

Sanders, C.R. and E. Lyon (1995) "Repetitive retribution: Media images and the cultural construction of criminal Justice." Pp. 25–44 in J. Ferrell, and C. R. Sanders (eds.), *Cultural Criminology*. Boston: Northeastern University Press,

Santoro, G. (1990) "How 2 b nasty." *The Nation* 251: 4–5.

Santoro, J.P., A.W. Dawood, and G. Ayral (1985) "The murder-suicide: A study of the postaggressional suicide." *The American Journal of Forensic Medicine and Pathology*, 6(3): 222–225.

Saunders, M. (1993) " 'Gangsta' Rap: Rising with a bullet." *Rocky Mountain News* (October 27): 24D.

Sayers, D.L., ed. (1929) *The Omnibus of Crime*. New York: Payson and Clarke.

Scala, M. (1990) "Virginia judge rules installation not obscene." *New Art Examiner*, 18: 13.

Schatz, T. (1981) *Hollywood Genres: Formulas, Filmmaking and the Studio System*. Philadelphia: Temple University Press.

Scheuer, S.H. (1992) *Movies on TV and Videocassette*. New York: Bantam.

Schichor, D. and Sechrest, D. (1996) *Three Strikes and You're Out*. Sage.

Schlesinger, P. (1978) *Putting Reality Together: BBC News*. London: Constable.

Schroeder, A. (1976) *Shaking It Rough*. New York: Doubleday.

Schwartz, J.A. (1989). "Promoting a good public image: Effective leadership, sound practice makes the difference." *Corrections Today* 51(1): 38, 40, 42.

Scott, J. (1992) "Official culture meets Jes Grew." *Lies of Our Times*, 3: 9–10.

Selkin, J. (1976) "Rescue fantasies in homicide-suicide." *Suicide and Life-Threatening Behavior*, 6(2): 79–85.

Sennett, R. and J. Cobb (1972) *The Hidden Injuries of Class*. New York: Vintage.

Shapiro, B. (1990) "The art cops." *The Nation*, 251: 40–41, 57.

Sheley, J.F. and C.D. Ashkins (1981) "Crime, crime news, and crime views." *Public Opinion Quarterly*, 45(4): 492–506.

Sheley, J. F. and C.D. Ashkins (1984) "Crime, crime news, and crime views." Pp. 124–140 in Ray Surette (ed.), *Justice and the Media*. Springfield, IL: Charles C. Thomas.

Sherizen, S. (1978) "Social creation of crime news: All the news fitted to print." Pp. 203–224 in C. Winick (ed.), *Deviance and Mass Media*. Beverly Hills, CA: Sage.

Sikor, E. (1989) *Screwball: Hollywood's Madcap Romantic Comedies*. New York: Crown.

Silverman, I.J., and M. Vega (1996) *Corrections: A Comprehensive View*. St. Paul, MN: West.

Simmons, D. (1994) "Gangsta rap reaches Capitol Hill." *Rocky Mountain News* (March 9): 28.

Singer, S.I., M. Levine, and S. Jou (1993, August) "Heavy metal music preference, delinquent friends, social control, and delinquency." *Journal of Research, Crime and Delinquency*, 30(3): 317–329.

Snow, R.P. (1983) *Creating Media Culture.* Beverly Hills, CA: Sage.

Snow, R.P. (1995) "Media and social order in everyday life." Pp. 77–92 in Richard V. Ericson (ed.), *Crime and Media.* Aldershot, England: Dartmouth.

Snyder, M. (1992) "Ice-T hailed as censorship foe." *Fort Worth Star-Telegram* (July 21): D2.

Soothill, K., and S. Walby (1991) *Sex Crime in the News.* London: Routledge.

Spring, J. (1992) *Images of American Life: A History of Ideological Management in Schools, Movies, Radio, and Television.* Albany: State University of New York Press.

Stark, R. (1972) *Police Riots.* Belmont, CA: Wadsworth.

Starker, S. (1989) *Evil Influences: Crusades Against the Mass Media.* New Brunswick, NJ: Transaction.

Stogdill, R.M. (1970) *The Process of Model-Building in the Behavioral Sciences.* Columbus: Ohio State University Press.

Strati, A. (1992) "Organizational culture." Pp. 578–584 in G. Szell (ed.) *Concise Encyclopedia of Participation and Co-Management.* Berlin and New York: de Gruyter.

Strinati, D. (1995) *An Introduction of Theories of Popular Culture.* London: Routledge.

Surette, R. (1984) *Justice and the Media.* Springfield, IL: Charles C. Thomas.

Surette, R. (1992) *Media, Crime and Criminal Justice: Images and Realities.* Pacific Grove, CA: Brooks/Cole.

Surette, R. (1994) "Predator criminals as media icons." Pp. 131–158 in Gregg Barak (ed.), *Media, Process and the Social Construction of Crime: Studies in Newsmaking Criminology.* New York: Garland.

Surette, R. (1995b) "Predator criminals as media icons." Pp. 131–158 in Gregg Barak (ed.), *Media, Process, and the Social Construction of Crime: Studies in Newsmaking Criminology.* New York: Garland.

Surette, R. (1995a) "A serendipitous finding of a news media history effect: A research note." *Justice Quarterly* 12(2): 355–364

Symons, J. (1985) *Bloody Murder: From the Detective Story to the Crime Novel,* Middlesex, England: Penguin.

Talleck, D.G. (1976) "William Faulkner and the tradition of tough-guy fiction." Pp. 247–264 in Larry N. Landrum, Pat Browne, and Ray B. Browne (eds.), *Dimensions of Detective Fiction.* Bowling Green, OH: Popular Press.

Tannenbaum, F. (1938) *Crime and the Community.* Boston: Ginn.

Taylor, E. (1989) *Prime Time Families: Television Culture in Postwar America.* Berkeley: University of California Press.

Taylor, J. (1995) "To die for." *The Nation,* 260: 440–441.

Taylor, L. and B. Mullan (1986) *Uninvited Guests.* London: Chatto and Windus.

Thomas, C. (1996, May 17) "Are media outlets smart enough to stem the decline in audience?" *Times Union,* (Albany, NY): A–15.

Time, "Psychiatry in Harlem," 1 December 1947, 50.

Toland, J. (1963) *The Dillinger Days.* New York: Random House.

Toll, R.C. (1982) *The Entertainment Machine: American Show Business in the Twentieth Century.* Oxford: Oxford University Press.

Travisono, A.P. (1980) "Brubaker: The crusader strikes out," *ON THE LINE,* 3(6): 1.

Tuchman, G. (1973) "Making news by doing work: Routinizing the unexpected." *American Journal of Sociology,* 79(1): 110–131.

Tuchman, G. (1978) *Making News: A Study in the Construction of Reality.* New York: Free Press.

Tunnell, K.D. (1992) "Film at eleven: Recent developments in the commodification of crime." *Sociological Spectrum* 12: 293–313.

Tunnell, K.D., ed. (1993) *Political Crime in Contemporary America: A Critical Approach.* New York and London: Garland.

Tunnell, K.D. (1995a) "A cultural approach to crime and punishment, bluegrass style." Pp. 80–105 in J. Ferrell and C. Sanders (eds.), *Cultural Criminology.* Boston: Northeastern University Press.

Tunnell, K.D. (1995b) "Silence of the left: Reflections on critical criminology and criminologists." *Social Justice* 22: 89–101.

TV Guide (Albany, NY edition) (1996, May 18–24) "Close-up: Death by demographics," 44(20): 91.

U.S. Department of Commerce (1992) *1990 Census of the Population: General Population Characteristics, United States.* Washington, D.C.

U.S. Department of Justice (1994) *Uniform Crime Reports for the United States.* Washington, D.C.

U.S. Senate (1954) Judiciary Subcommittee on Juvenile Delinquency Reports—Miscellaneous, 15 December, Hendrickson Papers, "A Resume of the Work of the Subcommittee on Juvenile Delinquency," pp. 2–4, Box 74, Syracuse University, Syracuse, New York.

U.S. Senate (1954) Judiciary Subcommittee on Juvenile Delinquency. *Juvenile Delinquency (Comic Books).* (83rd Congress, 2nd session, April 21, 22 and June 4): 10.

U.S. Senate (1955) *Comic Books and Juvenile Delinquency.* Interim report of the Committee on the Judiciary, Subcommittee of Juvenile Delinquency (84th Congress, 1st session).

U.S. Senate Subcommittee to Investigate Juvenile Delinquency Hearings (1954) Juvenile Delinquency (Comic Books) (83rd Congress, 2nd session, April 21, 22 and June 4).

USA Today (1994) "Across the USA." (January 27): 6A.

USA Today (1995) August 30: 3.

Vance, C.S. (1989) "The war on culture." *Art in America,* 77: 39, 41, 43.

Van Wormer, K. (1981) "Are males suited to police parole work?" *Police Studies* 3: 41–44.

van Zoonen, L. (1994) *Feminist Media Studies.* Thousand Oaks, CA: Sage.

Vaughn, S. (1990) "The origins of the motion picture production code." *The Journal of American History,* 77(1): 39–65.

Vold, G.B. and T.J. Bernard (1986) *Theoretical Criminology.* New York: Oxford University Press.

Voumvakis, S.E. and R.V. Ericson (1984) *News Accounts of Attacks on Women: A Comparison of Three Toronto Newspapers.* Toronto: Centre of Criminology, University of Toronto.

Walby, S. (1990) *Theorizing Patriarchy.* Oxford: Basil Blackwell.

Wald, P. (1988) "Women in the law." *Trial,* 24: 75–79.

Walker, S. (1994) *Sense and Nonsense about Crime and Drugs* (3rd. ed.). Belmont, CA: Wadsworth.

Wallerstein, I. (1983) *Historical Capitalism.* London: Verso.

Walsh, A.S. (1984) *Women's Film and Female Experience, 1940–1950.* New York: Praeger.

Walsh, F. (1996) *Sin and Censorship: The Catholic Church and the Motion Picture Industry.* New Haven, CT: Yale University Press.

Washington Post (1995, August 31): A16.

Weber, R.P. (1990) *Basic Content Analysis* (2nd ed.), Newbury Park, CA: Sage.

Weibel, K. (1977) *Mirror Mirror: Images of Women Reflected in Popular Culture.* Garden City, NY: Anchor Books.

Welch, M. (1996) *Corrections: A Critical Approach.* New York: McGraw-Hill.

Wells, C. (1929) *The Technique of the Mystery Story.* Springfield, MA: Home Correspondence School.

Wertham, Fredric (1954) *Seduction of the Innocent.* Port Washington, NY: Kennikat.

West, M. I. (1988) *Children, Culture and Controversy*. Hamden, Conn.: Archon.

West, D. (1967) *Murder Followed by Suicide*. Cambridge: Harvard University Press.

Williams, J. (1994) "Comics: A tool of subversion?" *Journal of Criminal Justice and Popular Culture*, 2(6): 129–147.

Williams, R. (1975) *Television: Technology and Cultural Form*. London: Fontana.

Wilmington, M. (1995) "Too much sex and violence?" Pp. 295–299 in Peter Keough (ed.), *Flesh and Blood: The National Society of Film Critics on Sex, Violence, and Censorship*. San Francisco: Mercury House.

Wilson, W. (1988) "Rape as entertainment." *Psychological Reports*, 63: 607–610.

Wimmer, R.D. and J.R. Dominick (1994) *Mass Media Research: An Introduction* (4th ed.). Belmont, CA: Wadsworth.

Wiseman, C. (1991) "The legal education of women: From 'treason against nature' to sounding a 'different voice.'" *Marquette Law Review*, 74: 325–344.

Wolfgang, M. E. (1958) "An analysis of homicide-suicide." *Journal of Clinical and Experimental Psychopathology and Quarterly Review of Psychiatry and Neurology*, 19(3): 208–218.

Woods, J. (no date) "Metal and Rap on Trial in Texas." *Rock Out Censorship*, 13: 3.

Wright, W. (1975) *Six-Guns and Society*. Berkeley: University of California Press.

Zaner, L. O. (1989, February) "The screen test: Has Hollywood hurt corrections' image?" *Corrections Today* 51(1): 64–65; 94–98

Zimmer, L.E. (1986). *Women Guarding Men*. Chicago: The University of Chicago Press.

Zipes, J. (1979) *Breaking the Magic Spell: Radical Theories of Folk and Fairy Tales*. Austin: University of Texas Press.

Zoglin, R. (1994) "Tim at the Top." *Time*, 144(24): 76, 78, 80–81.

Subject Index

Film Index

259

Author Index